T0185727

Pro Exchange Server 2013 Administration

Jaap Wesselius

Apress®

Pro Exchange Server 2013 Administration

Copyright © 2014 by Jaap Wesselius

This work is subject to copyright. All rights are reserved by the Publisher, whether the whole or part of the material is concerned, specifically the rights of translation, reprinting, reuse of illustrations, recitation, broadcasting, reproduction on microfilms or in any other physical way, and transmission or information storage and retrieval, electronic adaptation, computer software, or by similar or dissimilar methodology now known or hereafter developed. Exempted from this legal reservation are brief excerpts in connection with reviews or scholarly analysis or material supplied specifically for the purpose of being entered and executed on a computer system, for exclusive use by the purchaser of the work. Duplication of this publication or parts thereof is permitted only under the provisions of the Copyright Law of the Publisher's location, in its current version, and permission for use must always be obtained from Springer. Permissions for use may be obtained through RightsLink at the Copyright Clearance Center. Violations are liable to prosecution under the respective Copyright Law.

ISBN-13 (pbk): 978-1-4302-4695-4

ISBN-13 (electronic): 978-1-4302-4696-1

Trademarked names, logos, and images may appear in this book. Rather than use a trademark symbol with every occurrence of a trademarked name, logo, or image we use the names, logos, and images only in an editorial fashion and to the benefit of the trademark owner, with no intention of infringement of the trademark.

The use in this publication of trade names, trademarks, service marks, and similar terms, even if they are not identified as such, is not to be taken as an expression of opinion as to whether or not they are subject to proprietary rights.

While the advice and information in this book are believed to be true and accurate at the date of publication, neither the authors nor the editors nor the publisher can accept any legal responsibility for any errors or omissions that may be made. The publisher makes no warranty, express or implied, with respect to the material contained herein.

President and Publisher: Paul Manning
Lead Editor: Jonathan Hassell
Developmental Editor: Chris Nelson
Technical Reviewers: Michael Smith and David Stork
Editorial Board: Steve Anglin, Mark Beckner, Ewan Buckingham, Gary Cornell, Louise Corrigan, Jim DeWolf, Jonathan Gennick, Jonathan Hassell, Robert Hutchinson, Michelle Lowman, James Markham, Matthew Moodie, Jeff Olson, Jeffrey Pepper, Douglas Pundick, Ben Renow-Clarke, Dominic Shakeshaft, Gwenan Spearing, Matt Wade, Steve Weiss
Coordinating Editor: Jill Balzano
Copy Editor: Carole Berglie
Compositor: SPi Global
Indexer: SPi Global
Artist: SPi Global
Cover Designer: Anna Ishchenko

Distributed to the book trade worldwide by Springer Science+Business Media New York, 233 Spring Street, 6th Floor, New York, NY 10013. Phone 1-800-SPRINGER, fax (201) 348-4505, e-mail orders-ny@springer-sbm.com, or visit www.springeronline.com. Apress Media, LLC is a California LLC and the sole member (owner) is Springer Science + Business Media Finance Inc (SSBM Finance Inc). SSBM Finance Inc is a Delaware corporation.

For information on translations, please e-mail rights@apress.com, or visit www.apress.com.

Apress and friends of ED books may be purchased in bulk for academic, corporate, or promotional use. eBook versions and licenses are also available for most titles. For more information, reference our Special Bulk Sales–eBook Licensing web page at www.apress.com/bulk-sales.

Any source code or other supplementary material referenced by the author in this text is available to readers at www.apress.com/9781430257882. For detailed information about how to locate your book's source code, go to www.apress.com/source-code/.

This book is dedicated to my wife and sons.
Without their support it's not possible to live life as I do!

Contents at a Glance

Contents

About the Author

Jaap Wesselius is an architect at Amsio, one of the larger managed Service Providers in The Netherlands. At Amsio he is responsible for the entire Microsoft suite when it comes to hosting, which means Jaap is working with hosted Exchange, Lync, and SharePoint. Other than the Unified Communications solution, Jaap is also involved with private cloud solutions—in particular, Windows Azure Services and VMWare, to a lesser extent.

Before working at Amsio, Jaap had been working (and traveling) as an independent consultant, also primarily in the Microsoft Unified Communications area. He learned Unified Communications, especially Microsoft Exchange Server, in his years at Microsoft. He worked at Microsoft from 1997 to 2006, both in support as a Technical Account Manager and in MCS as an Infrastructure Consultant.

Besides work, Jaap spends a lot of time in the Exchange community, like the Dutch UC User Group and the Dutch Network User Group NGN. He is a frequent blogger on his own site www.jaapwesselius.com, but you can also find an extensive selection of his articles on Simple-Talk (www.simple-talk.com). As if that's not enough, Jaap is a regular speaker at major events like Microsoft TechEd, the Microsoft Exchange Conference, the Quest Experts Conference, and the Connections conferences. For his work in the community, Jaap was giventhe Exchange Server MVP award in 2007, a prize he has held ever since.

When time permits (it never permits enough, so spare time has to be created), Jaap savors life with his wife and three sons and also enjoys doing some serious hiking and cycling—the best way, he feels, for one to free one's mind. An ongoing dream is to cycle across Europe, but most likely this will remain a dream as long as he spends most of his time working, writing, and giving speeches.

About the Technical Reviewer

Dave Stork has more than 12 years' experience working in IT and has a great deal of Exchange experience starting with Exchange 2000. He is currently working as an IT Architect with a focus on Exchange (and a little bit of Lync and Office 365) at OGD ICT Diensten, an IT services company in the Netherlands, and is responsible for consultancy, designs, quality control, technical strategies and research & development and internal Exchange training programs.

Outside of work he is a speaker at events, blogs at http://bit.ly/dmstork, twitters with the account @dmstork and is a regular co-host of the www.TheUCarchitects.com podcast focused on Exchange and Lync news.

Acknowledgments

Although this is not my first book I was again surprised by the amount of work that needed to be done and the amount of people that contributed to this book in one way or another.

The first one is Tony Davis from Red Gate in the UK who put me in touch with Jonathan Hassel from Apress. This is how it all started again, a little over a year ago. Some special words for my Coordinating Editor at Apress, Jill Balzano who was chasing me all this time whenever I did not make my deadlines, but without ever saying one bad word. Thank you, Jill, for your patience.

My technical reviewers Michael B. Smith and Dave Stork of course, the latter is living close by which makes it easy to have good, in-depth discussions about several Exchange related topics, and the time we spend together at NGN of course. And speaking about the NGN I should not forget Johan Veldhuis, Maarten Piederiet and Michel de Rooij, countless are the amount of messages I've sent to these guys starting with "Hey, you know quite some stuff about Exchange, right?"

There are several people at Microsoft I'd like to thank, especially David Espinoza and Kern Hardman for getting me into the various Exchange TAP programs, which are one the most valuable resources one can think of.

I should not forget my collegues at Amsio and my manager Ruben van der Zwan, who supplied me with so many resources like hardware, virtual machines, load balancers, storage, public IP addresses, and so forth. Enough to start my own hosting company. ☺ Fellow MVPs, MCMs around the world I have had solid discussions with and everybody I forgot, thank you!

The last one is my wife and sons who always had a hard time when I needed to do some research, write down notes, do the intial writing or the reviews of the chapters. It will sound familiar to most authors when I rephrase my wife: "This is the last book you're gonna write, you hear me?" Thank you all for your support the past year, let's do it again, I love it.

Introduction

It is always difficult to write a book, especially about a dynamic server application like Exchange Server 2013. Microsoft is releasing a cumulative update of Exchange Server 2013 and every update contains new features and functionality. From a product point of view this is good of course, but from a book point of view it is difficult. This book is a point in time that is currently at Exchange Server 2013 CU3.

This book is aiming at the IT professionals, the Exchange administrators with a couple years of experience that need guidance in deploying and managing Exchange Server 2013 on-premises. Inside there are nine chapters, covering the following topics:

- Chapter 1 - Introduction to Exchange 2013. This chapter contains an overview of Exchange Server 2013 including new and removed features, integration with Active Directory and an architectural overview of the product.

- Chapter 2 - Installing Exchange Server 2013. This chapter covers the installation of Exchange Server 2013, both on Windows Server 2008 R2 and Windows Server 2012. The normal graphical setup is discussed, also the unattended setup with all the command-line switches that are available. The last part of this chapter discussses the post-installation configuration options.

- Chapter 3 - Coexistence and Migration. This chapter covers installation and configuration of Exchange Server 2013 into an exisitng Exchange Server 2007 or Exchange Server 2010 environment.

- Chapter 4 - Client Access Server. A theoretical chapter discussing details about the Exchange Server 2013 Client Access server.

- Chapter 5 - Mailbox Server. This chapter discusses the Exchange 2013 Mailbox server. Not only the mailbox database and its database internals are discussed, but also the types of mailboxes, the database availability group (DAG), the Transport service and the UM service which are now part of the Exchange 2010 Mailbox server.

- Chapter 6 - Managing Exchange Server 2013. This chapter discusses the way to manage your Exchange 2013 environment like the Exchange Admin Center (EAC) and its options as well as the Exchange Management Shell (EMS) with all the possibilities. After the basic this chapter continues with management tasks like certificate management, mailbox management and recipient management.

- Chapter 7 - Backup, Restore and Disaster Recovery. A pretty important chapter. It discusses how backups are made and what options you have for restoring information. The last part of this chapter discusses the new Exchange native data protection, sometime referred to as backup-less environment.

- Chapter 8 - Monitoring Exchange 2013. This chapter deals with various available otpions to monitor Exchange Server 2013. The Exchange Management Shell, Microsoft tools, 3rd party tools and System Center Operations Manager are discussed in this chapter.

- Chapter 9 - Troubleshooting Exchange 2013. This chapter is strongly related with the previous two chapters and discusses various ways to troubleshoot your Exchange 2013 servers.

I realize that I did not, and cannot cover all available options in an Exchange 2013 environment. Sometimes because the functionality is not available anymore, or is not yet available, like an Exchange 2013 Edge Transport server with anti-spam and anti-virus functionality. Things that will be added with the upcoming Service Pack 1 release of Exchange Server 2013. Other things that come to mind are Office 365 and its integration with Exchange 2013 on-premises for example, or in-depth coverage of mobile devices for a Bring Your Own Device (BYOD) implementation. Nevertheless I hope you find this book useful and a good source of information for deploying and maintaining an Exchange 2013 environment in your office.

CHAPTER 1

■ ■ ■

Introduction to Exchange Server 2013

In October 2012, Microsoft released the eighth version of its messaging and collaboration server, Exchange Server 2013. At first glance it didn't seem like a revolutionary change, but there was more than met the eye. Exchange Server 2013 is the first version from Microsoft that was designed from the ground up, with the "cloud" in mind—in particular, Office 365, of course. This is an area where Microsoft is facing tough competition from others—for example, Google. Google Mail and Google Apps have a slick underlying infrastructure, making it possible for users to add new features quickly and have good performance figures at the same time. This ability was something that hasn't been Microsoft's strongest point in the last couple of years, and therefore Microsoft decided to invest heavily in its cloud infrastructure. At the same time, Exchange Server was being redesigned to take advantage of these cloud developments.

What's important in a public cloud environment like Office 365? Of course, it's the scalability, but also it's the architecture and manageability of the platform that are extremely important. You'll see this in the new front-end and back-end architecture, where the front end is actually a protocol proxy. This is important in a multi-datacenter environment, perhaps in combination with a global, geographically based DNS solution. That is, in a datacenter environment, you want your application to run with as few administrators and as little administrator input as possible. A solid monitoring solution, with predefined actions and solutions, is key to achieving such an environment.

Look at the JBOD (Just a Bunch of Disks) solutions that Microsoft has been promoting since its introduction of Exchange Server 2010. This is a development driven by the ongoing need to lower the operational cost of running a large Exchange Server infrastructure. Running multiple copies of a Mailbox database on just simple SATA disks is easy to manage and low in cost in terms of replacement. When a disk fails, which is not uncommon with cheap SATA disks, the Exchange Server automatically moves over to another Mailbox database on another disk. Later on, it's a simple matter of rip-and-replace the faulty disk, reseed the Mailbox database, and you're back in business. This ability decreases the cost of maintaining the disk infrastructure and at the same time decreases the operational cost of administrative staff.

These are just a few key things for Microsoft datacenters running Office 365, and you'll see these features in the new Exchange Server 2013 as well.

Does this mean that Exchange Server 2013 is targeted toward large, multinational organizations? Well, yes and no. Yes, large, multinational organizations will certainly benefit from the new architecture with its front-end and back-end technologies. But smaller organizations, perhaps with datacenter resiliency, will certainly also benefit from Exchange Server 2013.

Larger organizations can move to Office 365 and create a combination of Exchange Server 2013 on-premises and Office 365. This is called a "hybrid environment," where the two are tightly integrated. Together they form one namespace with one address book, and yet are independent where the actual mailboxes are located. Also, e-mail sent between Exchange Server 2013 on-premises and Office 365 is fully secure because of the hybrid configuration.

Getting Started

To begin, let's take a general look at the Exchange Server 2013 release. First, we'll consider the two Exchange Server 2013 editions and review their features. Then, we'll look at the features that have been removed from Exchange Server and are not part of Exchange Server 2013.

The Editions

Exchange Server 2013 is available in two editions:

- **Exchange Server 2013, Standard Edition** This is a "normal" Exchange Server 2013, limited to only five (5) Mailbox databases per Mailbox server. This edition can also be used for non-Mailbox servers.

- **Exchange Server 2013, Enterprise Edition** This version can host up to 50 Mailbox databases per Mailbox server. (If you are familiar with Exchange Server 2010, you'll notice that this is a decrease in the number of Mailbox databases; in Exchange Server 2010, there were up to 100 Mailbox databases per server. In Chapter 3, I discuss this "limitation.")

Except for the number of Mailbox databases per Exchange Server, there are no differences between the two versions; the binaries are the same.

Entering the Exchange Server 2013 license key enforces the number of Mailbox databases per server. Besides the Exchange Server server license, there's also a Client Access License (CAL), a license that's required for each user or device accessing the server software.

There are two types of CALs available:

- **Standard CAL** This CAL offers standard e-mail functionality from any platform. The license is for typical Exchange and Outlook usage.

- **Enterprise CAL** This more advanced CAL offers functionality such as integrated archiving, compliance features, and information-protection capabilities. The CAL is an add-on to the Standard CAL, so both licenses need to be purchased!

This is not a complete list of all available features for the different CALs. For a complete overview, visit the Microsoft licensing page on www.microsoft.com/exchange/en-us/licensing.aspx.

What's New in Exchange Server 2013?

So, what are the new features and improvements in Exchange Server 2013? There are a lot of new features, valuable both from an administrator's point of view and from that of an enduser. Let's discuss the most important changes here:

- **A new look and feel of client interfaces** Exchange Server 2013 has a new appearance and tone across all messaging clients. Outlook 2013 has a new interface based on the new Microsoft design language. It's not an overloaded amount of information but, rather, offers a consistent view on all information, easy to find and easy to work with. This interface can also be found in the Outlook Web App (OWA), as shown in Figure 1-1, and it's obvious that the OWA team and the Outlook 2013 team have worked closely together. This new design can be seen on all kinds of devices, with all types of clients or browsers. Use Windows 8 with Outlook 2013, or Windows 7 with OWA, or Windows Phone 8 with the Outlook mobile mail client, and they all offer this consistent view and user experience.

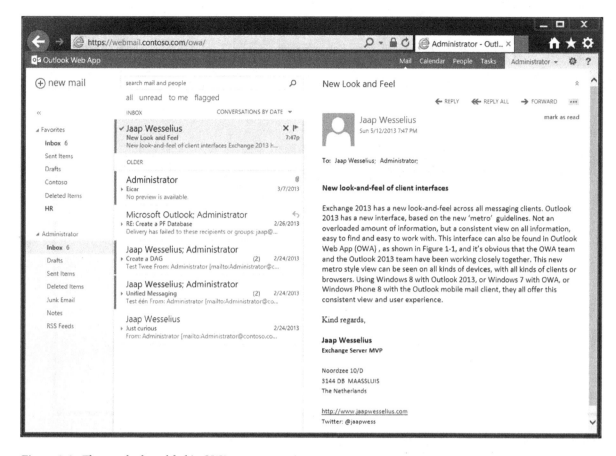

Figure 1-1. *The new look and feel in OWA*

OWA also has a great new feature: When using Internet Explorer 10 (or Firefox 12, Safari 5.1, or Chrome 18 or later), you'll find OWA is available also in offline mode, thus giving you the option of working with OWA in an airplane, for example. Not all information is cached within the browser; it is comparable to mobile clients' use of ActiveSync, where only a few days of data are stored. Only the default settings are different between ActiveSync and OWA offline.

- **Exchange Admin Center** The Exchange Admin Center (EAC) is the new Web-based management interface for Exchange Server 2013 (see Figure 1-2). Built on the new design for mail clients, it offers a management interface across various types of clients and Web browsers.

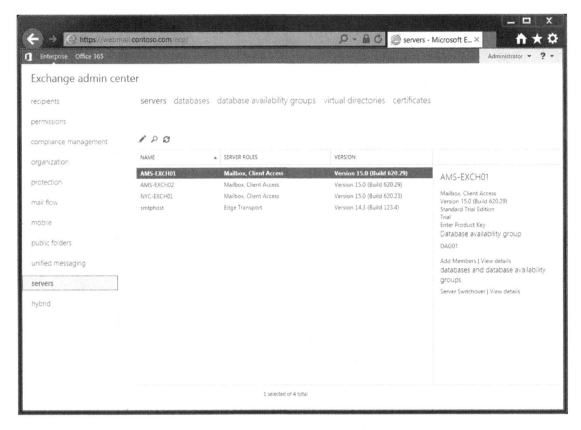

Figure 1-2. *The new EAC in Exchange Server 2013*

Under the hood, EAC is using role-based access control (RBAC) so that only the management options enforced by RBAC are visible to the administrator. That is, just like the Exchange Management Console in Exchange Server 2010, not all the nitty-gritty details are available in the EAC—only the basic management functions are present. For all other management functions, the Exchange Management Shell (EMS) is available.

- **Exchange Management Shell** It's not really new in Exchange Server 2013, but the Exchange Management Shell (EMS) is strongly enhanced in this version. It now runs on top of PowerShell 3.0 (by default, in Windows Server 2012), with approximately 300 new cmdlets making it a very powerful management tool.

- **Exchange 2013 architecture** There's a new architecture when it comes to server roles. In Exchange Server 2013, only two server roles, sometimes referred to as "building blocks," are available:

  - *Mailbox server role*: The Mailbox server role is the Exchange Server 2013 running in the back end, where all the mailboxes are stored. At the same time, the Mailbox server role contains the hub transport service and the unified messaging components.

  - *Client Access server role*: The Client Access server role is running in the front end and is the server all clients connect to. It is responsible for authenticating the connection requests and proxy (or redirect, in case of SIP traffic) the requests to the appropriate mailbox. The server also contains the Front-End Tranport (FET) and a UM call router.

- **Managed store** The "store" is the process running on the Exchange Server that's responsible for processing the mail transactions and storing the transactions in the Mailbox databases. In Exchange Server 2013, the store process is completely rewritten in "managed code." More important, every Mailbox database now has its own store process. So, even if one store process stops working, resulting in that particular Mailbox database to stop working, the other Mailbox databases on the same Mailbox server are unaffected. Earlier, in Exchange 2010, there was only one store process on a Mailbox server. When problems arose with the store process, all those Mailbox databases were affected. Now, this managed store is a great improvement in system stability.

- **Managed availability** One of the best new features of Exchange Server 2013 is its managed availability. It looks like some sort of "self-healing" feature, and it is responsible for monitoring all critical services on Exchange Server 2013. When needed, it takes appropriate action. Managed availability consists of probes, monitors, and actions. *Probes* are constantly checking for certain services, and they feed the results into the monitors. The *monitors* evaluate the results from the probes. And when needed, the managed availability can perform certain *actions*. For example, it can check if OWA is up and running; and if it's not, it can recycle the application pool where OWA is running or reset the Internet Information Services (IISRESET). Likewise, managed availability has probes for Mailbox databases; if a Mailbox database is found to be corrupted, managed availability can take action to automatically fail-over that Mailbox database to another Mailbox server in the DAG and perform an automatic reseed of the corrupted Mailbox database. This way, problems can be resolved even before end-users notice the failures, thereby reducing the number of calls to the help desk.

- **Outlook Anywhere** This feature is not really new, but what's new in the Exchange Server 2013 environment is the fact that Outlook clients no longer connect using RPC over TCP (the traditional MAPI way). All Outlook clients now use RCP over HTTPS (i.e., Outlook Anywhere, or OA). This is true for both internal and external clients. So even an internal Outlook client automatically connects to the Exchange Server 2013 Client Access server (CAS) using RPC/HTTPS. The Outlook client is authenticated on the Exchange Server 2013 CAS, and after authentication, the request is proxied (again using RPC/HTTPS) to the Mailbox server where the mailbox is located.

- **Anti-malware protection** Exchange Server 2013 has built-in anti-malware protection available, but unfortunately it is not as feature-rich as the former Forefront Protection for Exchange (FPE), nor does it have the features that were available in the Exchange Server 2010 edge transport server. For anti-spam and anti-virus solutions for SMTP in transit, Microsoft relies heavily on Exchange Online Protection (EOP), the successor to Forefront Online Protection for Exchange (FOPE), Microsoft's cloud solution for anti-spam and anti-virus. The good news is that both the Exchange Server 2010 and the Exchange Server 2007 edge transport server are running fine and are fully supported in combination with Exchange Server 2013, including edge synchronization. For this to work correctly, though, you need Exchange 2007 SP3 RU10 or Exchange Server 2010 SP3.

- **"Modern" public folders** Microsoft has invested heavily in public folders after years of uncertainty about the future of public folders. Microsoft is calling the new public folders the "modern public folders." The traditional public folder database has been discontinued in Exchange Server 2013, and the public folders have moved to the Mailbox database. Because of this, the public folders are now protected by means of the database availability group, or DAG, so that multiple copies of public folders can exist in a DAG. Public folders consist of the hierarchy (i.e., the folder structure) and the actual content. A writeable copy of the hierarchy is stored in a primary hierarchy mailbox, and there's only one writeable copy.The public-folder content is stored in secondary hierarchy mailboxes; this is a new type of mailbox introduced in Exchange Server 2013. Besides public-folder content, the secondary hierarchy mailboxes also contain a read-only copy of the hierarchy. Although public folders are migrated into these special mailboxes, Outlook clients and Outlook show them as "normal" public folders. Therefore, users will not notice the difference between the traditional public folders and the new public folders.

- **Site mailboxes** Site mailboxes are another new mailbox type in Exchange Server 2013, and they are a combination of Exchange Server 2013 and SharePoint Server 2013. That is, site mailboxes are designed for (temporary) project teams, where lots of Office documents are sent among members of the groups. Under the hood, these site mailboxes are actually a SharePoint team site that is much more capable of storing document-type information. For an Outlook client, it is fully transparent and the site mailbox is visible as a normal mailbox. This is a great example of "Exchange and SharePoint: Better Together."

- **Data loss prevention** Data loss prevention, or DLP, is a new security feature in Exchange Server 2013. It's designed to prevent sending out messages that contain confidential information, based on transport rules. For example, DLP can be used to filter messages that contain credit card numbers or Social Security numbers. It does this by checking the messages as they are submitted against certain predefined templates. If there's a match, a warning is displayed—much like mail tips—about what DLP has found to be a security issue. A number of predefined DLP policies are included in Exchange Server 2013, and the policies are customizable to fit company policies.

Of course, there are many more new features in Exchange Server 2013, but these are the most important ones.

What Has Been Removed from Exchange Server

With every new version of Exchange Server, new features are introduced, but at the same time other features are discontinued, deprecated, or available only in some other form or scenario. The most important changes or discontinued features are:

- **Support for Outlook 2003** Outlook 2003 is not supported in Exchange Server 2013. Not only it is not supported, it is just not working. Outlook 2003 depends on system folders, free/busy, and offline address book distribution folders in public folders, and these system folders have been discontinued.

- **RPC/TCP access for Outlook clients** The traditional RPC/TCP access for Outlook clients is no longer supported in Exchange Server 2013. All Outlook clients will connect using Outlook Anywhere (OA, formerly known as RPC/HTTPS), whether they are on the internal or external network. The reason is obvious; RPC/HTTPS is easily routable between Exchange Servers and between datacenters, which is not the case for the RPC/TCP protocol.

- **Transport service** The dedicated Hub Transport server that was used in Exchange Server 2007 and Exchange Server 2010 is no longer available as a dedicated server. Instead, it is integrated into the Mailbox server role, so that every Mailbox server automatically has a transport service installed. This transport service is responsible for routing SMTP messages, both inside the Exchange Service organization and to the Internet. The Exchange Server 2013 CAS is a protocol proxy for the transport service on the Mailbox server; the service on the Exchange 2013 CAS is called Front-End Transport (FET). External SMTP hosts connect to the FET on the Exchange Server 2013 Client Access server, which proxies the request to the transport service running on the Mailbox server where the recipient's mailbox is located.

- **Unified Messaging service** The dedicated Unified Messaging (UM) server role is no longer available as a dedicated server. Just like the Hub Transport server, it is now integrated with the Exchange Server 2013 Mailbox server. When you are installing an Exchange Server 2013 Mailbox server, the UM service is automatically installed. For SIP traffic, the Exchange Server 2013 CAS does not act as a proxy, but it does redirect the SIP request to the UM service on the Mailbox server where the recipient's mailbox is located.

- **Exchange Management Console and Exchange Control Panel** In Exchange Server 2010, the Exchange Management Console (EMC) was the primary graphical UI for managing the entire Exchange Service environment. While this worked fine in a smaller environment, it failed in large, multi-datacenter environments. In Exchange Server 2013, Microsoft has discontinued the EMC and its functionality is replaced by the Exchange Admin Center (EAC). The same is true for the Exchange Control Panel (ECP). It has been discontinued in Exchange Server 2013, and user self-management is now performed by the EAC.

- **Managed folders** Managed folders were introduced in Exchange Server 2007 as Microsoft's solution for information management and compliance. In Exchange Server 2010, Microsoft introduced the personal archive and retention policies; as a result, the managed folders in Exchange Service 2010 were deprecated. This was clearly visible in Exchange Server 2010 SP1, where the managed folders were manageable only from the EMS and they were not compatible with the personal archive. In Exchange Server 2013, the managed folders are decommissioned completely.

- **Anti-spam agent management** Anti-spam functionality as we knew it in Exchange Server 2010 is not available in Exchange Server 2013. The Exchange Service 2013 CAS does not perform any anti-spam duties, so all SMTP message are proxied to the transport service on the Mailbox servers. These do have some anti-spam functionality, but compared to Exchange Server 2010, they are very limited.

- **Anti-malware** The anti-malware that was built into Exchange Server 2013 is very limited and absolutely not comparable to Microsoft's Forefront Protection for Exchange (FPE), which was previously available. Now, anti-malware is available only on the Mailbox server in the back end. There are no options for managing the anti-malware solution other than to turn it on or off.

- **Exchange Edge Transport server** At first sight, it looks as if the Edge Transport server was discontinued with Exchange Server 2013. It is true that it is not available at the release to manufacturing (RTM) version, but it will be available with Exchange Server 2013 service pack 1. The good news is that Exchange Server 2013 is working fine with the Exchange Server 2010 and Exchange Server 2007 Edge Transport server, even with an edge synchronization between the Exchange 2013 Mailbox server and the down-level Exchange Edge Transport server.

A bit beyond the scope of this book is the Forefront Threat Management Gateway (TMG) 2010. At the end of 2012, Microsoft announced the end of life for TMG 2010. While TMG will be supported for another five years, it will continue to work with Exchange Server 2010—and with some minor adjustments, it will also work with Exchange Server 2013. For the long term, however, it is recommended you start looking for alternatives to this firewall and pre-authentication. The official Microsoft strategy on this is its Forefront Unified Application Gateway (UAG), which can act as a firewall and perform pre-authentication, but other third-party hardware vendors (like Cisco, Juniper, or F5) can deliver the same functionality, sometimes even with load-balancing functionality.

Integration with Active Directory

Active Directory is the foundation for Exchange Server 2013, as it has been for Exchange Server since it was issued 12 years ago. Earlier versions of Exchange Server—that is, Exchange 5.5 and older—relied on their own directory, which was separate from the (NT4) user directory.

A Microsoft Windows Active Directory Directory Service (AD DS) is best described as a forest; this is the highest level in the Directory Service and is the actual security boundary. The forest contains one or more Active Directory Directory domains, and a domain is a logical grouping of resources like users, groups, and computers. Exchange Server 2013 is bound to the forest, so even if you have an environment with over 100 domains, there's only one Exchange organization.

Active Directory sites also play an important role in Exchange deployment. An Active Directory site can be seen as a location, well connected with high bandwidth and low latency—for example, a datacenter or an office. Active Directory sites can contain multiple Active Directory domains, but an Active Directory domain can also span multiple Active Directory sites.

Exchange Server 2013 depends heavily on Active Directory Directory Services, and Active Directory Directory Services need to be healthy. The minimum levels in Active Directory Directory Services need to be Windows 2003 Forest Functional Level (FFL) and Windows 2003 Domain Functional Level (DFL). The domain controllers also need to be at a minimum level of Windows Server 2003 SP1, but this shouldn't be a problem for anyone anymore.

Active Directory Partitions

A Microsoft Windows Active Directory Directory Service consists of three system-provided partitions:

- **Schema partition** The schema partition is the blueprint for all objects and properties that are available in Active Directory. For example, if a new user is created, a user object is instantiated from the schema, the required properties are filled in, and the user account is stored in the Active Directory database. All objects and properties are in the schema partition, and therefore it depends which version is used. Windows 2012 Active Directory has much newer objects, and newer (and more) properties, than, for example, Windows 2003 Active Directory. The same is true, of course, for applications like Exchange Server. Exchange Server 2013 adds a lot of new objects and attributes to Active Directory that make it possible to gain functionality. Therefore, every new version of Exchange Server, or even the service packs, needs to make schema changes.

  There is only one schema partition in the entire Active Directory forest. Even if you have an Active Directory forest with 100 domains and 250 sites worldwide, there's only one schema partition. This partition is replicated between all domain controllers in the entire Active Directory forest. The most important, read-write copy of the schema partition is the schema master, which is typically the first domain controller installed in the forest.

- **Configuration partition** The configuration partition is where all nonschema information is stored that needs to be available throughout the entire Active Directory forest. Information regarding the Exchange is stored in the configuration partition, and as with the schema partition, there's only one configuration partition. It replicates all domain controllers so that all the Exchange Servers have access to the same consistent set of information. Information stored in the configuration partition is, for example, Exchange Server information, accepted domain information, policy information—in short, basically all the information that needs to be identical on all Exchange Servers, regardless of the number of Exchange Servers.

- **Domain partition** The domain partition is where all domain-specific information is stored. There's one partition per domain, so if you have 100 domains in your Active Directory forest, you have 100 separate domain partitions. User objects, contacts, and security and distribution groups are stored in the domain partition.

The best tool for viewing the three Active Directory partitions in the ADSI Edit MMC (Microsoft Management Console) is a snap-in, which is shown in Figure 1-3. But be careful; there's very little safeguarding in this tool, so it's easy to destroy critical parts in Active Directory when you're just clicking around!

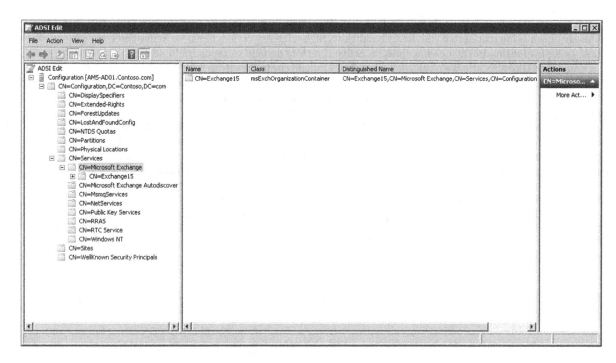

Figure 1-3. *The Exchange information is stored in the configuration partition*

The Active Directory Users and Computers (ADUC) MMC has a focus on the domain partition. In Windows Server 2012, the Active Directory Administrative Center (ADAC) is the preferred tool to manage the Active Directory environment. But using either tool is relatively safe, since the tool prevents messing around with objects in a way that Active Directory does not like. The Active Directory Sites and Services (ADSS) work in the configuration partition. All changes made here are visible to all domains in the forest; the same is true for the Active Directory domains and trusts MMC snap-in.

The last important tool regarding Active Directory is the Schema MMC snap-in, which is usually run on the domain controller that holds the schema master role. Using the Schema MMC snap-in, it is possible to make changes to the Active Directory schema partition.

■ **Warning**   Only do this when you're absolutely sure o f what you're doing, and when you have proper guidance—for example, from Microsoft support. Changes to the Active Directory in a wrong way here cannot be reversed!

Domain controllers also have tools like LDIFDE and CSVDE installed. These are command-line tools that can be used to import and export objects into or from Active Directory. LDIFDE can also be used to make changes to the Active Directory schema, and the Exchange Server 2013 setup application uses the LDIFDE tool to configure Active Directory for use with Exchange Server 2013. These tools are beyond the scope of this book.

Active Directory Sites

Active Directory sites play an important role in the larger Exchange Server 2013 deployments. As stated earlier, an Active Directory site can be seen as a (physical) location with good network connectivity, high bandwidth, and low latency—that is, a local LAN. An office or a datacenter is typically a good candidate for an Active Directory site.

An organization can have multiple locations or multiple datacenters, resulting in multiple Active Directory sites. Sites are typically interconnected with lower bandwidth, higher latency connections. An Active Directory site can also have multiple domains, but at the same time, an Active Directory domain can span multiple sites.

An Active Directory also is a replication boundary. Domain controllers in an Active Directory site replicate their information almost immediately among sites. If a new object is created, or if an object is changed, the other domain controllers in that same site are notified immediately and the information is replicated within seconds. All domain controllers in an Active Directory site should contain the same information.

Information exchanged between domain controllers in different Active Directory sites is replicated on a timed schedule, defined by the administrator. A typical timeframe can be 15 minutes, but depending on the type of connection, or the bandwidth used to a particular location (you don't want your replication traffic to interfere with normal production bandwidth), it can take up to hours. This means that when changes are made to Active Directory—for example, when installing Exchange Server 2013—it can take a serious amount of time before all the information is replicated across all the domain controllers and the new changes are visible to the entire organization.

Active Directory sites are created using the Active Directory Sites and Services MMC snap-in (see Figure 1-4). The first step is to define the network subnets in the various locations in the snap-in, and then tie the actual Active Directory site to the network subnet. For example, a datacenter in Amsterdam has the IP subnet `192.168.0.0/24` while the datacenter in New York has the IP subnet `192.168.10.0/24`.

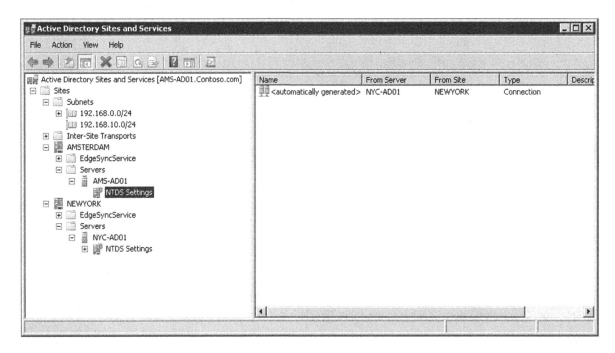

Figure 1-4. *Two different subnets and sites, as shown in Active Directory Sites and Services*

An Active Directory site can be "Internet facing" or "non-Internet facing," which of course indicates whether the site has Internet connectivity or not. This is important for Exchange Server 2013, since it determines how external clients are connecting to their mailboxes in the various locations.

Also, the routing of SMTP messages through the Exchange organization is based on Active Directory sites.

Exchange Server 2013 Architecture

Exchange Server 2013 at RTM is using so-called building blocks; there are two such building blocks:

- **Client Access Server** The Client Access server (CAS) is the server where all clients connect. The CAS consists of three parts: client access front end (CAFE), front end transport (FET), and the UM call router (UMCR). The CAS performs authentication and proxies the client request to the appropriate Mailbox server, where the actual client mailbox is located. The CAS in Exchange Server 2013 is sometimes also referred to as the front end, although according to the book, UMCR is not officially a front end.

- **Mailbox Server** The Mailbox server is the server where the actual mailbox data is stored. Clients do not access the Mailbox server directly; all requests are routed through the CAS. The Mailbox server in Exchange Server 2013 is sometimes also referred to as the back end.

In Exchange Server 2007 and Exchange Server 2010, the Hub Transport server and the Unified Messaging server were also dedicated servers. These four servers were tightly coupled and used RPC for inter-server communication. Although this works fine, it presents some challenges when it comes to a multi-datacenter environment and to site resiliency. One of the design goals for Exchange Server 2013 was to remove the tight coupling of the server roles and replace them with a more loosely coupled mechanism.

The four servers are no longer available in separate server roles, but are incorporated into the Mailbox server role. When installing the latter, note that the Hub Transport and Unified Messaging functions are automatically installed. The Mailbox server contains most of the business logic of Exchange Server 2013, and this is the server where all the processing takes place for all mailboxes located on that Mailbox server.

The Client Access Server

The Client Access server (CAS) performs only authentication of a client request, and after authentication, the request is proxied to the Mailbox server where the destination mailbox is located. The CAS in itself does not perform any processing with respect to mail data. Compared to previous versions of Exchange Server CAS, in Exchange Server 2013 it is basically a "thin" server. According to Microsoft, its connections are stateless (not clueless, though). But the connections are not really stateless, because the SSL connection is terminated at the CAS and then processed. If a CAS goes offline, all connections are terminated and they have to be set up again on another CAS (which would not be the case in a true stateless setup). The reason that Microsoft calls it "stateless" is that there's no persistent storage on Exchange Server 2013 CAS.

Unlike Exchange Server 2010 and Exchange Server 2007, the CAS no longer communicates with the Mailbox server using RPC; the original client request is instead proxied to the Mailbox server. If the initial request from the client to the Client Access server is from Outlook Web App (so HTTPS), the protocol between the CAS and the Mailbox server is also HTTPS. Note that the request from Internet to the CAS is using the regular port 443, but that the proxied request to the Mailbox server is using port 444.

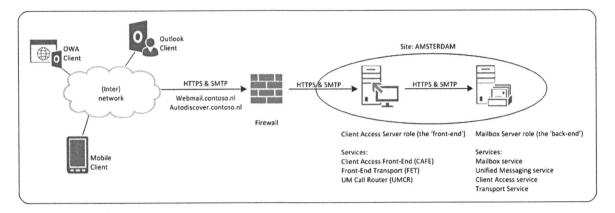

Figure 1-5. *The front-end and back-end architecture in Exchange Server 2013*

This architecture means that the actual Exchange Server 2013 servers are now loosely coupled, which offers huge advantages when multiple offices or multiple datacenters are used.

■ **Note**   The SMTP protocol can be seen as a client in this scenario, as well. Outbound SMTP can be also routed through the Client Access server.

As stated before, the CAS is a "thin" server and does not store any information from the sessions, except for the default logging in IIS, of course. This is true for both regular client requests and SMTP requests. SMTP requests are accepted on the CAS, but the message itself is not stored on the CAS as it is on an Exchange 2010 Edge Ttransport server, for example.

The front-end transport service that is responsible for handling SMTP messages on the CAS doesn't store messages on the server itself, but passes the SMTP messages directly to the appropriate Mailbox server where the intended recipient's mailbox is located, or to a downlevel Hub Transport server if the recipient is located on a downlevel Mailbox server. The front-end transport service does not inspect message content.

Because of the stateless connections from clients, the load-balancing solution needed when multiple CAS are used doesn't have to be a layer 7 load balancer, as used to be the case in Exchange 2010; Exchange Server 2013 works fine with (much simpler) layer 4 load balancers.

The Mailbox Server

The Mailbox server is where all the processing regarding messages takes place. Clients connect to the CAS, but the requests are proxied or redirected to the appropriate Mailbox server. All message rendering takes place on the Mailbox server, in contrast to Exchange Server 2010, where all rendering took place on the CAS. To achieve this, there's also a CAS component on the Mailbox server.

SMTP Transport is now also located on the Mailbox server and consists of three separate services:

- The Transport service
- The Mailbox Transport Delivery service
- The Mailbox Transport Submission service.

The Transport service can be seen as the successor to the "old" Hub Transport server, and it handles all SMTP message flow within the organization, such as routing, queueing, bifurcation, message categorization, and content inspection. Important to note is that the Transport service never communicates directly with the Mailbox databases. Communication between the Transport service and the Mailbox database is performed by the Mailbox Transport Delivery service and the Mailbox Transport Submission service. These services connect directly to the Mailbox database (using RPC!) to deliver or retrieve messages from the Mailbox database. As with the Front End Transport Service, the Mailbox Transport service does not queue any messages on the Mailbox server; the Transport service (notice the absence of the word *mailbox*) does queue information on the Mailbox server. (The transport mechanism is covered in detail in Chapter 3.)

The most important part of this, of course, is the mailbox components that run on the Mailbox server. The information store, or store process, is the process responsible for handling all mailbox transactions and for storing these transactions in a Mailbox database. The database is not a relational database like SQL Server; it's running on its own engine, the extensible storage engine or ESE. The ESE databases have been fully optimized for the past 15 years for use with Exchange Server, so they perform very well and also are very reliable. The ESE database is a transactional database using a database, log files, and a checkpoint file. (I'll get back to database internals in Chapter 4.)

The engine in Exchange Server 2013 is completely rewritten in managed code (i.e. C#) and in Exchange Server 2013, there's now one store process for each Mailbox database. So if one store process can crash, resulting in the accompanying database crash as well, the other databases on the server are unaffected.

The Exchange Replication service is another important service running on the Mailbox server. This service is responsible for replicating mailbox data from one Mailbox database on one Mailbox server to a Mailbox database running on another Mailbox server. The collection of Mailbox server replication data between sources is called the database availability group, or DAG. A DAG can take up to 16 Mailbox servers where there's only one active Mailbox database copy, and up to 15 passive Mailbox database copies.

The database in Exchange Server 2013 has been greatly improved compared to earlier versions. For instance, Exchange Server 2013 now generates 50% fewer IOs per second (IOPS compared with Exchange Server 2010), making it now possible to store multiple databases, including its log files, on one physical disk. This is something that Microsoft never recommended doing in the past, but now it is a viable solution. Of course, this is recommended only when there are multiple copies of a Mailbox database available for recovery purposes.

Clients

Clients are the most important part of every messaging system, since this is the interface the users are using. In Exchange Server 2013, there are a lot of major improvements and changes that are worth noticing.

Widely used are Outlook clients, but Outlook clients also uses Autodiscover and Exchange Web Services (EWS) for communicating with Exchange Server 2013. OWA and Activesync clients are also widely used. All three are running on the HTTPS protocol.

The last two client protocols are POP3 and IMAP4; these are legacy protocols but still in use by (old) clients or sometimes by business applications.

Outlook Clients

One of the most important changes in Exchange Server 2013 is that Outlook no longer uses direct MAPI (RPC over TCP); Exchange Server 2013 is accessible only using Outlook Anywhere, with RPC rather than HTTPS. This change reflects the loose coupling of the Exchange Server 2013 roles, as explained in the previous section. Direct MAPI is pretty rigid and it requires a fast and reliable network connection. Also, routing problems that occur when multiple datacenters are used contributed to this decision. So, only RPC over HTTPS, also known as Outlook Anywhere, is used by Outlook clients, both internally and externally.

I have mentioned Outlook 2013, but Outlook 2010 SP1 (with April 2012 Cumulative Update) and Outlook 2007 SP3 (with July 2012 Cumulative Update) are also fully supported in combination with Exchange Server 2013—but again, only with Outlook Anywhere. Outlook 2007, 2010, and 2013 rely heavily on the Autodiscover functionality. Autodiscover is used not only for creating the Outlook profile during the initial startup of the Outlook client but also hourly to request the latest configuration information from Exchange Server 2013.

Outlook 2007, 2010, and 2013 also rely heavily on EWS. Using EWS, the Outlook client can request free/busy information, set an out-of-office message, or download the offline address book. The tricky part here is that when Autodiscover is not functioning correctly, the Outlook client will not get the appropriate information from the Exchange 2013 server, resulting in a nonworking EWS environment, for example.

Since HTTPS is playing such an important role in an Exchange Server 2013 environment, SSL certificates have an even more important role than they did in previous versions of Exchange Server. If there's no proper SSL certificate on the Exchange Server 2013, CAS will most likely result in Outlook clients not being able to connect at all. As mentioned earlier in this chapter, Outlook 2003 clients are no longer supported. The oldest supported Outlook client working against an Exchange Server 2013 environment is Outlook 2007.

Outlook clients can run in cached mode or in online mode, where cached mode is the default (and preferred) mode. When running in cached mode, Outlook is working with a copy of the mailbox on the local machine, and all changes are made to this "cached" copy. Outlook automatically synchronizes this copy in the background with the mailbox on the Exchange Server. All processing takes place on the Outlook client's workstation, and not on the Exchange Server, thereby reducing processor cycles and (expensive) disk IO on the Exchange Server. Note that Outlook 2007 and Outlook 2010 will store a complete copy of the mailbox on the workstation's hard disk. Outlook 2013 can be adjusted to prevent a full copy on the local hard disk.

When running in online mode, Outlook is working directly against the Exchange Server, and there's no copy of the mailbox on the local workstation. It's obvious that this will increase the load on the Exchange Server, plus the Outlook client will always need to be online. Offline working—for example, while traveling—is not possible in this scenario. Outlook running in online mode can be seen when it is used in a terminal server environment, although Outlook 2010 running in cached mode on a terminal server is fully supported nowadays.

Outlook Web App Clients

Outlook Web App, or OWA, is the webmail client for Exchange Server 2013. A native part of Exchange Server 2013, it offers a rich client and a similar look and feel as for Outlook 2013. At the same time, OWA has a consistent view across different browsers on different operating systems. You can run OWA on IE9 and get the same user experience as when running OWA in a browser on an iPad or on Windows Surface. The Microsoft Exchange Team blog contains an interesting blog post about OWA running on different devices; see http://tinyurl.com/c2cdhru.

New in Exchange Server 2013 is the option to use OWA offline, with integrated apps for OWA that enrich the user interface and offer additional functionality.

Microsoft is offering cross-browser supportability, so besides Internet Explorer, Mozilla Firefox 17 or later, Google Chrome 24 or later, and Apple Safari 5 or later are fully supported for use with Exchange Server 2013. Of course, the latest versions of these browsers support most features, but for an up-to-date overview of available functionality per browser version, navigate to the Microsoft Technet site at http://tinyurl.com/buxyby9.

OWA Offline

In the past, a commonly requested feature was to be able to use OWA offline. This is now possible with Exchange Server 2013. For this feature to work, you need at least Internet Explorer 10, Safari 5.1(Mac only) or later, or Chrome 24 or later.

If your browser is capable of supporting offline OWA, it's just a matter of selecting Offline Settings from the settings menu in OWA, as shown in Figure 1-6, and you're ready to go.

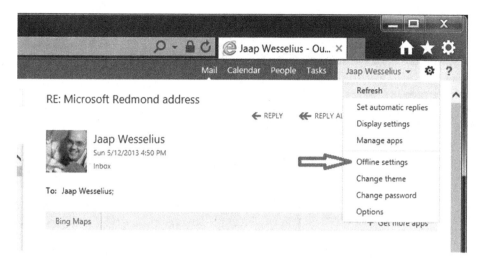

Figure 1-6. *To enable offline usage*

Not all information is available in OWA offline. It is comparable to, for example, the amount of information available in Windows Phone. Only three days of e-mail (or 150 items, whichever is larger) will be available; there are the current and next month calendar information, and there are no archive folders, for example.

The browser determines where to store the offline information, and this poses a security risk. Anyone who has access to the PC where OWA offline is used also has access to this information, so it should not be used on a PC that is shared by multiple users.

Outlook Apps

New in Exchange Server 2013 is the concept of using apps. Apps on the Exchange Server are integrated in OWA and Outlook 2013, and they give the user added functionality. For example, there is the default Bing Maps app (see Figure 1-7). If there's a street address in an e-mail, the Bing Maps app can look it up and provide additional information regarding the address, such as the location on a map or directions to the location. At the time of writing, only U.S. addresses are recognized, but Microsoft is actively working on regional support.

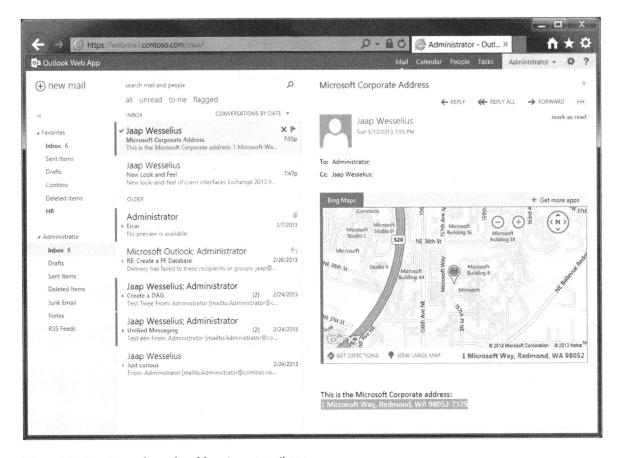

Figure 1-7. *Bing Maps shows the address in an e-mail app*

By default, there are four apps available out of the box: Bing Maps, Suggested Meetings, Unsubscribe, and Action Items. These four are globally enabled by default.

The Exchange administrator has the option to add, remove, disable, or enable apps in the EAC as a global setting (see Figure 1-8), but the user can also install, enable, or disable apps in the EAC.

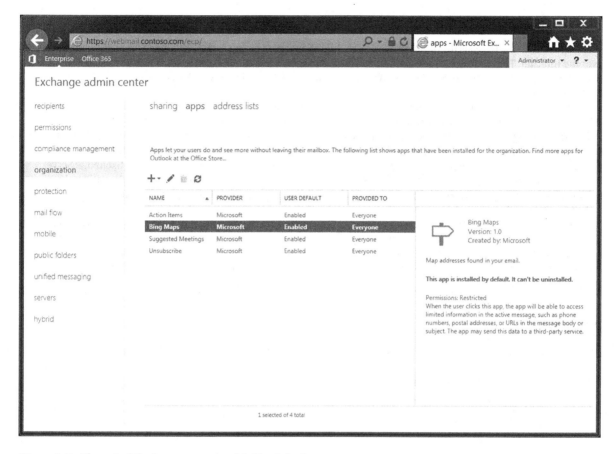

Figure 1-8. *The out-of-the-box apps are enabled by default*

Additional apps are available in the Office Store. Microsoft also encourages Independent Software Vendors (ISV) to write their own apps and distribute them through the Office Store.

Office Web Apps

In Exchange Server 2010, it was possible to use the attachment preview functionality in OWA. A technique called WebReady Document Viewing was used to provide this functionality.

In Exchange Server 2013, the attachment preview functionality is still available, but instead there's a completely new server application called Office Web Apps, which may be used to render the actual document and send the HTML information to the OWA client. That is, when an OWA client wants to preview an attachment, the request is forwarded to an Office Web Apps server. Exchange Server online users in Office 365 have this functionality available by default; for an Exchange Server on-premises deployment, a dedicated Office Web Apps server is needed.

■ **Note**   To offer this functionality in an Exchange Server 2013 on-premises environment, an additional Office Web Apps server needs to be installed.

Exchange ActiveSync Clients

Exchange ActiveSync (EAS) is the protocol used by mobile clients connecting to the Exchange Server 2013 environment over the Internet. This includes Windows Phone clients, iOS clients like iPhone and iPad, and Android clients. Also, the mail client on Windows 8 RT (i.e., Windows 8 running on a tablet) uses EAS to retrieve mail data from Exchange Server 2013.

Microsoft is licensing the EAS protocol and its interfaces to third parties and independent software vendors. It is up to the vendors to write actual applications to use the EAS protocol. One of the problems with this situation is that Microsoft "forgets" to enforce standard implementations or employ quality control. Therefore, each vendor has its own interpretation of how to use the EAS protocol, resulting in some applications that run fine and some that are horrible to use. Or, there are some applications that have a major performance impact on Exchange Server 2013. For instance, there are several known problems with iOS applications using the EAS protocol, resulting in poor performance or corrupted items in a user's mailbox. Recurring appointments being accepted on iOS devices are unfortunately well known in this scenario.

Mobile clients are typically very sensitive when it comes to SSL certificates, and not all SSL certificates are accepted by mobile clients. In order to get EAS working properly, there needs to be used a supported third-party SSL certificate.

Most mobile clients rely on the Autodiscover function of Exchange Server 2013, as do Outlook clients, so again having a fully working autodiscover environment is a prerequisite for running EAS successfully. I'll discuss this in more depth in Chapter 3.

Apple Clients

Apple Mac clients are fully supported with Exchange Server 2013, but this is true only for those Mac clients who are using Exchange Web Services (EWS) for connecting with the Exchange Server. This means that the following versions are supported with Exchange Server 2013:

- Entourage 2008 for Mac, Web Services Edition
- Outlook for Mac 2011

POP3 and IMAP4 Clients

Although still widely used and under active development, POP3 and IMAP4 are not commonly used in a Microsoft environment. POP3 and IMAP4 are primarily used in (low-cost) hosting environments running some Unix flavor, but they can also be configured to be used on Exchange Server 2013. There are also business applications that can access a particular mailbox using the POP3 protocol to retrieve messages.

POP3 and IMAP4 are installed on Exchange Server 2013 by default, but the relevant services are set to "manual start"; if needed, the POP3 or IMAP4 service has to be set to "automatically start." Also, the authentication (encrypted login or plain text login) needs to be set. Exchange Server 2013 allows the basic POP3 and IMAP4 protocol, but also allows the encrypted version—that is, POP/3 (POP3 over SSL) and IMAP/S (IMAP4 over SSL).

■ **Note** The POP3 and IMAP4 protocols are used only for retrieving messages. The mail client should be configured for sending outbound mail via a SMTP mailhost. Of course, this can be the Exchange Server 2013 Client Access server running the client front-end connector.

Summary

Exchange Server 2013 is the newest version of Microsoft's well-known messaging and collaboration solution. There are a lot of new features available, and a lot of changes as well. The most important differences are the changes in the architecture, resulting in only two server roles: the Client Access server and the Mailbox server roles—sometimes also referred to as the front end and the back end. The Exchange Server 2013 roles are now loosely coupled, and as a result it is much easier to implement a multi-datacenter Exchange Server environment.

Exchange Server 2013 offers a consistent view across multiple clients, so the look and feel of Outlook 2013 is similar to that of OWA, even if it is running on other operating systems, such as Apple or Linux. Also, mobile clients like Windows Phone, Windows RT, or the Apple iPad offer a great end-user experience.

From an administrator's view, management features of Exchange Server 2013 have been greatly improved. Managed availability offers a built-in monitoring solution and, tied into this, some self-healing functionality. If performance is degrading or parts of your Exchange Server are not working correctly, then this managed availability will automatically detect these problems and take appropriate action.

In the next two chapters, I'll discuss how to install Exchange Server 2013. Chapter 2 will be about a green-field installation, while Chapter 3 will discuss installing Exchange Server 2013 into an existing Exchange Server 2007 or Exchange Server 2010 environment.

CHAPTER 2

Installing Exchange Server 2013

Now that we've covered some of the new functions of Exchange Server 2013 and provided some background information, it's time to move on to actually installing Exchange 2013 and getting it working. In this chapter I will cover installation of both the Mailbox server and the Client Access server (CAS), including the prerequisite software. Installation can be performed using the GUI or from the command line, fully unattended. This chapter covers new, "green-field" installations. Chapter 3 covers upgrades from a previous version of Exchange Server.

An important decision to make is what operating system you will use for Exchange 2013. Normally I recommend using Windows Server 2012 as the underlying operating system, simply because it's newer, the scalability figures are better, and the support lifecycle is longer compared to Windows Server 2008 R2.

However, a lot of companies still have Windows Server 2008 R2 as their default operating system and they haven't switched to Windows Server 2012. Therefore, I will discuss both operating systems in this chapter.

Requirements and Prerequisite Software

When you are installing Exchange 2013, a number of requirements have to be met regarding the operating system where Exchange Server will be installed and the version of Active Directory Directory Services (AD DS) that will be used. There's also some prerequisite software that needs to be installed in advance, including Windows Server roles or features.

Software Requirements

Exchange 2013 can be installed on the following Windows operating systems:

- Windows Server 2008 R2 SP1 Standard Edition

- Windows Server 2008 R2 SP1 Enterprise Edition

- Windows Server 2008 R2 RTM Datacenter Edition

- Windows Server 2012 Standard Edition

- Windows Server 2012 Datacenter Edition

The Exchange 2013 management tools can be installed on the following Windows operating systems:

- Windows Server 2008 R2 SP1 Standard Edition

- Windows Server 2008 R2 SP1 Enterprise Edition

- Windows Server 2008 R2 RTM Datacenter Edition

- Windows Server 2012 Standard Edition

- Windows Server 2012 Datacenter Edition

- Windows 8 64-bit version (except home edition)

- Windows 7 SP1 64-bit version (except home edition)

■ **Important** Both Windows Server 2008 R2 and Windows Server 2012 need to be installed with the full GUI. Windows Server core is not supported for use with Exchange 2013.

When it comes to Active Directory, the following requirements can be identified:

- Schema master Windows Server 2003 SP2 or later

- Global catalog server Windows Server 2003 SP2 or later

- Domain controller Windows Server 2003 SP2 or later

- Active directory forest Active Directory at Windows Server 2003 forest functionality level or higher

---

■ **Note** Installation of Exchange 2013 on domain controllers is supported but not recommended. The recommended way of installing Exchange 2013 is on a member server of an Active Directory domain.

Hardware Requirements

Exchange 2013 has the following hardware requirements, but note that these are the absolute bare-minimum hardware requirements:

- X64 architecture-based processor (Intel Itanium IA64 is not supported).

- 8 GB of RAM for the Mailbox server.

- 4 GB of RAM for the Client Access server.

- 8 GB of RAM for combined Mailbox server and Client Access server.

- At least 30 GB of free space on the disk where Exchange 2013 will be installed. (Add an additional 500 MB for every UM language pack. All disks have to be formatted with the NTFS file system.)

For a full and up-to-date overview of all Exchange 2013 requirements, visit the Microsoft TechNet site at http://tinyurl.com/2chaju.

Prerequisite Software

Before installing Exchange 2013 on Windows Server 2012 or Windows Server 2008 R2 SP1, you need to have installed some prerequisite software. These can be default Windows Server roles or features, but also additional software.

To install Exchange 2013 on a server, you need the following preprequisite software, independent of the server roles that will be installed:

- .NET Framework 4.5

- Windows Management Framework 3.0, which includes PowerShell 3.0

The first Exchange 2013 server will typically be used for modifying the Active Directory schema as well, so this particular server also needs the Remote Server Administration Tools (RSAT). Both Exchange 2013 roles need (parts of) Internet Information Server (IIS) installed and both server roles also need the Unified Communciations Managed API 4.0 (UCMA).

■ **Note** The Active Directory schema can be modified from the first Exchange 2013 server that will be installed. Some administrators, however, prefer to change the Active Directory schema from the Active Directory domain controller that holds the Schema Master FSMO role.

There's some confusion regarding the use of the Office 2010 Filter Pack software. In earlier versions of Exchange Server, this software was used to perform attachment inspection on the Mailbox server role and the Hub Transport server role. Although the setup application still checks if this software is installed on the new Exchange Server, it is not really needed since this function is now included in the Exchange Server search function.

For more detailed information about the Exchange 2013 prerequisites, visit the Microsoft TechNet website on `http://tinyurl.com/dhnbxq`.

Virtualization

All Exchange 2013 server roles are supported in a server virtualization environment, but only if the virtualization solution is supported via the Microsoft Server Virtualization Validation Program (SVVP). Most major virtualization software vendors are supported via this program.

However, there are a few options that you should be aware of:

- Use of dynamic memory in a virtual machine (VM) is not supported. Using dynamic memory will severely impact the server's performance—in a negative way, that is.

- Use of dynamically expanding disks, differencing disks, and snapshots are not supported.

- Keeping the ratio of virtual processor to physical processor at 2:1 or lower, preferably 1:1. This means that if the virtualization host is offering 16 processor cores, the virtual processors of all your running VMs must not exceed 32.

- No "free processor cycles." Although the use of hyperthreading in the physical processor can be tempting, you can't count the additionally hyperthreading processor cores as "normal" processor cores, as that will not result in the desired performance.

- For a virtualized Exchange 2013 environment, the same design principles apply as for a physical environment. This means that if a physical design needs 32GB of server memory, a virtual design also needs 32GB of server memory.

- Storage requirements in a virtualized environment are identical to the storage requirements in a physical environment.

- Do not install (server) applications on the virtualization hosts, except for management software like monitoring software or backup software.

- Do not overcommit your environment. You cannot create processor cycles out of thin air!

Virtualization is not rocket science, so if you just keep these factors in mind, your virtualized Exchange 2013 environment should run fine.

Exchange Server 2013 Installation

It is my personal recommendation that you install Exchange Server 2013 on top of Windows Server 2012. It is more scalable than Windows Server 2008 R2 and its support lifecycle is better. Windows Server 2012 will be supported for 10 years after the time of this writing. Also, upgrading an underlying operating system on an Exchange 2013 server is not supported, so when you are installing Exchange 2013 on Windows Server 2008 R2, there's no way to upgrade later on.

However, not all companies have raised Windows Server 2012 to the company standard, and many are still running Windows Server 2008 R2 as their default operating systems. Therefore, I start the installation guide with installation of Exchange 2013 on Windows Server 2008 R2, and then I will switch to installation on Windows Server 2012.

Preparing Windows Server 2008 R2 SP1

When installing Exchange 2013 on Windows Server 2008 R2 SP1, the .NET Framework 4.5 and the Windows Management Framework 3.0 need to be installed first. Both can be downloaded from the Microsoft website:

- .NET Framework 4.5 at http://tinyurl.com/asuzq2d

- Windows Management Framework 3.0, which includes PowerShell 3.0, at http://tinyurl.com/bmro9o4

After you've installed both packages and rebooted the server, the Remote Server Administration Tools (RSAT-ADDS) can be installed. To install, log on to the server as an administrator, open a PowerShell command prompt, and enter the following commands:

```
Import-Module ServerManager
Add Windows Feature RSAT-ADDS
```

When the Remote Server Administration Tools are installed, as shown in Figure 2-1, reboot the server.

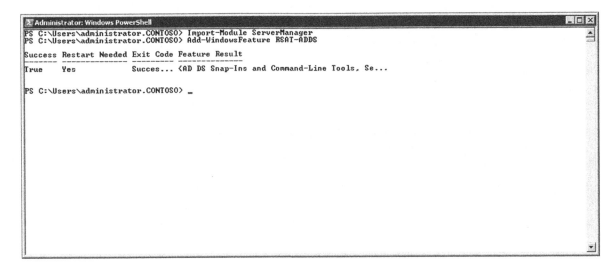

Figure 2-1. *Installing the Remote Server Administration Tools (Windows Server 2008 R2)*

Once rebooted, you install the additional prerequisite software. Which prerequisite software you install depends on the Exchange 2013 server role that you want to install. For a dedicated Exchange Mailbox server, or a combined Exchange Mailbox server and Client Access server, you log on as an administrator to the new server, open a PowerShell command window, and enter the following commands:

```
Import-Module ServerManager

Add-WindowsFeature Desktop-Experience, NET-Framework, NET-HTTP-Activation, RPC-over-HTTP-proxy,
RSAT-Clustering, RSAT-Web-Server, WAS-Process-Model, Web-Asp-Net, Web-Basic-Auth, Web-Client-Auth,
Web-Digest-Auth, Web-Dir-Browsing, Web-Dyn-Compression, Web-Http-Errors, Web-Http-Logging,
Web-Http-Redirect, Web-Http-Tracing, Web-ISAPI-Ext, Web-ISAPI-Filter, Web-Lgcy-Mgmt-Console,
Web-Metabase, Web-Mgmt-Console, Web-Mgmt-Service, Web-Net-Ext, Web-Request-Monitor, Web-Server,
Web-Stat-Compression, Web-Static-Content, Web-Windows-Auth, Web-WMI
```

For just a dedicated Exchange Client Access server, you use the following commands:

```
Import-Module ServerManager

Add-WindowsFeature Desktop-Experience, NET-Framework, NET-HTTP-Activation, RPC-over-HTTP-proxy,
RSAT-Clustering, RSAT-Web-Server, WAS-Process-Model, Web-Asp-Net, Web-Basic-Auth, Web-Client-Auth,
Web-Digest-Auth, Web-Dir-Browsing, Web-Dyn-Compression, Web-Http-Errors, Web-Http-Logging,
Web-Http-Redirect, Web-Http-Tracing, Web-ISAPI-Ext, Web-ISAPI-Filter, Web-Lgcy-Mgmt-Console,
Web-Metabase, Web-Mgmt-Console, Web-Mgmt-Service, Web-Net-Ext, Web-Request-Monitor, Web-Server,
Web-Stat-Compression, Web-Static-Content, Web-Windows-Auth, Web-WMI
```

After installing the prerequisite software and rebooting the new server, continue by installing the following updates on the Exchange 2013 server:

- Microsoft Unified Communications Managed API 4.0, Core Runtime 64-bit at http://tinyurl.com/axohycv

- Knowledge Base article KB974405 ("Windows Identity Foundation") at http://tinyurl.com/asdt348

- Knowledge Base article KB2619234 ("A hotfix is available to enable the association cookie/GUID that is used by RPC over HTTP to also be used at the RPC layer in Windows 7 and in Windows Server 2008 R2") at http://tinyurl.com/aklfexf

- Knowledge Base article KB2533623 ("Insecure library loading could allow remote code execution")at http://tinyurl.com/ap83ft5

■ **Note** It is possible that some of these updates were already installed as part of the Windows update when you installed the base operating system. If this is the case, you'll see the message "The update is not applicable to your computer."

When requested, reboot the server. Once it's rebooted, you'll see that the Windows Server 2008 R2 server is ready to install Exchange 2013, as described in the "Installing Exchange Server 2013" section later in this chapter.

Preparing Windows Server 2012

When installing Exchange 2013 on Windows Server 2012, there are fewer prerequisite software programs and updates to be installed first, since a lot of them are contained in Windows Server 2012 itself, such as the .NET Framework 4.5 and the Windows Management Framework 3.0.

So, as with Windows Server 2008 R2, the first step is to install the Remote Server Administration Tools (RSAT-ADDS). To do this, you log on to the server as an administrator, open a PowerShell command prompt, and enter the following command: `Add-WindowsFeature RSAT-ADDS`. Figure 2-2 shows the operation completed successfully.

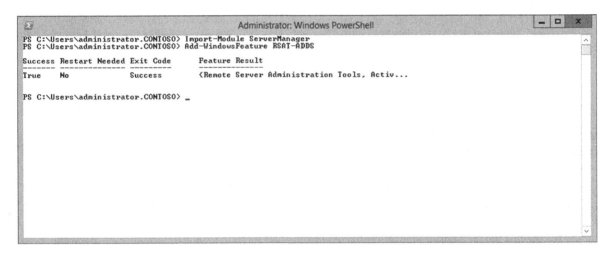

Figure 2-2. *Installing the Remote Server Administration Tools (Windows Server 2012)*

For a dedicated Exchange 2013 Mailbox server, or for combined Mailbox and Client Access server roles, log on as an administrator to the new server, open a PowerShell command window, and enter the following commands:

```
Install-WindowsFeature AS-HTTP-Activation, Desktop-Experience, NET-Framework-45-Features,
RPC-over-HTTP-proxy, RSAT-Clustering, RSAT-Clustering-CmdInterface, Web-Mgmt-Console,
WAS-Process-Model, Web-Asp-Net45, Web-Basic-Auth, Web-Client-Auth, Web-Digest-Auth,
Web-Dir-Browsing, Web-Dyn-Compression, Web-Http-Errors, Web-Http-Logging, Web-Http-Redirect,
Web-Http-Tracing, Web-ISAPI-Ext, Web-ISAPI-Filter, Web-Lgcy-Mgmt-Console, Web-Metabase,
Web-Mgmt-Console, Web-Mgmt-Service, Web-Net-Ext45, Web-Request-Monitor, Web-Server,
Web-Stat-Compression, Web-Static-Content, Web-Windows-Auth, Web-WMI, Windows-Identity-Foundation
```

For a dedicated Client Access server, use the following commands:

```
Install-WindowsFeature AS-HTTP-Activation, Desktop-Experience, NET-Framework-45-Features,
RPC-over-HTTP-proxy, RSAT-Clustering, Web-Mgmt-Console, WAS-Process-Model, Web-Asp-Net45,
Web-Basic-Auth, Web-Client-Auth, Web-Digest-Auth, Web-Dir-Browsing, Web-Dyn-Compression,
Web-Http-Errors, Web-Http-Logging, Web-Http-Redirect, Web-Http-Tracing, Web-ISAPI-Ext,
Web-ISAPI-Filter, Web-Lgcy-Mgmt-Console, Web-Metabase, Web-Mgmt-Console, Web-Mgmt-Service,
Web-Net-Ext45, Web-Request-Monitor, Web-Server, Web-Stat-Compression, Web-Static-Content,
Web-Windows-Auth, Web-WMI, Windows-Identity-Foundation
```

Figure 2-3 shows the commands executed successfully and the warning that a reboot is needed.

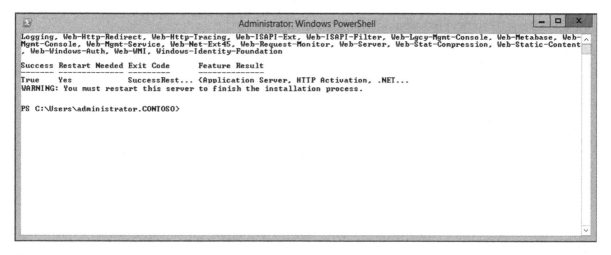

Figure 2-3. *Successfully installed prerequisite software in a PowerShell window*

After rebooting the server, there's onlyl one thing that needs to be installed: the Unified Communications Managed API 4.0 Runtime, at www.microsoft.com/en-us/download/details.aspx?id=34992

As mentioned earlier, there's no need to install the Office 2010 Filter Pack software, since this functionality is contained in the Exchange 2013 Search function.

Installing Exchange Server 2013

After you've installed all the prerequisite software, it's time to continue with the real installation of Exchange 2013. Exchange 2013 uses the Net.Tcp port sharing service. Unfortunately, this service startup is set to manual, so you need to change it to automatic.

Start the MMC services snap-in and scroll down to the Net.Tcp port sharing service, then double-click it. By default, the startup type is set to manual, so change this to automatic (see Figure 2-4). If you forget this step, the setup application will fail during the prerequisite check.

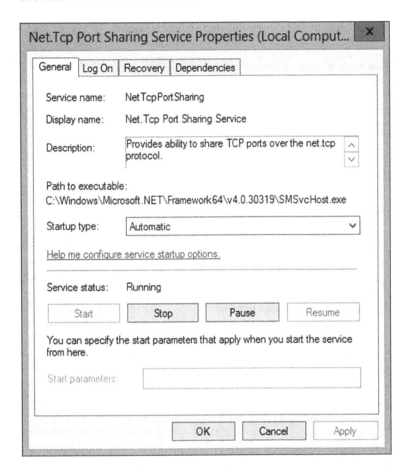

Figure 2-4. *Changing the startup type to automatic*

Now, to install Exchange 2013 on the new server, follow these steps:

1. Log on to the server as a member of the Domain Administrators security group. Besides being a member of the Domain Administrators security group, you need to make sure the account is also a member of the Enterprise Administrators security group and the Schema Administrators security group. You need to be a member of these groups in order to write to the configuration partition and the schema partition.

2. Navigate to the installation media. This can be a physical DVD, an ISO image mounted to a virtual machine, or the extracted binaries on a fileshare on the network. Start the setup application with setup.exe.

3. Note that Microsoft has made significant changes to the Exchange Server setup process. The first window that's shown asks whether the setup application needs to check for updates. If updates are available, the setup application will download them and automatically install them as well. Leave the default (Connect to the Internet and Check for Updates), and click Next to continue and follow the wizard.

4. Setup will now start copying the files needed to install Exchange 2013. When the introduction screen appears, click Next to continue.

5. Read the license agreement, select I Accept the Terms in This License Agreement, and click Next to continue.

6. The window for recommended settings asks you to select whether or not you want to use the recommended settings. There's not much information on this screen, but when you select Use Recommended Settings, it enables the error reporting and the Customer Experience Improvement Program (CEIP) that collect information on your hardware and how you use Exchange Server. If you agree with this, select Use Recommended Settings; if not, select Don't Use Recommended Settings. Click Next to continue.

7. The next screen, shown in Figure 2-5, is the most important in the installation process, as it's here that you select which server roles to install. Select the Mailbox role and the Client Access role to have both installed on the server, and click Next to continue.

MICROSOFT EXCHANGE SERVER 2013 CUMULATIVE UPDATE 1 SETUP   ? ✕

Server Role Selection

Select the Exchange server roles you want to install on this computer:

☑ Mailbox role

☑ Client Access role

☑ Automatically install Windows Server roles and features that are required to install Exchange Server

E⊞ Exchange   back   next

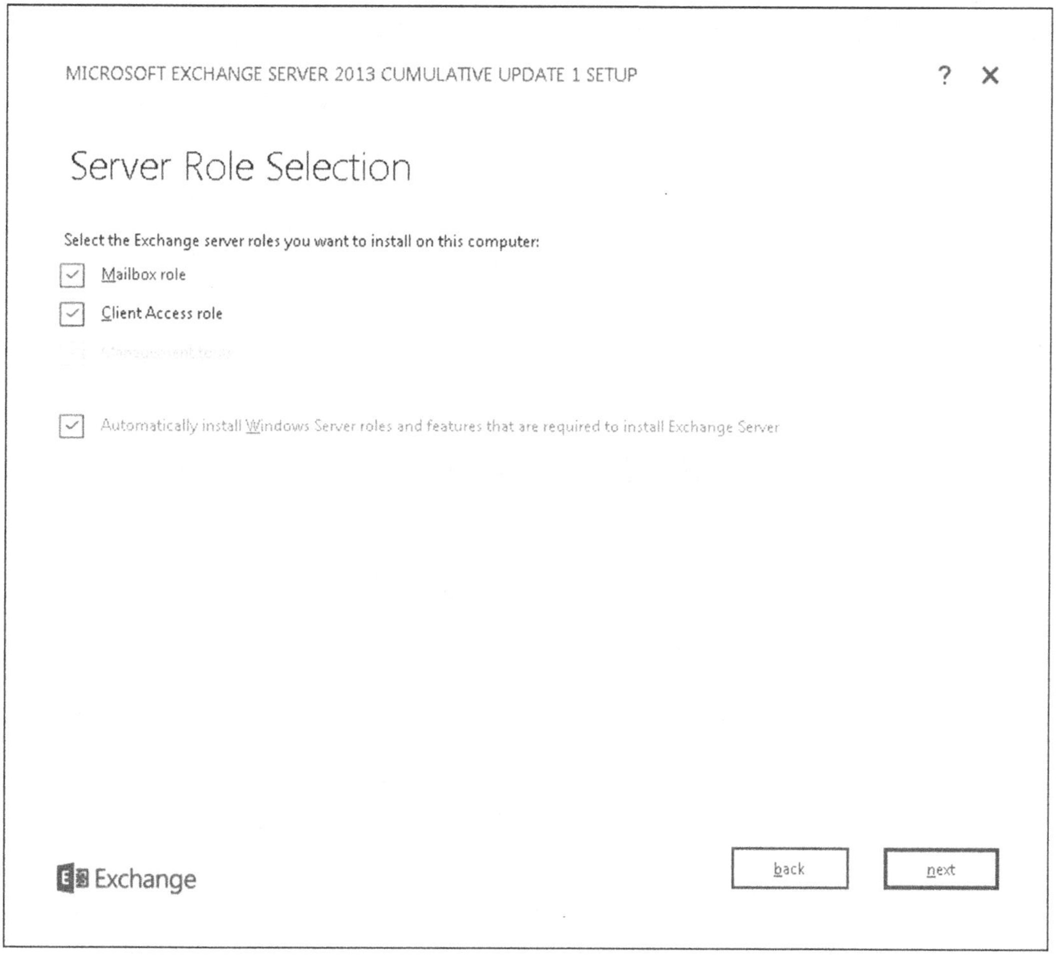

Figure 2-5. *Server Role Selection window during setup*

8. If you want to install only the Mailbox server, make sure *only* the Mailbox server role is selected. If you want to install a dedicated Client Access server, make sure only the Client Access server role is selected.

9.   On the Installation space and location screen, you can change the location where the Exchange 2013 files are installed, if needed. Click Next to continue.

10. Exchange 2013 comes with a default anti-malware solution. It is not as complete as, for example, the earlier Forefront protection for Exchange Server, but it can certainly help keep your messaging environment clean. By default, the anti-malware is enabled; you can disable it if you want to use another (third-party) solution, but check with your anti-malware vendor first. Internet access is required, though, to download the latest anti-malware updates. Click Next to continue.

11. The setup program has now gathered enough information to proceed with the installation and will perform a readiness check. When no problems are found, select Install to start the actual installation. Now it's time to wait. . . .

     The setup consists of 14 different steps. The screen is updated with every step, and within every step, the progress is indicated by a blue bar, as shown in Figure 2-6.

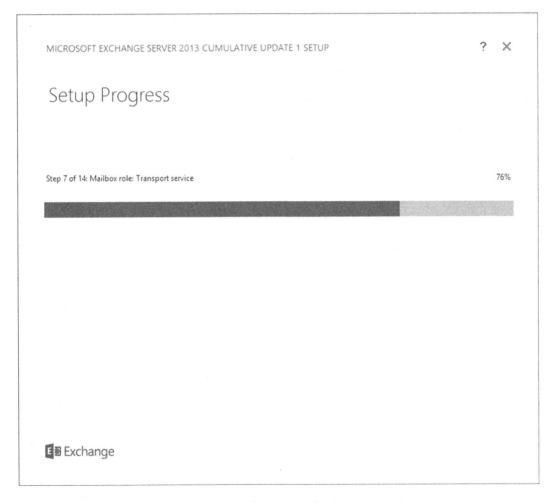

Figure 2-6. The blue bar indicating progress in the setup application

12. When setup is completed, you're given the option of selecting Launch Exchange Administration Center After Finishing Exchange Setup. Doing so will start the Exchange Admin Center (EAC) so that you can continue the postconfiguration tasks. But whether you select this or not, click the Finish button to finish the setup application.

To continue the installation from here, see the section "Postinstallation Configuration" later in this chapter.

Unattended Exchange Server 2013 Installation

If you want to install multiple Exchange 2013 servers, and you want to minimize your console interaction, it is possible to do an unattended installation. Also, for example, if your IT organization has multiple departments for Active Directory administration and Exchange Server administration, the unattended setup can be useful, since it offers a granular way of configuring Active Directory and installing Exchange 2013.

The unattended installation is the same setup application as found on the installation media (setup.exe), but it is started from a command prompt and includes multiple setup switches.

It is possible to make the changes to Active Directory using the command line setup, as well as installing the actual Exchange 2013 servers.

Setup Switches

For installing Exchange 2013, the setup.exe application has a number of switches that can be used while executing the command. Table 2-1 lists these switches, with descriptions of their purposes.

Table 2-1. *Exchange 2013 Setup Switches*

Switch	Description
/IAcceptExchangeServerLicenseTerms	Mandatory switch for legal reasons
/PrepareSchema	Prepares the schema for Exchange 2013
/PrepareAD	Prepares the configuration partition in Active Directory and creates the Exchange 2013 organization in Active Directory
/OrganizationName	Defines the name of the configuration, used for preparing Active Directory. Used in conjunction with the /PrepareAD switch in a new Exchange environment
/PrepareDomain	Prepares the current domain for implementation of Exchange 2013
/Mode	Indicates installation mode, like Install, Uninstall, or Upgrade
/Roles	Defines the server roles that need to be installed, like Client Access or Mailbox
/InstallWindowsComponents	Installs the Windows roles and features needed for Exchange 2013
/Targetdir	Indicates the directory where the Exchange binaries will be installed
/Sourcedir	Indicates the directory where the installation files can be found
/Updatesdir	Names a directory where Exchange 2013 updates can be found. These will be installed automatically when a new server is installed
/Domaincontroller	Names a specific domain controller to be used during installation

(continued)

Table 2-1. (*continued*)

Switch	Description
/Answerfile	Indicates a file containing more specific configuration settings
/EnableErrorReporting	Enables or disables error reporting during setup
/CustomerFeedbackEnabled	Enables or disables the customer feedback option
/AddUMLanguagepack	Adds a specific unified messaging language pack
/RemoveUMLanguagepack	Removes a specific unified messaging language pack
/NewProvisionedServer	Provisions an Exchange Server object in Active Directory
/RemoveProvisionedServer	Removes an Exchange Server object from Active Directory
/Mdbname	Names the mailbox database that will be created during setup
/Dbfilepath	Locates the initial mailbox database
/Logfolderpath	Locates the mailbox database log files and checkpoint file
/ActiveDirectorySplitPermissions	Configures a split permissions model
/DoNotStartTransport	Does not start the Transport service (SMTP) during setup to prevent "strange" routing problems

Not all options are mandatory when installing Exchange 2013 unattended, but the more options you use, the more granular will be your setup application. I'll discuss some of these in the following sections.

Preparing the Schema Partition

The first step in an unattended installation is to update the schema. You do this by using the setup application with the /PrepareSchema switch. When it comes to permissions, make sure that the account you use for executing this is a member of the Schema Administrators and Domain Administrators security groups in Active Directory.

1. Log on to the Exchange 2013 server, open a command prompt, and enter the following command:

   Setup.exe /PrepareSchema /IAcceptExchangeServerLicenseTerms

The /IAcceptExchangeServerLicenseTerms is a mandatory switch owing to legal reasons. It does not auto-complete; you have to manually enter this switch to indicate that you agree to the license terms. Figure 2-7 shows this first step completed successfully.

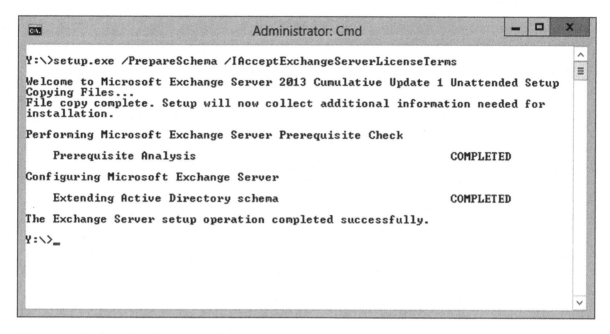

Figure 2-7. Changing the schema for Exchange Server 2013

2. Next, you check the schema update using the ADSIEdit tool. Start the ADSIEdit tool, and open the schema partition. All the schema entries will appear in the right-hand pane.

3. Scroll down to the CN=ms-Exch-Schema-Version-Pt entry, and open its properties. The rangeUpper attribute should contain the value 15254 for Exchange 2013 CU1, as shown in Figure 2-8.

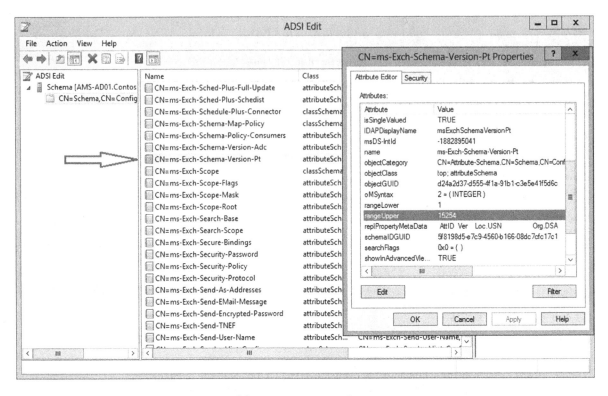

Figure 2-8. *Checking for the correct version of the Active Directory schema*

If you are PowerShell adept and do not want to use the GUI for checking the Active Directory schema version, you can also use these PowerShell commands:

```
$root = [ADSI]"LDAP://RootDSE"
$m = [ADSI]("LDAP://" + "CN=ms-Exch-Schema-Version-Pt," + $root.schemaNamingContext)
$m.rangeUpper
```

Every version of Exchange Server has its own value for the rangeUpper attribute, and this value even changes with service pack. Table 2-2 lists all the values up until Exchange 2013.

Table 2-2. *Schema Values for Earlier Exchange Server Versions*

Exchange Server version	Corresponding value for rangeUpper attribute
Exchange Server 2000	4397
Exchange Server 2000 SP 3	4406
Exchange Server 2003 RTM	6870
Exchange Server 2003 SP 2	6936
Exchange Server 2007	10628
Exchange Server 2007 SP 1	11116
Exchange Server 2007 SP 2	14622
Exchange Server 2007 SP 3	14625
Exchange Server 2010	14622
Exchange Server 2010 SP 1	14726
Exchange Server 2010 SP 2	14732
Exchange Server 2010 SP 3	14734
Exchange Server 2013	15137
Exchange Server 2013 CU1	15254
Exchange Server 2013 CU2	15281

Once the Active Directory schema is updated to the Exchange 2013 level, and the domain controllers have replicated all the schema information, you continue with preparing the Active Directory configuration container, which is the location where the actual Exchange 2013 information is stored.

Preparing the Configuration Partition

As explained in Chapter 1, the Exchange 2013 information is stored in the configuration partition in Active Directory, and this partition is shared across all domain controllers in all domains in the Active Directory forest.

To change the Active Directory configuration partition, and to create the actual Exchange 2013 organization, log on to the server as an enterprise administrator and open a command prompt. Navigate to the installation media and enter the following command:

```
Setup.exe /PrepareAD /OrganizationName:Exchange15 /IAcceptExchangeServerLicenseTerms
```

Figure 2-9 shows the operation completed successfully.

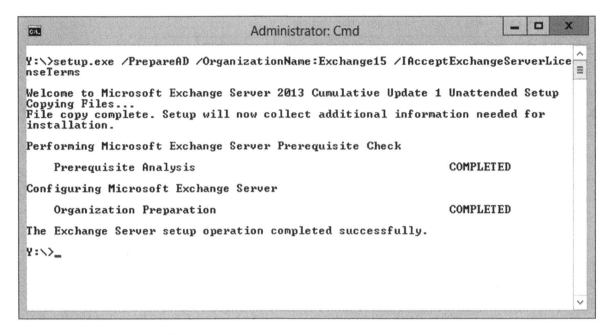

Figure 2-9. *Creating a new Exchange Server organization in Active Directory*

A lot or work is done behind the curtains when you are executing this step. The entire Exchange 2013 organization is created, including all objects and entries in Active Directory. When you use ADSIedit (use caution!) and open the configuration container, you can navigate to the CN=Services leaf and see the entire Exchange 2013 organization (see Figure 2-10).

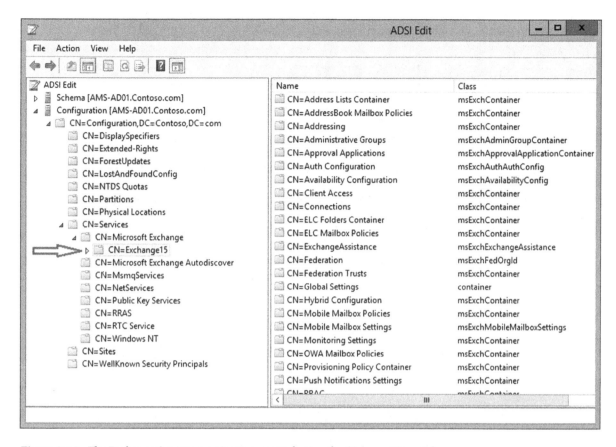

Figure 2-10. *The Exchange Server organization, created using the /PrepareAD switch*

Also, 20 or so universal security groups are created in Active Directory. When you use Active Directory Users and the Computers MMC snap-in, you'll find these security groups in Microsoft Exchange Security Groups, as shown in Figure 2-11.

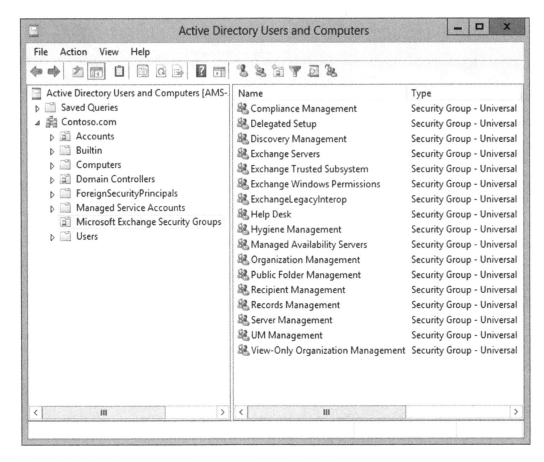

Figure 2-11. *Security groups created with the /PrepareAD switch*

Wait for replication among all the domain controllers to be completed before you continue to the next step.

Preparing the Domain Partition

The last step in configuring Active Directory is to prepare the domain where Exchange 2013 will be installed and where the recipients are located. If you have multiple domains in your Active Directory, your Exchange 2013 environment is in domain A and your recipients are in domain B, so you will have to prepare both domains!

To do this, log on to the server as a domain administrator and open a command prompt. Navigate to the installation media and enter the following command:

```
Setup.exe /PrepareDomain /IAcceptExchangeServerLicenseTerms
```

Figure 2-12 shows the operation completed.

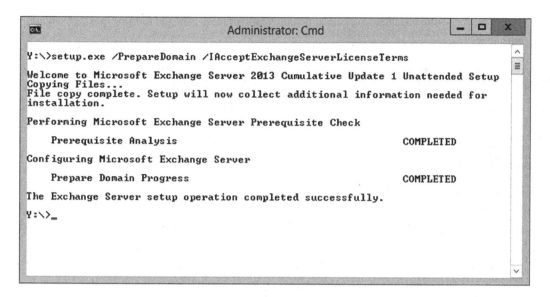

Figure 2-12. *The Active Directory domain prepared successfully*

If you have multiple domains and want to prepare all domains to receive the installation of Exchange 2013, you can also use the /PrepareAllDomains switch: Setup.exe /PrepareAllDomains /IAcceptExchangeServerLicenseTerms

---

■ **Note**   Enterprise administrator privileges are required to perform this step.

When replication is complete, then Exchange 2013 can be installed. This is achieved by using a regular installation with the setup graphical user interface (GUI), as well as the command-line interface, as described in the next section.

Installing Exchange Server 2013

Before Exchange Server 2013 can be installed, you need to have the preprequisite software. This is no different from a normal setup procedure as discussed earlier in this chapter, so it won't be repeated here. When performing an unattended server installation, the setup application will do a prerequisite check, though.

To install a typical Exchange 2013 with both the Client Access server role and the Mailbox server role, log on to the server as a domain administrator. Open a command prompt, navigate to the installation media, and enter the following command:

```
Setup.exe /mode:install /role:clientaccess,mailbox /IAcceptExchangeServerLicenseTerms
```

This action will perform a default installation of the Client Access server role and the Mailbox server role. If you want to modify the initial mailbox database and its location during installation, you can use something like the following command:

```
Setup.exe /mode:install /role:clientaccess,mailbox /IAcceptExchangeServerLicenseTerms
/Mdbname:MDB01 /DbFilePath:F:\MDB01\MDB01.edb /LogFolderPath:F:\MDB01\LogFiles
```

Figure 2-13 shows the successful installation of CAS and Mailbox server roles. Note the warning messages about the Office 2010 Filter Pack.

Figure 2-13. *Successful unattended installation of the CAS and Mailbox server roles*

After the setup has finished, reboot the server and continue with the postinstallation tasks, as described in the next section.

Postinstallation Configuration

After the initial installation of Exchange 2013, there is still quite some more work to do before you have the server fully operational. Tasks that need to be performed are:

- Creating accepted domains

- Creating an email address policy

- Configuring SSL certificates

- Creating a send connector

- Configuring a receive connector

- Setting anti-malware settings

I'll discuss these topics in the following paragraphs.

Accepted Domains

An accepted domain in Exchange 2013 is an SMTP domain for which a Exchange 2013 server is responsible. This means that it's going to accept mail for this SMTP domain, but it can also be used to send email. The initial accepted domain that's configured on the server is the domain name that's used in the Active Directory domain; in our example, this is the domain contoso.com. If this is the only domain that's going to be used, you're fine; but maybe you want to add additional SMTP domains?

When you want to create another accepted domain—for example, Fabrikam.com—you follow these steps:

1. Log on to the new Exchange 2013 server as an administrator, open a browser, and navigate to the Exchange Admin Center (EAC)—that is, https://localhost/ecp. (For now you can ignore the SSL security warning; this is caused by the self-signed certificate, combined with the fact that you are accessing the server using the localhost name.)

2. On the logon page, use the domain administrator account to log on to the EAC. This account should also be a member of the Enterprise Administrators security group in Active Directory. If this account is *not* the account that was used to install Exchange 2013, make sure that this account is also a member of the Organization Management security group in Active Directory. In Chapter 7, I will discuss how this is achieved using Role-Based Access Control (RBAC) in Exchange 2013.

3. To configure an accepted domain, select Mail Flow in the navigation menu on the left, and then select Accepted Domains in the top navigation bar.

4. Click the + icon to start the new accepted domain wizard. Give the new accepted domain a display name (this is just a cosmetic name; it's how the accepted domain will show up in the EAC) like "Fabrikam," and then enter the actual SMTP domain name—that is, fabrikam.com. Leave the new accepted domain as an authoritative domain and click Save to continue.

If you want to create an accepted domain using the Exchange Management Shell (EMS), shown in Figure 2-14, you can use the following command:

```
New-AcceptedDomain -Name Fabrikam -DomainName Fabrikam.com -DomainType Authoritative
```

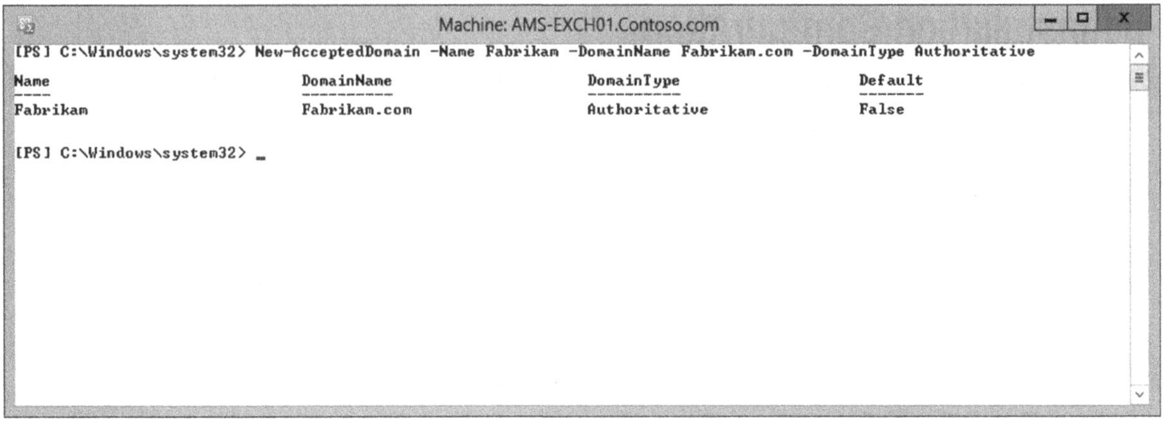

Figure 2-14. *Using the Exchange Management Shell to create an accepted domain*

Email Address Policies

An email address policy is a policy in Exchange 2013 that is responsible for assigning email addresses to recipients according to a predefined set of filters and formats. When a new recipient is created and it fits into such a filter, the accompanying email address is automatically assigned to the new recipient based on the defined format.

By default, there's one email address policy that filters all recipients and assigns the default accepted domain to all these new recipients.

To create a new email address policy using the fabrikam.com SMTP domain, for users in the OU=Accounts organizational unit, you can follow these steps:

1. Assuming you're still logged on to the EAC, select Mail Flow from the navigation menu, and then Email Address Policies next to Accepted Domains. In the wizard, click the + icon to add a new email address policy.

2. Give the policy a name. As with the accepted domain, this is only for display purposes; enter something like "Contoso."

3. Click the + icon to select an SMTP domain. This is one of the accepted domains available on the Exchange 2013 server. Use the drop-down box to select the accepted domain fabrikam.com, which was configured in the previous section.

4. Select the proper format of the email address that will be assigned to users. When chosen, click Save to continue with the wizard.

5. By default, a new email address policy will be used on all recipients, but in the wizard it's also possible to select other recipients, such as mail users, resource mailboxes, or mail-enabled groups.

6. Scroll down and click the Add a Rule button. Here, you select a predefined set of rules that can be used to filter recipients. For example, you can select an organizational unit in Active Directory, or recipients with a certain value in the "company" attribute, or those with one of the 15 custom attributes. In our example, we select Recipient Container and in the popup, we single-click on the correct container—that is, Accounts. Click OK to continue and click Save to finish the wizard.

To create this email address policy using the Exchange Management Shell, you can use the following command:

```
New-EmailAddressPolicy -Name Fabrikam -IncludedRecipients AllRecipients -RecipientContainer
"contoso.com/accounts" -EnabledEmailAddressTemplates "SMTP:%1@fabrikam.com"
```

To apply this newly created email address policy, you can use the following command:

```
Update-EmailAddressPolicy -Identity Fabrikam
```

Figure 2-15 shows the process completed successfully.

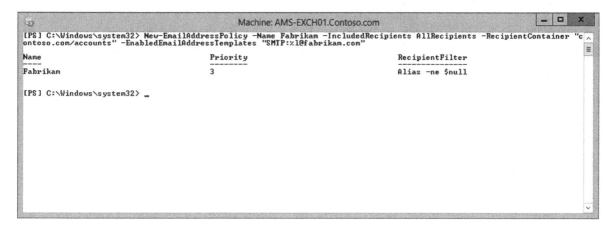

Figure 2-15. *Creating and applying an email address policy using the Exchange Management Shell*

SSL Certificates

By default, a self-signed certificate is installed on the Client Access server during installation of Exchange Server 2013. This self-signed certificate has the NetBIOS name of the server as its common name and the fully qualified domain name (FQDN) of the server configured in the subject alternative name field of the certificate (see Figure 2-16).

Figure 2-16. *The self-signed certificate of Exchange Server 2013*

This works fine for testing OWA and the EAC, but it will cause headaches when you try to use it for Outlook Anywhere or other Web services of the Client Access server.

Request an SSL Certificate Using the EAC Wizard

The easiest way to request a new certificate is by using the wizard in EAC:

1. Assuming the EAC is still open in your browser, navigate to the Servers option in the left-hand navigation menu and then select Certificates in the top menu.

2. Click the + icon to start a new certificate request. Select Create a Request for a Certificate from a Certification Authority and click Next to continue.

3. Enter a friendly name for the certificate—something like "Contoso SSL certificate" and click Next to continue.

4. A wildcard certificate is fully supported, but since we want to use a unified communications SSL certificate with a subject alternative name, leave this blank and click Next to continue.

5. Use the Browse button to select a Client Access server for this certificate and click Next to continue.

6. In the next screen, there's the option to specify an FQDN for every service offered by Exchange 2013. The most important ones are the FQDN for OWA (webmail.contoso.com) and the FQDN for autodiscover (autodiscover.contoso.com). Scroll down to make sure you covered all the services. For services not used, or when using the same FQDN as OWA, you can empty the field using the small pencil icon. When done, click Next to continue.

7. When there are multiple accepted domains in the Exchange environment, the wizard will show them all and there's the option to add them to the certificate as well. For a simple scenario, remove all additional names until only the autodiscover.contoso.com and webmail.contoso.com are left.

Figure 2-17 shows the names Contoso.com and Fabrikam.com that you need to remove.

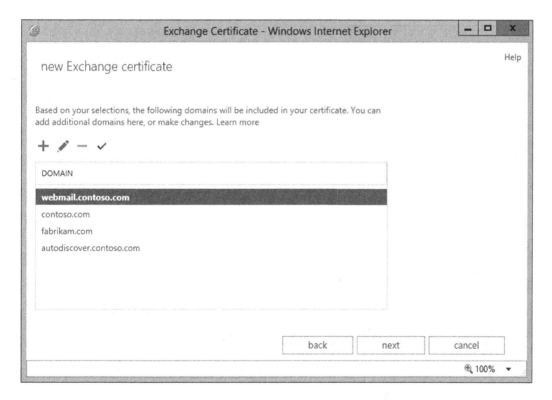

Figure 2-17. *Removing additional names from the certificate request*

8. Click Next to continue.

9. Fill in the required information, such as organization name, country, city, and so on, as shown in the WHOIS database where all the Internet domain details are stored. If there's a mismatch, the certification authority will most likely push back the certificate request. Click Next to continue.

10. Enter the location where the request file will be stored (see Figure 2-18). This location is a UNC path. Don't forget to enter the filename of the request file as well.

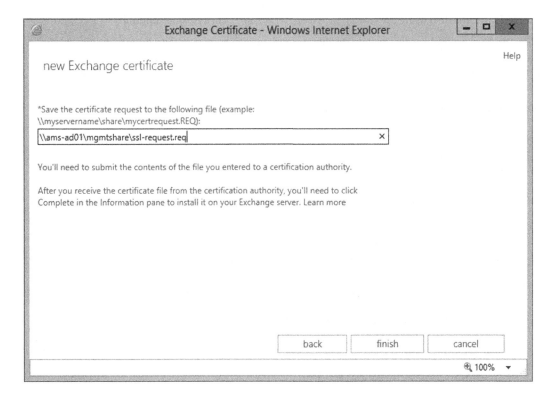

Figure 2-18. *Location of the request file, entered in UNC format*

■ **Note** The universal security group Exchange Trusted Subsystem needs write permissions on the file share where the request will be stored.

11. Click Finish to save the request file and end the new Exchange Certificate wizard.

The request file is a text file with a lot of characters in a fully random order, not readable for a normal human being. The content of this request file is used to request the SSL certificate from a certification authority (CA).

12. Once processed by the CA, the certificate is returned. Store this file in the same location or in another location that is accessible over the network, and return to the EAC.

13. In the EAC, select servers in the left-hand menu and select certificates in the top menu. Select the Contoso SSL Certificate request created earlier; you'll see that its status is "Pending request".

14. In the right-hand pane under Status, click Complete. In the pop-up screen, enter the location where the file that was returned by the CA is stored—that is, \\ams-ad01\mgmtshare\certnew.p7b and click OK.

The certificate is now imported onto the Exchange Server. If all goes well, it should be listed as "valid" and it's almost ready to use. The last step to accomplish this is to assign services like IIS to the certificate.

15. To assign services to the certificate, make sure it is selected in the EAC and then click on the pencil icon in the top menu. In the certificate details in the left-hand pane, select Services. Select the IIS service and click Save to continue.

The certificate should now have IIS listed as the assigned service (see Figure 2-19).

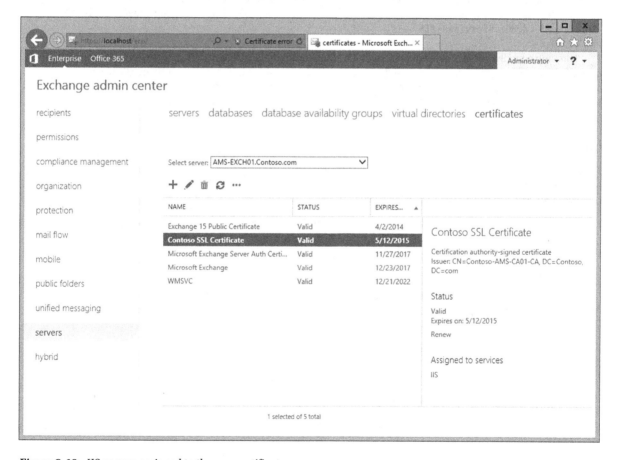

Figure 2-19. *IIS as now assigned to the new certificate*

Request an SSL Certificate Using EMS

To use the Exchange Management Shell to request, install, and configure an SSL certificate is a bit more complex. To do this, use the following commands:

```
$Data = New-ExchangeCertificate -FriendlyName "Contoso SSL Certificate" -GenerateRequest
-SubjectName "c=US, o=Contoso, cn=webmail.contoso.com" -DomainName
webmail.contoso.com,autodiscover.contoso.com -PrivateKeyExportable $true

Set-Content -path "\\ams-ad01\mgmtshare\SSLCertRequest.req" -Value $Data
```

After ordering the certificate from your certificate authority (or have it created using your internal Active Directory CA, of course), store the new certificate on the same share and continue with the following commands:

```
Import-ExchangeCertificate -Server AMS-EXCH01 -FileData ([Byte[]]$(Get-Content -Path
"\\ams-ad01\mgmtshare\certnew.cer" -Encoding byte -ReadCount 0)) | Enable-ExchangeCertificate
-Server AMS-EXCH01 -Services IIS
```

This step actually consists of two commands. The first command is the Import-ExchangeCertificate, which imports the .cer file that was returned from the CA into the local certificate store of the Exchange 2013 server. The output is then sent to the Enable-ExchangeCertificate, which enables the newly imported certificate to be used with Internet Information Server.

Import an Existing SSL Certificate

There's also the possibility that you already have a valid and usable SSL certificate, possibly from another deployment or another server, and you have it exported to a .pfx file (certificate export file). If so, you copy the .pfx file to the management share on the network share we used earlier.

1. Log on to the EAC, select Servers in the left-hand menu, and select Certificates in the top menu.

2. Click on the three dots just above the list of certificates and select Import Exchange Certificate.

3. In the Import Exchange Certificate wizard, enter the location where the .pfx file is stored and enter the password used while exporting (see Figure 2-20). Click Next to continue.

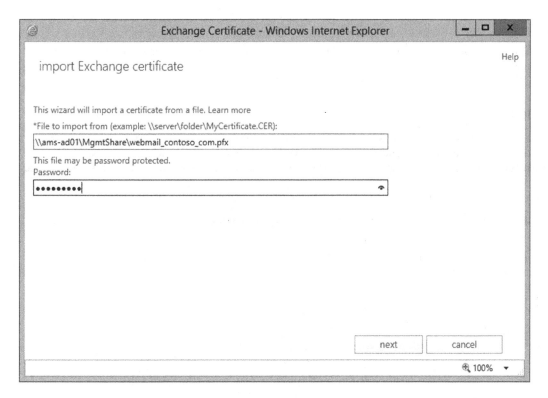

Figure 2-20. *Importing an existing SSL certificate in Exchange 2013*

4. Click on the + icon to add the Exchange 2013 server that you want to import the SSL certificate onto and click Finish to close the window. The SSL certificate is now imported and Exchange services can now be assigned to the SSL certificate, just as when you create new SSL certificates.

If you want to import an exisiting SSL certificate on the Exchange 2013 server, you can use the following command:

```
Import-ExchangeCertificate -Server AMS-EXCH01 -FileData ([Byte[]]$(Get-Content -Path
"\\ams-ad01\MgmtShare\webmail_contoso_com.pfx" -Encoding byte -ReadCount 0))
-Password:(Get-Credential).password | Enable-ExchangeCertificate -Server AMS-EXCH01 -Services IIS
```

The -Password:(Get-Credential).password parameter shows a Windows pop-up where you have to enter the password while exporting the certificate. The output of Import-ExchangeCertificate command is piped directly to the Enable-ExchangeCertificate command to assign the IIS service to the imported SSL certificate.

Connectors

In Exchange 2013, connectors are used for sending and receiving messages. These are called send connectors and receive connectors.

Send Connector

An Exchange server is by default not able to send messages to any other server. To achieve this function, however, a send connector has to be created. The send connector is a connector in Exchange 2013 with a namespace, permissions, and one or more source transport servers. The Exchange server uses this to route messages, for example, to the Internet.

To create a new connector that will send messages to the Internet, use the following steps:

1. Log on to the EAC and select Mail Flow in the left-hand menu and then select Send Connectors in the top menu.

2. Click on the + icon to start the new send connector wizard. Enter a name for the send connector—something like "Internet send connector"—and click the Internet radio button. Click Next to continue.

3. There are two ways the connector can send messages:

    a. Use MX, which means the Exchange Hub Transport service uses the MX records found on the Internet and then accesses the destination SMTP host directly.

    b. A smart host, which means all messages are delivered to one SMTP host, typically an Internet service provider, which in turn delivers the message to the destination SMTP host.

4. In our example. we use MX, which is selected by default. Click Next to continue.

5. The address space for an Internet connector is typically an asterisk (*), which basically means all external SMTP domains. Click the + icon, type * in the FQDN field, and click Save, then click Next to continue.

6. A send connector also needs a source transport server. This is a mailbox server (with the Hub Transport service on it) that will deliver the messages to the Internet. Click the + icon and select an Exchange server that will act as the source transport server. Choose Add to add the source server to the list, and click OK. Click Finish to close the new send connector wizard and save all the information (see Figure 2-21).

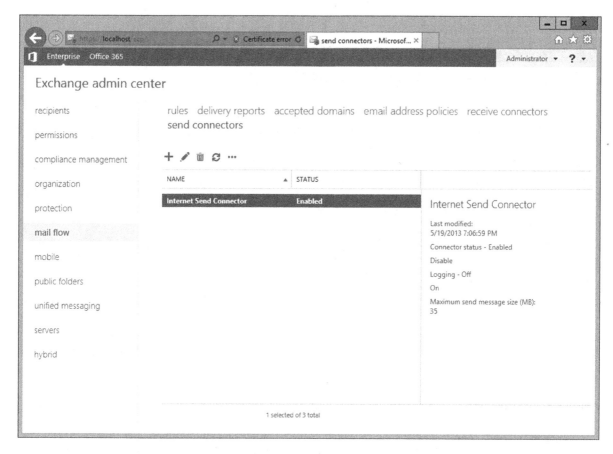

Figure 2-21. *The Internet send connector, now ready to use*

To create a new Internet send connector using the Exchange Management Shell, use the following command:

```
New-SendConnector -Name "Internet Send Connector" -Internet -AddressSpaces "*"
-DNSRoutingEnabled:$TRUE -SourceTransportServers "AMS-EXCH01"
```

Receive Connector

Besides send connectors, Exchange 2013 also has receive connectors. A receive connector is configured on a Mailbox server and on a Client Access server, and is capable of receiving SMTP messages. There are default receive connectors for receiving messages from other SMTP hosts, and there are client receive connectors that are used so that authenticated clients can send SMTP messages. The latter can sound strange, but the Exchange 2013 server is actually receiving messages from the client and, when needed, routes the messages to the Internet.

As one server, with both the Client Access server and the Mailbox server roles installed, Exchange 2013 actually has five receive connectors (see Figure 2-22): three receive connectors for the Client Access server role and two receive connectors for the Mailbox server role.

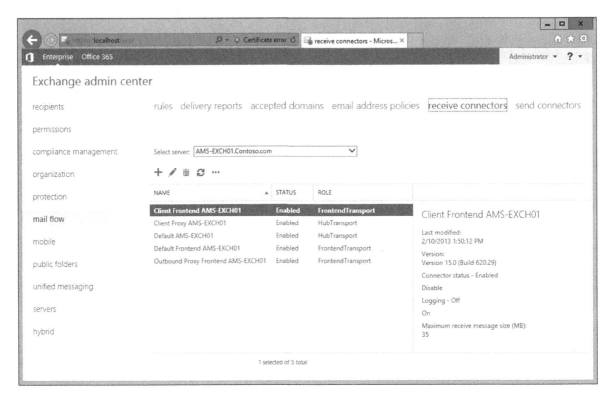

Figure 2-22. *With two server roles on one server, there are five receive connectors*

To prevent all kinds of protocol problems, the default receive connector on the Mailbox server role is actually listening on port 2525, while the default receive connector on the Client Access server role is listening on port 25.

Out of the box, there's no need to configure anything on the receive connector; it just works. You configure the firewall to forward SMTP to port 25 on the Exchange 2013 Client Access server, and you're ready to go.

Outlook Anywhere

On the Exchange 2013 Client Access server, Outlook Anywhere is enabled by default. The only step an administrator needs to take is to install a valid (third-party) SSL unified communications certificate and to configure an external hostname—that is, the name of the proxy server that the Outlook clients connect to.

Installing and configuring the SSL certificate has been explained earlier in this chapter. To configure Outlook Anywhere on the Client Access server, open the Exchange Management Shell and enter the following command:

```
Get-OutlookAnywhere -Server AMS-EXCH01 | Set-OutlookAnywhere
-ExternalHostname webmail.contoso.com -ExternalClientsRequireSsl:$true
```

External URLs

As designed, all virtual directories in Exchange 2013 are configured with their local FQDN—that is, https://ams-exch01.contoso.com/owa. While this works fine if there's only one Exchange server, it becomes challenging when multiple Exchange servers are installed. In this scenario, you would use one namespace spanning multiple Exchange servers. For example, use https://webmail.contoso.com/owa to cover all Client Access servers in your organization.

Microsoft recommends that you use one namespace for both the external URLs and the internal URLs for all virtual directories. This means that webmail.contoso.com on the Internet points to your public IP address on the Internet; but at the same time, webmail.contoso.com points to private IP address on the internal network. This is called a "split-brain DNS" configuration.

In Exchange 2013, the following directories need to be configured:

- OWA virtual directory

- ECP virtual directory

- EWS (Web services) virtual directory

- Activesync virtual directory

- OAB (offline address book) virtual directory

- PowerShell virtual directory

- Autodiscover virtual directory

In the EAC, click on the servers in the left-hand navigation menu and choose Virtual Directories in the top navigation menu. All virtual directories will be shown here (see Figure 2-23). If there are multiple servers, you can use the Select Server drop-down box to select a particular Exchange server to configure.

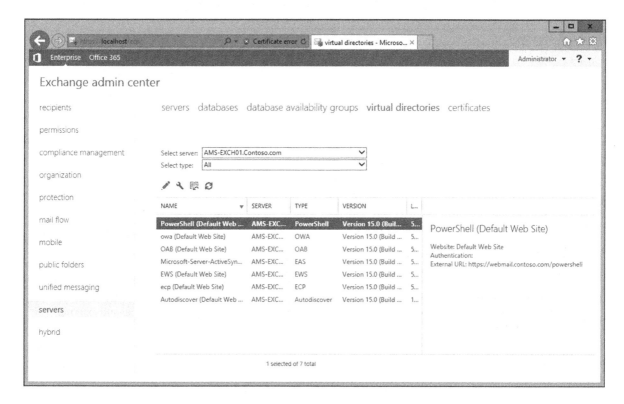

Figure 2-23. *Using the EAC to configure the virtual directories*

To configure the virtual directories for use on the Internet, click on the wrench icon in the top menu. In Configure External Access Domain, use the + icon to select one or more Client Access servers to configure. In the text box shown in Figure 2-24, you would enter the externally accessible domain name, such as webmail.contoso.com.

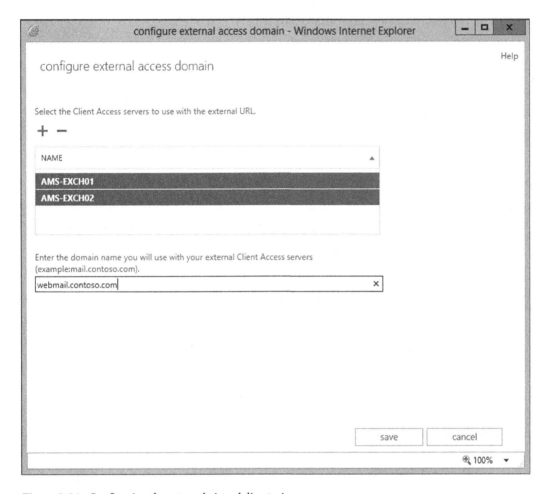

Figure 2-24. *Configuring the external virtual directories*

In EAC, it is unfortunately not possible to use a similar wizard to configure the virtual directories for internal usage, so these have to be configured manually, step by step.

To begin, open the virtual directory by double-clicking on it and then change both the internal and external URLs according to Table 2-3.

Table 2-3. *Virtual Directory Settings*

Virtual Directory	Internal URL	External URL
OWA virtual directory	https://webmail.contoso.com/owa	https://webmail.contoso.com/owa
ECP virtual directory	https://webmail.contoso.com/ecp	https://webmail.contoso.com/ecp
Activesync virtual directory	https://webmail.contoso.com/Microsoft-Server-ActiveSync	https://webmail.contoso.com/Microsoft-Server-ActiveSync
EWS virtual directory	https://webmail.contoso.com/ews/exchange.asmx	https://webmail.contoso.com/ews/exchange.asmx
OAB virtual directory	https://webmail.contoso.com/oab	https://webmail.contoso.com/oab
PowerShell virtual directory	https://webmail.contoso.com/powershell	https://webmail.contoso.com/powershell
Autodiscover virtual directory	https://autodiscover.contoso.com/autodiscover	https://autodiscover.contoso.com/autodiscover

Making all these changes manually using the EAC is quite some work and it's prone to error, so it's better to use the Exchange Management Shell to make all the settings. Copy and past this small script in the Notepad on the Client Access server and save it as change_vdir_settings.ps1 on the local hard drive.

```
# Change_vdir_Settings.ps1
# You can use this small script to change the virtual directories on your exchange (2013) server
# starting point is a split DNS configuration, so internalURL and externalURL are identical
#
# usage: .\Change_vdir_settings.ps1 contoso.com
#

$ServerName = $env:COMPUTERNAME
$Domain = $args[0]
$Server = "webmail"

$External = $Server +"." + $Domain
$AutoD = "autodiscover." + $Domain

Write-Host "The following FQDN will be used for configuring the virtual directories: " $External
Write-Host "The following FQDN will be used for configuring autodiscover: " $AutoD

Get-OWAVirtualDirectory -Server $ServerName | Set-OWAVirtualDirectory -ExternalURL
https://$External/owa -InternalURL https://$External/owa
Get-ECPVirtualDirectory -Server $ServerName | Set-ECPVirtualDirectory -ExternalURL
https://$External/ecp -InternalURL https://$External/ecp
Get-ActiveSyncVirtualDirectory -server $ServerName | Set-ActiveSyncVirtualDirectory -ExternalURL
https://$External/Microsoft-Server-ActiveSync -InternalURL https://$External/Microsoft-Server-ActiveSync
Get-WebServicesVirtualDirectory -Server $ServerName | Set-WebServicesVirtualDirectory -ExternalURL
https://$External/ews/exchange.asmx -InternalURL https://$External/ews/exchange.asmx
Get-OABVirtualDirectory -Server $ServerName | Set-OABVirtualDirectory -ExternalURL
https://$External/OAB -InternalURL https://$External/OAB
```

```
Get-PowershellVirtualDirectory -Server $ServerName | Set-PowershellVirtualDirectory -ExternalURL
https://$External/Powershell -InternalURL https://$External/Powershell

Get-ClientAccessServer -Identity $ServerName | Set-ClientAccessServer
-AutoDiscoverServiceInternalUri https://$AutoD/autodiscover/autodiscover.xml

Get-OutlookAnywhere -Server $ServerName | Set-OutlookAnywhere
-ExternalHostname $External -ExternalClientsRequireSsl:$true

Write-Host "Do not forget to issue an IISRESET command."
```

Open the Exchange Management Shell, navigate to the script, and run it with your external domain
as a parameter, like: .\change_vdir_settings.ps1 contoso.com

Now, all your virtual directories will be configured with the correct internal and external URLs.
Also, the autodiscover service connection point will be correctly configured.

Service Connection Point

Outlook 2007 and higher use a so-called service connection point in Active Directory for autodiscover purposes.
This will be covered more in detailed in Chapter 4.

The service connection point can only be configured using EMS. Use the following command to configure the
service connection point:

```
Get-ClientAccessServer -Identity AMS-E15SRV01 | Set-ClientAccessServer -AutoDiscoverServiceInternalUri
https://autodiscover.contoso.com/autodiscover/autodiscover.xml
```

This setting was included in the script in the preceding section.

Summary

Installation of Exchange Server 2013 can be performed on Windows Server 2008 R2 or Windows Server 2012.
Installing on Windows Server 2012 has the advantage of being the better operating system, plus the lifecycle of the
product is way longer.

Before Exchange 2013 can be installed, however, prerequisite software needs to be installed, such as .NET
Framework 4.5, Windows Management Framework 3.0, Remote Server Administration Tools, and Internet
Information Server.

Installation can be done using the graphical user interface, which is relatively foolproof, but it always needs
attention during actual installation. Another option is to install Exchange 2013 using the unattended setup, which can
be a useful alternative if multiple Exchange servers need to be installed. This way a consistent setup is created.

After installing Exchange 2013, you need to perform some postinstallation tasks, such as the installation and
configuration of a valid SSL certificate and configuration of the virtual directories. This is quite some work, but if you
use a script, you'll achieve a consistent configuration.

This chapter covered the installation of Exchange 2013 in a new Active Directory environment, sometimes
referred to as a green-field environment. In the next chapter, we will cover the installation of Exchange 2013 in an
existing Exchange Server 2007 or Exchange Server 2010 environment.

CHAPTER 3

■ ■ ■

Coexistence and Migration

The previous chapters were about installing a brand-new Exchange Server 2013 environment, a so-called green-field installation. While there's nothing wrong with this, chances are you already have an older Exchange environment running in your organization. If this existing environment is based on Exchange Server 2007 or Exchange Server 2010, then it is possible to create a coexistence scenario into which the new Exchange Server 2013 can be installed, and you can gradually transition your mailboxes to Exchange Server 2013.

If your existing environment is based on Exchange Server 2003, however, then you'll run into difficulties. A coexistence scenario is not supported by Exchange Server 2003, and therefore it cannot work with Exchange Server 2013. In this case, you have to either (1) upgrade Exchange Server 2003 to Exchange Server 2010 and then move on to Exchange Server 2013; or (2) build a brand-new Active Directory with a green-field Exchange Server 2013 and perform a so-called *interorg migration*; that is, you move your user accounts and mailboxes to the new environment using a tool like Active Directory Migration Toolkit (ADMT), or you use a third-party migration tool. Updating from Exchange Server 2003, using these options, is beyond the scope of this book.

This chapter covers how to transition from either Exchange Server 2007 or Exchange Server 2010 to Exchange Server 2013. In the preparation and installation phases, the transitions from Exchange Server 2007 or Exchange Server 2010 to Exchange Server 2013 are similar. The differences occur when you start to implement Exchange Server 2013. Proxying and redirection differ greatly in an Exchange Server 2010/2013 secenario compared to an Exchange Server 2007/2013 scenario.

Therefore, this chapter deals initially with both scenarios, up to the point when things start to be different. Then, each scenario is discussed individually. Also, when I talk about "previous versions of Exchange Server," I am referencing *both* Exchange Server 2007 and Exchange Server 2010 unless otherwise noted.

■ **Note**   Creating a coexistence scenario with Exchange Server 2007 or Exchange Server 2010 is possible only with Exchange Server 2013 CU1 or higher.

Transition to Exchange Server 2013

Transitioning from Exchange Server 2007 or 2010 is relatively easy because Exchange 2013 is simply introduced *into* the current Exchange Server environment. This saves you the hassle of building a new Active Directory environment, moving all your resources to that new Active Directory, and working around the problems that might occur when you're keeping both directories in sync during the coexistence phase.

I deliberately say "relatively easy" since it still takes quite some time to accomplish this task and to work around some difficulties caused by incompatibilities between the previous versions and Exchange 2013. Just as in the past, it's not possible to have the Exchange 2013 Client Access server (CAS) work directly with an earlier version's Mailbox server. Even worse, an Exchange 2013 CAS won't work directly with an Exchange Server 2007 CAS (like proxying requests). As a result, in the coexistence scenario, all client requests need to be redirected to the 2007 CAS. The client in this case creates a new connection with the 2007 CAS and continues working. This is the reason you need an additional namespace with a name like `legacy.contoso.com`. (This is discussed in more detail later on in this chapter.) If you have been working with Exchange Server for a long time, this requirement will probably sound familiar, as the same situation existed when upgrading from Exchange Server 2003 to Exchange Server 2010.

Upgrading from Exchange Server 2010 to Exchange Server 2013 works better in this case. When you access an Exchange 2013 CAS while trying to retrieve information from an Exchange 2010 Mailbox server, the request will be proxied to the Exchange 2010 CAS, so there's no need for Exchange 2013 to redirect the request to the other CAS. In this case, the client keeps its connection with the Exchange 2013 CAS, and this server is responsible for communication with the Exchange 2010 CAS.

The upgrade path from Exchange Server 2007 or Exchange Server 2010 to Exchange 2013 is as follows:

1. Prepare Active Directory.

2. Install the first Exchange 2013 Mailbox server.

3. Install the first Exchange 2013 Client Access server.

4. Configure namespaces and client access redirection (only needed for Exchange Server 2007).

5. Change client access to contact Exchange 2013 CAS directly.

6. Change SMTP routing from the previous version of Exchange Server to Exchange 2013.

7. Move resources from the previous version of Exchange Server to Exchange Server 2013.

8. Decommission the previous version of Exchange Server.

Prerequisites

To begin the transition, you have to prepare the current environment. If you're running Exchange Server 2007, all servers in the existing environment need to be at Exchange Server 2007 service pack 3, update rollup 10, or higher. If you're running Exchange Server 2010, all servers have to be at Exchange Server 2010 service pack 3 or higher.

The domain controllers need to be running at least version Windows Server 2003 service pack 2, while the Active Directory forest must be at Windows Server 2003 forest functionality mode or higher.

When it comes to Active Directory namespaces—that is, the naming conventions within the Active Directory forest, trees, and domains—Exchange 2013 supports the following:

- *Contiguous namespace*. This is an Active Directory namespace where all domains share a common namespace—for example, `contoso.com`. All child domains also end with `contoso.com`—for example, `research.contoso.com` or `factory.contoso.com`.

- *Noncontiguous namespace*. This is an Active Directory namespace where multiple trees are implemented—that is, one tree named `contoso.com` and another tree named `fabrikam.com`.

- *Single-label domain.* This is an Active Directory namespace that does not follow the regular naming conventions with a top-level domain (TLD), but only have their name—for example, contoso or fabrikam without the .com suffix. These domains cannot be registered by an Internet registrar and also need additional client configuration when it comes to DNS name resolution.

- *Disjoint namespace.* This is a situation where the fully qualified domain name of the server or workstation does not match the DNS name of the Active Directory domain—for example, a mail server called mail.contoso.com that's a member of the Active Directory domain called corp.contoso.com.

When these prerequisites are met, the Active Directory itself can be upgraded to the Exchange 2013 level.

Preparing Active Directory

To transition to Exchange 2013, you need to prepare the schema partition, the configuration partition, and the domain partition by upgrading to Exchange 2013 level.

Preparing the Schema Partition

Before upgrading the Active Directory schema to the appropriate level, you should install the Remote Server Administration Tools (RSAT) on the server where you want to perform the upgrade, typically the first Exchange 2013 server, although this can be done on a domain controller as well. The RSAT tools include the normal Active Directory mangement tools like Active Directory users and computers or Active Directory sites and services, but also low-level tools like ADSIEdit and LDIFDE. The latter is the tool used for making changes to the Active Directory.

To install the RSAT tools on a Windows 2012 Server, log on to the server, open a PowerShell window, and enter the following commands:

```
Import-Module ServerManager

Install-WindowsFeature RSAT-ADDS
```

■ **Note**   When using Windows Server 2008 R2, replace the last command with the Add-WindowsFeature RSAT-ADDS command.

The schema partition should be on an acceptable level. You can check this by using ADSIEdit. Open the schema partition and search for the CN=ms-Exch-Schema-Version-Pt object. Open its properties and request the rangeUpper property; this value should read "14625" for Exchange Server 2007 SP3 (see Figure 3-1) or "14732" for Exchange Server 2010 SP3.

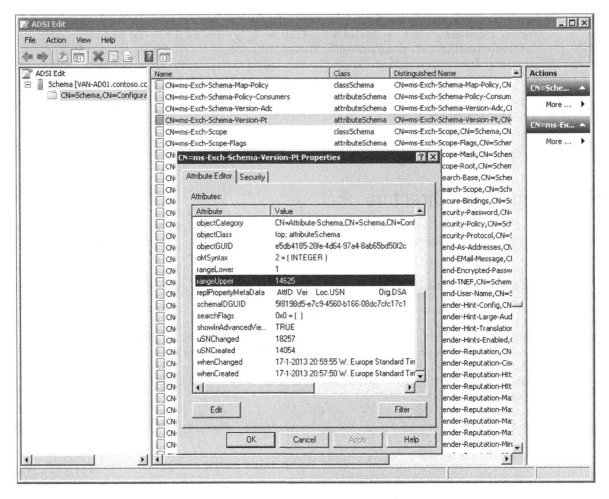

Figure 3-1. *The level of the Active Directory schema. The rangeUpper should read "14625" for Exchange Server 2007*

To prepare the Schema for Exchange Server 2013, log on to the server as a domain administrator, but be sure that this account is added to the Schema Admins security group. Open a command prompt, navigate to the installation media, and enter the following command:

```
Setup.exe /PrepareSchema /IAcceptExchangeServerLicenseTerms
```

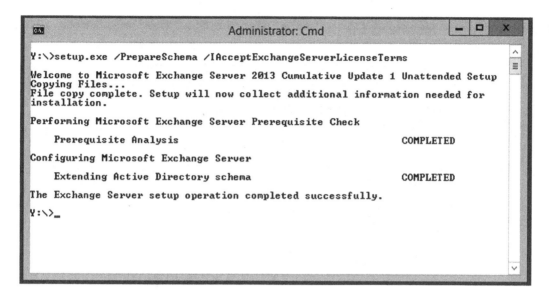

***Figure 3-2.** Extending the schema to Exchange 2013*

The setup program will read all the LDIF files, which actually describe all schema changes and make these changes to Active Directory. Depending on the hardware that's being used for the domain controllers, the schema changes should not take longer than a couple of minutes. When done, the schema should be at level 15254; use the procedure as shown in Figure 3-1 to check this schema version.

■ **Note**   The schema level 15254 is for Exchange Server 2013 CU1, but this will change with subsequent versions of Exchange 2013. For the actual versions you can check the Microsoft website at `http://tinyurl.com/pm2wnjt`.

Before continuing with the next step, make sure that all schema changes have been replicated to all the domain controllers in the entire Active Directory forest. If you have only one location, then it should not take too long, but if you have multiple locations and slow links between them, it can take quite some time.

Preparing the Configuration Partition

The configuration partition is the location in Active Directory where all Exchange-specific data is stored, as we've seen in Chapter 1. Most likely you know which version of Exchange Server you are running currently, but for a quick check you can open the Exchange Management Console, or EMC (see Figure 3-3). This will show the version you are running.

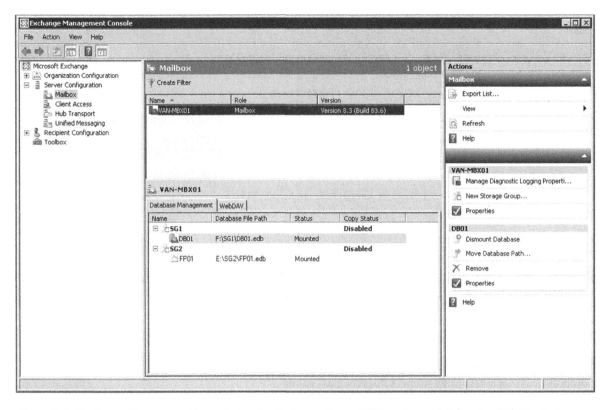

Figure 3-3. *Exchange Management Console showing Exchange Server 2007 service pack 3 (version 8.3). For Exchange Server 2010, the view is similar*

To upgrade the configuration partition to the Exchange 2013 level, log on to the new server as an enterprise admininstrator (or with any administrator account with sufficient permissions in the configuration container) and open a command prompt. Navigate to the installation media and enter the following command:

```
Setup.exe /PrepareAD /IAcceptExchangeServerLicenseTerms
```

Figure 3-4 shows the operation completed successfully.

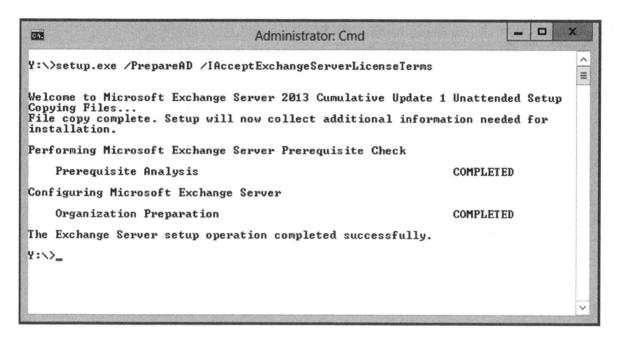

Figure 3-4. *Preparing the Active Directory configuration partition*

■ **Note** There's no need to use the /OrganizationName parameter, as in a green-field setup, since the organization was already named during the previous Exchange Server installation, whichever version that may have been.

Now, how do you check if this upgrade was successful? Obviously, if you didn't get any error messages when you executed the setup.exe /PrepareAD /IAcceptExchangeServerLicenseTerms command, you can be relatively sure everything went fine. In Active Directory, there are no Exchange 2013 server objects yet to check, but if you open Active Directory Users and Computers (shown in Figure 3-5) after the upgrade, you'll find 20 universal security groups in the Microsoft Exchange Security Groups folder in the root of the Active Directory domain, compared to the seven universal security groups in Exchange Server 2007.

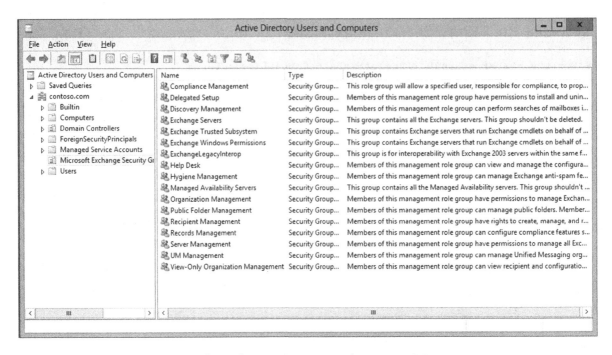

Figure 3-5. Universal security groups for implementing RBAC in Exchange 2013 CU1

As mentioned, in Exchange Server 2007 there were only seven universal security groups in this container in Active Directory:

- Exchange Organization Administrators

- Exchange Public Folder Administrators

- Exchange Recipient Administrators

- Exchange Servers

- Exchange Trusted Subsystem

- Exchange View-Only Administrators

- ExchangeLegacyInterop

These universal security groups in Exchange Server 2007 are used for setting the delegation of control—for example, delegating permissions to other (sub) administrators or helpdesk employees. In Exchange 2013, however, the delegation of control is no longer used for delegating permissions; instead, a new model called Role Based Access Control (RBAC) is used. Under the hood, RBAC is using these universal security groups as well, but since RBAC is much more granular than the old delegation-of-control model, many more groups are needed. This RBAC model is the same as in Exchange Server 2010, so not much difference there.

For the nitty-gritty details, you can also check the properties of the organization object in the configuration container in Active Directory. This object can be found in CN=contoso, CN=Microsoft Exchange, CN=Services, CN=Configuration, DC=Contoso, DC=Com. This object has an attribute called *objectVersion* and its value should read "15614" for Exchange Server 2013 CU1 (see Figure 3-6).

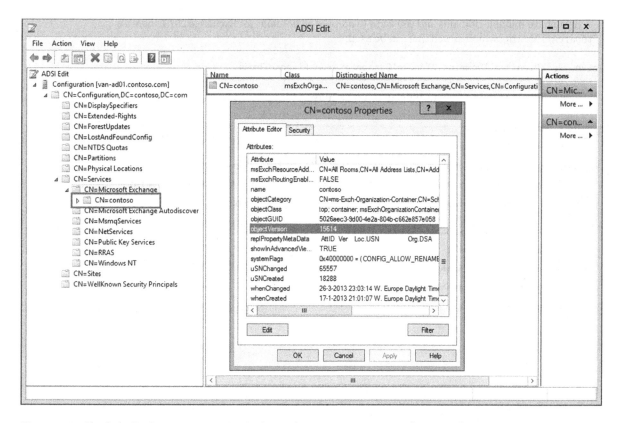

Figure 3-6. *Check the Exchange 2013 version in the configuration partition. In this example it is CU1*

Another check is the msExchProductID attribute of the organization object; this should have the value of at least 15.00.0620.027.

Preparing the Domain Partition

The last step in preparing Active Directory is the actual preparation of the Active Directory domain where the Exchange recipients are located. To prepare this domain, log on with an administrator account that is a member of the Enterprise Admins security group, open a command prompt, navigate to the installation media, and enter the following command:

```
Setup.exe /PrepareAD /IAcceptExchangeServerLicenseTerms
```

If you have multiple domains and you want to prepare all domains for Exchange 2013, there's a /PrepareAllDomains switch as well that can be used:

```
Setup.exe /PrepareAllDomains /IAcceptExchangeServerLicenseTerms
```

Figure 3-7 shows the operation completed successfully.

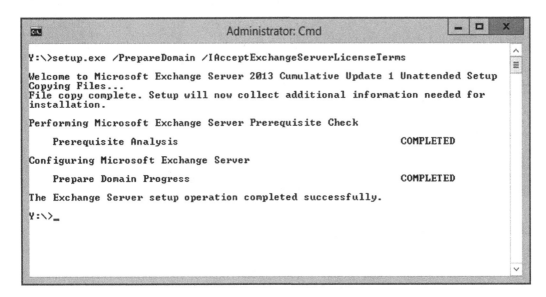

Figure 3-7. *Prepare the current domain for Exchange 2013*

To check if this command has run successfully, you can use ADSIEdit to verify the version of the Microsoft Exchange System Objects container in the root domain you're preparing. To check this you have to use ADSIEdit and open the Default Naming Context. This container has a property called *objectVersion* and its value should read "13236" for Exchange 2013 (see Figure 3-8).

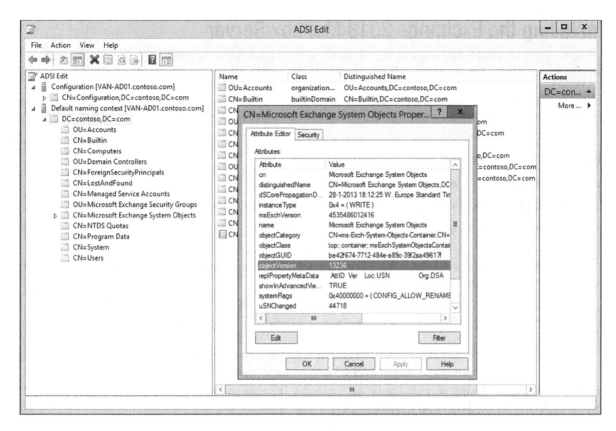

Figure 3-8. *Check the objectVersion of the Exchange System Objects container*

The setup application of Exchange 2013 also logs everything in log files in the directory `C:\ExchangeSetupLogs`, but this is not really informational for a normal human being because of the amount of information in the log files. The log files are stored on disk for troubleshooting purposes by Microsoft, should something goes terribly wrong during setup and you want to submit a call to Microsoft support. But I have to admit, in all those years, I have never seen the setup application fail at this point.

■ **Note** It is not really necessary to prepare the Active Directory manually. When the graphical setup of Exchange 2013 is started on the first Exchange 2013 server and the installation is executed, the Active Directory partitions are automatically upgraded to the right level. However, performing these steps manually is much more granular; it can be performed by, for example, Active Directory administrators; and it can be monitored on a step-by-step basis.

Installing the Exchange 2013 Mailbox Server

When the Active Directory is fully prepared, the first Exchange 2013 server can be installed. Typically, this is the Mailbox server since all business logic is located in this server role and this is where PowerShell commands are actually executed. On the other hand, the Exchange 2013 Client Access server is the server responsible for the namespaces, so you need both servers to actually start configuring your Exchange 2013 environment. But before you install the Exchange 2013 server role, you need to install some prerequisite software that will hold the Mailbox server.

Prerequisite software

The prerequisite software for an Exchange 2013 Mailbox server includes:

- .NET Framework 4.5 - `http://msdn.microsoft.com/library/5a4x27ek.aspx`

- Management Framework 3.0 - `www.microsoft.com/en-us/download/ details.aspx?id=34595`

- Exchange-specific Windows features like Internet Information Server, Management Consoles, or the Identity Foundation, which will be installed using a PowerShell command, as explained in the following section

- Unified Communications Managed API 4.0 Runtime - `www.microsoft.com/en-us/download/ details.aspx?id=34992`

■ **Note**   The Unified Communications Managed API 4.0 Runtime has a dependency on the Desktop-Experience module which is installed using PowerShell, as outlined in the third bullet. Therefore, the Unified Communications Managed API 4.0 Runtime is the last prerequisite software to install.

The Exchange 2013 Mailbox server also requires filter components (which used to be installed on the Exchange server with the Office 2010 filter pack, but these filters are now included in the search components of the Mailbox server so there's no need to install the filter pack separately). Keep in mind that the setup application will generate a warning message when the filter pack is not installed, but this warning can be ignored.

The .NET Framework 4.5 and Management Framework 3.0 are included in Windows Server 2012; for Windows Server 2008 R2, they need to be downloaded from the Microsoft website and installed manually.

Before installing the Mailbox server on Windows Server 2008 R2, have the startup type for the Net.Tcp port sharing service set to automatic and start the service. Open the services MMC snap-in, select the Net.Tcp port sharing service, and request its properties, changing the settings as appropriate (see Figure 3-9).

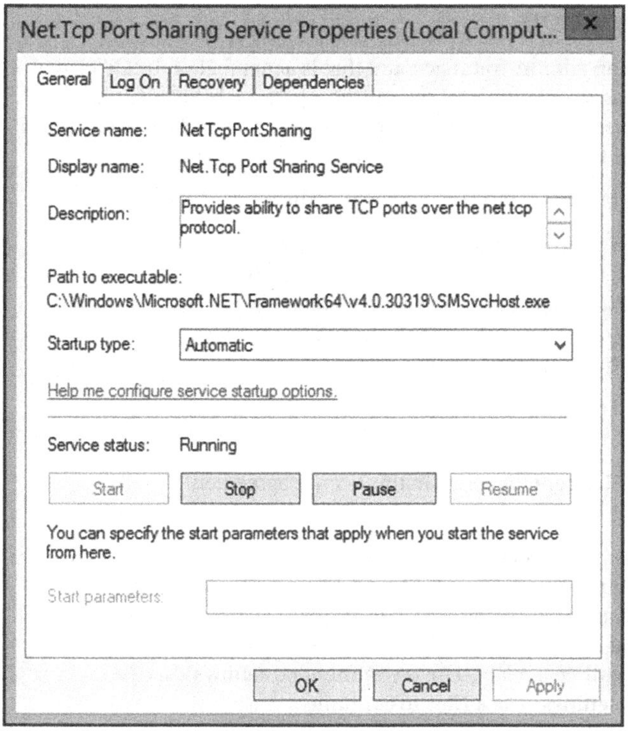

Figure 3-9. *Change the startup type of the Net.Tcp port sharing service to automatic*

To install the prerequisite server roles and features, log on to the new server with an administrator account, open the Windows PowerShell, and enter the following command:

```
Import-Module ServerManager

Install-WindowsFeature AS-HTTP-Activation, Desktop-Experience, NET-Framework-45-Features,
RPC-over-HTTP-proxy, RSAT-Clustering, RSAT-Clustering-CmdInterface, Web-Mgmt-Console,
WAS-Process-Model, Web-Asp-Net45, Web-Basic-Auth, Web-Client-Auth, Web-Digest-Auth,
Web-Dir-Browsing, Web-Dyn-Compression, Web-Http-Errors, Web-Http-Logging, Web-Http-Redirect,
Web-Http-Tracing, Web-ISAPI-Ext, Web-ISAPI-Filter, Web-Lgcy-Mgmt-Console, Web-Metabase,
Web-Mgmt-Console, Web-Mgmt-Service, Web-Net-Ext45, Web-Request-Monitor, Web-Server,
Web-Stat-Compression, Web-Static-Content, Web-Windows-Auth, Web-WMI, Windows-Identity-Foundation
```

When installed, reboot the server; once it reboots, log on again with an administrator account and install the Unified Communications Managed API 4.0 Runtime prerequisite software. Once it's installed, continue with the installation of the actual Exchange 2013 Mailbox server binaries.

Exchange 2013 Mailbox Server Installation

To install the Exchange 2013 Mailbox server, log on with an administrator account that is a member of the Delegated Setup universal security group or the Organization Management universal security group. If you have *not* prepared Active Directory at this point and want setup to take control of this, the administrator account should be a member of the Enterprise Admins security group. Follow these steps to install the Exchange 2013 Mailbox server:

1. On the installation media, double-click setup.exe to start the setup application.

2. Microsoft has made significant changes to the setup process compared to Exchange Server 2010. The first window that's shown is whether the setup application needs to check for updates. If updates are available, the setup application will download them and automatically install them as well. Leave the default "Connect to the Internet and check for updates" and click Next to continue and follow the wizard.

3. Setup will now start copying the files needed to install Exchange 2013. At the introduction screen, click Next to continue.

4. Read the license agreement (…), select the "I accept the terms in this license agreement," and click Next to continue.

5. The window for Recommended Settings lets you select if you want to use the recommended settings or not. There's not much information on this screen, but when you select "Use recommended settings," it enables the error reporting and the Customer Experience Information Program (CEIP) that collects information on your hardware and how you use Exchange Server. If you agree with this, select "Use recommended settings"; otherwise, select "Don't use recommended settings." Click Next to continue.

6. The next screen is the most important screen since you can select what server roles to install. For a dedicated Mailbox server, select the Mailbox role and just leave the Client Access role unchecked (see Figure 3-10). Note the checkbox for "Automatically install Windows Server roles and features that are required to install Exchange Server." This will install all roles and features needed for the Mailbox server. (This was already installed in a previous step using Windows PowerShell and the Server Manager module, but it doesn't do any harm to leave this checked.) Click Next to continue.

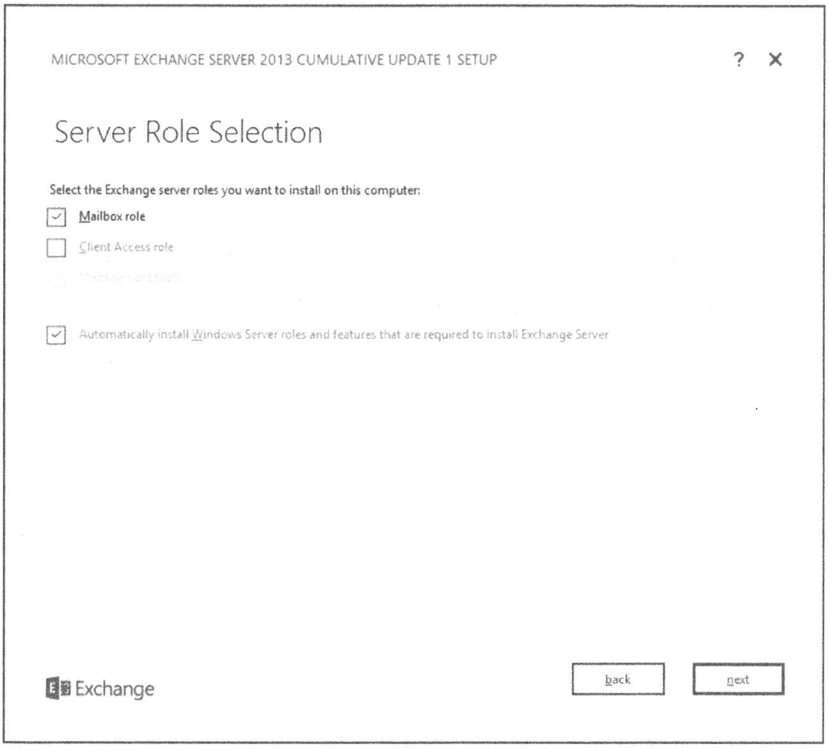

Figure 3-10. *The server selection with the Windows Server roles and features option*

7. On the Installation Space and Location screen, you can change the location where the Exchange 2013 files are installed if needed. Click Next to continue.

8. Exchange 2013 comes with a default anti-malware solution. It is not as complete as, for example, Forefront Protection for Exchange(FPE) was, but it can certainly help keep your messaging environment clean. By default the anti-malware is enabled, but you can disable it if you want to use another (third-party) solution. Internet access is required to download the latest anti-malware updates. Click Next to continue.

9. The setup program has now gathered enough information for the installation and will perform a readiness check. When no problems are found, click "Install to start the actual installation." Now it's time to wait. . . .

   The setup consists of 12 different steps; the screen is updated with every step, and within every step the progress is indicated by a blue bar (see Figure 3-11).

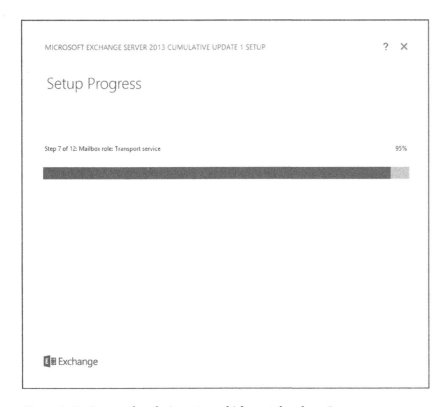

Figure 3-11. *Progress bar during setup, which can take a long time*

When setup is completed, a Setup Completed page is shown congratulating you for finishing the setup successfully. Click Finish and reboot the Mailbox server. The installation of the Exchange 2013 Mailbox server is now finished and it's time to continue with installation of the Exchange 2013 Client Access server.

Installing the Exchange 2013 Client Access Server

Once the Mailbox server is installed, the Exchange 2013 Client Access server (CAS)can be installed as well. The Client Access server can be installed on Windows Server 2012 or on Windows Server 2008 R2.

Prerequisite Software

As with the Mailbox server, the Client Access server needs some prerequisite software:

- .NET Framework 4.5 - `http://msdn.microsoft.com/library/5a4x27ek.aspx`

- Management Framework 3.0 - `www.microsoft.com/en-us/download/ details.aspx?id=34595`

- Exchange-specific Windows features like Internet Information Server, Management Consoles, or the Identity Foundation, which will be installed using a PowerShell command, as explained in the following section

- Unified Communications Managed API 4.0 Runtime - `www.microsoft.com/en-us/ download/details.aspx?id=34992`

■ **Note** The Unified Communications Managed API 4.0 Runtime has a dependency on the Desktop-Experience module that is installed using PowerShell, as outlined in the third bullet. Therefore, the Unified Communications Managed API 4.0 Runtime is the last prerequisite software to install.

Exchange 2013 Client Access Server Installation

Since the Client Access server is the second Exchange server to be installed, no changes to Active Directory need be made. It's also not necessary to install the remote server administration tools unless you want the Active Directory tools on your Client Access server. If so, log on as an administrator, open a PowerShell command prompt, and enter the following commands:

```
Import-Module ServerManager
```

```
Install-WindowsFeature RSAT-ADDS
```

■ **Note** When installing Exchange 2013 on Windows Server 2008 R2, replace the second command with Add-WindowsFeature RSAT-ADDS.

To install the prerequisite server roles and features on the new Client Access server, log on to the server as an administrator, open a PowerShell command prompt, and enter the following command:

```
Install-WindowsFeature AS-HTTP-Activation, Desktop-Experience, NET-Framework-45-Features,
RPC-over-HTTP-proxy, RSAT-Clustering, Web-Mgmt-Console, WAS-Process-Model, Web-Asp-Net45,
Web-Basic-Auth, Web-Client-Auth, Web-Digest-Auth, Web-Dir-Browsing, Web-Dyn-Compression,
Web-Http-Errors, Web-Http-Logging, Web-Http-Redirect, Web-Http-Tracing, Web-ISAPI-Ext,
Web-ISAPI-Filter, Web-Lgcy-Mgmt-Console, Web-Metabase, Web-Mgmt-Console, Web-Mgmt-Service,
Web-Net-Ext45, Web-Request-Monitor, Web-Server, Web-Stat-Compression, Web-Static-Content,
Web-Windows-Auth, Web-WMI, Windows-Identity-Foundation
```

You will be prompted to reboot before proceeding to the next step (see Figure 3-12).

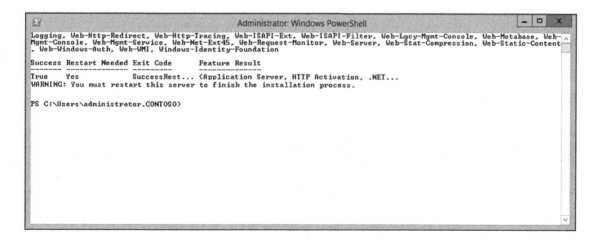

Figure 3-12. *Installing the prerequisite server roles and features for the Client Access server*

After rebooting, the Client Access server binaries can be installed. This process is not very different from installing the Mailbox server, as described in the previous section of this chapter.

Log on as an administrator who is a member of the Enterprise Admins group, navigate to the installation media, and double-click setup.exe to start the setup application. Follow the wizard until you reach the Server Role Selection window. Select the Client Access role and then select the "Automatically install Windows server roles and features that are required to install Exchange Server" option (see Figure 3-13). Although this checkbox is optional, and you've installed the prerequisite software in the previous step, there's always the risk that Microsoft subsequently changed something in the setup application that is not reflected in the prerequisite software that needs to be installed.

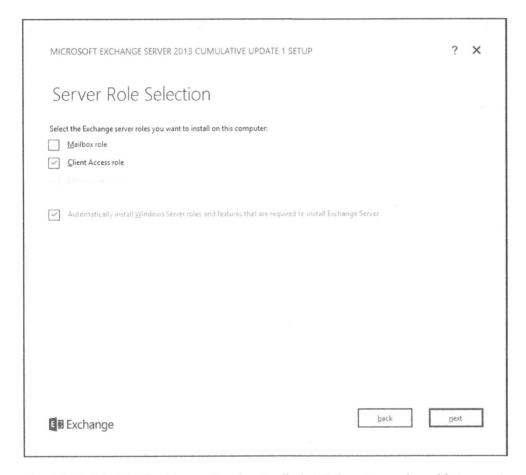

Figure 3-13. *Select the Client Access role and optionally the Windows Server roles and features option*

Continue the wizard and wait for the readiness check to finish. If all goes well and all prerequisite checks are met, you can continue the installation by clicking Install. The installation will continue, and after some time the installation should finish successfully. Once installation is completed, you can immediately start the Exchange Admin Center (EAC) by checking the box for "Launch Exchange Admin Center after finishing Exchange setup." The browser will then automatically start and the EAC will be opened. Since only a self-signed SSL certificate is configured on the new Client Access server, you'll receive a certificate warning, but you can safely ignore this warning.

After logging on, you'll immediately see the recipients in your Exchange organization (see Figure 3-14). Needless to say, these recipients still exist on your previous Exchange Server.

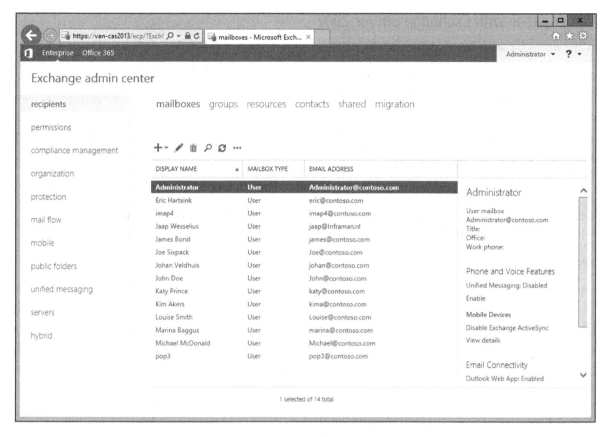

Figure 3-14. *The recipients from the previous Exchange installation, shown in the EAC after the first logon*

At this moment, leave the EAC for what it is and reboot the server. Up to this point there are no major differences between the upgrades from Exchange Server 2007 and Exchange Server 2010. But things are different in the namespace and coexistence phase.

Configuring Namespaces and Coexistence

When installing Exchange Server 2013 into an existing Exchange Server 2010 or Exchange Server 2007 environment, you have to configure what are called *namespaces*. A namespace is a name that clients use to access the Exchange services, like webmail.contoso.com or autodiscover.contoso.com. As you will see in the following sections, there are differences in how Exchange Server 2007 and Exchange Server 2010 handle namespaces.

Namespaces and Coexistence with Exchange Server 2007

When you are installing Exchange 2013 into an Exchange Server 2007 environment, namespaces are extremely important because they determine how a particular client can access the platform. Clients use these namespaces to make a distinct difference between accessing Exchange 2013 and accessing Exchange Server 2007. They use a technique called *redirection* to switch from Exchange 2013 to Exchange Server 2007.

Namespaces with Exchange Server 2007

In the original Exchange Server 2007 environment, two namespaces are typically used:

- webmail.contoso.com - used for all HTTPS-based services, including Outlook Anywhere

- autodiscover.contoso.com - used by external Outlook clients for discovering the internal Exchange configuration

In Exchange 2013, this namespace planning is not very different, but since Exchange Server 2007 and Exchange 2013 are not compatible with each other, we have to come up with a solution for the coexistence scenario whereby both Exchange Server 2007 and Exchange 2013 are accessible. Needless to say, this does not work with a single namespace.

When Exchange 2013 is initially installed into an existing Exchange Server 2007 environment, nothing happens when it comes to clients. At one point, the client access is changed from the Exchange Server 2007 CAS to the Exchange 2013 CAS. When the mailbox is located on an Exchange 2013 Mailbox server, this is fine, but when the mailbox is still located on the Exchange Server 2007 Mailbox server, things will break. The client request is redirected from the 2013 CAS to the 2007 CAS to be processed there. You will see this happen in OWA where the URL in the navigation bar changes from the 2013 CAS to the 2007 CAS.

Since the FQDN webmail.contoso.com is pointing to the 2013 CAS, a new FQDN has to be created to access the old 2007 CAS. Microsoft typically uses the FQDN legacy.contoso.com for this (see Figure 3-15).

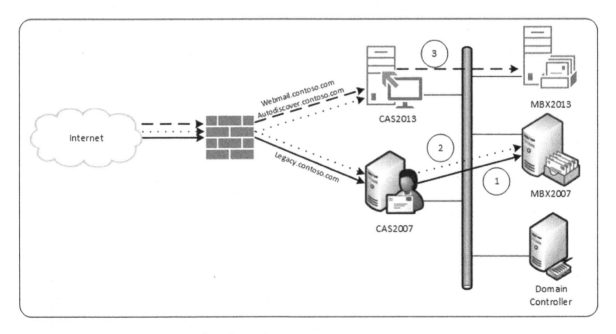

Figure 3-15. *Coexistence scenario with Exchange Server 2007*

In Figure 6-13, the three scenarios are clearly visible.

1. The solid line is the original situation, in which clients connect via webmail.contoso.com and autodiscover.contoso.com to the 2007 CAS. The CAS retrieves the information from the 2007 Mailbox server.

2. The dotted line is the coexistence scenario. Clients connect using webmail.contoso.com and autodiscover.contoso.com to the Exchange 2013 CAS. Requests for webmail.contoso.com are now redirected to the 2007 CAS using the legacy.contoso.com FQDN. The 2007 CAS retrieves the information from the 2007 Mailbox server and returns the information directly to the clients.

3. The dashed line is the final situation. Clients connect to the Exchange 2013 CAS using the webmail.contoso.com and autodiscover.contoso.com FQDN, and the requests are proxied directly to the Exchange 2013 Mailbox server.

Unfortunately this is not identical for all protocols:

- *Outlook Web App* is redirected from the Exchange 2013 CAS to the 2007 CAS. This conforms with the three bullets mentioned above.

- *Outlook Anywhere* is not redirected, but the client requests (HTTPS) are proxied from the Exchange 2013 CAS to the 2007 CAS. This server retrieves the information from the 2007 Mailbox server and the information is returned to the clients through the 2013 CAS.

- *Exchange activesync and Exchange web services* are proxied from the Exchange 2013 CAS to the 2013 Mailbox server, and then proxied to the 2007 CAS.

- *POP3 and IMAP4* are proxied from the Exchange 2013 CAS to the 2007 CAS.

- *Autodiscover* is a bit different. In an Exchange Server 2007/2013 coexistence scenario, the Autodiscover requests are sent to the Exchange 2013 CAS, which proxies them to the 2013 Mailbox server. This server processes all requests, regardless of the location of the mailbox. This is true both for internal clients who get the 2013 CAS from the service connection point (SCP) and for external clients who construct the URL based on the user's SMTP address.

Outlook clients in an Exchange Server 2007 environment on the internal network connect directly to the Mailbox server where the mailbox is hosted. When Exchange 2013 is introduced into the existing Exchange Server 2007 environment this does not change the way Outlook clients connect to the Exchange Server 2007 mailbox. But as soon as the mailbox is moved to the 2013 Mailbox server, the Outlook client automatically switches to Outlook Anywhere and starts to connect to the 2013 CAS.

■ **Note** There's a distinct difference between *proxying* and *redirection*. In a proxy situation, the client keeps the connection with the Exchange 2013 server, which forwards the request to the Exchange 2007 server. This server returns the information to the Exchange 2013 server, which returns the information to the client. Thus, connection with the Exchange 2013 server never gets lost.

In a redirection situation, the connection with the Exchange 2013 server is closed after the authentication request and the client sets up a new connection with the Exchange 2007 server.

Coexistence with Exchange Server 2007 and SSL Certificates

When configuring the Exchange 2007 CAS for coexistence scenario with the Exchange 2013 CAS, the SSL certificates need to be changed. The webmail.contoso.com and autodiscover.contoso.com names are used on the SSL certificate on the 2013 CAS, and the legacy.contoso.com name is used on the SSL certificate on the 2007 CAS.

The easiest and cheapest way to achieve this is to use one SSL certificate on both Client Access servers, whereby:

- webmail.contoso.com is used as the common name (CN). autodiscover.contoso.com is added to the subject alternative names (SAN) field.

- legacy.contoso.com is added to the subject alternative names (SAN) field.

An advantage of using the same SSL certificate on both the 2007 CAS and the 2013 CAS is that the moment of switching the FQdN from Exchange 2007 to Exchange 2013 is fully independent of the SSL certificate activities.

To request a certificate like this, log on as an administrator to the 2013 CAS and open the EAC using the URL https://localhost/ecp?ExchClientVer=15. This ?ExchClientVer15 suffix is very important in a coexistence scenario. Since the administrator mailbox is still on Exchange Server 2007, the EAC cannot be contacted directly and so Exchange Server wants to redirect the request, but the EAC does not exist on Exchange Server 2007.

■ **Note** If the new Exchange 2013 Client Access server already has an external Internet connection, you can also use that one instead of the localhost.

To request the new certificate, follow these steps:

1. In the EAC, log on with an administrator account. In the left-hand menu, select Servers and in the top menu, select Certificates. In the box "Select server drop down," select the appropriate Client Access server and click on the "+" symbol.

2. In the new Exchange Certificate window, select "Create a request for a certificate from a certification authority" and click Next.

3. In the next window, enter a friendly name for the new certificate—something like "Contoso Client Acess Certificate"—and click Next to continue.

4. Skip the wildcard option and click Next to continue.

5. For "Store certificate request on this server," use the Browse button to select the 2013 CAS (see Figure 3-16). Please note that this is not the server where the request file, typically newcert.req, is stored; it is the server where the request is generated and, very important, where the private key of the new certificate is generated. Click Next to continue.

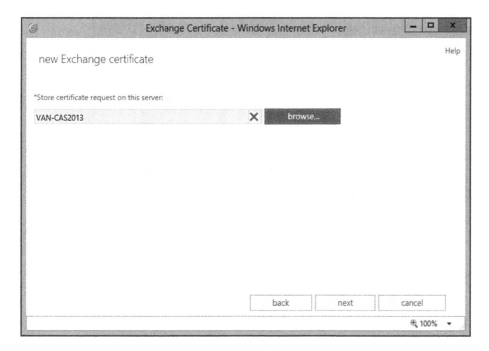

Figure 3-16. *Store the request on the Client Access server*

6. The next window lets you specify the various domain names. For example, for Outlook Web App (when accessed from the Internet), enter webmail.contoso.com; for Autodiscover (when accessed from the Internet), enter autodiscover.contoso.com. Clear all other entries and click Next to continue.

7. In the "Based on your selections . . ." window, use the "-" symbol to delete the contoso.com entry and use the "+" symbol to add the legacy.contoso.com entry. Typically, the highlighted entry is the common name (CN) of the SSL certificate. Your list should look similar to Figure 3-17.

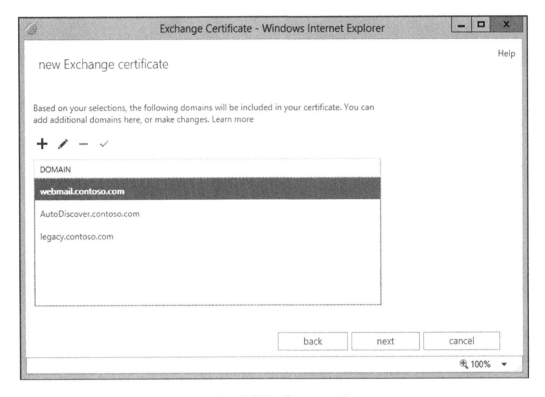

Figure 3-17. These domain names will be included in the SSL certificate

8. Click Next to continue.

9. Specify the organization information, such as organization name, department name, or other. When requesting a certificate at a third-party vendor, make sure that all information is valid. This will speed up the certificate-issuing process. Click Next to continue.

10. The actual request file will be stored on a fileshare on the network. Enter the UNC path of this certificate request file, like \\van-ad01\Management\newcert.req. This share can be anywhere on the network as long as the Exchange Trusted Subsystem universal security group has *full access* permissions on the share. Click Next to continue.

11. The request is now finished and the request file is stored on the share in the previous step. Use the contents of this file to request the new certificate at a certificate authority (CA). For example, this can be an internal (Active Directory) certificate authority or a third-party CA like Digicert or Entrust. For a complete overview of all supported partners, check the Microsoft knowledgebase article KB929395: http://support.microsoft.com/kb/929395.

12. In the EAC, you'll see the new certificate request and that its status is "pending request." When you have received a new certificate from your CA, select the pending certificate request and click Complete under "Status" in the right-hand pane.

13. In the Complete Pending Request window, select the new certificate you got from your CA (use the UNC naming convention here, such as \\van-ad01\Management\certnew.cer) and click OK.

14. In the EAC, you'll see the status of the certificate change from "pending" to "valid." To assign services to the newly created certificate, select the new certificate and click the "pencil" button.

15. In the window that pops up, select "services" in the left menu. In the Specify the Services window, select the appropriate services, like IIS, and click Save. The SSL certificate is now fully configured.

When you check the new certificate, using either the certificates MMC snap-in or your browser, and you navigate to the Exchange 2013 CAS, you'll see all entries, similar to those shown in Figure 3-18.

Figure 3-18. *The new SSL certificate with the subject alternative names entries*

The final step is to export this SSL certificate on the Exchange 2013 CAS and import it on the 2007 CAS. Don't forget to assign the services on the 2007 CAS to the newly imported SSL certificate.

■ **Note**   Unfortunately, it turned out that Exchange Server 2013 CU1 had a nasty bug that would cause the switching of several parameters, like city and province, in the actual certificate. This should be fixed in subsequent cumulative updates.

Exchange Server 2007 and Virtual Directories

Now that there are two separate and different Exchange CASs, you need to take special care when it comes to configuring the virtual directories that are part of those Client Access servers.

In Exchange 2013, all virtual directories should point to the Exchange 2013 server, so this is no different from a normal green-field installation. All mailboxes that have been moved to Exchange 2013 will use these settings (see Table 3-1).

Table 3-1. *Virtual Directory Settings on the Exchange 2013 Client Access Server*

Virtual Directory	Internal URL	External URL
OWA virtual directory	`https://webmail.contoso.com/owa`	`https://webmail.contoso.com/owa`
EAC virtual directory	`https://webmail.contoso.com/ecp`	`https://webmail.contoso.com/ecp`
Activesync virtual directory	`https://webmail.contoso.com/` `Microsoft-Server-ActiveSync`	`https://webmail.contoso.com/` `Microsoft-Server-ActiveSync`
EWS virtual directory	`https://webmail.contoso.com/` `ews/exchange.asmx`	`https://webmail.contoso.com/` `ews/exchange.asmx`
OAB virtual directory	`https://webmail.contoso.com/oab`	`https://webmail.contoso.com/oab`
PowerShell virtual directory	`https://webmail.contoso.com/` `powershell`	`https://webmail.contoso.com/` `powershell`
Autodiscover virtual directory	`https://autodiscover.contoso.com/` `autodiscover`	`https://autodiscover.contoso.com/` `autodiscover`
Outlook Anywhere	`Webmail.contoso.com`	`Webmail.contoso.com`

To configure the virtual directories for external access, log on to the EAC, but do not forget to add the `/?ExchClientVer=15` suffix in the ECP request. This is necessary because the administrator mailbox is still on Exchange Server 2007 at this point, and if you do not add the suffix, the request will fail with an HTTP 403 error. So the request will be `https://localhost/ecp/?ExchClientVer=15`.

In the left navigation menu, select "servers" and in the top level menu, select "virtual directories." In the Select Server drop-down box, select the 2013 CAS you want to change; in this example, it's `VAN-CAS2013.contoso.com` (see Figure 3-19).

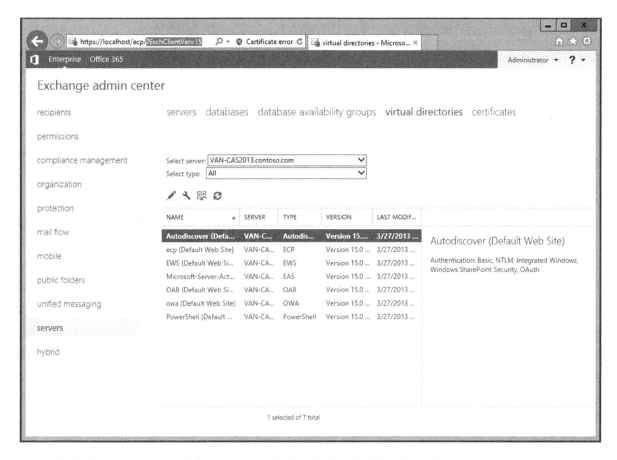

Figure 3-19. *Configure the virtual directories. Note the ?ExchClientVer=15 option in the navigation bar*

To configure the virtual directories, click on the little "wrench" icon to start the Configure External Access Domain wizard. In the wizard, click the "+" symbol to add an 2013 CAS to the list of servers to be configured, and in the text box, enter the external domain name—for example, webmail.contoso.com–and click Save to continue. When the wizard is finished processing, click the Close button to return to the EAC. Unfortunately, this will only change the External URL parameter of the virtual directories; the Internal URL is untouched.

To change the Internal URL settings on the virtual directories, you have to open all virtual directories (except the Autodiscover virtual directory) and change the Internal URL appropriately (see Figure 3-20).

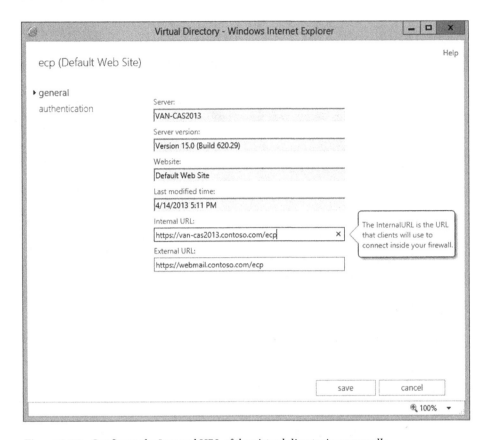

Figure 3-20. *Configure the Internal URL of the virtual directories manually*

To change both the External URL and the Internal URL at the same time, the Exchange Management Shell (EMS) can be used as well, with the following commands:

```
Set-OWAVirtualDirectory -Identity van-cas2013\owa* -InternalURL
https://webmail.contoso.com/owa -ExternalURL https://webmail.contoso.com/owa

Set-ECPVirtualDirectory -Identity van-cas2013\ecp* -InternalURL
https://webmail.contoso.com/ecp -ExternalURL https://webmail.contoso.com/ecp

Set-ActiveSyncVirtualDirectory -Identity van-cas2013\microsoft* -InternalURL
https://webmail.contoso.com/Microsoft-Server-ActiveSync -ExternalURL
https://webmail.contoso.com/Microsoft-Server-ActiveSync
```

```
Set-WebServicesVirtualDirectory -Identity van-cas2013\ews* -InternalURL
https://webmail.contoso.com/ews/exchange.asmx -ExternalURL
https://webmail.contoso.com/ews/exchange.asmx

Set-OABVirtualDirectory -Identity van-cas2013\oab* -InternalURL
https://webmail.contoso.com/OAB -ExternalURL https://webmail.contoso.com/OAB

Set-PowershellVirtualDirectory -Identity "van-cas2013\powershell (def*" -InternalURL
https://webmail.contoso.com/Powershell -ExternalURL https://webmail.contoso.com/Powershell

Set-ClientAccessServer -Identity van-cas2013 -AutodiscoverServiceInternalUri
https://autodiscover.contoso.com/autodiscover/autodiscover.xml
```

■ **Note**   The internal URL needs to be resolvable on the Client Access servers, or else a warning message will be shown that it is not resolvable.

On the new 2013 CAS, Outlook Anywhere has to be configured as well. Remember that Outlook Anywhere is enabled by default, since all Outlook clients on Exchange 2013 use Outlook Anywhere. The internal hostname and the external hostname need to be configured as well as the SSL requirement parameter:

```
Set-OutlookAnywhere -Identity van-cas2013\rpc* -InternalHostname webmail.contoso.com
-InternalClientsRequireSSL $true -ExternalHostname webmail.contoso.com -ExternalClientsRequireSSL
$true -ExternalClientAuthenticationMethod Basic
```

■ **Note**   It is not possible to configure Outlook Anywhere using the EAC; these settings can only be changed using the EMS. So even if you're trying to avoid using the EMS at all and attempt to use the EAC only, you don't have much choice, I'm afraid.

It is also possible to use the change_vdir_settings.ps1 script, as explained in Chapter 2. Open the EMS, navigate to the script, and run it with your external domain as a parameter, just like:

```
.\change_vdir_settigns.ps1 contoso.com
```

When a mailbox has not been moved to the Exchange 2013 Mailbox server, the 2013 CAS will detect this during the initial client request when the user is authenticated. The request will either be redirected or it will be proxied to the 2007 CAS, depending on the protocol being used.

The virtual directories on the 2007 CAS (see Table 3-2) either should point to the legacy URL when the request is redirected or should point to the 2013 CAS when the request is proxied or handled by the 2013 Mailbox server.

Table 3-2. *Virtual Directory Settings on the Exchange Server 2007 Client Access Server*

Virtual Directory	Internal URL	External URL
OWA virtual directory	https://legacy.contoso.com/owa	https://legacy.contoso.com/owa
ECP virtual directory	n/a	n/a
Activesync virtual directory	https://webmail.contoso.com/ Microsoft-Server-ActiveSync	https://webmail.contoso.com/ Microsoft-Server-ActiveSync
EWS virtual directory	https://webmail.contoso.com/ ews/exchange.asmx	https://webmail.contoso.com/ ews/exchange.asmx
OAB virtual directory	https://legacy.contoso.com/oab	https://legacy.contoso.com/oab
PowerShell virtual directory	https://legacy.contoso.com/ powershell	https://legacy.contoso.com/ powershell
Autodiscover virtual directory	https://autodiscover.contoso.com/ autodiscover	https://autodiscover.contoso.com/ autodiscover

■ **Note**   When enabling Outlook Anywhere on Exchange Server 2007 in a coexistence scenario, the same settings apply as when enabled in a pure Exchange Server 2007 scenario. The Outlook clients who will access 2013 CAS are proxied to the 2007 CAS.

Please note that it is not possible to manage Exchange Server 2007 settings from the EMS running on the Exchange 2013 environment, nor is it possible from the EAC. Exchange Server 2007 settings should be managed from the 2007 Exchange Management Console or the 2007 Exchange Management Shell. Since you are reading this, you should be familiar with Exchange Server 2007 and how to configure the virtual directories in the 2007 Exchange Management Console or the 2007 Exchange Management Shell, so I won't go into detail here.

■ **Note**   Don't make changes to the Exchange 2007 virtual directories yet, since that will immediately change the client behavior. Make these changes at the moment when you are actually changing the access method, when all clients access the 2013 CAS and are redirected to the 2007 CAS.

Making the Change for Clients

If all servers have been installed and configured, it's time to change how these clients access the Exchange platform. This is an important moment since one mistake here can potentially have an impact on all clients.

I've said before that Outlook clients connect directly to the 2007 Mailbox server, and this does not change when you make the change to the 2013 CAS. While this is true, Outlook clients use Autodiscover and the Exchange web services at the same time, and these protocols are impacted by a change to the 2013 CAS.

For internal clients, it is just a matter of changing the internal DNS records for webmail.contoso.com and autodiscover.contoso.com to the 2013 CAS and creating a new record for legacy.contoso.com. If there are multiple CAS in a load-balanced array, you have to change the IP address from the old load-balanced array to the new load-balanced array.

For external clients, the forwarding address on the firewall needs to be changed from the 2007 CAS to the 2013 CAS.

· If the Microsoft Threat Management Gateway (TMG) 2010 is used, more steps are involved:

1. Import the new SSL certificate that includes the `legacy.contoso.com` domain name to the TMG server, and bind it to the web listener that's used by the Exchange servers.

2. Create a new web publishing rule in the TMG console for publishing the `legacy.contoso.com` Exchange 2007 server. The existing web listener can be used for this new web publishing rule.

3. The web listener for `webmail.contoso.com` needs to be changed so that it now points to the 2013 CAS. If the self-signed certificate is used on the CAS, make sure it is imported in the trusted root certification authorities store on the TMG server so that the self-signed certificate is trusted. This certificate is only used for communication between the TMG server and the CAS.

■ **Note**   It is possible to create the legacy web publishing rule before making the actual network changes. This way you have the possibility of testing the new legacy rule.

Figure 3-21 outlines how clients connect in a coexistence scenario with Exchange Server 2007:

1. Clients use the `webmail.contoso.com` FQDN to connect to the 2013 CAS.

2. When the mailbox is still on Exchange Server 2007, the client will be redirected to 2007 CAS and the client will use the `legacy.contoso.com` FQDN to connect to the legacy CAS. Since one web listener is used by both web publishing rules, one authentication is sufficient.

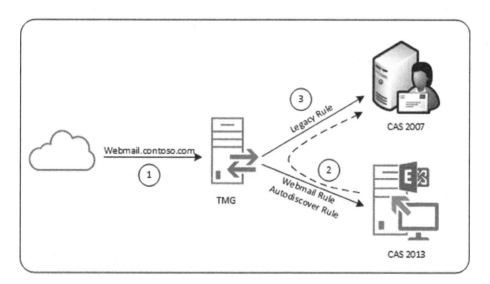

Figure 3-21. *TMG rules in a coexistence scenario*

■ **Note**   Make sure that the authentication settings on the TMG publishing rules match the authentication settings on the virtual directories in Exchange Server 2007 and Exchange Server 2013.

When these changes are made, the last step to perform is to change the virtual directories on the 2007 CAS using the 2007 Exchange Management Console or the 2007 Exchange Management Shell, according to settings shown in Table 3-2, and then you're ready to go.

A client will now use the `http://webmail.contoso.com/owa` URL to connect to the Exchange 2013 CAS and the Exchange 2013 logon form is presented. This is the first change for users! When the user's mailbox is on the Exchange 2013 Mailbox server, the mailbox is shown directly after authentication. When the user's mailbox is still on Exchange Server 2007, a second logon screen is displayed. This is the logon screen from the Exchange 2007 legacy publishing rule; after entering the credentials a second time, the client is shown the Exchange 2007 mailbox (see Figure 3-22).

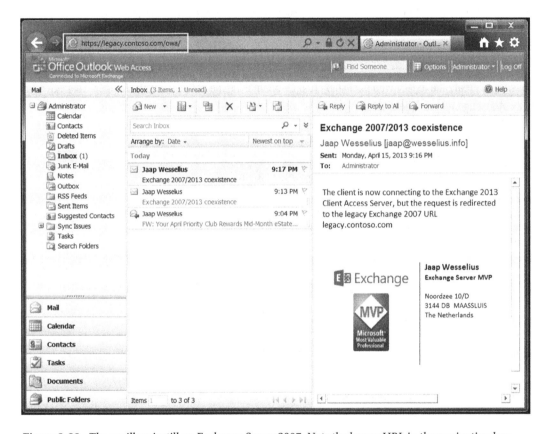

Figure 3-22. The mailbox is still on Exchange Server 2007. Note the legacy URL in the navigation bar

■ **Note**   There's been a major change in Exchange Server 2013 CU2. This update of Exchange 2013 offers single sign-on in a coexistence scenario so users need only log on once and their credentials are passed on to the 2007 CAS.

If TMG is used, the client still sees the initial TMG logon screen. But after authentication, the client is redirected to the 2007 CAS; the TMG listener makes sure a single sign-on is used, so there's no need to authenticate a second time.

Once you've made this change, you've finished one the most important steps in the transition, and it's time to relax a bit and enjoy the Exchange 2013 CAS. Moving mailboxes is the next step in the transition process, and this will be explained after we've covered namespaces and coexistence with Exchange Server 2010.

Namespaces and Coexistence with Exchange Server 2010

Life is a little easier when you're installing Exchange 2013 into an existing Exchange Server 2010 environment. Exchange 2013 works quite well with Exchange Server 2010, making use of an additional namespace unnecessary. There's only one namespace, so there's not a lot of change needed.

Namespaces with Exchange Server 2010

In a typical Exchange Server 2010 environment, two namespaces are used:

- `webmail.contoso.com` - used for all HTTPS-based services, including Outlook Anywhere.
- `autodiscover.contoso.com` - used by external Outlook clients for discovering the internal Exchange configuration.

The namespace planning is identical in Exchange 2013. Also, the Exchange 2013 CAS works smoothly with the 2010 CAS. Requests that hit the 2013 CAS for a mailbox running on Exchange Server 2010 are automatically proxied to the 2010 CAS (see Figure 3-23). For the end user, this is a seamless experience; his connection is set up to the 2013 CAS, and this connection is preserved as long as his session is kept alive. So, in this scenario there's no need for an additional namespace as was needed for the Exchange Server 2007/2013 coexistence.

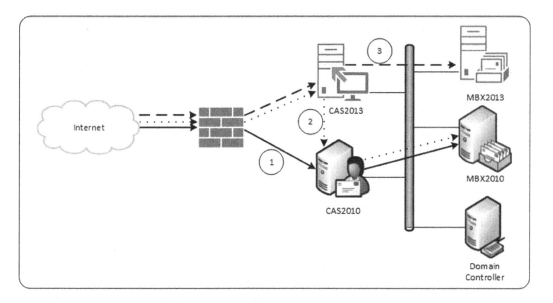

Figure 3-23. *Coexistence scenario with Exchange Server 2010*

Figure 3-23 shows what happens in an Exchange Server 2010/2013 coexistence scenario:

1. The solid line is the original situation, where clients connect via webmail.contoso.com and autodiscover.contoso.com to the Exchange Server 2010 CAS. The CAS retrieves the information from the 2010 Mailbox server.

2. The dotted line is the coexistence scenario. Clients connect using webmail.contoso.com and autodiscover.contoso.com to the 2013 CAS. Requests are proxied to the 2010 CAS, which retrieves the information from the 2010 Mailbox server and returns the information via the 2013 CAS to the client. No connection is set up between the client and the 2010 CAS, and this is fully transparent for the end user.

3. The dashed line is the final situation. Clients connect to the 2013 CAS using the webmail.contoso.com and autodiscover.contoso.com FQDN, and the requests are proxied directly to the 2013 Mailbox server.

In an Exchange Server 2010/2013 coexistence scenario, this is true for all protocols:

- *Outlook Web App* is proxied from the 2013 CAS to the 2010 CAS when the mailbox is still on the 2010 Mailbox server. The interface for those mailboxes is still 2010 and will not benefit from the new 2013 Outlook Web App features.

- *Autodiscover* requests are proxied to the 2010 CAS when the user mailbox is still on the 2010 Mailbox server. This is true for both internal and external clients. Internal clients get the 2013 CAS via the service connection point (SCP) while external clients construct the URL from the SMTP email address of the user.

- *Outlook Anywhere* connections (HTTPS) from Outlook clients are proxied from the 2013 CAS to the 2010 CAS as long as the mailbox is on the 2010 Mailbox server.

- *Exchange activesync and Exchange web services* are proxied from the 2013 CAS to the 2010 CAS as long as the mailbox is running on the 2010 Mailbox server.

- *POP3 and IMAP4* are proxied from the 2013 CAS to the 2010 CAS.

So, all requests are proxied from the 2013 CAS to the 2010 CAS. If there are multiple 2013 Client Access servers, they are load-balanced using a layer-4 load balancer. If there are multiple 2010 Client Access servers, though, there's no need for a load-balancer solution on Exchange Server 2010. The 2013 CAS picks a 2010 CAS randomly from Active Directory so the load is automatically distributed across all 2010 Client Access servers in this particular site.

Outlook clients in an existing Exchange Server 2010 environment connect to the RPCClientAccess service running on the Exchange Server 2010 Client Access server. If multiple Exchange 2010 Client Access servers are used, a load-balanced array of Client Access servers is used—the so-called CAS Array. When Exchange 2013 is introduced into the existing Exchange Server 2010 environment, nothing changes in the way internal Outlook clients connect to the CAS Array. Only if the mailbox is moved from Exchange Server 2010 to Exchange 2013 does the Outlook client no longer connect to the CAS Array; instead, the client starts using Outlook Anywhere and then connects to the 2013 CAS.

Coexistence with Exchange Server 2010 and SSL Certificates

In an Exchange Server 2010/2013 coexistence scenario, there's no need to worry about SSL certificates. The existing SSL certificate on the 2010 CAS in a typical environment should have domain names webmail.contoso.com and autodiscover.contoso.com. At one point, the clients connect to the 2013 Client Access servers using the same domain names, so it's just a matter of exporting the SSL certificate from the 2010 CAS to the 2013 CAS.

Client requests are proxied to the 2010 CAS, but the information is only encrypted using the SSL certificate; the SSL certificate is *not* used for server authentication. Since the 2010 CAS is a member of the same Active Directory environment, it is automatically trusted by the 2013 CAS.

To use an existing SSL certificate from the 2010 CAS, you follow these steps:

1. On the 2010 CAS, use the Exchange Management Console to export the SSL certificate to a PFX file and store this PFX file on a network share—for example, \\eml-ad01\Management\.

2. Log on to the EAC with an administrator account, and don't forget to add ?ExchClientVer=15 to the URL. In the left-hand menu, select "servers" and in the top menu, select "certificates." In the Select Server drop-down box, select the appropriate Client Access server and click on the "three dots" symbol. In the pop-up window, select "Import Exchange Certificate."

3. In the Import Exchange Certificate wizard, enter the filename where the certificate export is stored, such as \\eml-ad01\Management\Contoso.pfx, and enter the password. Click Next to continue.

4. In the next window, click the "+" symbol to add a 2013 CAS where the certificate needs to be imported. When selected, click Finish.

5. The newly imported certificate will now show up in the list of certificates. Select this new certificate, and in the top menu, select the "pencil" icon. The Certificate Details window is shown, and in this window, select "services." Check the box next to IIS and click Save to bind the certificate to the IIS service.

Exchange Server 2010 and Virtual Directories

Now that there are two separate and different Client Access servers, you need to take special care when it comes to configuring the virtual directories that are part of those Client Access servers.

In Exchange 2013, all virtual directories should point to the Exchange 2013 server, so this is no different than a normal green-field installation. All mailboxes that have been moved to Exchange 2013 will use these settings (see Table 3-3).

Table 3-3. *Virtual Directory Settings on the Exchange 2013 Client Access Server*

Virtual Directory	Internal URL	External URL
OWA virtual directory	https://webmail.contoso.com/owa	https://webmail.contoso.com/owa
EAC virtual directory	https://webmail.contoso.com/ecp	https://webmail.contoso.com/ecp
Activesync virtual directory	https://webmail.contoso.com/ Microsoft-Server-ActiveSync	https://webmail.contoso.com/ Microsoft-Server-ActiveSync
EWS virtual directory	https://webmail.contoso.com/ ews/exchange.asmx	https://webmail.contoso.com/ ews/exchange.asmx
OAB virtual directory	https://webmail.contoso.com/oab	https://webmail.contoso.com/oab
PowerShell virtual directory	https://webmail.contoso.com/ powershell	https://webmail.contoso.com/ powershell
Autodiscover virtual directory	https://autodiscover.contoso.com/ autodiscover	https://autodiscover.contoso.com/ autodiscover
Outlook Anywhere	webmail.contoso.com	webmail.contoso.com

To configure the virtual directories for external access, log on to the EAC; again, do not forget to add the /?ExchClientVer=15 suffix in the ECP request. In the left navigation menu, select "servers," and in the top-level menu, select "virtual directories." In the Select Server drop-down box, select the 2013 CAS you want to change—in this example, it's EML-CAS2013.contoso.com (see Figure 3-24).

Figure 3-24. *Virtual directories on the Exchange 2013 Client Access server*

To configure the virtual directories, click on the little "wrench" icon to start the Configure External Access Domain wizard. In the wizard, click the "+" symbol to add an 2013 CAS to the list of servers to be configured, and in the text box, enter the external domain name—for example, webmail.contoso.com—and click Save to continue. When the wizard is finished processing, click the Close button to return to the EAC. Unfortunately, this will only change the External URL parameter of the virtual directory; the Internal URL is untouched.

To change the Internal URL settings on the virtual directories, you have to open all virtual directories (except the autodiscover virtual directory) and change the Internal URL appropriately.

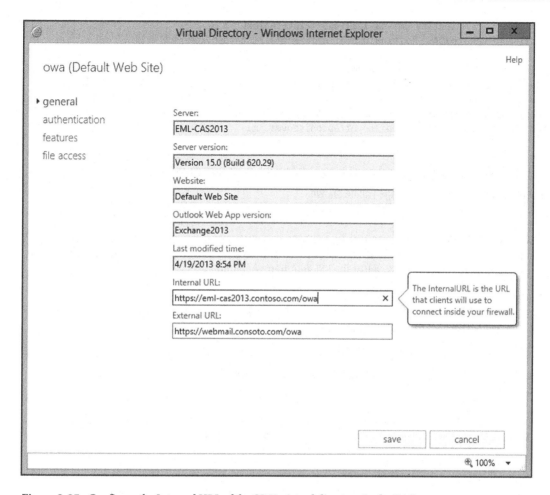

Figure 3-25. *Configure the Internal URL of the OWA virtual directory in the EAC*

To change both the External URL and the Internal URL at the same time, you can use the EMS as well, with the following commands:

```
Set-OWAVirtualDirectory -Identity eml-cas2013\owa* -InternalURL
https://webmail.contoso.com/owa -ExternalURL https://webmail.contoso.com/owa

Set-ECPVirtualDirectory -Identity eml-cas2013\ecp* -InternalURL
https://webmail.contoso.com/ecp -ExternalURL https://webmail.contoso.com/ecp

Set-ActiveSyncVirtualDirectory -Identity eml-cas2013\microsoft* -InternalURL
https://webmail.contoso.com/Microsoft-Server-ActiveSync -ExternalURL
https://webmail.contoso.com/Microsoft-Server-ActiveSync

Set-WebServicesVirtualDirectory -Identity eml-cas2013\ews* -InternalURL
https://webmail.contoso.com/ews/exchange.asmx -ExternalURL
https://webmail.contoso.com/ews/exchange.asmx
```

```
Set-OABVirtualDirectory -Identity eml-cas2013\oab* -InternalURL
https://webmail.contoso.com/OAB -ExternalURL https://webmail.contoso.com/OAB

Set-PowershellVirtualDirectory -Identity "eml-cas2013\powershell (def*)" -InternalURL
https://webmail.contoso.com/Powershell -ExternalURL https://webmail.contoso.com/Powershell

Set-ClientAccessServer -Identity eml-cas2013 -AutodiscoverServiceInternalUri
https://autodiscover.contoso.com/autodiscover/autodiscover.xml
```

■ **Note**   As with Exchange Server 2007, make sure the Internal URL is resolvable as well when making changes. When this is not resolvable, a warning message will be shown.

On the new 2013 CAS, Outlook Anywhere has to be configured as well. Remember that Outlook Anywhere is enabled by default, since all Outlook clients on Exchange 2013 use Outlook Anywhere. The internal hostname and the external hostname need to be configured, as well as the SSL requirement parameter:

```
Set-OutlookAnywhere -Identity eml-cas2013\rpc* -InternalHostname webmail.contoso.com
-InternalClientsRequireSSL $true -ExternalHostname webmail.contoso.com -ExternalClientsRequireSSL
$true -ExternalClientAuthenticationMethod Basic
```

■ **Note**   It is not possible to configure Outlook Anywhere using the EAC; these settings can only be changed using the EMS.

It is also possible to use the change_vdir_settings.ps1 script, as explained in Chapter 2. Open the EMS, navigate to the script, and run it with your external domain as a parameter, as with:

```
.\change_vdir_settigns.ps1 contoso.com
```

If a mailbox has not been moved to the 2013 Mailbox server, the 2013 CAS will detect this when the user is authenticated during the initial client request, and the request will be proxied to the 2010 CAS. In this situation, the same settings (see Table 3-4) are used since all client requests are proxied from the 2013 CAS to the 2010 CAS. For the client, what happens on the Exchange Server level is fully transparent, so the same virtual directory settings apply as for mailboxes that are already on Exchange 2013. In the original environment, the namespaces used were the same as in the coexistence scenario, so if all is correct, there's no need to change anything on the Exchange Server 2010 virtual directory settings.

Table 3-4. *Virtual Directory Settings on the Exchange 2013 Client Access Server*

Virtual Directory	Internal URL	External URL
OWA virtual directory	`https://webmail.contoso.com/owa`	`https://webmail.contoso.com/owa`
ECP virtual directory	`https://webmail.contoso.com/ecp`	`https://webmail.contoso.com/ecp`
Activesync virtual directory	`https://webmail.contoso.com/` `Microsoft-Server-ActiveSync`	`https://webmail.contoso.com/` `Microsoft-Server-ActiveSync`
EWS virtual directory	`https://webmail.contoso.com/ews/` `exchange.asmx`	`https://webmail.contoso.com/ews/` `exchange.asmx`
OAB virtual directory	`https://webmail.contoso.com/oab`	`https://webmail.contoso.com/oab`
PowerShell virtual directory	`https://webmail.contoso.com/powershell`	`https://webmail.contoso.com/` `powershell`
Autodiscover virtual directory	`https://autodiscover.contoso.com/` `autodiscover`	`https://autodiscover.contoso.com/` `autodiscover`

■ **Note** Outlook Anywhere in a coexistence scenario is similar to Outlook Anywhere in a native Exchange 2010 environment, so no additional changes are necessary.

Please note that it is not possible to manage Exchange Server 2010 settings from the EMS running on the Exchange 2013 environment, nor from the EAC. Exchange Server 2010 settings should be managed from the 2010 Exchange Management Console or 2010 Exchange Management Shell.

Making the Change for Clients

If all servers have been installed and configured, it's time to make the change for how clients access the Exchange platform. This is an important moment; one mistake here can potentially have an impact on all clients.

Although this change is important, the impact is different for every client. Outlook clients, for example, will connect to the Exchange 2010 CAS array, and this will not change when the switch to the 2013 CAS is made. But those same Outlook clients also use Autodiscover and the Exchange web services, and these protocols are impacted during the change.

For internal clients, it is just a matter of changing the internal DNS records for `webmail.contoso.com` and `autodiscover.contoso.com` to the 2013 CAS. If there are multiple Client Access servers in a load-balanced array, you have to change the IP address from the old load-balanced array to the new load-balanced array. However, this is the case only for HTTP services; the CAS Array IP address should not be changed, of course.

For external clients, the forwarding address on the firewall needs to be changed from the 2010 CAS to the 2013 CAS.

If Microsoft Threat Management Gateway (TMG) 2010 is used, an additional step is needed. The web listener for `webmail.contoso.com` needs to be changed so that it now points to the 2013 CAS. If the self-signed certificate is used on the CAS, you need to make sure it is imported in the trusted root certification authorities store on the TMG server so that the self-signed certificate is trusted. This certificate is used only for communication between the TMG server and the CAS. Figure 3-26 outlines how clients connect with an Exchange Server 2010/2013 TMG coexistence scenario:

1. Clients use the `webmail.contoso.com` FQDN to connect to the 2013 CAS.

2. When the mailbox is still on Exchange Server 2010, the client request is proxied to 2010 CAS. For the client, this step is fully transparent.

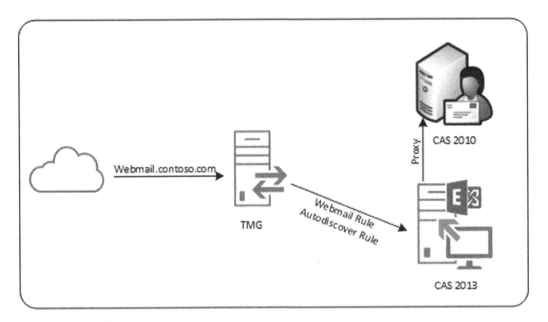

Figure 3-26. *TMG in an Exchange 2010/2013 coexistence scenario*

■ **Note**   Make sure that the authentication settings on the TMG publishing rules match the authentication settings on the virtual directories in both Exchange Server 2010 and Exchange Server 2013

The client now uses the webmail.contoso.com FQDN to connect to the 2013 CAS and the Exchange 2013 logon form is presented. As with the Exchange 2007 coexistence scenario, this is the first change for users! When the user's mailbox is on the 2013 Mailbox server, the mailbox is shown directly after authentication. When the user's mailbox is still on Exchange Server 2010, the request is proxied to the 2010 CAS and the mailbox data is retrieved. No second logon attempt is needed.

When TMG is operating, clients stll use the webmail.contoso.com FQDN and users still have the TMG logon screen presented. After logging on, they hit the 2013 CAS, but the request is proxied to the 2010 CAS, which then returns the proper data. The end user with his mailbox doesn't see any difference at this point until his mailbox is moved to Exchange 2013.

SMTP Mail in a Coexistence Scenario

During the coexistence phase, the SMTP mail flow has to be changed from the previous version of Exchange Server to Exchange 2013. It does not matter when the mail flow is changed, however. It can be changed in the beginning of the transistion process, halfway through the process, or just before the previous version of Exchange Server is decommissioned. The Edge Transport server from the previous versions can also play a role in the Exchange 2013 environment.

Changing the SMTP Mail Flow

Initially, SMTP messages are delivered to the previous Exchange Hub Transport servers, and inbound SMTP messages are delivered to the recipients' mailboxes. When mailboxes are moved to Exchange 2013, the previous Hub Transport server sends inbound messages using SMTP to the Exchange 2013 Mailbox server, where they are delivered to the recipients' mailboxes.

Specifically, an inbound SMTP message is delivered to the 2013 Client Access server, which proxies the inbound SMTP connection to a 2013 Mailbox server. An inbound SMTP message intended for a recipient still on Exchange Server 2007 is sent from the 2013 Mailbox server using SMTP to an old Exchange Server Hub Transport server. From there it is delivered to the recipient's mailbox. Needless to say, if the mailbox is moved to Exchange 2013, the Hub Transport service on the 2013 Mailbox server delivers the message to the 2013 Mailbox server hosting the recipient's mailbox.

Is there a guideline or best practice for when to change the mail flow? I don't know. I have seen customers change the SMTP mail flow as their first step in the transition process so that they know their platform is running fine. At the same time, I have seen customers change the mail flow after the last mailbox move, a step that concludes their transition process. It depends on your own preferences.

Using an Edge Transport Server

In the previous versions of Exchange Server there was an additional server role called the Edge Transport server, a server typically located in the perimeter network. The permiter network is also referred to as the DMZ. The Edge Transport Server is responsible for SMTP message hygiene. The MX records on the public DNS point to the Edge Transport servers, and therefore these Edge Transport servers accept messages from the Internet. They apply a set of anti-spam rules to the inbound messages, ensuring that only legitimate messages are sent to the internal Exchange organization. After cleaning, the messages are delived to the internal Exchange Hub Tranport server, which delivers the messages to the recipients' mailboxes. The Edge Transport server is tied to the internal Hub Transport server using the Edge subscription, a mechanism whereby information from the internal Exchange structure is pushed to the Edge Transport server.

In a coexistence scenario, mail continues to be delivered to the Exchange Server's Hub Transport server, and this server delivers the message to an Exchange 2013 Mailbox server when the recipient's mailbox is moved to Exchange 2013. The good news is that the previous Exchange Edge Transport servers continue to work with the 2013 Mailbox server, including the Edge synchronization.

Therefore, when changing the mailbox in combination with the Edge Transport server, it's just a matter of removing an old Edge synchronizaton between the previous Exchange Hub Transport server and creating a new Edge synchronization between the Edge Transport server and the 2013 Mailbox server. Mail from the Internet will then be delivered to the Exchange 2010 Edge Transport server and then sent from the Edge Transport server to the 2013 Mailbox server (see Figure 3-27).

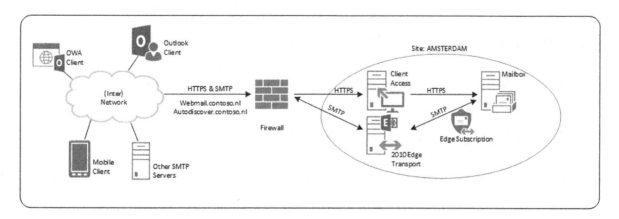

Figure 3-27. *The 2010 Edge Transport server in an Exchange 2013 environment*

▪ **Note**   The previous Edge Transport server needs to be at Exchange Server 2007 SP3 RU10 or Exchange Server 2010 SP3 level for coexistence to work.

To change the Edge synchronization from an Exchange 2007 or 2010 Hub Transport server to a new Exchange 2013 Mailbox server, you need to create a new Edge subscription. To do this, follow these steps:

1. On the previous Exchange Edge Tranport server, open the Exchange Management Console.

2. Log on to the Edge Transport server as a local administrator, open the EMS, and enter the following command: `New-EdgeSubscription -FileName C:\Temp\Edge01.xml`

3. A warning message is shown, basically saying the subscription file is valid for 1440 minutes (which equals 24 hours). (If the subscription file is not processed within this timeframe, a new subscription has to be created.) Enter "Y" to confirm the warning message and the subscription file will be created.

4. Copy the `Edge01.xml` subscription file to a directory on the local disk of the 2013 Mailbox server in the appropriate site. On the 2013 Mailbox server, open the EMS and enter the following commands:

```
New-EdgeSubscription -FileData ([byte[]]$(Get-Content -Path "C:\Temp\edge01.xml"
-Encoding Byte -ReadCount 0)) -Site "Default-First-Site-Name" -CreateInternetSendConnector $true
-CreateInboundSendConnector $true
```

```
Start-EdgeSynchronization
```

The first command is an instruction to read the contents of the subscription file, import it, and bind it against the Active Directory site. Also, an Internet send connector and an inbound send connector are created. The second command starts the Edge synchronization process. It's as easy as that.

▪ **Note**   The Exchange 2010 Edge Transport server should be able to resolve the Exchange 2013 Mailbox server, and vice versa. This can be achieved using DNS, but using a HOSTS file for resolving an Edge Transport server is quite common as well.

Moving Resources to Exchange 2013

The most important step in this transition process is moving the mailboxes and other resources from the previous version of Exchange Server to the new Exchange Server 2013. Other resources in this respect are the address lists and the offline address book.

Moving Mailboxes to Exchange 2013

Moving the mailboxes to Exchange 2013 is an online process, which means the client stays connected to the mailbox until the very last step of the migration. Even when the contents are moved to Exchange 2013, the user can continue to work. This is called an *online migration*. When the migration process for a mailbox is finished, the user receives a message that the Outlook client needs to be restarted. At that point, the migration is finished and the user starts to connect to the Exchange 2013 environment.

The reason for restarting the Outlook client is basically that the client was connected to a particular mailbox server in Exchange Server 2007 or to the CAS array in Exchange Server 2010. This was reflected in the Outlook profile where the server was shown. In Exchange 2013, this is no longer the case and the mailbox is no longer connected to that particular mailbox server. You can see this in the Outlook profile, where there is no longer a server or CAS array shown; instead, the GUID of the mailbox is followed by the end user's primary SMTP address.

The process responsible for moving the mailboxes is the Mailbox Replication Service (MRS), a service that's running on the Exchange 2013 CAS or, better, on every 2013 CAS (see Figure 3-28).

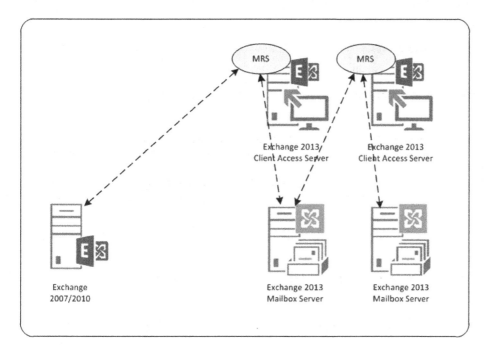

Figure 3-28. *The mailbox replication service*

When a mailbox needs to be moved from one mailbox database to another mailbox database, the actual mailbox move is initiated with a *move request*. With a move request, a flag is set in the system mailbox of the source mailbox database, and this flag is picked up by the MRS. The MRS then creates a copy of that mailbox in the target mailbox database, and it starts moving the mailbox data from the source to the target. This is an online and fully transparant mechanism; the recipient can be online and won't notice anything about moving data. When the MRS is about to finish the migration of data, the source mailbox is closed and all remaining data is written into the target mailbox; the properties in Active Directory are updated as well.

When the source mailbox is:

- *Exchange Server 2007 **or** Exchange Server 2010*. The user gets a warning message that the administrator has made major changes to the mailbox and that Outlook needs to be restarted.

- *Exchange 2013*. The user won't notice anything. The source mailbox is closed, the Active Directory properties are updated, and there's no need to restart Outlook.

The MRS is running on every Exchange 2013 Client Access server, so if there are five CASs, there are also five instances of MRS running in the Exchange environment. It is possible to tune the MRS to the 2013 CAS. By default, very few mailboxes are moved concurrently, so as to prevent the Mailbox server from becoming overwhelmed as mailboxes are moved. This otherwise tremendous amount of traffic might impact users when mailboxes are being moved during business hours.

The configuration of the MRS is stored in a config file located in the C:\Program Files\Microsoft\Exchange Server\V15\Bin directory called MSExchangeMailboxReplication.exe.config. When you open this file and scroll to the end, there's a section called "Mailbox Replication Service Configuration," where all the default, minimum, and maximum values are stored. There's also a section called "MRSConfiguration," where the actual settings are stored. You can changes the values stored in this config file, but don't be surprised if your Exchange servers are overwhelmed with move requests; it's best to leave the default values.

New in Exchange 2013 is the concept of "batch moves" whereby mailboxes are moved in (large) batches. Using these batches, it is possible to:

- Set email notifications.

- Set prioritization of mailbox moves.

- Set automatic retry options when mailbox moves fail.

- Set options for finalizing move requests.

- Use incremental syncs to update migration changes.

The move-requestion finalization is an interesting feature that was also available in Exchange Server 2010. It makes it possible to move mailboxes from a source mailbox database to a target mailbox database, but without finalizing the actual move. When the move is around 90 percent finished, the movement of mailbox data stops and the source and the target are kept in sync. It is then possible to finalize the actual move at a later time—for example, during off-business hours—so that the user doesn't receive the (disruptive) message about restarting the Outlook client at an inconvenient time.

■ **Note** Moving mailboxes is a "pull" mechanism, so the move process is initiated from the Exchange 2013 Mailbox server. To initiate a move request, the EAC or the 2013 Exchange Management Shell can be used.

To initiate a mailbox move for a user called joe@contoso.com, either the EAC or the EMS can be used. To use the EAC, use the following steps:

1. Log on to the EAC with an administrator account. When the EAC opens on the Recipients page, select a mailbox that's still on the previous Exchange Server.

2. In the actions pane on the right, scroll down and, under Move Mailbox, select "to another database."

3. In the move configuration window, give this request a name, like "contoso – one user"; and in the target database field, use the Browse button to select a mailbox database that's running on an Exchange 2013 Mailbox server. If needed, you can also select a mailbox database being used to store the user's archive mailbox.

4. If you click on More Options, you can set a *bad item limit*. By default, if MRS encounters a corrupt message it will stop the migration and log an error. To avoid this, you can set a bad item limit. That is, if MRS encounters a corrupt item, it will skip this item and continue the move until it reaches the number of bad items you've set. Important to note, however, is that if MRS skips any corrupt messages, these messages are lost and this will result in data loss! There's no way to work around this; a corrupt item is lost anyway, so it's better to skip it during the migration and thereby prevent stalling the mailbox move.

5. Click Next to continue, select a mailbox that will receive a result message when the move is completed (or aborted), and click Next. A new move request will be generated and a popup is shown asking if you want to go to the migration dashboard. If so, click Yes.

6. In this migration dashboard, which can be found under migration in the recipient's window in EAC, you can follow the status of the migration.

7. When the migration has finished, an email is sent to the administrator mailbox (in this example); open the message to view the migration details.

Exchange Server 2010 has a mailbox for discovery search purposes; this mailbox is shown in the 2010 Exchange Management Console, but not in the EAC. To move this mailbox, you need to use the EMS on Exchange 2013. To do this, open the EMS on Exchange 2013 and enter the following command:

```
get-mailbox -id discovery* | New-MoveRequest -TargetDatabase "Mailbox Database 1321634995"
```

You can also monitor the move of the mailbox by using the EMS; just enter the following command:

```
Get-MoveRequest -id discovery* | Get-MoveRequestStatistics
```

Exchange Server uses system mailboxes and arbitration mailboxes for approval functionality—for example, when messages need to be moderated before they are sent out. Messages that need moderation are stored temporarily in these mailboxes. The mailboxes are hidden but can be migrated only by using the EMS.

To retrieve a list of all system mailboxes on Exchange Server 2010, do the following:

1. Log on to an Exchange 2010 Mailbox server as an administrator and open the EMS.

2. Use the following command to retrieve a list of system mailboxes: `Get-Mailbox -Server EML-MBX01 -Arbitration`. This action will return all system mailboxes on Exchange Server 2010.

3. To move these mailboxes, simply pipe the output of the previous command into the `New-MoveRequest` command:

```
Get-Mailbox -Server EML-MBX01 -Arbitration | New-MoveRequest -TargetDatabase "Mailbox Database 1321634995"
```

If you don't specify a target database, Exchange Server will select a mailbox database on Exchange 2013 automatically, based on the availability of mailbox resources.

When the regular mailboxes, the discovery mailbox, and the system mailboxes are moved to Exchange 2013, then the mailbox databases on the previous Exchange Server should be empty and ready for removal.

Moving Address Lists to Exchange 2013

When all the mailboxes are moved to Exchange 2013, it's time to move your other resources as well. Regular address lists reside in Active Directory, so when moving them to Exchange 2013, there's no need to pay extra attention; they will be used automatically by Exchange 2013.

Since the address lists were created in the previous version of Exchange Server, they should also be managed with the previous EMS or the Exchange Management Console. But to make them "ready" for Exchange 2013, just touch the address lists and store them without changing any values. To do this, use the `Get-AddressList | Set-AddressList` command in the 2013 Exchange Management Shell. This will show something like this on the Exchange Management Console:

```
[PS] C:\Windows\system32>Get-AddressList | Set-AddressList
WARNING: The command completed successfully but no settings of '\All Contacts' have been modified.
WARNING: The command completed successfully but no settings of '\All Groups' have been modified.
WARNING: The command completed successfully but no settings of '\All Rooms' have been modified.
```

```
WARNING: The command completed successfully but no settings of '\All Users' have been modified.
WARNING: The command completed successfully but no settings of '\Public Folders' have been modified.
[PS] C:\Windows\system32>
```

Moving the Offline Address Book to Exchange 2013

A nice feature for Outlook clients is that they can work offline, also referred to as *cached mode*. When working in cached mode, clients need an address book, and so the offline address book (OAB) is used. This is a list of addresses agregated in files that can be downloaded by the Outlook client for offline use. This way, clients can use the address lists at all times, even when not connected to the network.

Exchange 2010 uses an offline address book called *Default Offline Address Book*. Its format is version 3 or version 4, and it's distributed to clients using public folders (especially for Outlook 2003 clients) or web distribution—that is, a virtual directory on the Exchange 2010 CAS.

Exchange 2013 uses a new offline address book. It is based on version 4 and exclusively uses web distribution. The name of Exchange 2013's offline address book is *Default Offline Address Book (2013)*. You can use the 2013 Exchange Management Shell to view the available offline address books via the Get-OfflineAddressBook command:

```
[PS] C:\Windows\system32>Get-OfflineAddressBook

Name                                  Versions               AddressLists
----                                  --------               ------------
Default Offline Address Book          {Version3, Version4}   {\Default Global Address List}
Default Offline Address Book (Ex2013) {Version4}             {\Default Global Address List}

[PS] C:\Windows\system32>
```

Outlook clients will automatically pick up the new default offline address book, so there's no need to change anything here.

All existing clients who rely on an OAB will see this new default OAB the next time they look for an OAB update. This will cause the clients to perform a full OAB download. To prevent this from happening, you can configure your existing mailbox databases to explicitly point to the current default OAB prior to introducing the first Exchange 2013 server. More information on how to achieve this can be found on the Microsoft Exchange Product Group website: http://tinyurl.com/cwv2t2b.

If you have custom offline address books in your organization, you cannot move them to Exchange Server 2013. Instead, you have to recreate them on Exchange Server 2013 using the New-OfflineAddress book command in the EMS.

When all the mailboxes are moved to Exchange 2013, the previous version's default offline address book is no longer needed and you can remove it using the previous Exchange Server's EMC. You will find the default offline address list by opening the EMC, expanding the organization configuration, and selecting the Mailbox option. In the results pane, select the tab for the offline address book and remove that address book by right-clicking it.

Decommissioning the Previous Exchange Server

When all resources have been moved or removed, you can decommission the previous Exchange Server. This is not really a big deal at all, and involves the following steps:

1. Make sure the old Hub Transport server is not responsible anymore for any mail traffic. This not only includes SMTP from and to the Internet but also third-party appliances or (custom) applications that might have been using the Hub Transport server for receiving or relaying messages. Caution: You don't want to remove the previous Exchange Server version and find out that your multifuncational devices cannot send out messages anymore.

2. Remove the mailbox databases from the previous Exchange Server by using the Exchange Management Console or the Exchange Management Shell.

3. Remove the previous Exchange Mailbox server role. This can be done by opening the control panel on the particular server and uninstalling the Exchange Server. Uncheck the Mailbox server roles and the Exchange mangement tools option in the setup application. This will remove the Mailbox server role for this particular server.

4. Remove the previous Exchange CAS and Hub Transport server roles. Again, this can be achieved by opening the control panel and uninstalling the Exchange Server. Uncheck the Client Access server role, the Hub Transport server role, and the Exchange management tools to completely remove these from the previous Exchange Server.

When all of these steps are successfully executed, the previous Exchange Server is now fully removed and only the Exchange 2013 servers remain in the Exchange organzations.

■ **Important Note**   Decommissioning the previous version is not just like turning it off. Now this may sound silly, but it happens frequently in a virtualized server environment. It's tempting to turn off the virtual machines and just delete them, but this is absolutely *wrong*. When you do this, all information regarding previous versions of Exchange Server remain in Active Directory; from an Exchange 2013 point of view, they are still there (but not responding, of course). This can lead to erratic behavior. So, *fully uninstall* the previous Exchange Server!

Summary

Exchange 2013 fits perfectly into an existing Exchange organization, as long as this Exchange organization consists of Exchange Server 2010 or Exchange Server 2007. If the Exchange organization is Exchange Server 2003, the Exchange 2013 setup application will halt the deployment.

When introducing Exchange 2013 into an existing Exchange environment, the following prerequisites have to be met for implementation to be successful:

- Active Directory needs to be at least Windows 2003 SP2, the domains need to be in native mode, and the forest should be in Windows 2003 forest functional level.

- If current use is Exchange Server 2007, it needs to be at service pack 3 update, rollup 10 level, for all Exchange 2007 servers in the organization.

- If current use is Exchange Server 2010, it needs to be at least at service pack 3 level; no update rollups on SP3 are required.

- The Exchange 2013 version itself needs to be at CU1 level or higher.

When introducing Exchange 2013 into an existing organization, the network flow will change dramatically when it comes to clients. All Internet clients will connect to the 2013 CAS. When the mailbox is still on Exchange Server 2010, the requests will be proxied to the 2010 CAS. If the mailbox is still on Exchange Server 2007, the request will be redirected to the 2007 CAS. In the latter case, an additional namespace, typically referred to as legacy.contoso.com, will be used.

Since Outook will no longer use direct MAPI (RCP/TCP), all clients will gradually move to Outlook Anywhere (RCP/HTTPS). When the mailbox is still on Exchange Server 2007, the Outlook client will connect to the old Mailbox server; if the mailbox is still on Exchange Server 2010, the Outlook client will use the CAS array. When the mailbox is moved to Exchange 2013, the Outlook client will automatically move to Outlook Anywhere.

When all existing resources are moved or decommissioned, the previous Exchange Server can be uninstalled and then only Exchange 2013 will reside in the Exchange organization.

## CHAPTER 4

Client Access Server

The Client Access server is one of the most important server roles in any Exchange environment. As someone from Microsoft once said during a conference, "You can have the most beautiful and redundant Mailbox server environment with a DAG and everything, but without a Client Access server you cannot access it and it's useless."

And that's true. The Client Access server is used by all clients, whether they connect from the internal network or from the Internet. And whether they are Outlook clients or browser-based clients, or POP3 and IMAP4 clients, all clients connect to the Client Access server and then are routed to the correct Mailbox server.

So, whenever a Mailbox server is used, a Client Access server needs to be used as well. This can be on the same server as the Mailbox server, but it can also be a dedicated server.

This is a relatively odd chapter, though. It is about the Client Access server, but at the same time there are Client Access components on the Mailbox server as well. The other way around is true also. The Hub Transport server in Exchange Server is now part of the Mailbox server, but there are parts of transport in the Client Access server—the Front End Transport service—as well. Therefore, this chapter and the next chapter (discussing Mailbox server) are complementary and should be read one after the other.

Overview of Client Access Technologies

Microsoft has made major infrastructural changes to the Client Access server role, ensuring it is possible to use it in a multi-datacenter environment. In earlier versions of Exchange Server, this was possible to some extent, but it was far from optimal. Some parts of the technology haven't changed that much, like the Autodiscover technology, the virtual directories, the SSL certificates, and use of the single unified namespace. All of this is covered in the following sections.

Introducing the Client Access Infrastructure

In previous versions of Exchange Server (Exchange Server 2007 and 2010), the various server roles were "tightly coupled." The Client Access server and the Hub Transport server roles needed a high-bandwidth, low-latency network connection with the Mailbox server to facilitate the RPC traffic between them. This worked fine as long as all server roles were located on the same network in the same datacenter, but when someone was using multiple locations, that person faced some serious challenges.

One of the objectives in developing Exchange Server 2013 was to create a "loosely coupled" infrastructure where the server roles are less dependent on each other and on a good network connection. In Exchange 2013, the servers are no longer tied together using the RPC protocol; rather, they are now more independent, and they communicate using the same protocol as the original client connection. But most important, all client protocols are Internet protocols, and as such they are easy to route through the network, as well as not being 100% dependent on a tight network connection as were the previous versions of Exchange Server. Sometimes you hear the comment "Every server is an island" and that's a good description of this arrangement.

The Client Access server is a domain-joined server in the internal Active Directory forest. The Client Access server comprises three different components:

- Client access protocols (HTTP, IMAP4, POP3)
- SMTP
- UM call router

Compared to Exchange 2010, now almost all business logic has been removed from the Client Access server and moved to the Mailbox server. At the same time, all the processing and rendering now takes place on the Mailbox server, whereas in Exchange 2010 this took place on the Client Access server.

The result is that the Exchange 2013 Client Access server is a thin and stateless server that handles all incoming connections in a load-balanced configuration. It is not truly stateless, though; the SSL connection is terminated at the Client Access, the client is authenticated, and then is proxied to the correct Mailbox server or other downlevel server. When a Client Access server is lost, all connected clients need to re-authenticate against another Client Access server. The fact that no data is stored on the Client Access server is the reason that Microsoft refers to the Client Access server as "stateless." Stateless, but not clueless, is a good description here.

Since all processing is taking place on the Mailbox server, and no longer on the Client Access server, session affinity or persistence is no longer needed on the Client Access server and therefore a layer-4 load balancer can be used in combination with the Exchange 2013 Client Access servers (see Figure 4-1).

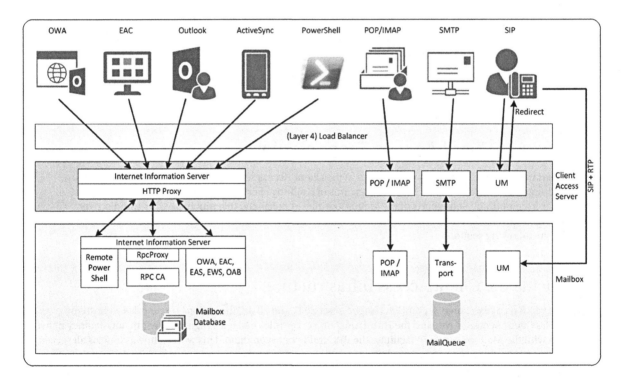

Figure 4-1. *Protocol flow through the Client Access server and Mailbox server*

■ **Note** Since the Exchange 2013 Client Access server is a domain-joined server in the corporate forest, it is automatically located on the internal network. An Exchange 2013 Client Access server located in the perimeter network is not supported!

So, all clients on the internal and external networks connect to the load balancer and then to the Client Access server. Outlook Web App, Exchange Admin Center (EAC), Outlook Anywhere, Exchange ActiveSync, and PowerShell all use HTTP as their protocol. All requests are sent to the Internet Information Server running on the Client Access server. After authentication, the Client Access server determines which Mailbox server hosts the active mailbox database copy, and the client request is proxied to this Mailbox server.

POP3 and IMAP4 have their own services running on both the Client Access server and the Mailbox server. Again, after authentication the POP3 or IMAP4 service determines the active copy of the mailbox database and proxies the request to this Mailbox server.

SMTP is a bit different. The SMTP connection request is sent to the Client Access server. The Front End Transport service running on the Client Access server proxies the request to a Mailbox server that accepts the actual SMTP message. The Client Access server does not accept the message, and therefore it does not store any information regarding that message.

When it comes to Unified Messaging (UM), there's no proxying. When a SIP request is sent to the Client Access server—for example, from a Lync Server 2010 or Lync Server 2013 Front End server—it is accepted by the UM call router service running on the Client Access server. The UM call router service determines which Mailbox server hosts the active copy of the mailbox database where the recipient is hosted, and it redirects the SIP request to the Unified Messaging service running on that particular Mailbox server. From that moment on, the Lync server communicates directly with the Mailbox server.

The Death of RPC/TCP

Clearly visible in Figure 4-1 is that all major clients are HTTP based and the traditional MAPI (or RPC over TCP) is no longer used. That's right, Outlook clients now only connect to the Client Access server using Outlook Anywhere, sometimes still referred to as RPC over HTTP.

But how does Outlook Anywhere actually work? The Outlook client sets up an HTTPS connection with the Exchange 2013 Client Access server. This is a normal HTTPS connection and as such, it is fully routable via the Internet. The Client Access server then terminates the SSL connection, authenticates the request, and determines the correct Mailbox server to proxy the request to. This means that the connection between the Client Access server and the Mailbox server is also a normal HTTPS connection, although it's using a different TCP port. The HTTPS connection is then terminated on the Mailbox server—more specifically, on IIS on the Mailbox server, and the AppPool on the back end decapsulates the RPC traffic from the HTTPS stream. A local connection is then set up using local RPC (LRPC) to the mailbox service running on the Mailbox server.

So, the Outlook client connects to the Client Access server using HTTPS, and an SSL certificate is used on the Client Access server for making this connection. Outlook is very sensitive to the type of certificate being used and only accepts normal, prefereably third-party Unified Commmunications (UC) certificates, although UC certificates issued by an Active Directory Certifcation Authority can be used as well.

Since the Outlook clients now connect to the correct Mailbox server, it is no longer necessary to use the RPC Client Access server array (earlier CAS array). This CAS array was introduced in Exchange 2010, used as the MAPI endpoint for Outlook clients. The FQDN of the CAS array was also the server name that was visible in the Outlook profile. But in Exchange 2013, the RPC CAS array is no longer needed. The FQDN being used in the Outlook profile has been replaced with the mailbox GUID, followed by the domain name (see Figure 4-2).

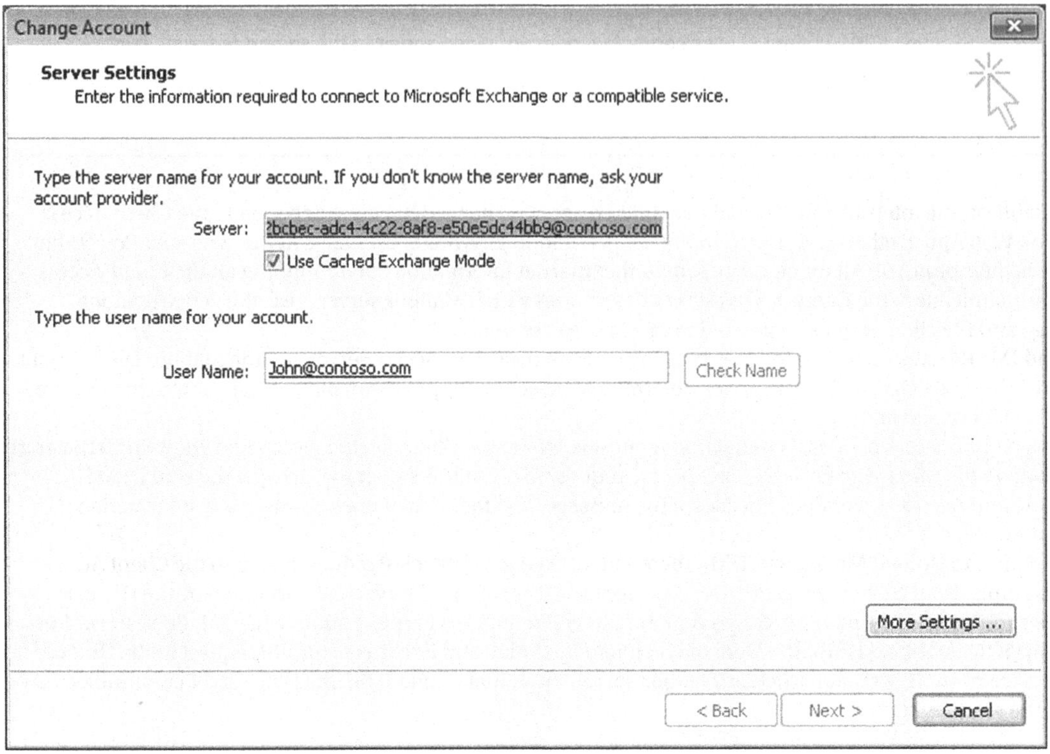

Figure 4-2. *Instead of the RPC CAS array, the mailbox GUID is shown*

The good thing is that this mailbox GUID is unique within the entire Exchange organization. If a mailbox is moved from one server to another, from one Database Availability Group to another, or from one datacenter to another, the mailbox GUID does not change. Therefore, the dreaded message "The Exchange administrator has made a change that requires you to quit and restart Outlook" no longer appears after whatever mailbox move you have performed.

In summary, the advantages of substituting the earlier MAPI client connectivity in Exchange 2013 have been:

- A much more reliable connection between the Outlook client and the mailbox.

- The RPC CAS array no longer needed.

- No more restarting Outlook after moving mailboxes.

So, the Client Access server is used to intercept connections from clients and to proxy these connections to the correct Mailbox server. But besides this traffic, there are a couple of other connections that are set up from the Outlook client to the Client Access server:

- Autodiscover

- Exchange Web Services (EWS)

- Offline address book downloads

Outlook Anywhere is enabled by default, but it is not configured at all. Therefore, Outlook Anywhere should be configured with the appropriate server name used for the proxy servers. Also, the SSL requirements must be set manually, for both internal and external clients. Unfortunately, this cannot be configured using the EAC, so you need to use the Exchange Management Shell (EMS) for this. To configure Outlook Anywhere, open EMS and enter the following command:

```
Set-OutlookAnywhere -Server AMS-EXCH01 -ExternalHostname webmail.contoso.com
-ExternalClientsRequireSsl:$true –InternalHostname webmail.contoso.com –InternalClientsRequireSsl:$true
```

What actually happens is that Outlook Anywhere on Exchange Server AMS-EXCH01 is configured with the external hostname `webmail.contoso.com`, which is the Client Access server running the RPC proxy service. At the same time, the SSL use is enforced by the `-ExternalClientsRequireSsl` parameter. The same settings in the command shown above are used for internal clients.

Autodiscover

Autodiscover was introduced in Exchange 2007 to support Outlook 2007, and it has been developed into one of the most important parts in the Exchange environment. It is also one of the most important protocols. If you don't have a proper Autodiscover implementation, you will experience all kinds of nasty problems, like not being able to check free/busy information when scheduling a meeting, not being able to download an Offline Address Book, or not being able to set the out-of-office message using the Outlook client.

Autodiscover is the most visible for end users when they intially set up their Outlook client. Users only have to enter their names, their email addresses, and their Active Directory passwords, and the Outlook client will configure itself automatically. It actually discovers all the information regarding the Exchange Server implementation and uses this information to configure the Outlook profile. But not only does it do this on the initial setup, it also performs this action every hour to check for any changes in the Exchange environment.

Autodiscover works by an XML request sent from the Outlook client to the Client Access server. The Client Access server then forwards the request to the Mailbox server hosting the user's mailbox. There, the request is handed over to the Outlook Anywhere provider, which in turn queries the Services Discovery (which is a set of XSO API calls) to retrieve all information from Active Directory (see Figure 4-3).

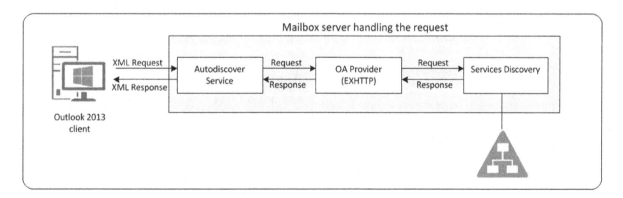

Figure 4-3. *Autodiscover information flow*

How does the Outlook client discover which Client Access server to send its request to? The answer is twofold:

- Domain-joined Outlook clients that are actually logged on to the Active Directory domain retrieve this information directly from Active Directory.

- Non-domain-joined Outlook clients, or domain-joined Outlook clients that cannot access Active Directory (when working at home, for example), build the Autodiscover URL based on the user's SMTP address.

Domain-Joined Clients

When a Client Access server is installed, a computer object is created in Active Directory. Besides this computer object, a so-called service connection point is also created in Active Directory. For every Client Access server that's installed, a corresponding service connection point is created. So, if you have six Client Access servers, you also have six service connection points.

A service connection point has a GUID (Global Unique Identifier) that's unique for the type of application that's using the service connection point. All service connection points that are created by installing Client Access servers have the same (well-known) GUID, and Outlook clients query Active Directory for this GUID. This GUID is stored in the keywords attribute together with the Active Directory site name where the Client Access server is installed.

Once found, the serviceBindingInformation attribute is queried, and this attribute is filled in with the FQDN of the Client Access server—that is, ams-exch01.contoso.com. If there are multiple Client Access servers in the Active Directory, a virtual IP (VIP) on the load balancer should be created. This VIP should be the IP address of a load-balanced FQDN (for example, autodiscover.contoso.com) and this VIP should contain all Client Access servers.

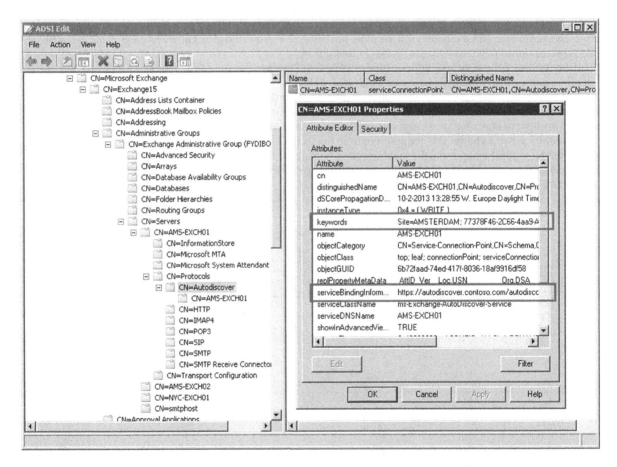

Figure 4-4. *The service connection point in Active Directory, with keywords and ServiceBindingInformation properties*

The Outlook client retrieves the Autodiscover FQDN from Active Directory and sends an HTTP post command to this URL. The Client Access server then accepts the request and proxies it to the Mailbox server. The Mailbox server gathers all the required information and returns this as an XML package to the Outlook client. The Outlook client then can use the XML package to configure its profile (when it's a new setup) or reconfigure its profile (when changes are detected in the Exchange environment).

This process happens always, not only during the initial setup of the Outlook client; the request is sent once an hour to determine if there are any changes in the Exchange configuration. Since it is an HTTP request that's secured on the server, the SSL certificates come into play. The autodiscover.contoso.com needs to be in the certificate as well, next to the webmail.contoso.com name.

The Autodiscover URL is configurable only by using EMS. Open the shell and enter the following command:

```
Get-ClientAccessServer -Identity AMS-EXCH01 | Set-ClientAccessServer -AutoDiscoverServiceInternalUri
https://autodiscover.contoso.com/autodiscover/autodiscover.xml
```

Or, if all the Client Access servers need to be configured with this URL, the following command can be used:

```
Get-ClientAccessServer | Set-ClientAccessServer -AutoDiscoverServiceInternalUri
https://autodiscover.contoso.com/autodiscover/autodiscover.xml
```

■ **Note** If there are no Outlook clients connecting via the Internet, or there are only domain-joined clients, or you want to use service records (SRV records) in the public DNS, it is possible to configure the Client Access server with webmail.contoso.com for the Autodiscover URL.

Autodiscover will retrieve all information from the Exchange environment, as well as other information, such as virtual directories for OWA, EAC, Offline Address Book downloads, or Exchange web services. And these web services in turn are used for retrieving free/busy information or setting the out-of-office information.

Therefore, if there are problems with Autodiscover, most likely these will result in your not being able to check free/busy information when creating a meeting request or in setting the out-of-office message in Outlook. And to make it more confusing, if this is the case, the free/busy information is visible in OWA, and you can set the out-of-office message in OWA as well.

In 99 percent of cases, any complications with Autodiscover are caused by SSL certificate errors. When using a browser to connect to a Client Access server and a certificate error arises, it is possible to continue, despite the error. Outlook, and thus Autodiscover, however, does not have this ability. When Outlook enters an Autodiscover certificate error, it just stops working.

It is possible to verify the Autodiscover functionality from within Outlook. When Outlook is running, check the system tray for the Outlook icon. Control-right-click this Outlook icon, and select Test Email AutoConfiguration (see Figure 4-5).

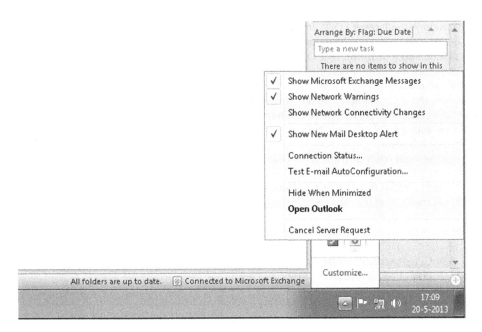

Figure 4-5. *Test Autodiscover from within the Outlook client*

Enter the email address and password, clear Use Guessmart and Secure Guessmart Authentication, and click the Test button. The Outlook client will perform an Autodiscover check against the Exchange server and display the information in the console, as shown in Figure 4-6.

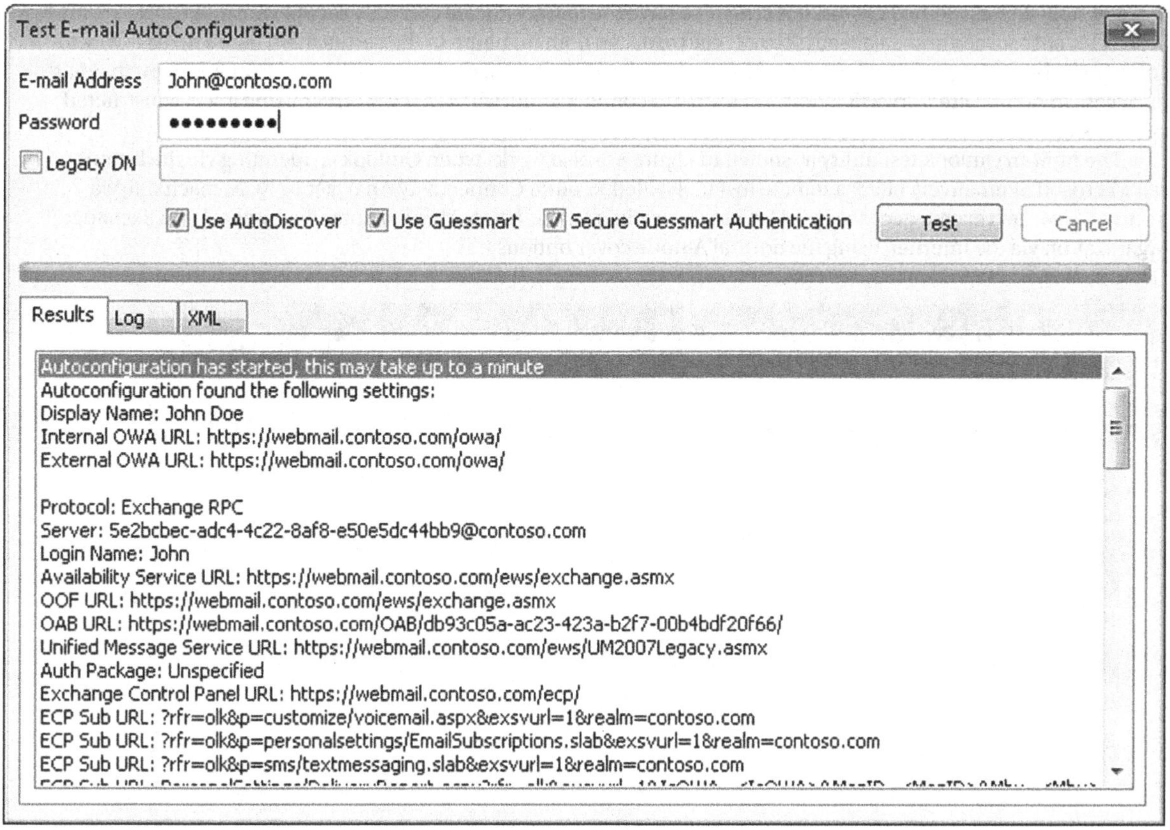

Figure 4-6. *Autodiscover information returned from Exchange Server*

There are three tabs visible:

- Results tab: The returned information is shown in a readable format.

- Log tab: The various options are shown for how the Outlook client tried to retrieve the information.

- XML tab: The raw XML data that is returned from the Exchange server is shown.

This utility is extremely useful when troubleshooting the Exchange environment.

Non-Domain-Joined Clients

Non-domain-joined clients, or domain-joined clients that do not have access to Active Directory, use a different approach for getting Autodiscover information.

To get to the Client Access server, Outlook constructs the URL automatically. This URL always starts with the hostname Autodiscover, followed by the right-hand part of the user's primary email address. So, if a user's email address is john@contoso.com, Outlook will automatically create the FQDN autodiscover.contoso.com. The URL in this case is https://autodiscover.contoso.com/autodiscover/autodiscover.xml.

Once the URL is constructed, Outlook will automatically send an HTTP post request to the Autodiscover URL and get all the necessary information, as it does for an internal Outlook client.

For non-domain-joined clients, it is crucial to have the SSL certificate correctly set up, with an FQDN webmail.contoso.com and an autodiscover.contoso.com domain name in the certificate. There's no easy way to get around this, unless you implement a solution based on SRV records in public DNS. Any Outlook client that has no access to Active Directory will automatically try to connect to the Client Access server using a self-constructed URL autodiscover.contoso.com. This is hard-coded in the Outlook application!

The built-in Outlook test utility as shown in Figure 4-5 also works when Outlook is operating via the Internet, but Microsoft alternatively offers a remote test tool called Remote Connectivity Analyzer or RCA, reachable via https://www.testexchangeconnectivity.com/ (see Figure 4-7). This tool will automatically check the Exchange organization via the Internet, using the normal Autodiscover options.

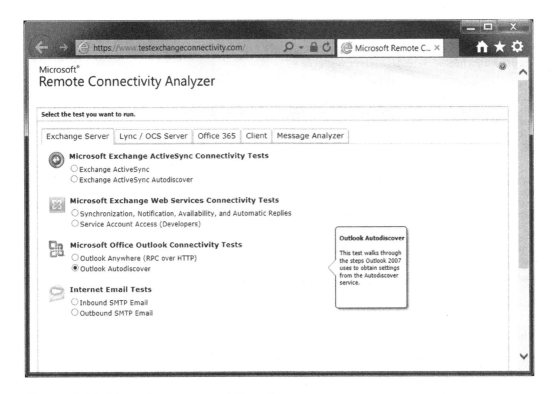

Figure 4-7. *The Microsoft remote connectivity analyzer*

To use this, select Outlook Autodiscover; enter the email address, username, and password; select the I Understand that I Must Use the Credentials of a Working. . . check box and enter the verification string. Select Perform Test, and the RCA will start testing the Exchange environment using the Autodiscover methods; the results are shown in seconds.

Since there are multiple methods for retrieving Autodiscover information, these are shown when *not* successful. In Figure 4-8, for example, the test using https://contoso.com/autodiscover/autodiscover.xml has failed, and this is shown. There's no reason to panic, however; the next test step is automatically performed, using https://autodiscover.contoso.com/autodiscover/autodiscover.xml, and this is successful. A warning message is shown, though, because in this example there's a chain issue with the SSL certificate on the load balancer. But other than that, the RCA test is successful and Autodiscover is working correctly over the Internet.

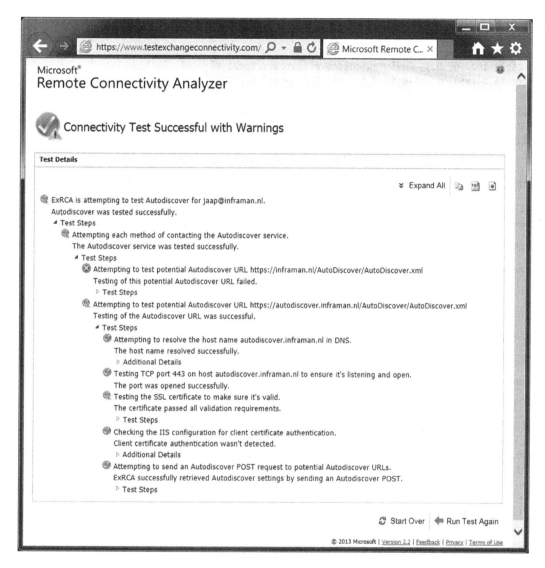

Figure 4-8. *The RCA results*

■ **Note** The remote connectivity analyzer is a publicly available tool to test your Exchange environment. Since it has to access your Exchange environment from the Internet, your Client Access server needs to be accessible from the Internet. It also needs a valid third-party UC certificate on the Client Access server. Important: it *does not work* with the default self-signed certificate.

Remember that the Autodiscover process works for Outlook 2007 clients and later (earlier versions are not supported by Exchange 2013) connecting from an internal network as well as those connecting from the external network.

If you check the IIS log files, which can be found by default on %SystemDrive%\inetpub\logs\LogFiles\W3SVC1, you'll see numerous entries like:

```
2012-12-29 09:05:31 192.168.0.55 POST /autodiscover/autodiscover.xml - 443 CONTOSO\jaap 80.101.27.11
Microsoft+Office/14.0+(Windows+NT+6.1;+Microsoft+Outlook+14.0.6129;+Pro) - 200 0 64 156
```

Using the IIS log files, it is possible to troubleshoot your Autodiscover process. Visible here are, for example, the URI that's used, the port number, the account, the source IP address, the client (okay, I'm still running Windows 7 and Office 2010 on my laptop), and that the request returned a "200" response.

Virtual Directories

By now it should be clear that Exchange 2013 uses the HTTP protocol extensively. The following Exchange 2013 services have their own virtual directories, which are also visible in the Internet Information Server (IIS) Manager:

- Autodiscover (/Autodiscover)
- Outlook Web App (/OWA)
- Exchange Admin Center (/ECP)
- Exchange Web Services (/EWS)
- Exchange ActiveSync (/Microsoft-Server-ActiveSync)
- Offline Address Book (/OAB)
- Remote PowerShell (/Powershell)
- RPC Proxy (/RPC)

For normal maintenance tasks, the IIS Manager is not used; all Exchange 2013 maintenance is done using the EAC or the EMS. Using the EAC, it is possible to establish the most important settings, like the external URL and the authentication methods. For more detailed configuration options, you need to use the EMS.

The internal and external URLs are the most important settings. These settings determine which URL clients connect to via the internal network or via the external network (i.e., Internet) and they are stored in Active Directory. For OWA and EAC, it's not a big deal—you can use any URL to access OWA as long as the name is resolved to the IP address of the Client Access server. You'll see a certificate warning that the name in the request does not match the name on the certificate, but other than that, you can access the service.

For Outlook clients and mobile clients, it's different because these clients get their Exchange configuration from Autodiscover. And if something is configured incorrectly, the wrong data is returned to the client and the client in turn cannot connect to the various services.

When the Exchange 2013 Client Access server is installed, none of the virtual directories are configured properly with the Internal URL and External URL. To configure the External URL, use the option in the EAC to do this for all virtual directories in one step.

In the EAC, select the servers in the navigation menu and then select the virtual directories in the top-level menu. Select the wrench icon and you'll see the Configure External Access Domain window. Add the Client Access servers you want to configure, and enter the FQDN, like webmail.contoso.com, that need to be used (see Figure 4-9).

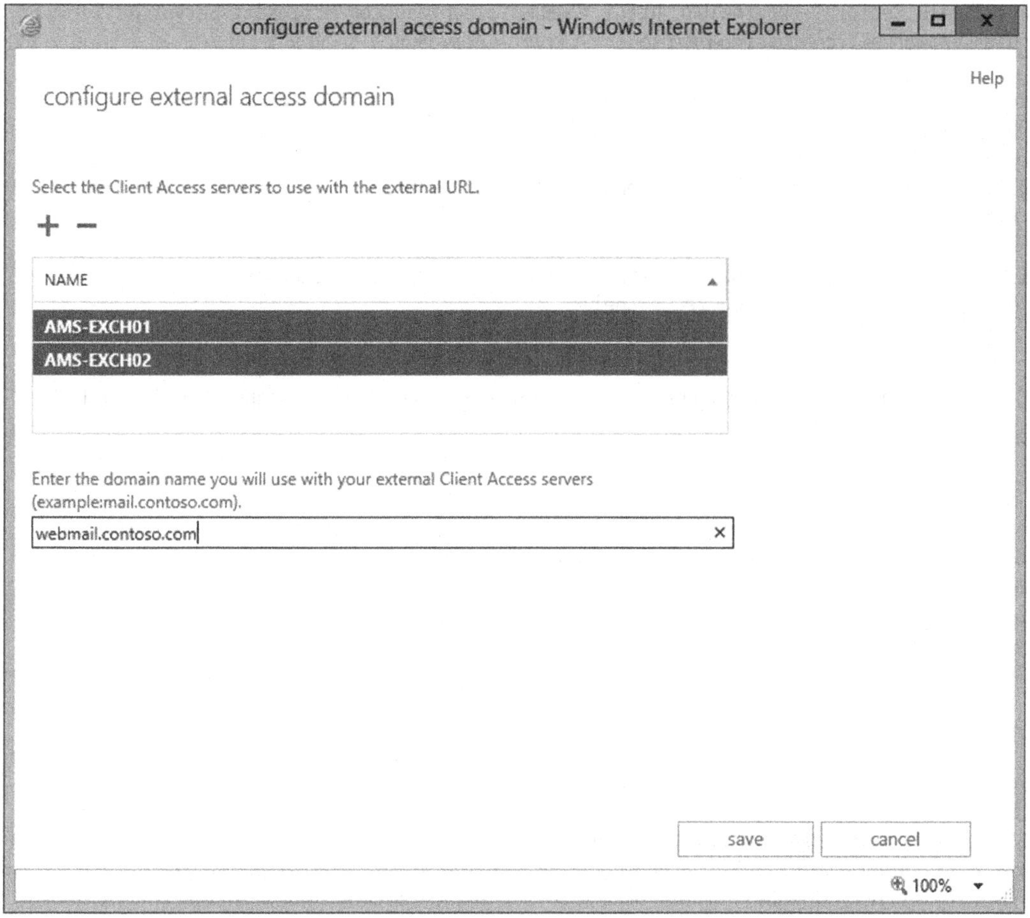

Figure 4-9. *Configuring the external access domain name in EAC*

It is not possible to use EAC to change the Internal URL properties of the virtual directories. For the most granularity, you can use the EMS to set all the options of the virtual directories. To change the Internal URL and External URL, you can use the following commands in the EMS:

```
Set-OWAVirtualDirectory -Identity AMS-EXCH01 -ExternalURL https://webmail.contosol.com/owa
-InternalURL https://webmail.contoso.com/owa

Set-OWAVirtualDirectory -Identity AMS-EXCH01 -ExternalURL https://webmail.contosol.com/owa
-InternalURL https://webmail.contoso.com/owa

Set-ECPVirtualDirectory -ExternalURL https://webmail.contoso.com/ecp
-InternalURL https://webmail.contoso.com/ecp
```

```
Set-ActiveSyncVirtualDirectory -ExternalURL https://webmail.contoso.com/Microsoft-Server-ActiveSync
-InternalURL https://webmail.contoso.com/Microsoft-Server-ActiveSync

Set-WebServicesVirtualDirectory -ExternalURL https://webmail.contoso.com/ews/Exchange.asmx
-InternalURL https://webmail.contoso.com/ews/Exchange.asmx

Set-OABVirtualDirectory -ExternalURL https://webmail.contoso.com/OAB
-InternalURL https://webmail.contoso.com/OAB

Set-PowershellVirtualDirectory -ExternalURL https://webmail.contoso.com/Powershell
-InternalURL https://webmail.contoso.com/Powershell
```

■ **Note** See Chapter 2 for more detail on configuring the virtual directories. This chapter also includes a PowerShell script to automate this process.

If there are multiple Client Access servers, be very careful when configuring the various options in the virtual directories, however; this is even more critical when using multiple Client Access servers in a load-balanced array. If one of the Client Access servers in the array is misconfigured, you'll see erratic results. This won't be consistent because the remaining servers might be configured correctly. You'll see problems arise every now and then, and these are the toughest to troubleshoot.

SSL Certificates

Since Exchange 2013 extensively uses HTTP to communicate between the client and the CAS, and between the CAS and the Mailbox server, the SSL certificates become very important. When a Client Access server is installed, a self-signed SSL certificate is created (see Figure 4-10). This self-signed certificate contains only the NetBIOS name of the server as its common name and the FQDN of the server in the Subject Alternative Name field. Such a certificate can be used for encryption, but it cannot be used for server authentication since its issuer (the Exchange server itself) is not trusted by any other machine. For the Client Access server, this self-signed certificate can be used for testing purposes to see if OWA and EAC are working correctly and to configure the server, but it is not meant for production purposes.

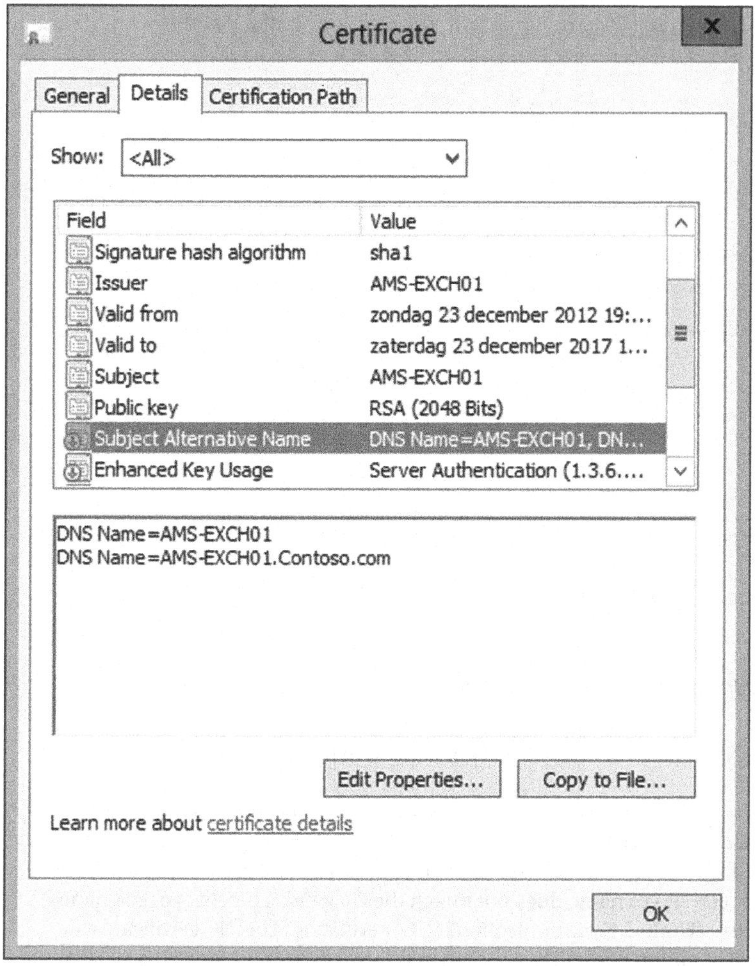

Figure 4-10. *The self-signed certificate on a Client Access server*

A normal SSL certificate has only one name on it; this is the certificate's common name (CN), and it will work perfectly when the server that's configured with this certificate is accessed by a URL that's equal to the common name. For example, a webshop can be accessed using a URL like `https://shop.contoso.com`; its certificate would have a common name of `CN=shop.contoso.com`. If this site is accessed with a URL like `https://webshop.contoso.com`, it will result in a certificate error like the one shown in Figure 4-11, saying "The security certificate presented by this website was issued for a different website's address."

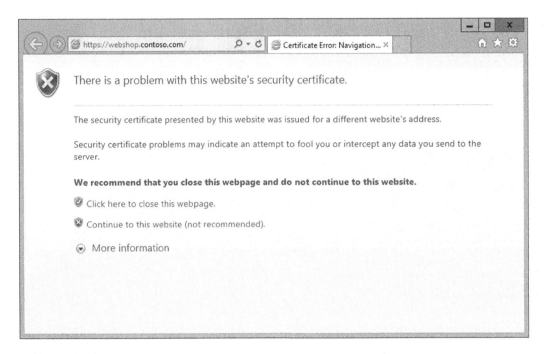

Figure 4-11. Certificate warning when the URL does not match the certificate's CN

If you select Continue to This Website (Not Recommended), you can continue with access but you'll see a certificate warning in the navigation bar.

The "problem" with a Client Access server is that this server can be accessed using a normal URL like webmail.contoso.com, but external Outlook clients (that do not have access to Active Directory) automatically try to access the Client Access server using the URL autodiscover.contoso.com. If you have a normal SSL certificate, this will fail because the autodiscover.contoso.com server name does not match the CN=webmail.contoso.com name.

To work around this problem, you can use a Unified Communications (UC) certificate. This UC certificate can hold multiple server names next to its normal common name. These additional server names are stored in an attribute called "subject alternative name." A typical UC certificate for contoso.com would have a CN=webmail.contoso.com, an autodiscover.contoso.com. If a split-DNS configuration is used in your environment, these server names are sufficient (see Figure 4-12); this is also according to Microsoft best practices. However, there are plenty of successful Exchange Server installations where the local hostname (for example, ams-exch01.contoso.com) is included in the subject alternative names attribute without any complications. Some organizations, however, see this as a possible security matter and prefer not to include the local hostname in the UC certificate.

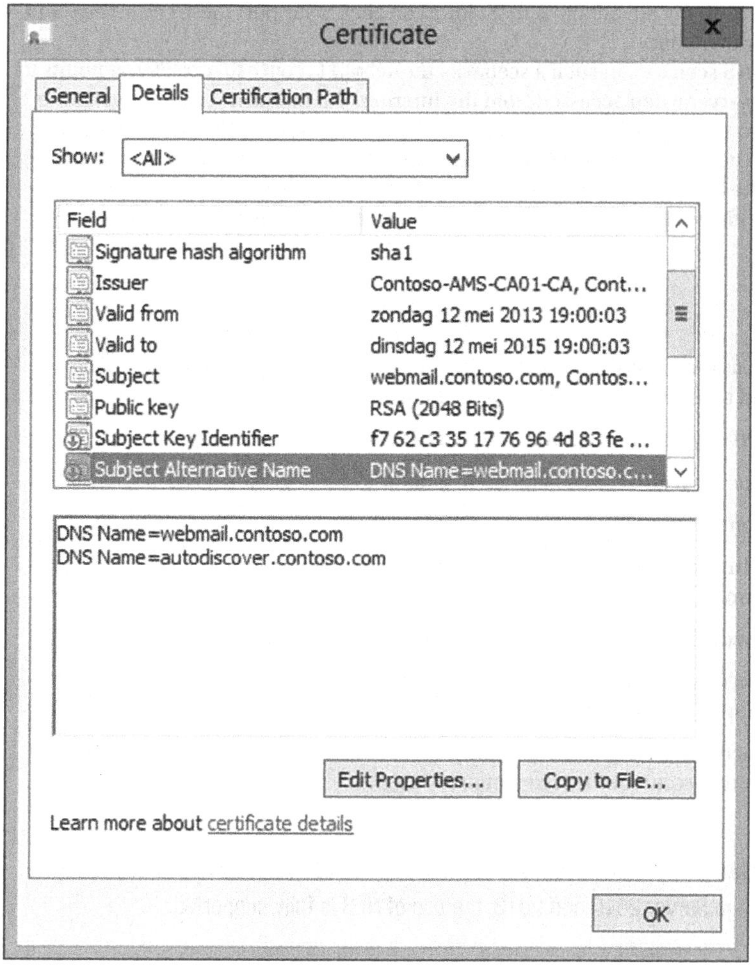

Figure 4-12. *The contoso UC certificate*

A UC SSL certificate can be issued by an Active Directory integrated certificate authority (CA), as shown in Figure 4-12; but this works fine only for other servers and members that are in this particular Active Directory domain. They don't have to be connected to the Active Directory domain, though, so domain-joined laptops should work fine when you are working at home or in a hotel and connecting via the Internet. Non-domain-joined computers will work fine as well, but you have to add the root certificate of the CA to the local certificate store of the client.

Doing the latter can become challenging when you're using mobile devices. You can add the root certificate of the CA to these devices, but it takes a considerable amount of work. You have to ask yourself if you want to spend your money on this additional labor or if it would be better buy a third-party certificate.

The preferred way, of course, is to use a third-party certificate from a trusted CA. Both well-known and Microsoft-supported CAs include, for example, Verisign (now owned by Symantec), Entrust, Comodo, and Digicert.

■ **Note**   A list of all supported SSL certificates can be found in the Microsoft knowledge base article KB929395, "Unified Communications certificate partners," at `http://support.microsoft.com/kb/929395`.

Of course, these certificates are not free, but the advantage is that almost all clients support these certificates and there's less certificate management to take care about.

Microsoft recommends using a split-DNS scenario. In such a scenario, the webmail.contoso.com FQDN points to the external IP address of the Client Access server when accessed from the Internet. But on the internal network, the same webmail.contoso.com FQDN points to the internal IP address of the Client Access server. The sames goes for the autodiscover.contoso.com FQDN; on the Internet, it points to the external IP address of the Client Access server, while on the internal network, it points to the internal IP address of the Client Access server.

The advantage of these third-party certificates is a simple Exchange configuration and fewer server names on the SSL UC certificate.

Load Balancing

In the early days of Exchange Server there was hardly any load balancing, and so the Microsoft solution for load balancing was to use Windows network load balancing (NLB). Although NLB works fine, it has some drawbacks:

- NLB is a service in Windows Server, and thus dependant on the server.

- Scalability of an NLB cluster is not that great and is limited to 8 nodes.

- The only option for affinity is source IP.

- When you are adding or removing nodes to or from an NLB cluster, all clients are disconnected and have to reconnect.

- When NLB is used in unicast mode, it is possible that port- or switch-flooding occurs.

- NLB cannot be combined with a Database Availability Group (DAG) on a single server, since a DAG is running on top of Windows fail-over clustering software.

Starting with Exchange Server 2010, Microsoft began recommending the use of hardware load balancers in front of Client Access servers, a recommendation that continues for Exchange 2013.

■ **Note**   A recommendation to use a hardware load balancing does not mean that use of NLB is no longer supported; this is absolutely not the case. In both Exchange Server 2010 and 2013, the use of NLB is fully supported.

But in Exchange 2013, layer-4 load balancing is recommended, whereas in Exchange 2010 it was layer-7 load balancing that was necessary. Layer-4 load balancing is a relatively "dumb" load-balancing mechanism since it does not have access to the information within the requests.

Compare load-balancing layers to the OSI model. A layer-7 load balancer is a solution where the load balancing takes place on the application layer. The SSL session is terminated at the load balancer, and the load balancer can do pretty smart things to the connection, like modifying the HTTP headers or using cookie information in the HTTP stream. This information is then employed to identify the session and make sure the session is always connected to the same Client Access server.

With a layer-4 load balancer, the load balancing takes place on the network layer. An incoming connection is accepted and distributed across multiple Exchange 2013 Client Access servers "as is." No processing takes place at all. The Client Access server in turn accepts the connection, and after authentication, the connection is forwarded to the appropriate Mailbox server. Since the connections to the Client Access server are stateless, there's no need to worry about affinity. If a Client Access server fails, the connected is rerouted to another Client Access server. There will be a minor performance penalty, owing to re-authentication, but the connection on the Mailbox server is preserved.

The load balancer is configured with a virtual service, and this virtual service has an FQDN (like webmail.contoso.com) and an IP address. The IP address is referred to as the Virtual IP, or VIP. A client connects to this VIP and connects to the load balancer. The load balancer keeps track of the source IP of the connection request and forwards the request to one of the Exchange 2013 Client Access servers. Since all the processing takes place on the Exchange 2013 Mailbox server, instead of the Exchange 2013 Client Access server, the affinity or stickyness of the connection is not important.

Please keep in mind that in a layer-4 load balancer the SSL connection is terminated at the Client Access server, and not at the load balancer. Therefore, the load balancer cannot inspect any of the traffic between the client and the Client Access server. If multiple services, OWA, EAC, Outlook Anywhere, PowerShell, and ActiveSync all use the same VIP at the load balancer, the load balancer cannot inspect the traffic, nor can it inspect the destination virtual directory for health concerns.

If one service on the Exchange 2013 Client Access server fails, the load balancer only detects that the Client Access server in general has failed and will initiate a fail-over to another Client Access server. To overcome this problem, there are two possible solutions:

- Use multiple VIPs for various services so that the individual VIPs can be checked for health (see Figure 4-13).

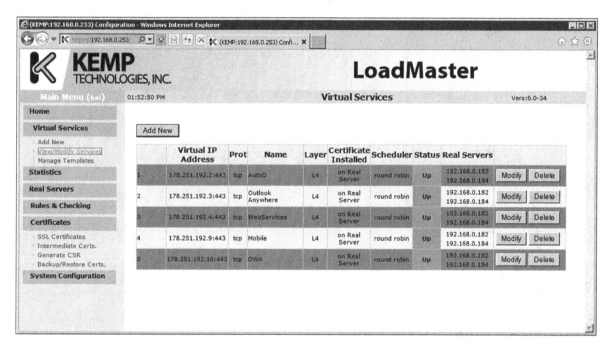

Figure 4-13. *Multiple VIPs on the load balancer for Exchange 2013*

- Use a layer-7 load balancer so that the load balancer can inspect the traffic and the individual services.

Single Common Namespace

One of the advantages of the loosely coupled architecture of Exchange 2013 is its unified namespace. It is now possible to use only one or two namespaces for the entire Exchange organization. It is even possible to use only one namespace, webmail.contoso.com, for all Exchange servers, even if there's a worldwide deployment.

Say, a user called John logs on to webmail.contoso.com when he's in Amsterdam. This is where his mailbox is located. He is authenticated by the local Exchange 2013 Client Access server, and his request is proxied to the appropriate Mailbox server.

When John is traveling to New York, he still accesses webmail.contoso.com. The Geo-DNS solution resolves to a local Exchange 2013 Client Access server, where his request is authenticated. The Client Access server detects that John's mailbox is located in Amsterdam, and thus proxies the request, over the internal network, to the Mailbox server in Amsterdam (see Figure 4-14).

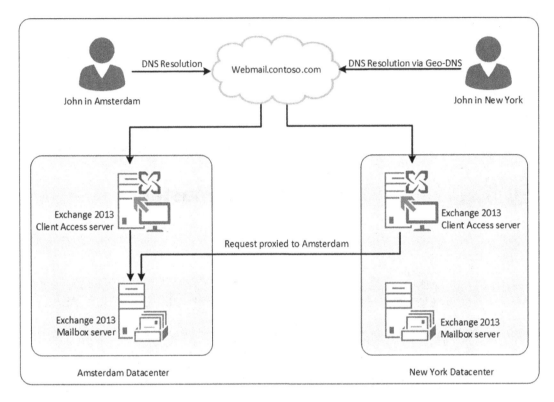

Figure 4-14. *A single, common namespace using a Geo-DNS solution*

Front-End Transport Service

In Exchange 2013, the complete set of services, components, connections, and queues that deal with item transport is called the transport pipeline.This transport pipeline is made up of three different services:

- **Front End Transport service (FETS):** FETS is the part that is running on the Client Access server. It acts as a stateless SMTP protocol proxy for inbound and outbound SMTP traffic. FETS accepts connections from the Internet and routes them to the appropriate Mailbox server or downlevel Hub Transport server. FETS does not store any information in a queue on the local disk and therefore it cannot do any content inspection.

- **Transport service:** The Transport service is comparable to the Hub Transport server role in Exchange Server 2010 and 2007, except that it is no longer a dedicated server role; instead, it is part of the Mailbox server. Because of this, the message routing, especially in multi-site database availability groups, is much more efficient. The Transport service performs message categorization and can perform message inspection. All internal routing between Exchange servers is always performed by the Transport service, but the Transport service never communicates with the mailbox databases.

- **Mailbox Transport service:** The Mailbox Transport service runs on all Mailbox servers and is made up of two different services:

    - Mailbox Transport Delivery service accept messages from the Transport service and delivers the message to the mailbox database via a local RPC connection with the mailbox database.

    - Mailbox Transport Submission service connects to the mailbox database using local RPC, but retrieves messages from the mailbox database that are in the user's outbox and delivers those messages, using SMTP to the Transport service for further processing.

So, FETS running on the Client Access server accepts messages from the Internet and from the Transport service running on the Mailbox server. For receiving messages, so-called receive connectors are used. For sending messages, a send connector is used. A send connector is used by the Transport service on the Mailbox server, but it can use the Client Access server as a local proxy that is controlled with the FrontEndProxyEnabled parameter when creating the send connector.

To use the front-end proxy function in the Exchange 2013 Client Access server, you first have to create a new send connector. Once created, the Proxy Through Client Access Server option is available when you request the properties of the newly created send connector, as shown in Figure 4-15.

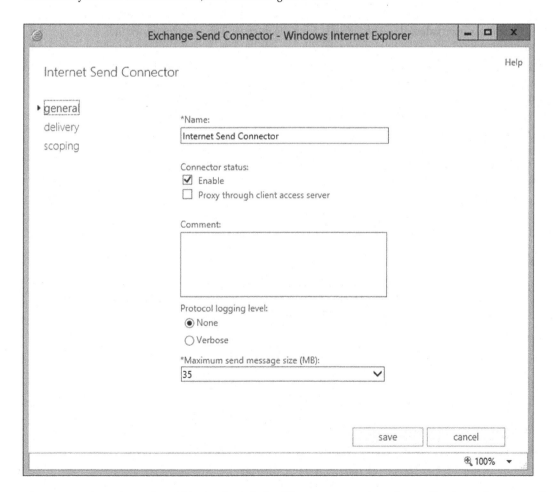

Figure 4-15. Proxying outbound SMTP through the Client Access server can be set after the send connector is created

It is also possible to create the send connector using the Exchange Management Shell. When using EMS to do this, you can set the front-end proxy function directly, using the following command:

```
New-SendConnector -Name " Send Connector" -Internet -AddressSpaces "*" -DNSRoutingEnabled:$TRUE
-SourceTransportServers "2012E15BE01","2012E15BE02"  -FrontendProxyEnabled:$TRUE
```

In Exchange 2013, there's no Edge Transport server available in the RTM (Release to Manufacturing) version. This server role will be added to Exchange 2013 in the future. FETS does not replace the Edge Transport server role; the Exchange 2007 and 2010 Edge Transport server role can both be used in conjunction with Exchange 2013. In this latter case, an edge synchronization is set up between the Transport service on the Mailbox server and the Edge Transport server, and then all messages can be routed via this Edge Transport server.

Receive Connectors

Receive connectors in Exchange 2013 are responsible for accepting SMTP messages from other messaging servers. These messaging servers can be internal Exchange servers or external SMTP servers.

By default, an Exchange 2013 Client Access server has three receive connectors:

- *Default front end <<server name>>:* The default front-end receive connector is used to receive SMTP messages from external servers—that is, from the Internet. This receive connector is listening on port 25.

- *Client front end <<server name>>:* The client front-end receive connector is used for sending SMTP messages by clients—that is, users needing an SMTP host to send messages. These users are authenticated before they are able to send messages. The client front-end receive connector uses port 587 to receive messages.

- *Outbound proxy front end <<server name>>:* The outbound proxy front-end receive connector is used by the Client Access server to receive messages from the Mailbox server that are proxied to external hosts—for example, on the Internet. The outbound proxy front-end server uses port 717 to receive messages.

When the Exchange 2013 Client Access server is installed, all receive connectors are automatically created and configured properly, so with out-of-the-box installations there's no need to configure them manually.

Anti-Spam Features

In Exchange 2013, anti-spam features are configured on the Mailbox server and not on the Client Access server. Therefore, all SMTP messages are accepted at the Client Access server and are proxied to the Mailbox server, where anti-spam processing takes place. The following anti-spam features are available:

- Sender filtering

- Recipient filtering

- Sender ID filtering

- Content filtering

- Sender reputation filtering

Unfortunately, connection filtering is not available in Exchange 2013 transport.

■ **Note** Since anti-spam features are running on the Mailbox server, they will be discussed in more detail in Chapter 5.

A good alternative for anti-spam and anti-virus activity with Exchange 2013 is to use Exchange Online Protection (EOP), Microsoft's cloud solution for anti-malware. EOP covers all anti-spam and anti-malware options currently available. In this scenario, mail destined for your SMTP domain is sent first to Microsoft's datacenters, where it is scanned for malware and cleaned up. From there it is sent to your Exchange 2013 Client Access servers, which then proxy the messages to the appropriate mailboxes.

Load-Balancing SMTP

It is obvious by now that a hardware load balancer is strongly recommended in front of the Exchange 2013 Client Access servers. This is true not only for handling client protocols like HTTPS, POP3, and IMAP4, but also for SMTP. Keep in mind that SMTP can also use DNS Round Robin for load-balancing purposes.

The load balancer can be used for inbound SMTP traffic from other SMTP hosts from the Internet on port 25 or for client SMTP submissions on port 587. The load balancer can be a layer-4 solution whereby the connections are directly sent to the Client Access server.

Scalability in this scenario is based on the number of connections. If more and more users or SMTP hosts are using the Client Access servers, you need only add more servers and reconfigure the load balancer.

Summary

The Exchange 2013 CAS is a relatively thin server that acts as a stateless protocol proxy. It does this not only for the standard client protocols like HTTP, POP3, and IMAP4, but also for the SMTP protocol. SIP traffic destined for the Unified Messaging (on the Mailbox server) is initially handled by the Exchange 2013 Client Access server, but the request is not proxied; it is redirected to the correct Mailbox server.

Since Exchange 2013 has a loosely coupled architecture, the servers are not using RPC anymore between the server roles. Instead, the original client protocol is proxied to the correct Mailbox server. As a result, all protocol handling now takes place on the Mailbox server and no longer on the Client Access server, as it did in Exchange 2010.

Consequently, load balancing is much simpler; a layer-4 load balancer without affinity settings will do perfectly in Exchange 2013, but you still have to be very careful about the server configuration when using a load-balanced array of Client Access servers.

Autodiscover becomes even more important with Exchange 2013. The oldest client supported on Exchange 2013 is Outlook 2007, which means that all clients preferentially use Autodiscover to create their initial Outlook profile, but also check the Exchange infrastructure every hour. Please note that Outlook clients and any other EWS clients do NOT use the autodiscover function.

SSL plays an important role in Autodiscover. Any SSL certificate misconfiguration automatically means Autodiscover problems and partially failing Outlook functionality when using HTTPS to communicate with the Exchange server.

SMTP message transport is now part of the Mailbox server, and all SMTP routing takes place on the Mailbox server. The Client Access server acts only as a "stateless" proxy, according to Microsoft, although this is not entirely accurate. It accepts SMTP messages from the Internet and proxies them to the correct Mailbox servers. If needed, the Client Access servers can also act as an outbound SMTP proxy where the Client Access servers are "visible" as the source servers sending the SMTP messages.

The next chapter will discuss not only the mailbox function but also the other services running on the back-end server, such as the Transport service and the Unified Messaging service.

## CHAPTER 5

Mailbox Server

The primary role of the Mailbox server is to host mailbox databases where the recipient mailboxes are hosted. But in Exchange Server 2013 there's more done besides hosting those mailboxes. The Hub Transport service is also running on the Mailbox server, and this service is responsible for all SMTP message routing in the Exchange organization. The Unified Messaging service is also part of the Mailbox server role, and there's a Client Access service running on the Mailbox server as well. As explained in the previous chapter, the Client Access server is a stateless protocol proxy, proxying user requests to the Mailbox server.

In this chapter I explain the most important features and functions of the Exchange 2013 Mailbox server, such as the processing of items in the mailbox database and the routing functions. I also cover the Unified Messaging role.

The Mailbox Server role

The Exchange 2013 Mailbox Server role is similar to the earlier Mailbox server role in Exchange Server 2010. It is responsible for processing all mail items, storing those items in the mailbox database, and showing them in the user's inbox.

All mail items are stored in a mailbox, and all mailboxes are stored in a mailbox database. This mailbox database is stored by default on the local hard disk of the Mailbox server, in the `C:\Program Files\Microsoft\Exchange Server\V15\Mailbox\<<database name>>` directory. Figure 5-1 shows this arrangement for a mailbox database called `Mailbox Database 9361956222`.

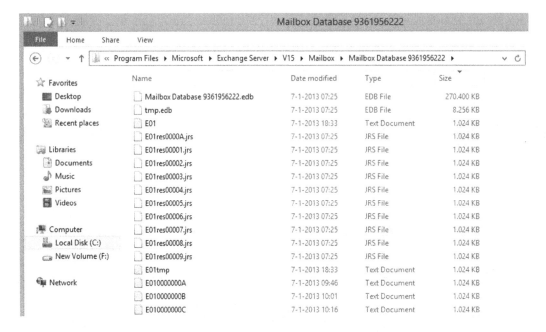

Figure 5-1. *Mailbox database files on disk*

The following files are available, as can be seen in Figure 5-1:

- The file `Mailbox Database 9361956222.edb` is the actual database where all the individual mail items are stored.

- `Tmp.edb` is a temporary file used by Exchange.

- E01 and subsequent log files are log files used for the transactional processing of information.

- E00.chk is a checkpoint file that keeps track of the transactions still in the log files, as well as those that are already written in the mailbox database. This file is not visible in Figure 5-1.

- `E01res00001.jrs` - `E01res0000A.jrs` are temporary log files reserved by Exchange Server in case of disk-full problems.

- `E01tmp.log` is a temporary log file used by Exchange Server.

All of these files belong together, and together they make up one database. One Exchange 2013 Enterprise Mailbox server can host up to 100 mailbox databases. Exchange 2013 now fully supports multiple mailbox databases on one physical disk if you have multiple copies of the mailbox databases in a database availability group.

■ **Note**   In Exchange 2013 Enterprise RTM and Enterprise CU1, the number of mailbox databases was limited to 50. In Exchange 2013 Enterprise CU2, this maximum was increased to 100. The maximum number of mailbox databases on an Exchange 2013 Standard, however, is limited to 5, independent of any cumulative update.

When you install a Mailbox server, a new mailbox database is automatically created on the boot- and system disk, as shown in Figure 5-1. When you create additional mailbox databases, they have a preference for this boot- and system disk as well. However, using this disk is not a good idea. It is best practice to store the mailbox databases on a dedicated disk that's capable of handling the load generated by processing the mailbox items.

The Mailbox Database

The mailbox database is the primary repository of the Exchange Server information; it's where all the Exchange data is stored. In theory, the mailbox database can be 16TB in size, but it is normally limited to a size you can handle within the constraints of your Service Level Agreement (SLA). The recommended maximum database size for a normal Exchange 2013 Mailbox server is 2TB when you have multiple copies of the mailbox database. If this is not the case, the maximum recommended size is 200GB—but in practice it is limited by your backup and restore solution and by the accompanying SLA.

The mailbox database in Exchange 2013 is an Extensible Storage Engine (ESE) database. ESE is a low-level database technology, sometimes also referred to as a JET database. The ESE database has been used since Exchange Server 4.0. The Active Directory database, the WINS database, and the DHCP database also use an ESE database.

The data within a database is organized in a binary tree, or B+ tree. This binary arrangement can be envisioned as an upside-down tree where the leaves are in the lowest part, as illustrated in Figure 5-2. The actual mail data is stored in the leaves. The mid-level pages contain the pointers. The upper level is the root. This binary tree design is an efficient way of storing data, since it requires only two or three lookups to find a particular piece of data and all the pointers can be kept in memory.

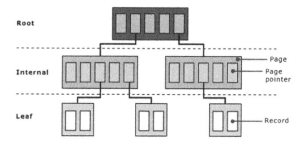

Figure 5-2. *A binary tree setup*

One or more trees in a database make up a table. There are several kinds of tables in Exchange Server:

Mailbox table

Folders table

Message table

Attachment table

The tables hold the information that appears in the inbox. The tables consist of columns and records; the columns are identified as MAPI properties, and the records contain the actual information.

Multiple trees make up a database and sometimes the trees need to be split, as when the tree fills up with information. Exchange Server's internal processes reorganize the tree's information when it is divided into two trees. This is called a "split." It is not possible to predict how many trees will make up a particular database, but it can be hundreds or even thousands. This can be seen in the header of the database, which will be explained later in this chapter.

Database Pages

A *page* is the smallest unit of data in an Exchange environment. It consists of a header, pointers to other pages, checksum information to ensure that page is not corrupt, and data from Exchange Server regarding messages, attachments, or folders. A database file can consist of millions of pages. For Exchange 2010 and 2013, the size of a page was 32KB. The total number of pages can easily be calculated by dividing the total size of the database by this page size of 32KB. If, for example, the size of a database is 250GB, it consists of 250GB times 32KB, or approximately 8.2 million pages.

Each page is sequentially numbered. Whenever a new page is created, it gets a new, incremented number. When the pages are read from the database and altered, they also get new numbers before being written to the log file and flushed to the database file. Needless to say, this sequential number must be very large. In fact, it's a 64-bit number, which means that 18 quintillion changes can be made to a database!

Transaction Log Files

Mailbox items are processed by the Mailbox server in what are termed "transactions." A transaction can be:

> The creation of a new message or a new calendar item.
>
> The storage of a message received from SMTP in the mailbox.
>
> The creation of a new folder in the mailbox.
>
> The deletion of a message in the mailbox.
>
> The renaming of a folder in the mailbox.
>
> The creation of new Mailbox database.

And so on. All transactions are created and processed in the Mailbox server's memory, and when a transaction is finished, it is immediately stored in a transaction log file. If you look back at Figure 5-1, you'll see these files identified as `E01.log`, `E01000000A.log`, `E01000000B.log`, and `E01000000C.log`. Transactions are a sequential process, so subsequent transaction log files are numbered accordingly. Note that a hexadecimal notation is used, so after writing a transaction log file that ends with a number 9, the letter A is added. Only after writing a transaction log file ending with the letter F does Exchange Server start a new sequence.

By storing the transactions in a transaction log file, you safeguard the data against server failures—for example, a power failure. In fact, the transaction log files can be used for recovery purposes. When a server fails, or a mailbox database fails, the information can be recovered and reconstructed because it has been stored in those transaction log files. For this reason, it is not a good idea to manually delete the transaction log files from your server (unless you have no other option); keep in mind that doing so will destroy your recovery options.

Transaction log files are automatically removed from Exchange Server when you run a backup solution, as will be explained in Chapter 7.

Checkpoint File

When transactions are stored in the transaction log files, they are not written to the mailbox database but, rather, they are kept in memory for some time. This technology is called "write ahead logging." That is, the information stored in the transaction log files is always "ahead of" the information stored in the mailbox database.

After some time, transactions that remain in server memory are then stored in the mailbox database. At this point, they can also be removed from the server's memory. To keep track of which transactions are stored in the transaction log files and which are stored in the mailbox database, you need a *checkpoint file*.

The checkpoint file is an 8KB file stored in the same location as the transaction log files, but it contains only a pointer. This pointer "points to" the transaction that has just been stored in the mailbox database. All transactions that are older than the pointer in the checkpoint file are stored in the mailbox database; all transactions that are newer, therefore, remain in the server's memory and in the transaction log files. In case of a problem, Exchange Server knows which information is stored where, and thus it knows how it can start recovering the information. This is a simple and safe solution for trouble-free processing of database information.

How This All Fits Together

As outlined above, there are four locations that are imports with respect to Exchange Server data:

> The internal server memory
>
> The transaction log files
>
> The mailbox database file
>
> The checkpoint file

This is shown in Figure 5-3.

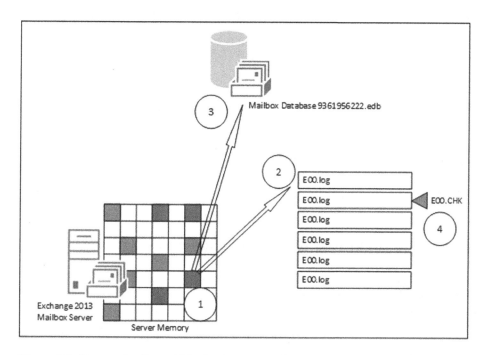

Figure 5-3. *Transaction flow within database processing*

As you might have guessed, server memory is very important. The more memory there is in the Exchange 2013 Mailbox server, the better it will perform. The other way around is also true: if there's not enough memory in the Exchange 2013 Mailbox server, the server will have to flush transactions to the mailbox database too early, and eventually it will have to read these items back from the database. Each item added costs valuable performance, so when there's not enough server memory for the Exchange services, performance will suffer dramatically.

One important point to remember is that the transition log files are always written in advance of writing those transactions to the mailbox database, so there's always data not yet written to the database that is available in those log files. This data can cover a number of log files, and the number of log files or amount of data is called the *checkpoint depth*. That is, the database that is running is always in a nonconsistent state, or what's termed a *dirty shutdown*. When a database is dismounted, it is brought into a consistent state. All data not yet written to disk is flushed to the database, and all files are then closed. This is called a *clean shutdown* of the database.

The transition log files needed to get the database into a consistent state, and then the clean shutdown is recorded in the header of the database. The header of the database is written into the first page of the database file, and it contains information regarding that database. The header information can be retrieved using the ESEUTIL tool. Just enter the following command in the directory where the database file resides:

```
ESEUTIL /MH "DB01.edb"
```

This will result in an output such as:

```
Extensible Storage Engine Utilities for Microsoft(R) Exchange Server
Version 15.00
Copyright (C) Microsoft Corporation. All Rights Reserved.

Initiating FILE DUMP mode...
        Database: db01.edb

DATABASE HEADER:
Checksum Information:
Expected Checksum: 0x5cdc5390
  Actual Checksum: 0x5cdc5390

Fields:
        File Type: Database
         Checksum: 0x5cdc5390
   Format ulMagic: 0x89abcdef
   Engine ulMagic: 0x89abcdef
 Format ulVersion: 0x620,20
 Engine ulVersion: 0x620,20
Created ulVersion: 0x620,20
     DB Signature: Create time:12/23/2012 18:32:24.362 Rand:4071177377 Computer:
         cbDbPage: 32768
           dbtime: 4256402 (0x40f292)
            State: Dirty Shutdown
     Log Required: 2764-2764 (0xacc-0xacc)
    Log Committed: 0-2765 (0x0-0xacd)
    Log Recovering: 2765 (0xacd)
  GenMax Creation: 03/08/2013 18:09:34.936
         Shadowed: Yes
        Last Objid: 14500
     Scrub Dbtime: 0 (0x0)
       Scrub Date: 00/00/1900 00:00:00
     Repair Count: 0
      Repair Date: 00/00/1900 00:00:00.000
 Old Repair Count: 0
```

```
    Last Consistent: (0x9E9,19,594)  02/27/2013 20:20:43.313
       Last Attach: (0x9EA,2,268)  02/27/2013 20:20:43.407
       Last Detach: (0x0,0,0)  00/00/1900 00:00:00.000
     Last ReAttach: (0xAC7,2,0)  03/08/2013 16:18:35.779
             Dbid: 1
     Log Signature: Create time:12/23/2012 18:32:24.268 Rand:2709814512 Computer:
        OS Version: (6.2.9200 SP 0 NLS ffffffff.ffffffff)


Previous Full Backup:
        Log Gen: 0-0 (0x0-0x0)
          Mark: (0x0,0,0)
          Mark: 00/00/1900 00:00:00.000

Previous Incremental Backup:
        Log Gen: 0-0 (0x0-0x0)
          Mark: (0x0,0,0)
          Mark: 00/00/1900 00:00:00.000

Previous Copy Backup:
        Log Gen: 0-0 (0x0-0x0)
          Mark: (0x0,0,0)
          Mark: 00/00/1900 00:00:00.000

Previous Differential Backup:
        Log Gen: 0-0 (0x0-0x0)
          Mark: (0x0,0,0)
          Mark: 00/00/1900 00:00:00.000

Current Full Backup:
        Log Gen: 0-0 (0x0-0x0)
          Mark: (0x0,0,0)
          Mark: 00/00/1900 00:00:00.000

Current Shadow copy backup:
        Log Gen: 0-0 (0x0-0x0)
          Mark: (0x0,0,0)
          Mark: 00/00/1900 00:00:00.000


    cpgUpgrade55Format: 0
    cpgUpgradeFreePages: 0
cpgUpgradeSpaceMapPages: 0

      ECC Fix Success Count: none
  Old ECC Fix Success Count: none
        ECC Fix Error Count: none
    Old ECC Fix Error Count: none
    Bad Checksum Error Count: none
Old bad Checksum Error Count: none

  Last checksum finish Date: 03/12/2013 18:29:58.184
```

```
Current checksum start Date: 00/00/1900 00:00:00.000
     Current checksum page: 0

Operation completed successfully in 0.15 seconds.
```

There's quite a lot of information to retrieve from the mailbox database header:

- **DB Signature** A unique value of date, time, and an integer that identifies this particular database. This value is also recorded in the log files and the checkpoint files, and this ties them together.

- **cbDbPage** The size of the pages used in this database; in Exchange 2013, the page size is 32KB.

- **Dbtime** (Part of) the number of changes made to this database.

- **State** The state of the database—that is, whether it is in a consistent state or not. The database in this example is in a dirty shutdown. (I killed the Information Store using Task Manager.) It needs a certain number of log files to get to a clean shutdown.

- **Log Required** If the database is not in a consistent state, these log files are needed to bring it into that consistent state. To make this database a consistent state again, the log files E0000000ACC.log through E0000000ACC.log are needed. Exchange Server will perform the recovery process when mounting a database, so under normal circumstances no EAC action is needed.

- **Last ObjID** The number of B+ trees in this particular database. In this example there are 14,500 B+ trees in the database.

- **Log Signature** A unique value of date, time, and an integer that uniquely identifies a series of log files. As with the database signature, this ties together the database file, the log files, and the checkpoint file.

- **Last Attach** The date and time when the database was last mounted. "Mounting" is actually attaching the mailbox database to a stream of log files, hence the entry label "Last Attach."

- **Last Detach** The date and time when the database was last dismounted, or detached from the stream of log files. In this example, the database was never dismounted; I only crashed it.

- **Backup information** Entries used by Exchange Server to keep track of the last full or incremental (or VSS) backup that was made on this particular database.

The same kind of information is logged in the header of the transaction log files (ESEUTIL /ML E00.LOG) and in the header of the checkpoint file (ESEUTIL /MK E00.CHK). As these file are grouped together, you can match the files using the header information.

Disk-Full Scenarios

When the Mailbox server is running, the log files are continually flushed to disk as an ongoing process. There's no automatic clean-up process because the log files are needed for recovery purposes, so at one point the disk where the log files are being stored can completely fill up.

When the Information Store is not able to store the transactions safely to disk, it will automatically dismount the mailbox database. Before it dismounts, however, it uses the 10 reserved log files, E01res00001.jrs to E01res0000A.jrs. These 10 log files are created automatically when the database is first mounted, and they are kept on disk until this moment. When the disk is full, Exchange Server dismounts the mailbox database and flushes all remaining data to these 10 log files.

The mailbox database will not mount again before disk space is freed up. Obviously, this will lead to downtime, as users aren't able to access their mailboxes. But monitoring, correct sizing, and capacity management can help to prevent this. There's no automatic clean-up process in Exchange 2013, so to avoid a disk-full scenario, there are two supported ways of removing log files from the disk:

- **Create a full backup**. When a full backup is created, the mailbox database and the log files are written to the backup media. The log files included in the backup are no longer needed for recovery purposes, since the backup itself is the recovery medium. Once the backup has successfully finished writing the data to the backup medium, the log files are automatically purged.

- **Enable circular logging.** When circular logging is enabled, only a small set of log files are kept on disk. As soon as the data is flushed from the server memory to the mailbox database file, the data in the log file is no longer needed and the log file is removed.

If circular logging is enabled and there's only one mailbox database, there's a risk of losing data, however. To explain, if the mailbox database crashes, there's only a limited amount of data available in the log files and there's *no way to recovery this lost data*. Therefore, using circular logging is generally speaking not a good idea unless there are multiple copies of the mailbox database in a database availability group.

Single-Instance Storage

Up until the 2007 version, Exchange Server had a feature called *single instance storage* (SIS). Using SIS, Exchange Server stored items in the mailbox database only one time per database. When an item had to be delivered to multiple mailboxes, it was stored once and the other mailboxes contained only a pointer to this particular item. In the early days, when 4GB SCSI disks were used, this method could save valuable disk space and would increase performance dramatically. It made sense, since writing a large item takes much more time than writing only a pointer.

Microsoft started to move away from SIS starting with Exchange Server 2007, and Exchange Server 2013 does not use SIS at all. Newer disk technology and improved ESE technology make it possible to use large 3TB SATA disks (or larger) without impacting disk performance. That is, of course, if the disk subsystem is not overcommitted. Microsoft's getting rid of SIS made it possible for the Exchange developer to create a less complex database structure, which in turn lowered the IOPS requirements.

Is this a bad development? No, it hasn't led to "exploding" mailbox databases, as a lot of people feared. Over the years, Microsoft has improved its compression techiques in the mailbox database, which balances the loss of SIS.

Microsoft Exchange Information Store

While ESE is just the database engine, it stores the transactions in the transaction log files and in the mailbox database, as explained above. If you open this database file with some sort of binary editor, however, there's absolutely no readable information. The same is true for the transaction log files—no readable information.

The *Information Store* is the process running on the Mailbox server that's responsible for the logical part of the database processing. It transforms the information read from the mailbox database into something readable, like your inbox, the folders in the inbox, or the individual message items. In essence, this process hasn't changed since the original release of Exchange Server 4.0 in 1997. Of course, there have been changes, such as increasing the number of mailbox databases or expanding the page size to 8KB in 2007 and to 32KB in 2010, but the overall concept hasn't changed.

In Exchange 2013, however, the Information Store process has been completely rewritten in managed code—in other words, it is now a .NET application. More interesting, for every mailbox database that is mounted on an Exchange 2013 Mailbox server, a new Information Store worker process is spawned and responsible for this particular database (see Figure 5-4). The huge advantage to this system is that all mailbox databases and the accompanying processes are fully independent of each other. That is, if you have an Exchange 2013 Mailbox server with 25 mailbox databases mounted, and one of those databases crashes, including the Information Store, the other 24 mailbox databases are not affected. (This is in contrast to earlier versions of Exchange Server, where all mailbox databases were dismounted if such a scenario took place.) Besides a new Information Store worker process, an additional search instance is started, minimizing the risk of affecting other mailbox databases in the event of a problem.

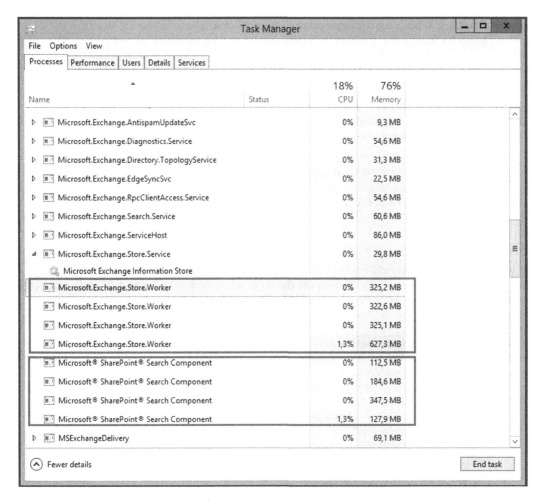

Figure 5-4. *Multiple databases means multiple Information Store worker processes*

Database Caching

For optimal performance, the Information Store wants to do only one thing: cache as much information as possible. Reading and writing in memory is much faster than reading and writing on disk. The more information that is kept in the server's memory, the better the server's performance will be.

The amount of memory assigned to a particular mailbox database is determined at the start time of the Information Store process. This also means that when additional mailbox databases are added, the server's memory used for database caching needs to be redistributed. This is the reason why a warning message such as "Please restart the Microsoft Exchange Information Store service on server <<name>> after adding new mailbox databases" appears (see Figure 5-5).

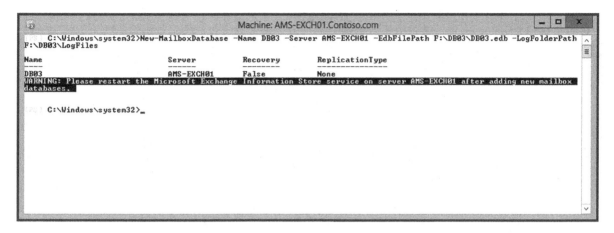

Figure 5-5. *The Information Store needs to be restarted after adding a mailbox database*

Creating a New Mailbox Database

To create a new mailbox database, follow these steps:

1. Open the Exchange Administration Center (EAC), either from the server itself or remotely from another server, and log in as an administrator.

2. In the EAC. select Servers in the left-hand menu and then select Databases in the top menu. A list of existing mailbox databases will appear on the screen.

3. Click on the + symbol to start the new database page. Fill in the fields for mailbox database name, select a Mailbox server, and enter the paths for the mailbox database file and for the accompanying log files. If you want, you can leave the checkbox for "Mount this database" checked to have it automatically mounted after creation (see Figure 5-6).

Figure 5-6. Creating a new mailbox database using the EAC

4. Click Save to create the new database and automatically mount it. A warning will be shown that the Microsoft Exchange Information Store service needs to be restarted on the server.

5. To enable circular logging, select the appropriate mailbox database and click on the little pencil icon in the top menu to edit the mailbox database properties. In the navigation menu, select Maintenance and in the results pane, check the Enable Circular Logging box and then click Save to continue.

6. A warning message will be shown that circular logging will only be applied when the mailbox database is dismounted and mounted again. Click OK.

7. To dismount the mailbox database, click on the three dots in the top menu; a dismount option will appear. Click on Dismount to dismount the mailbox database. To mount it again, click on the three dots and a mount option will appear. Click on Mount to mount the mailbox database. The mailbox database is now running with circular logging enabled.

Of course, it is also possible to create new mailbox databases using the Exchange Management Shell (EMS). To do so, log on to the Exchange 2013 Mailbox server, open an EMS window, and enter the following commands:

```
New-MailboxDatabase -Name DB03 -Server AMS-EXCH01 -EdbFilePath F:\DB03\DB03.edb -LogFolderPath
F:\DB03\LogFiles
Mount-Database -Identity DB03
```

To change the mailbox database to use circular logging, enter the following commands:

```
Set-MailboxDatabase -Identity DB03 -CircularLoggingEnabled:$true
Dismount-Database -Identity DB03 -Confirm:$false
Mount-Database -Identity DB03
```

Mailboxes

There are multiple types of mailboxes available in Exchange 2013:

- **User mailboxes** Regular mailboxes used by individuals to send and receive email messages.

- **Resource mailboxes** Mailboxes that are not assigned to human beings but to resources, like a conference room or a beamer in an office; as such they can be scheduled for meeting purposes.

- **Linked mailboxes** Regular mailboxes, tied to user accounts in another Active Directory forest and not to user accounts in the same Active Directory forest as the Exchange 2013 servers.

Although they are all mailboxes, there are differences between them, as outlined in the following sections.

Creating a User Mailbox

To create a new mailbox you can use the EAC or EMS. You can also create a new mailbox on an existing user account in Active Directory; this is called "mailbox-enabling" the user. The advantage of this last option is that users are provisioned in advance, using, for example, the Active Directory Users and Computers or another provisioning tool in any location of Active Directory. Also, all properties that need to have values can be configured in advance—something that's not always possible when creating a new user and a new mailbox using the EAC. However, to create a new user and a new mailbox using the EAC, log on to it with an administrator account that has sufficient permission.

1. The EAC opens directly on the mailbox recipients. Click on the + symbol and select User Mailbox to start the New Mailbox wizard. To create a new mailbox with a new user account in Active Directory, select the radio button next to New User.

2. Fill in all fields as needed, and use the Browse button to select an organizational unit in Active Directory where the user account will be stored; for example, contoso.com/accounts/contoso.

3. Continue with the user logon name and enter a password. Note that the user logon name is not necessarily the same as the alias of the new mailbox, but it will keep things easier if they are the same.

4. Click on More Options to expand the wizard and use the Browse button to select a mailbox database where the new mailbox will be stored. (This is optional; if you don't select a mailbox database, Exchange will automatically determine the best location based on available resources.)

   At the same time, it is possible to define an archive mailbox for this new mailbox where old email data can be stored. Just like the primary mailbox, it is possible to manually assign a mailbox database where the archive mailbox will be stored or have Exchange automatically determine the best location.

The algorithm used here first determines which mailbox databases are available in the appropriate Active Directory and are not excluded for provisioning. Then it looks at the number of mailboxes in each mailbox database and picks the mailbox database with the lowest number of mailboxes.

5. Select an address book policy, but this is optional as well.

6. Click Save to store the new mailbox and user account.

The new mailbox will automatically appear in the EAC, but when you check the organizational unit in Active Directory, the new user will show up there as well. If needed, you can use Active Directory Users and Computers to enter additional properties on the new user account.

As stated above, it is also possible to add a mailbox to an existing user account in Active Directory. Suppose there's a user account called Michael McDonald in the Contoso organizational unit in Active Directory, and this user should have a mailbox attached to it. Here's how you do it.

1. Log on to the EAC and it automatically opens the mailbox recpients. Click on the + symbol and select User Mailbox. This time keep the radio button on Existing User and use the Browse button to find the user account. A list of user accounts that are *not* mailbox enabled is shown. In this case, select user account "Michael McDonald" and click OK.

2. It is possible to add an alias for the new mailbox or have Exchange Server automatically determine an alias. Please note that the attributes that were used to create a new mailbox are now grayed out, since they are already populated on the existing user account. Use More Options (you may have to scroll down) to select a mailbox database, create an archive mailbox, or select an address book policy if needed.

3. Click Save to store the user account and mailbox.

When the mailbox is created, it is automatically listed in the EAC. You can double-click the mailbox to open it and check or alter its properties, which are divided into several categories (see Figure 5-7).

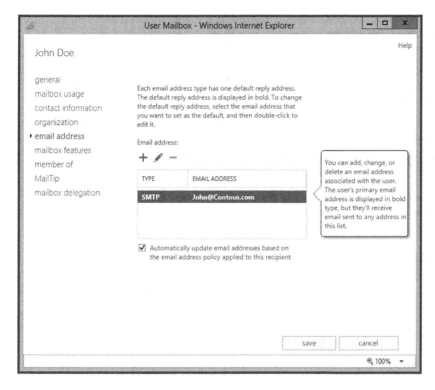

Figure 5-7. *Properties of a mailbox, in this case the mailbox email address*

Additional Email Addresses

The email address is automatically set by the email address policy that was created during the postinstallation tasks discussed in Chapter 2. When the "Automatically update email address based on the email address policy applied to this recipient" is checked, any future updates in the email address policy will automatically be reflected in the user's email address.

It is also possible to add email addresses manually. Click on the + symbol to start the New Email Address wizard. In this wizard, it is possible to add SMTP addresses, EUM addresses (Exchange Unified Messaging), or a custom email address like an X.500 address (which can be useful in an interorg migration scenario).

Select the SMTP radio button and in the email address field enter a new email address, like John.Doe@contoso.com. Click OK and then click Save to store the new email address.

Mailbox Delegation

Another important item I'd like to point out is the *mailbox delegation*, a feature that's widely used in a manager and assistant scenario where the manager needs to grant access to his mailbox to his assistant. There are three types of mailbox delegation available in the EAC:

- **Send As permission** Using the Send As permission, the assistant can send a message from the manager's mailbox. The recipient will only see the manager as the sender of the email message.

- **Send on Behalf permission** Using the Send on Behalf permission, the assistant can send email on behalf of the manager. The recipient of the message will see that the message was sent on behalf of the manager, and the sender of the message will be shown as "Assistant on behalf of Manager."

- **Full Access permission** Using Full Access permission, the assistant has full access (read, write, edit, and delete) to all items in the manager's entire mailbox.

For example, if Cindy McDowell is a manager at Contoso and John Doe is her assistant, you can follow these steps to grant her Send on Behalf permission.

1. Log on to the EAC with sufficient permission and navigate to Cindy McDowell's mailbox, then open its properties.

2. In the user mailbox menu, select Mailbox Delegation. Right under Send on Behalf, click the + symbol to open the user picker. Select John Doe, as in Figure 5-8, and click OK to continue. Then click Save to store the information.

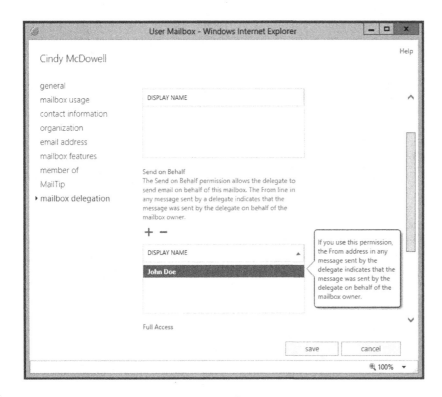

Figure 5-8. *Granting John "Send on Behalf" permission to Cindy McDowell's mailbox*

Now John can use his own mailbox, but when he sends a message he can select his manager (i.e., Cindy McDowell) in the From field. When he does, and sends a message to Michael McDonald, Michael sees in his mailbox the sender information as shown in Figure 5-9.

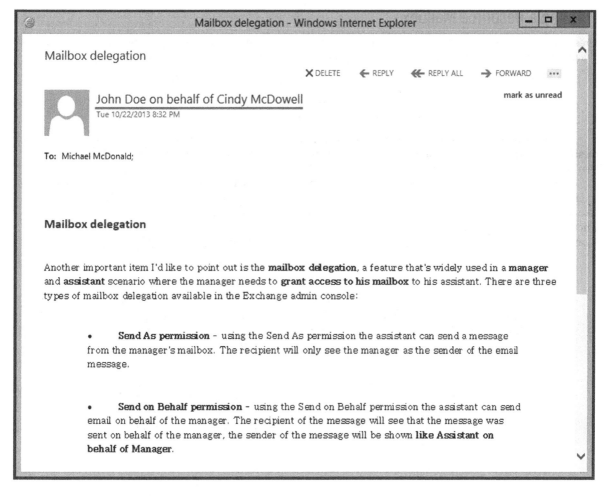

Figure 5-9. *The message Michael sees when John sends a message on behalf of his manager*

To grant the Send As permission to user Cindy on John Doe's mailbox using the EMS, you can use the following command: `Add-ADPermission -Identity Cindy -User John -ExtendedRights "Send As"`

To grant the Send on behalf of permission to user Cindy on John Doe's mailbox using the EMS, you can use the following command: `Set-Mailbox -Identity Cindy -GrantSendOnBehalfTo John`

To grant Full Access permissions to user John on Cindy McDowell's mailbox using the EMS, you can use the following command: `Add-MailboxPermission -Identity Cindy -User John -AccessRights FullAccess -InheritanceType all`

▪ **Note**　When a user is granted Full Access permission to a mailbox, this user cannot send email messages from the mailbox he's been granted permission to. To achieve this, the user also needs the Send As or Send on Behalf permission.

Creating a Resource Mailbox

A resource mailbox is a normal mailbox with the exception that it does not belong to a normal user; instead, it belongs to a resource. In Exchange 2013, there are two types of resource mailboxes:

- **Room mailbox** A room mailbox represents a conference room in your office.

- **Equipment mailbox** An equipment mailbox represents some sort of equipment, like a beamer, that's not tied to a conference room.

A resource mailbox represents something that can be booked by regular users when scheduling meetings. Since these resources cannot log on to the mailbox, the accompanying user account in Active Directory is disabled. They also do not require any user licences.

However, they are quite useful. It is possible to use a resource mailbox to schedule meetings, such as a conference room, thereby indicating when this resource is available. Like a regular email, this meeting request is sent to the resource mailbox, but in contrast, the request is automatically accepted when the resource is available. The response, whether the meeting is accepted or not, is sent back to the sender to confirm that availability. To create this type of room mailbox—say, with a capacity of 16 persons—you use the following procedure.

1. Log on to the EAC. It automatically opens the list of mailbox recipients. In the top-level menu, select Resources. Click on the + symbol and select Room Mailbox.

2. Enter a name for the room mailbox and email address. Use the Browse button to select an organizational unit where the accompanying user account will be created—for example, the contoso.com/accounts/contoso organizational unit. If needed, enter a location or a phone number. In the capacity field, enter the number of persons that the conference room can hold—in this example, enter 16.

3. When it comes to the booking request there are two options: (a) have the meeting requests automatically accepted when the resource is available; or (b)assign a delegate of the resource mailbox that can accept or deny the request on behalf of the resource. This delegate is selected using the + symbol in the Delegates option, as shown in Figure 5-10.

Figure 5-10. *Creating a room mailbox with the user Beau as a delegate, for booking purposes*

4. When More Options is selected, you can enter an alias for the resource mailbox, which is the mailbox database where the resource mailbox is stored and assign an address book policy.

5. When done, click Save to store all information and have the resource mailbox created.

When the room mailbox is created, it is automatically listed in the EAC. You can then double-click the newly created room mailbox to open its properties and edit them as needed. The booking options properties, for example, are interesting. Here you can define whether or not recursive meetings will be allowed, you can set the number of days a meeting can be into the future (by default, 180 days from now), and you can set a maximum duration (by default, 24 hours) for a requesting a resource mailbox (see Figure 5-11).

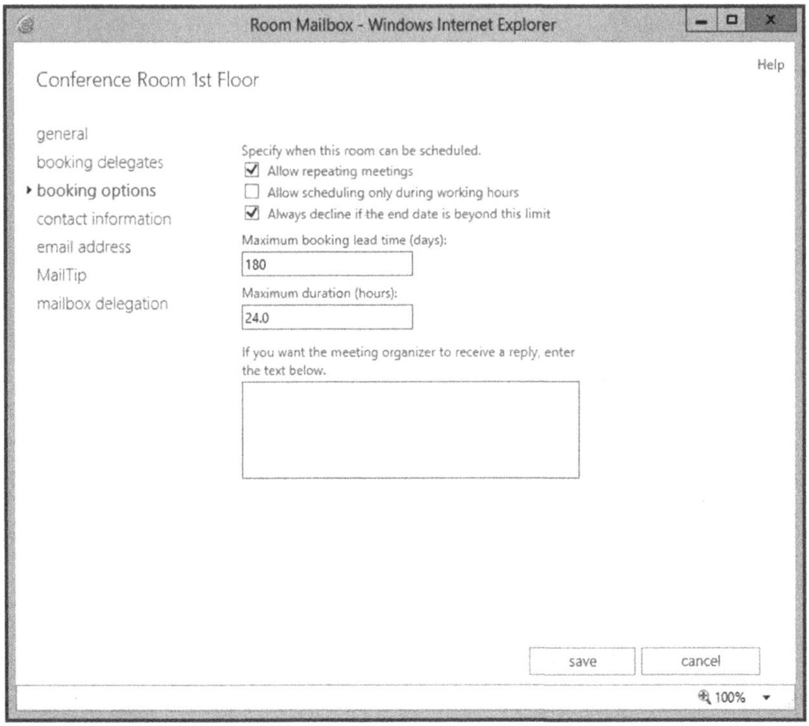

Figure 5-11. *Booking options for a room mailbox*

Creating an equipment mailbox is very similar; the only difference is that there is a little less to configure. There's no location, no phone number, and no capacity to enter, but otherwise the process is similar.

Creating a Linked Mailbox

A *linked mailbox* differs from a regular mailbox in that it does not have an active user account in Active Directory. Instead, it is used by a normal user, and that user is created in another Active Directory forest. There's a forest "trust" between the forest holding the user accounts and the forest holding the mailboxes. Thus, the user account is linked to the mailbox. The forest that holds the Exchange servers, and thus the mailboxes, is sometimes also referred to as a *resource forest*.

A regular mailbox always has an accompanying user account, but when a linked mailbox is used, this accompanying user account is disabled. For this scenario, you need some sort of provisioning process. This is the means by which the user account in forest A and the mailbox in forest B are linked, as can be seen in Figure 5-12. Note that the Active Directory forest A does not have any Exchange servers installed, and thus the user accounts do not have any Exchange-related properties. Since there's a trust relationship, users in forest A can log in and seamlessly access their mailboxes in forest B.

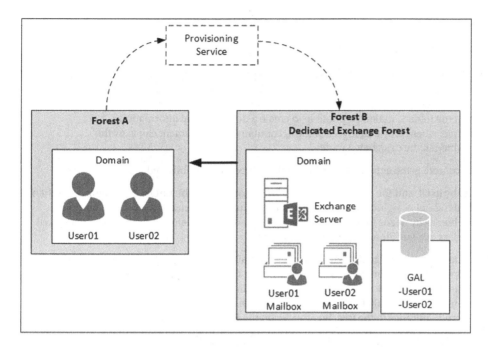

***Figure 5-12.** A linked mailbox scenario consists of an account forest (A) and an Exchange forest (B)*

The advantage of this scenario is that it makes it possible to have multiple, fully separated Active Directory forests where the user accounts reside, but have only one Exchange forest with all the mailboxes of all the (trusted) Active Directory accounts.

You may want to implement linked mailboxes if you have multiple Active Directory forests holding user accounts that are governed by strict security policies that do not allow multiple departments in one Active Directory forest. Using linked mailboxes makes it possible to create one Exchange environment for multiple, fully separated departments. While this might seem strange from an Active Directory point of view, when viewed from an Exchange perspective it is a fully supported scenario.

Modern Public Folders

Public folders have been around since the first version of Exchange Server, back in 1996. Public folders are another repository of information where messages, appointments, or contacts can be stored and shared among recipients. Starting with Exchange Server 2007, Microsoft decommissioned these public folders, a decision that was not popular with Exchange customers; after endless debate, Microsoft decided to restore and completely redesign the public folders for Exchange Server 2013. This has resulted in the so-called *modern public folders.*

History of Public Folders

From their start, public folders were a repository for information; it was even possible to store office documents in these public folders, although the negative side effect of this capability was ever-growing public folders.

These public folders used to have their own databases, called *public folder databases.* The databases were the same as mailbox databases, using the same ESE database technology and managed by the same Information Store. Only the database scheme and the information inside the database were different. The public folder databases also had their own replication mechanism, making it possible to create multiple databases with the same information and thus offering database redundancy. And to make these folders even more compelling, they used a multi-master replication technology, so that it was possible to make changes to documents on different servers, with the two copies in sync.

The public folders consisted of two parts:

- **The hierarchy** This is the structure of the items kept in the public folder database, or how and where the individual items are stored in the folders. The hierarchy is similar to a directory structure on a local hard disk, with all its folders and subfolders. In public folders, you can set permissions on the folders, making it possible to create a departmental information solution, for example, where only employees of the accompanying department can view the information contained in the designated folder.

- **The content** The content is the actual information that is stored in the public folders.

The hierarchy is an entity by itself, and the entire folder structure is stored in the hierarchy. The hierarchy is then replicated across all public folder databases, including all public folders and their permissions. When a new public folder database is created, the hierarchy needs to be replicated to this new database before the database can be used.

There are two types of folders in a traditional public folder database:

- **System folders** These are system-generated folders that contain free/busy information and the offline address book. The system folders are used by older Outlook clients—Outlook 2003 and earlier. Without the system folders, these older Outlook clients would not even be able to get started! When using Outlook 2003 or earlier, the calendering information is stored locally and published every 15 minutes to the free/busy folder on the Exchange server. The offline address book is generated once a day, typically in the middle of the night, and stored in the offline address book folder. Outlook clients then download a copy of the offline address book during business hours.

- **Public folders** These are the normal public folders where recipients can store information, where permissions are set, and whose contents can be replicated across multiple public folder databases.

Public folder replication is set on a per-public-folder basis; this means that data from one server—say, Public Folder A—can be replicated to a second Exchange server, while data from another server—say, Public Folder B—can be replicated to a third Exchange server, making it possible to create a flexible, distributed, and powerful information solution.

For accessing public folder information, Outlook would connect directly to the Exchange 2010 public folder database, whereas the same Outlook client would connect to the RPC Client Access service running on the Exchange 2010 CAS to retrieve information from the inbox. So one Outlook client connects in two different ways. Using the RPC Client Access service running on multiple Exchange 2010 CAS servers created a redundant connection mechanism, something that was not possible for the public folders. There can be multiple copies of a particular public folder on multiple public folder databases, but there is no automatic failover mechanism built into the "old" public folder solution. However, this situation was corrected in Exchange Server 2010 SP2 RU2, when an alternate server tag was introduced. This alternate server tag introduced a public folder failover function.

The bad thing is that there wasn't much development involving public folders after the early 2000s. As mentioned earlier, by Exchange Server 2007, Microsoft had started to decommission the public folders. However, in the development phase of Exchange 2013, Microsoft decided to reinstate the public folders. At that point, they decided to completely rewrite the public folder architecture and bring it back to life.

Public Folders in Exchange Server 2013

The basic idea behind the public folders has not changed. There still is a hierarchy containing the public folder structure, and there still is the actual content that is stored in the public folders. However, the completely redesigned public folders no longer use a separate public folder database; the public folders are now stored in mailbox databases. This makes it possible to:

- Use the Client Access server to access the public folder information, offering redundancy on the way clients connect to public folders.

- Use the database availability group (DAG) for redundancy on the public folder and mailbox database level, as discussed in the next part of this chapter.

The hierarchy in Exchange Server 2013 public folders is now stored in a new type of mailbox: the *public folder mailbox*. If new public folders are created, they are stored in the hierarchy in this public folder mailbox. It is possible to create multiple hierarchies in an Exchange 2013 environment, but there's only one primary or master public folder mailbox (also referred to as the *primary Hierarchy mailbox*). The public folder mailbox is stored in a normal mailbox database, which can be identified during creation of the public folder database. For redundancy, this mailbox database can be located in a database availability group, but it is important to note that there's only one writeable copy of the public folder mailbox.

Once the hierarchy mailbox is created, the public folders can be created and permissions can be assigned to these new public folders.

Creating a Public Folder Mailbox

Initially, nothing is configured regarding public folders so the first step is to establish the public folder settings on the organizational level in Exchange 2013, and then create a new hierarchy located in a public folder mailbox. By default, the sizing quotas for public folders are set to unlimited, and the deleted items retention and moved item retention are set to 14 days. Organizational settings can be set only using the EMS, so to change these settings and reflect your company's standards, open the EMS and enter a command similar to this:

```
Set-OrganizationConfig -DefaultPublicFolderIssueWarningQuota 1.9GB
-DefaultPublicFolderProhibitPostQuota 2.3GB -DefaultPublicFolderMaxItemSize 200MB
-DefaultPublicFolderDeletedItemRetention 30.00:00:00 -DefaultPublicFolderMovedItemRetention
30.00:00:00
```

The public folder mailbox can be created using the EAC or the EMS. To create one using the EAC, follow these steps:

1. Log on to the Exchange 2013 server and open the EAC. In the left-hand menu, navigate to Public Folders and in the top-level menu, select the Public Folder Mailboxes tab.

2. Click on the + symbol to start the New Public Folder Mailbox wizard.

3. Enter a name for the public folder mailbox and, if needed, select an organizational unit where the corresponding user object will be stored and a mailbox database where the public folder mailbox will be stored (see Figure 5-13). Both are optional. (If no organizational unit is selected, the corresponding user will be created in the CN = Users container in Active Directory. If no mailbox database is selected, a mailbox database will be automatically selected by Exchange based on the available resources.)

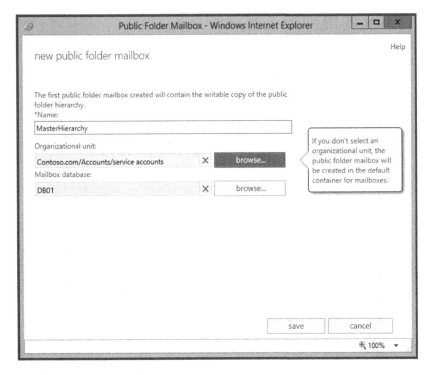

Figure 5-13. *Creating a new public folder mailbox using the EAC*

It is also possible to create the public folder database using the EMS; just use the following command:

```
New-Mailbox -PublicFolder -Name MasterHierarchy -OrganizationalUnit
"contoso.com/accounts/service accounts" -Database DB01
```

Creating Public Folders

After the public folder database is created, the "normal" public folders can be created. For example, suppose a root folder called CONTOSO needs to be created, and you also need multiple subpublic folders called HR, Marketing, Sales, and Support; the corresponding security groups also need to have the permissions assigned.

1. In the EAC, click on Public Folders in the left-hand menu and select the Public Folders tab. Click on the + symbol to start the New Public Folder wizard. Enter the name "Contoso" to create the root folder. Note that the path shows "\" to indicate that it is the root location of the public folders. Click Save to store the public folder.

2. The Contoso public folder now appears in the public folder list in the EAC (see Figure 5-14). To create the HR subfolder in the Contoso root folder, click on the Contoso folder to open it.

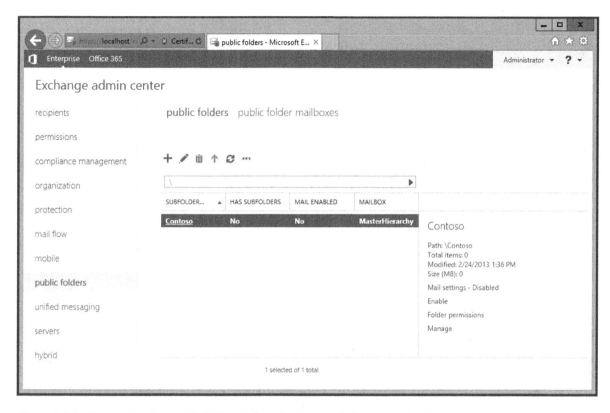

Figure 5-14. *The new Contoso public folder; click on the Contoso link to open it*

3. Once the folder is open, click on the + symbol again to restart the New Public Folder wizard. Enter the name "HR" and notice that the path now shows "\Contoso". Click Save to continue.

4. To grant permissions to the mail-enabled security group called "HR Staff," select the public folder that was just created and select Manage under the Folder Permissions in the right side pane to open the Public Folder Permissions window. Click the + symbol to start the Permissions wizard. (Don't let the system fool you with the *User selection box.) It is also possible to select mail-enabled security groups here. Use the Browse button to select the HR Staff security group. In the permissions-level drop-down box, select the appropriate permissions that need to be assigned. Click Save to continue.

5. To mail-enable a public folder so that users, both internal and external, can send email messages to these public folders, select the public folder and click Enable under Mail Settings. A warning message appears: "Are you sure you want to enable email for the selected public folders?" Click Yes to continue.

6. When the public folder is mail-enabled, click the little pencil icon to open the public folder properties. In the left-hand menu, select Email Address, and in the results pane, you'll see the public folder's email address (in the example, HR@contoso.com), as shown in Figure 5-15.

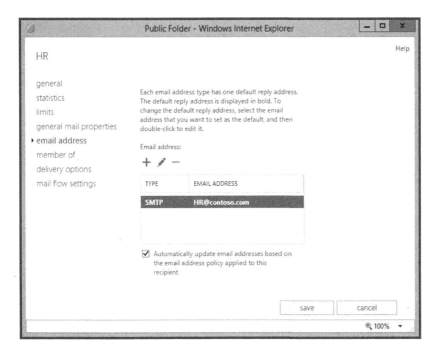

Figure 5-15. *The email address of the HR public folder*

7. Repeat the previous steps for the public subfolders Marketing, Sales, and Support; and grant the Marketing Staff, the Sales Staff, and the Support Staff security groups the appropriate permissions.

It should not be a surprise to learn that it is also possible to create new public folders in the EMS, including assigning permissions and mail-enabling them. Open the EMS and enter the following commands:

```
New-PublicFolder -Name Contoso -Path \ -Mailbox MasterHierarchy
New-PublicFolder -Name Marketing -Path \Contoso
Enable-MailPublicFolder -Identity \Contoso\Marketing
Add-PublicFolderClientPermission -Identity \Contoso\Marketing -User Marketing -AccessRights
PublishingEditor
```

Database Availability Group

In Exchange Server 2003 and earlier, it was possible to use Windows Clustering to create some sort of high availability in Exchange Server. On the underlying Windows operating system, a failover cluster was created that consisted of two or more physcial servers called *cluster nodes*. These nodes used shared storage—that is, storage that could be used by only one of the nodes at a time. Exchange Server was installed as a *virtual server* on this cluster. When one cluster node failed, another cluster node in the cluster could take over the Exchange virtual server. While this concept works fine for server redundancy, there's still a single point of failure: the mailbox database.

For Exchange Server 2007, Microsoft improved the cluster technology, which led to the concept of Cluster Continuous Replication (CCR), whereby a cluster is combined with two copies of a mailbox database. Each cluster node holds one copy of the mailbox database, and if one server fails, the other cluster node takes over the Exchange virtual server, including the other copy of the mailbox database.

To lower the complexity, and to minimize the downtime in case of a server failure, the CCR technology evolved into the database availability group (DAG) in Exchange Server 2010, a technology that's also available in Exchange 2013. A DAG is a logical grouping of a set of Exchange 2013 Mailbox servers that can hold copies of each other's mailbox databases. So, when there are six Mailbox servers in a DAG, mailbox database MBX01 can be active on the first server in the DAG, but it will have a copy on the fourth and sixth servers in the DAG. When the first server in the DAG fails, the mailbox database copy on the fourth server becomes active and continues servicing the user requests with minimal downtime for the user.

Under the hood, a DAG is using components of Windows Failover Clustering, and as such we have to discuss some of these components in more detail.

Cluster Nodes and the File Share Witness

A DAG usually consists of at least two Exchange 2013 Mailbox servers. It is possible to have a DAG with only one Exchange 2013 Mailbox server, but in this case there's no redundancy, of course. Another server is involved in a DAG as well, and this is the witness server.

By way of explanation, the DAG uses some Windows Failover Clustering software. From an Exchange Server point of view, this is fully transparent so there's no need to start worrying about clusters, and there's no need to start managing the DAG with the Failover Cluster Manager. All management of the DAG is performed using the EAC or the EMS. In fact, I strongly recommend *not* using the Windows Failover Cluster Management tool.

The witness server and the file share witness (the latter which is a shared directory on the witness server) are used only when there is an even number of Mailbox servers in the DAG. Furthermore, the witness server stores no mailbox information; it has only a cluster quorum role.

The following are the prerequisites for the witness server:

- The witness server cannot be a member of the DAG.

- The witness server must be in the same Active Directory forest as the DAG.

- The witness server must be running Windows Server 2003 or later.

- A single server can server as a witness for multiple DAGs, but each DAG has its own witness directory.

The witness server plays an important role when problems arise in the DAG—for example, when an Exchange 2013 Mailbox server is not available anymore. The underlying principle is based on a $N/2+1$ number of servers in the DAG. This means that for a DAG to stay alive when disaster strikes, at least half of the number of Mailbox servers plus 1 need to be up and running.

So, if you have a six-node DAG, the DAG can survive the loss of two Exchange 2013 Mailbox servers (6/2 +1). The fileshare witness, however, is an additional server or vote, in this process as well. Again, if there are six Exchange 2013 Mailbox servers in the DAG and three servers fail, the file share witness is the +1 server or vote, and the DAG will survive with four members: three Mailbox servers plus the additional file share witness.

Microsoft recommends you use an Exchange server as a file share witness, which of course cannot be an Exchange 2010 Mailbox server that is part of the DAG. The reason for this is that an Exchange server is always managed by the Exchange administrators in the organization, and the universal security group Exchange Trusted Subsystem has control over all Exchange servers in Active Directory.

When you're using a multi-role setup, which is the Exchange 2013 Client Access server and Mailbox server on the same box, and these servers are DAG members, there's no additional Exchange server that can assume the file share witness role. In this case it is also possible to use another Windows server as the file share witness. The only prerequisite is that the Exchange Trusted Subsystem have full control over the Windows server, so the Exchange Trusted Subsystem needs to be a member of the local administrators security group of the Windows server. As domain controllers do not have local groups, it would be necessary to add the Exchange Trusted Subsystem to the Domain Administrators security group. However, this imposes a security risk and it is therefore not recommended.

There's no reason to configure the file share witness in a high-availability configuration such as on a file cluster. Exchange Server periodically checks for the file share witness—by default, every four hours—to see if the file share witness is still alive. If it's not available at that moment, the DAG continues to run without any issues. The only time the file share witness needs to be available is during DAG changes, when an Exchange 2013 Mailbox server fails, or when Exchange 2013 Mailbox servers are added to or deleted from the DAG.

A question that pops up on a regular basis is whether or not to store the file share witness on a DFS share, especially when the company is using a server with multiple locations. This is not a good idea. Imagine this: There are two locations, A and B, and the Exchange location has three Exchange 2013 Mailbox servers configured in one DAG. The file share witness is located on a DFS share, and thus potentially available in both locations. Now, suppose the network connection between locations A and B fails for some reason. The DAG will notice the connection loss and in both locations, Exchange will try to determine the number of available Mailbox servers and attempt to contact the file share witness. In location A, this will succeed and the DAG will continue to run with four nodes (three Exchange 2013 Mailbox servers plus the file share witness). In location B, the same will happen, so Exchange will try to contact the file share witness as well. Since the file share witness is available via the DFS share in location B also, the DAG will claim the file share witness in location B and continue to run as well. And Exchange 2013 in each location will assume that the DAG members in the other location have been shut down—which of course is not the case. This is called a *split-brain scenario*, a highly undesirable situation that will lead to unpredictable results, and is a situation that is not supported at all.

■ **Note**   Using a DFS share for the file share witness is not supported and can lead to undesirable results and should therefore never be done.

Replication

A database availability group consists of a number of Exchange 2013 Mailbox servers, and these Mailbox servers have multiple mailbox databases (see Figure 5-16). There's only one copy of a mailbox database on a Mailbox server in a DAG, so the total number of copies of a specific mailbox database can never exceed the number of Mailbox servers in the DAG.

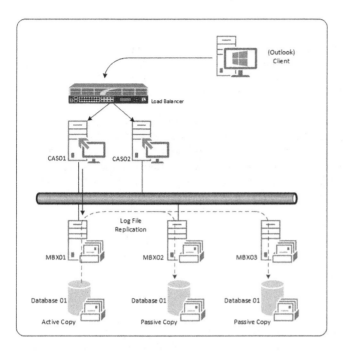

Figure 5-16. *Schematical overview of a database availability group (DAG)*

The mailbox databases can be either active or passive copies. The *active* copy is where all the mailbox data processing takes place, and it's no different from a normal Exchange 2013 Mailbox server that's not part of a DAG. Now, another Exchange 2013 Mailbox server in the DAG can host another copy of this same database; this is called a *passive* copy. The passive copy is 100 percent identical to the active copy, and it is kept up to date by a technology called *log shipping* or *log file replication*. As explained earlier in this chapter, all transactions are logged in the transaction log files. When the Mailbox server has stored all the transactions in one log file, a new log file is generated and the "old" log file is written to disk. At this moment, the log file is also copied to the second Mailbox server, where it is stored in disk. The log file is then inspected; if it's okay, the contents of the log file are replayed into the passive copy of the mailbox database. Since the log file on the passive copy is identical to the log file on the active copy, all contents are the same in both the active and the passive copies.

The process of copying is called *file mode replication,* since all log files are copied to the other Mailbox server. Another mode, which was actually introduced in Exchange 2010 SP1, is *block mode replication*. In this process the transactions are written into the active server's log buffer (before they are flushed into the active log file) and at the same time the transactions are copied to the passive server and written into that server's log buffer. When the log buffers are full, the information is flushed to the current log file and a new log file is used. Both servers do this at the same time. When the Mailbox server is running block mode replication, the replication of individual log files is suspended; only individual transactions are copied between the Mailbox servers. The advantage of block mode replication is that the server holding the passive copy of the Mailbox database is always 100 percent up to date and therefore failover times are greatly reduced.

The default process is block mode replication, but the server falls back to file mode replication when that server is too busy to cope with replicating individual transactions. If this happens, the Exchange server can replicate the individual transaction log files at its own pace, and even queue some log files when there are not enough resources.

An active mailbox database copy can have multiple passive copies on multiple Mailbox servers (remember that one server can hold only one copy of a specific mailbox database, active or passive). The active copy of a mailbox database is where all the processing takes place and all the replication, whether it is file mode or block mode, takes place from this active copy to all passive copies of the mailbox database. There's absolutely no possibility that one passive copy will replicate log files to another passive copy—never.

Seeding

Creating the passive copy of an active mailbox database is called *seeding*. In this process, the mailbox database is copied from one Mailbox server to another Mailbox server. When seeding, the complete mailbox database (the actual mailbox database.edb) is copied from the first Mailbox server to the second Mailbox server. This is not a simple NTFS file copy, though; the information store *streams* the file from one location to another—a process that's very similar to the streaming backup process that was used in Exchange server 2003 and earlier.

Here's how it works: The information store reads the contents of the mailbox database page by page, automatically checking them. If there's an error on a particular page (i.e., a corrupt page) the process stops and the error is logged. This way, Exchange prevents any copying to another location any mailbox database that has corrupt pages. Since the pages of the mailbox database are copied from one Mailbox server to another Mailbox server, the passive copy is identical to the active copy. When the entire mailbox database is copied to the other Mailbox server, the remaining log files are copied to the other Mailbox server as well.

When a new mailbox database is seeded, the process takes only a couple of minutes since there's not too much data to copy. But imagine if a mailbox database of 1TB in a normal production environment has to be seeded; this can take a considerable amount of time. And not only is the timing an important factor but also the process puts additional load on the servers. The 1TB of data needs to read and checked, copied via the network, and written to disk on the other Mailbox server.

Replication Queue and Replay Queue

In the ideal situation, log files are replicated to other Exchange 2013 Mailbox server directly after the log file is written to disk, and it is processed immediately after it is received by the other Exchange 2013 Mailbox server. Unfortunately we don't live in an ideal world, so there might be some delay anywhere in the system.

When the Exchange 2013 Mailbox servers are extremely busy, it can happen that more log files are generated than the replication process can handle and transmit. If this is the case, the log files will queue on the Mailbox server holding the active copy of the mailbox database. This queue is called the *replication queue*. Queueing always happens, and it is normally not reason for concern as long as the number of log files in the queue is low and the log files don't stay there too long. However, if there are thousands of messages waiting in line, it's time to start troubleshooting. (Troubleshooting is explained more in detail in Chapter 9.)

When the transaction log files are received by the Exchange 2013 Mailbox server holding the passive copy of the mailbox database, those transaction log files are stored in the *replay queue*. Queuing up in the replay queue always happens as well, and is generally speaking also not reason for concern when the number of transaction log files is low. There can be small spikes in the number of transaction log files in the replay, but when the number of log files is constantly increasing, there's something wrong. It can happen that the disk holding the mailbox database is generating too many read-and-write operations. There may not be enough resources to flush the queue, and so the queue will grow. As long as the system is able to flush the queue in a reasonable timeframe, and there aren't thousands and thousands of messages in the queue, you should be fine.

Lagged Copies

Regarding the replay queue, there's one exception to note: lagged copies. If you have implemented lagged copies in your DAG, and you experience a large number of log files in the replay queue, then there's nothing to worry about. Lagged copies are passive copies of a mailbox database that aren't kept up to date. This means that log files are replicated to the Exchange 2013 Mailbox server holding the lagged copy, but the log files themselves are kept in the replay queue. This lag time between replication and writing to the server can be as little as 0 second (the log file is replayed immediately) or up to 14 days. A very long lag time will have a serious impact on scalability, of course. A full 14 days' worth of log files can be a tremendous amount of data being stored in the queue; also, replaying the log files of a passive copy can take quite some time when longer timeframes are used.

A lagged copy of a mailbox database is no different from a regular copy of a mailbox database. To set a lag time of seven days to a copy of mailbox database DB02 on server AMS-EXCH01, use the following command in the EMS:

```
Set-MailboxDatabaseCopy -Identity DB02\AMS-EXCH01 -ReplayLagTime 7.0:00:00
```

When you execute this command, you'll see a warning message on the console saying that the safety net hold time is lower than the replay lag time. (The safety net and its settings are discussed later in this chapter.) Lagged copies are not a high-availability solution; rather, they are a disaster recovery solution. (Lagged copies and disaster recovery are explained in detail in Chapter 7.)

Active Manager

The Active Manager is a component of Exchange 2013 and it runs inside the Microsoft Exchange Replication Services on all Exchange 2013 Mailbox servers. The Active Manager is the component that's responsible for the high availability inside the database availability group.

There are several types of Active Manager:

- **Primary Active Manager** (PAM) The PAM is the role that decides which copy of a mailbox database is the active copy and which ones are the passive copies; as such, PAM reacts to changes in the DAG, such as DAG member failures. The DAG member that holds the PAM role is always the server that also holds the quorum resource or the default cluster group.

- **Standby Active Manager** (SAM) The SAM is responsible for providing DAG information—for example, which mailbox database is an active copy and which copies are passive copies—to other Exchange components like the Client Access service or the Hub Transport service. If the SAM detects a failure of a mailbox database, it requests a failover to the PAM. The PAM then decides which copy to activate.

- **Standalone Active Manager** The Standalone Active Manager is responsible for mounting and dismounting databases on that particular server. This Active Manager is available only on Exchange 2013 Mailbox servers that are not members of a DAG.

DAG Across (Active Directory) sites

In the previous examples, the DAG has always been installed in one Active Directory site. However, there's no such boundary in the DAG, so it is possible to create a DAG that spans multiple Active Directory sites, even in different physical locations. For instance, it is possible to extend the DAG for anticipating two potential scenarios:

- **Database Disaster Recovery** In this scenario, mailbox databases are replicated to another location exclusively for off-site storage. These databases are safe there should disaster, like a fire or flood, strike at the primary location.

- **Site Resiliency** In this scenario, the DAG is (most likely) evenly distributed across two locations (see Figure 5-17). The second location, however, also has (multiple) Exchange 2013 Client Access servers with a full-blown Internet connection. When disaster strikes and the primary site is no longer available, the second site can take over all functions.

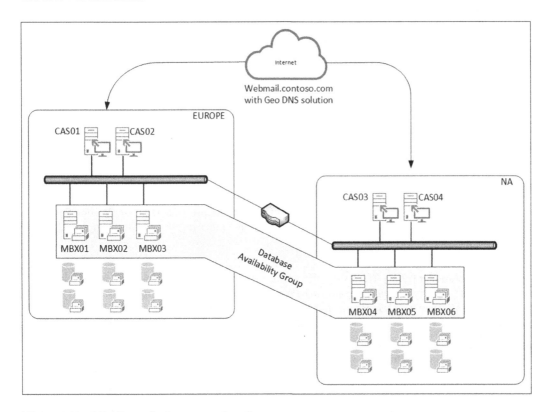

Figure 5-17. *A DAG stretched across two locations*

When using a Geo DNS solution, only one FQDN (i.e., `webmail.contoso.com`) can be used. For example, in Figure 5-17, there are two Active Directory sites, one location in Europe and another in North America (NA). When a user tries to contact `webmail.contoso.com` when traveling in Europe, he's automatically connected to the EUROPE site. When trying to access `webmail.contoso.com` in the United States, he's connected to the NA site. In either case, after authentication the client is automatically proxied to the correct Mailbox server to get the mailbox information.

By default, a site failover is not an automated process. If a datacenter failover *needs* to happen, especially when the site holding the file share witness is involved, administrative action is required. However, with Exchange 2013, it is possible to work around this limitation by placing the file share witness in a third Active Directory site.

It is possible to create an active/active scenario whereby both datacenters are active, servicing users and processing mail data. In this case, two DAGs have to be created; each DAG is active in one datacenter and its passive copies are located in the other datacenter. Note, however, that an Exchange Mailbox server can be a member of only one DAG at a time. This could mean that you need more servers in an active/active scenario, a downside of having two DAGs.

Creating a site-resilient configuration with multiple DAGs requires careful planning, plus asking yourself a lot of questions, both technical and organizational. Typical ones are:

- What level of service is required?

- What level of service is required when one datacenter fails?

- What are the objectives for recovery point and recovery time?

- How many users are on the system and which datacenters are these users connecting to?

- Is the system designed to service all users when one datacenter fails?

- How are services moved back to the original datacenter?

- Are there any resources available (like IT Staff) for these scenarios?

These are just basic planning questions to be answered before you even think about implementing a site-resilient configuration. And remember: the more requirements there are and the stricter they are, the more expensive the solution will be!

DAG Networks

A DAG uses one or more networks for client connectivity and for replication. Each DAG contains at least one network for client connectivity, which is created by default, and zero or more replication networks. In Exchange 2010, this default DAG network was called *MAPI Network*. The MAPI is no longer used in Exhange 2013 as a native client protocol, but the default DAG network is still called MapiDagNetwork.

While it is fully supported to run a DAG with only one network, Microsoft recommends using at least two networks—one for client connectivity and one for replication traffic. In Exchange 2013, the network is automatically configured by the system. If additional networks need to be configured, you set the DAG to manual configuration, then create the additional DAG networks.

When using multiple networks, it is possible to designate a network for client connectivity and the other networks for replication traffic. When multiple networks are used for replication, Exchange automatically determines which replication to use for replication traffic. When all the replication networks are offline or not available, Exchange automatically switches back to the MAPI network for the replication traffic.

Default gateways need to be considered when you are configuring multiple network interfaces in Windows Server. The only network that needs this configuring with a default gateway is the client connectivity network; all other networks should not be configured with a default gateway.

Other recommendations important for replication networks are the following:

- Disabling the DNS registration on the TCP/IP properties of the respective network interface.

- Disabling the protocol bindings, such as Client for Microsoft Networks and File and Printer Sharing for Microsoft networks, on the properties of the network interface.

- Rearrange the binding order of the network interfaces so that the client connectivity network is at the top of the connection order.

When using an iSCSI storage solution, make sure that the iSCSI network is *not used at all* for replication purposes. Remove any iSCSI network connection from the replication networks list.

■ **Note**   Although Microsoft recommends using multiple network interfaces, I see a lot of customers using only one network interface for both MAPI and replication traffic, especially with a blade infrastructure with a 10Gbe backbone. While separation of traffic is certainly true, the blade infrastructure uses only one path for network traffic, so selecting one network interface in Windows is not a big deal.

DAG Creation Process

Creating a database availability group (DAG) consists of several steps. The first step in the process is to create the cluster name object, followed by creation of the DAG itself, adding the Mailbox servers to the DAG, configuring the DAG networks, and adding the Mailbox database copies. But let's take each step in order.

Creating Cluster Name Object

As explained earlier, under the hood a DAG is using Windows Failover Clustering binaries. From a Failover Clustering perspective, the DAG is nothing more than a failover cluster, and this cluster is using a cluster name, formally known as the *cluster name object,* or CNO. When creating a DAG in Exchange 2013 that's running on Windows Server 2008 R2, the CNO is created automatically. In Windows Server 2012, however, this is no longer the case because of tightened security, and thus the CNO needs to be created manually.

The CNO is established as a new computer object in Active Directory and is assigned the appropriate permissions.To create the CNO, follow these steps.

1. Log on to the server as an administrator and open the Active Directory Users and Computers, then navigate to the organizational unit (OU) where you want to create the computer object. Right-click the OU, select New, and then select Computer. Give the computer object the name you want to use for your database availability group—for example, DAG01.

2. When the computer object is created, disable it. Right-click it again, and select Properties. Make sure that you have enabled the Advanced Features in Active Directory Users and Computers. In the properties window, select the Security tab.

3. Click the Add button and select the Exchange Trusted Subsystem Universal Security Group. Once added, check the Allow box next to Full Control to grant this group full access to the new computer object; press OK to finalize.

Creating the DAG

Now that the computer account needed for the DAG is in Active Directory, you continue with the DAG itself. To create the DAG with the EAC, use the following steps:

1. Log on to the EAC locally on the Exchange Server or remotely from another server with an administrator account. Select Servers in the left-hand menu and DAG in the top-level menu.

2. Click on the + symbol to start the New DAG wizard. Fill in the boxes for the DAG name, the witness server, and the witness directory, and enter an IP address for the DAG (see Figure 5-18). When finished, click Save to store all the information in Active Directory.

Figure 5-18. *Creating the new DAG*

Creating the DAG is simple—it's only an entry written in the configuration partition of Active Directory. If you want to check it, you can use ADSIEdit and navigate to

CN=DAG01, CN=Database Availability Groups, CN=Exchange Administrative Group (FYDIBOHF23SPDLT), CN=Administrative Groups, CN=<<organization name>> CN=Microsoft Exchange, CN=Services, CN=Configuration, DC=Contoso, DC=com.

Of course, the DAG that's visible in the EAC shows this object in Active Directory.

■ **Note** Microsoft recommends that the file share witness best be another Exchange server. This Exchange server cannot be a DAG member; however, this is not always possible and another server must be used as a file share witness. In this example, a fileserver called AMS-FS01 is used. Since Exchange Server cannot control a non-Exchange Server, the Active Directory's security group Exchange-trusted subsystem should be add to the local administrator's security group on the file share witness server.

Adding Mailbox Servers

Once the DAG exists, the Mailbox servers can be added to it, which is a straightforward process, as follows:

1. The DAG shows up in the EAC. Select it, and click on the little cogwheel in the taskbar. If you hover your mouse on it, it will show "Manage DAG Membership," which is the wizard.

2. In the wizard, click the + symbol and select the first Exchange 2013 Mailbox server that needs to be added to the DAG. Click the Add button and click OK.

3. Click Save to store the information and to have the Mailbox server added to the DAG. The wizard will continue checking for all prerequisites and installing the Windows Failover Clustering components on the Mailbox server (see Figure 5-19).

Figure 5-19. *Installing the Windows Failover Clustering binaries*

4. When the first server is joined to the DAG, the second member can be added as well. To do this, repeat steps 4 and 5.

At this point, a DAG is created with two members using a third server; in this example, a Windows fileserver is a witness server.

Configuring DAG Networks

In our example, the DAG is now configured with two Mailbox servers; by default, only one DAG network is configured, the default MapiDagNetwork. You can easily see this in the EAC, in the lower right part of the DAG view.

To add an additional DAG network (assuming that the servers have multiple network interfaces of course), the DAG itself should be set to manual configuration, as mentioned earlier. This can only be done using the EMS with the following command:

```
Set-DatabaseAvailabilityGroup -Identity DAG01 -ManualDagNetworkConfiguration $true
```

1. Click the server icon with the little + symbol to start the New DAG Network wizard.

2. Enter a name for the new network, like `Contoso Replication Network`, and enter a description when needed. In the subnets part, click the + symbol to add a new subnet that corresponds with the additional network in the server. It should be formatted like `192.168.0.0/24` (see Figure 5-20). Click Save to continue.

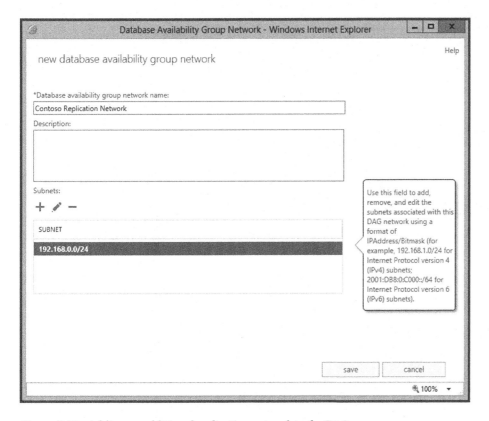

***Figure 5-20.** Adding an additional replication network to the DAG*

3. The DAG network that was just created appears in the EAC, in the lower right-hand corner of the DAG view. To disable replication via the normal MAPI network, click on the Disable Replication instruction just under `MapDagNetwork`. On the Warning page, if you're sure you want to do this, click OK to continue.

4. When you click the View Details option of a DAG network, you can see network details such as the subnet, but you'll also see the attached network interfaces—that is, the IP addresses of both Mailbox servers.

Adding Mailbox Database Copies

Now that the DAG is fully up and running, it's time for the last step: making additional copies of the mailbox databases. Initially there's only one copy of the mailbox database, but you can create redundancy when you add multiple copies on other Mailbox servers in the DAG. Here's how to do that:

1. Navigate to Servers in the left-hand menu and then to Databases in the top menu. Select a mailbox database and click on the three dots in the top menu; select Add Database Copy.

2. In the window that pops up, use the Browse button to select a Mailbox server that will host the additional copy, and enter an activation preference number. A list of servers already hosting a copy of this particular mailbox database is shown in the bottom (see Figure 5-21). Click Save to continue, and in the confirmation window, click Close to finish the wizard.

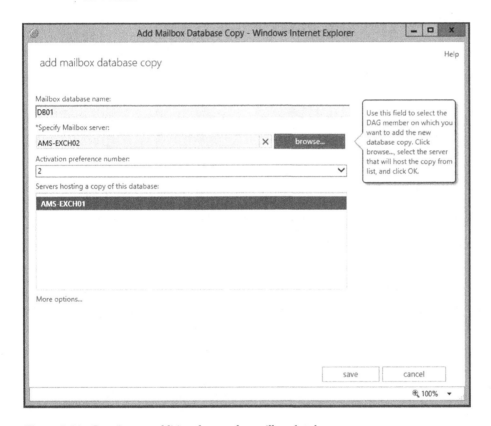

Figure 5-21. *Creating an additional copy of a mailbox database*

Repeat these steps for any other mailbox databases for which you want to have multiple copies. In the EAC, when you navigate to databases, you'll see the mailbox databases and the servers that hold the additional copies. If you click on a mailbox database, you'll see more information shown on the right-hand side. If you click on View Details under database copies, you'll see more details regarding the copy and its replication (see Figure 5-22).

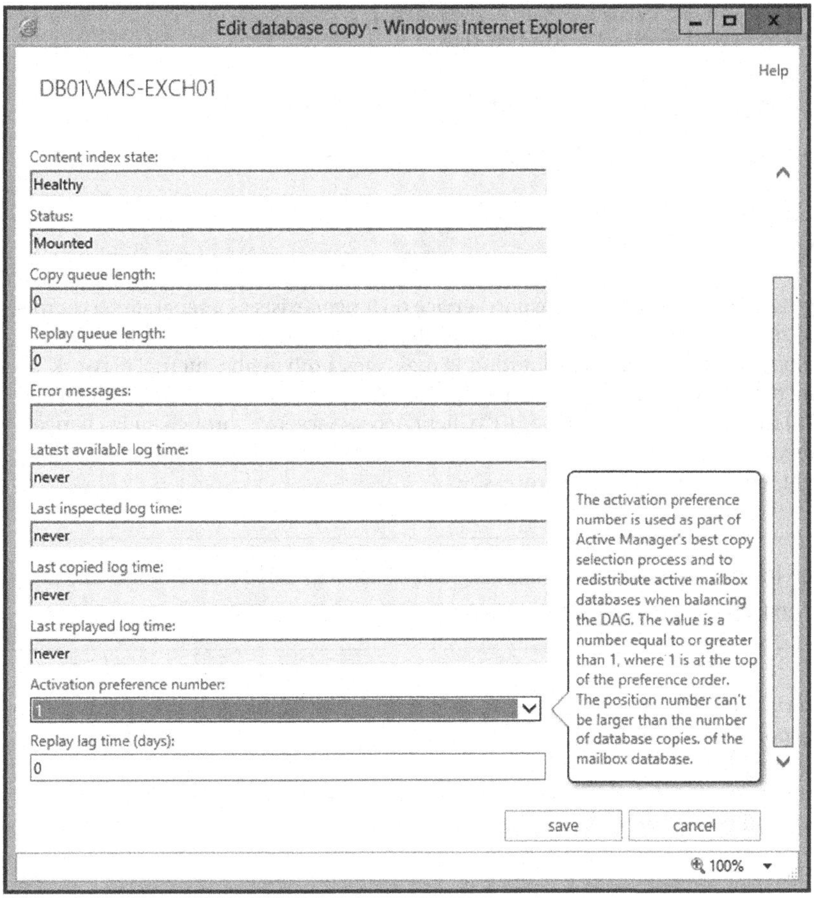

Figure 5-22. *Details regarding the mailbox database copies*

Needless to say, the creation of the DAG, adding Mailbox servers, and creating additional mailbox database copies can be done using the EMS as well. Open the EMS and enter the following commands to achieve the same results:

```
New-DatabaseAvailabilityGroup -Name DAG01 -WitnessServer AMS-FS01.contoso.com -WitnessDirectory
C:\DAG01\DAG01_FSW -DatabaseAvailabilityGroupIPAddresses 192.168.0.187

Add-DatabaseAvailabilityGroupServer -Identity DAG01 -MailboxServer AMS-EXCH01

Add-DatabaseAvailabilityGroupServer -Identity DAG01 -MailboxServer AMS-EXCH02

Set-DatabaseAvailabilityGroup -Identity DAG01 -ManualDagNetworkConfiguration $true

New-DatabaseAvailabilityGroupNetwork -DatabaseAvailabilityGroup DAG01
-Name "Contoso Replication Network" -Subnets 10.10.10.0/24 -ReplicationEnabled:$true
```

```
Get-DatabaseAvailabilityGroupNetwork -Identity DAG01\MapiDagNetwork |
Set-DatabaseAvailabilityGroupNetwork -ReplicationEnabled:$false

Add-MailboxDatabaseCopy -Identity DB01 -MailboxServer AMS-EXCH02 -ActivationPreference 2

Add-MailboxDatabaseCopy -Identity DB02 -MailboxServer AMS-EXCH01 -ActivationPreference 2
```

The Transport Service

One of the major changes in Exchange 2013 is that the Hub Transport service no longer exists as a separate server role, as it did in Exchange Servers 2007 and 2010. It is now integrated into the Exchange 2013 Mailbox server role. Thus the Hub Transport service on the Mailbox server is responsible for routing messages, both on the internal network between various Exchange servers and to the Internet. Outbound messages to the Internet can be routed through the Front End Transport service (FETS) running on the Exchange 2013 Client Access server, or through an Exchange Server 2007 or 2010 Edge Transport server. Both versions of the Edge Transport server can be synchronized with the Exchange 2013 Mailbox server throught the edge subscribtion process.

■ **Note**   A native Exchange 2013 Edge Transport server was not available when Exchange 2013 was released, and at the time of this writing it is unknown if and when that server will be released.

Inbound messages can be routed via the Exchange 2013 Client Access server or the Exchange Server 2007 or 2010 Edge Transport server. The Edge Transport server can perform default out-of-the-box anti-spam functions such as connection filtering, IP allow list, recipient filtering, or sender ID filtering.

Exchange 2013 does have some anti-spam features, but they are pretty limited. Exchange 2013 also comes with a default anti-malware engine, but this is limited as well.

The Transport Pipeline

The complete, end-to-end mail delivery process, from accepting external SMTP messages on the Exchange 2013 Client Access server to delivering the actual message to the mailbox, is called the *transport pipeline* (see Figure 5-23 for a graphic view of the pipeline). The transport pipeline consists of several individual components:

- **Front End Transport service** (FETS) FETS is running on the Exchange 2013 Client Access server and is responsible for accepting SMTP messages from external SMTP hosts. FETS can also be configured as a front-end proxy on send connectors to proxy all messages through the Exchange 2013 Client Access servers.

- **Transport Service** The Transport service runs on the Exchange 2013 Mailbox server and is responsible for processing all inbound and outbound SMTP messages. It receives messages on the receive connector from the FETS, from Transport service running on other Exchange 2013 Mailbox server, or the Exchange Server 2007 or Exchange Server 2010 Hub Transport servers. When the messages are received, they are queued in the submission queue.

The submission queue also receives messages from the pickup directory and from the replay directory. When messages are properly formatted (in an .EML format), you can drop them into the pickup directory and they will be automatically processed.

From the submission queue, the messages are sent to the categorizer. This is the process whereby the Transport service determines whether the message has to be delivered locally or remotely, whether it is on an internal Exchange server or an external one on the Internet. When categorized, the messages are delivered to a send connector. It is important to note that the Transport service never communicates directly with the mailbox databases.

- **Mailbox Transport Service** The Mailbox Transport service is also running on the Exchange 2013 Mailbox server and consists of two parts:

  - *Mailbox Transport Submission Service* Responsible for picking up messages from a user's drafts folder. In earlier versions of Exchange Server, this used to be the user's outbox, but that no longer exists in Exchange 2013. Instead, RPC (Remote Procedure Call) is used to communicate with the information store to pick up messages and then the SMTP is used to deliver messages to the local Transport service or to the Transport service running on other Exchange 2013 Mailbox servers in the organization.

  - *Mailbox Transport Delivery Service* Responsible for receiving messages from the Transport service and delivering those messages to the user's inbox. Messages are accepted from the local Transport service or from the Transport service running on other Exchange 2013 Mailbox servers running in the organization. Then the RCP is used to communicate with the information store to deliver the messages to the inbox and the SMTP is used to communicate with the Exchange 2013 Transport service.

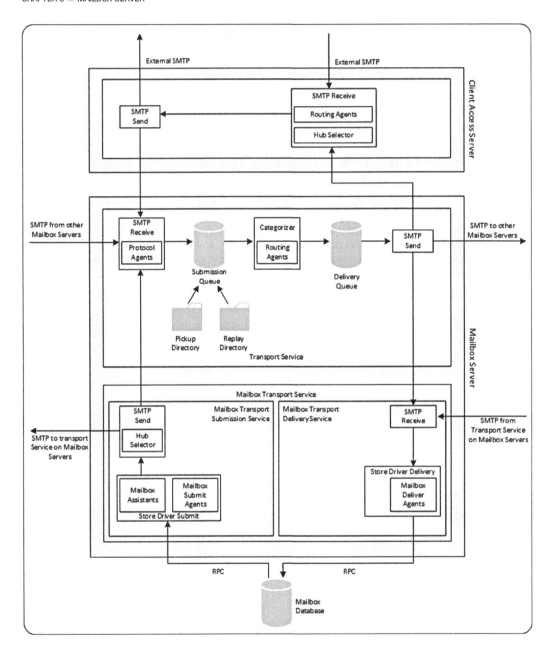

Figure 5-23. *The transport pipeline in Exchange 2013*

The Transport service running on an Exchange 2013 Mailbox server can work with other Exchange 2010 Mailbox server (naturally), but also with the Exchange 2007 and 2010 Hub Transport servers. The Mailbox Transport service only works with the Transport service running on the Exchange 2013 Mailbox server in the same Active Directory site.

The transport pipeline is the *complete* Transport service, on both the Exchange 2013 Mailbox server and the Client Access server. Regarding the transport pipeline, there are topics to address, such as the routing destinations, delivery groups, queues and how to manage them, and some redundancy features like shadow redundancy and Safety Net.

Routing Destinations

When a message arrives at the Hub Transport service on an Exchange 2013 Mailbox server, it has to be categorized—that is, the recipient or recipients need to be determined. Once Exchange 2013 knows the list of recipients, the server knows where to route the message.

The destination for a message is called the *routing destination*. Routing destinations can be:

- A mailbox database containing a mailbox or a public folder.

- A connector responsible for sending a message to another Active Directory site with Exchange server or to an external SMTP server.

- A distribution group expansion server, or an Exchange server that's responsible for extracting recipients from a distribution group if the message is destined for a distribution group.

Delivery Groups

The concept of delivery groups was created in Exchange 2013. A *delivery group* is a collection of Exchange 2013 Mailbox servers (holding the Hub Transport service) or a collection of Exchange 2010 Hub Transport servers. These servers are responsible for delivering SMTP messages within this group of servers. The following delivery groups can be identified in Exchange 2013:

- **Routable DAG** These are all the Exchange 2013 Mailbox servers that are members of a DAG. The mailbox databases in this DAG are the routing destinations of the delivery group. A message can be delivered to one particular Exchange 2013 Mailbox server in a DAG, and this Mailbox server is responsible for routing the message to the Exchange 2013 Mailbox server that holds the active copy of the mailbox database in the DAG. Since the DAG can span multiple Active Directory sites, the routing boundary for the routable DAG is the DAG itself, not the Active Directory site.

- **Mailbox Delivery Group** This is a collection of Exchange 2010 or Exchange 2013 Mailbox servers in one Active Directory site that is *not* a member of a DAG. In a mailbox delivery group, the routing boundary is the Active Directory site itself. Mailboxes located on Exchange 2013 mailbox databases are processed by the Hub Transport service running on the Exchange 2013 Mailbox servers in that Active Directory site. Mailboxes located on Exchange 2010 mailbox databases are processed by the Hub Transport servers in that Active Directory site.

- **Connector Source Server** This is a collection of Exchange 2010 Hub Transport or Exchange 2013 Mailbox servers that act as the source server for a particular send connector. These are only the source servers of a particular send connector; Exchange servers that are not defined as source servers of the send connector, but that are in the same Active Directory site, are *not* part of this delivery group.

- **Active Directory Site** This is an Active Directory site that's not the final Active Directory site—that is, the message is in transit through this particular Active Directory site. For example, it can be a hub site or a connecting Active Directory site for an Exchange 2007 or 2010 Edge Transport server. An Exchange 2013 Mailbox server cannot contact an Exchange 2010 Edge Transport server that has an Edge subscription to an Exchange 2013 Mailbox server in another site, so the message has to pass through this Active Directory site in order to be relayed via the Exchange 2010 Edge Transport server.

- **Server List** This is one or more Exchange 2013 Mailbox servers or Exchange 2010 Hub Transport servers that are configured as distribution group expansion servers.

Queues

Generally speaking, in Exchange Server, a queue is a destination for a message as well as a temporary storage location on the Exchange server. For every destination there's a queue, so there are queues for other submissions, for message delivery to the mailbox, for routing to other Exchange servers in the organization, or for routing to an external destination.

■ **Note**   Queues are a Transport service feature and thus they exist on Exchange 2013 Mailbox server, but also on Exchange 2007 and 2010 Hub Transport service, as well as on Exchange 2007 and2010 Edge Transport service.

When messages arrive at the Transport service they are immediately stored on the local disk of the Exchange server. The storage technology used is the Extensible Storage Engine (ESE), which is the same engine as used for the mailbox databases. The mailqueue database and its accompanying log files and checkpoint file can be found on C:\Program Files\Microsoft\Exchange Server\V15\TransportRoles\data\Queue (see Figure 5-24). The ESE database has circular logging enabled. This means that log files that are no longer needed are automatically deleted and, as such, there's no recovery method such as replay of log files.

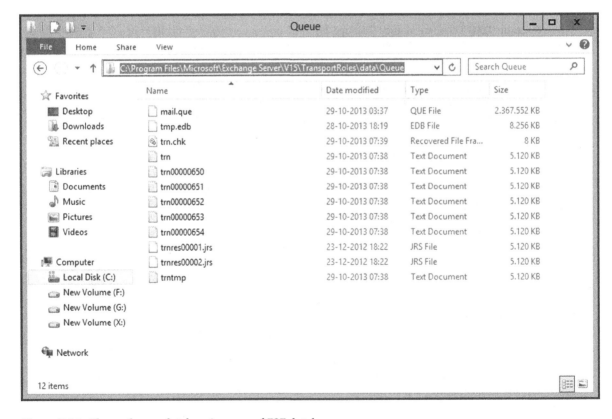

Figure 5-24. *The mailqueue database is a normal ESE database*

It is possible to change some of the configuration options of the queue database. When Exchange Server 2013 is installed in the default location, all configuration settings are stored in the EdgeTransport.exe.config file that can be found in C:\Program Files\Microsoft\Exchange Server\V15\bin. Most settings in this file can be left at their default values, but it is possible to change the location of all mailqueue-related files and directories to another disk. The advantage of doing this is that if there's unexpected growth in these files, that won't affect the normal system and boot drives. If these fill up there's always the possibility that the services running on this particular server will gradually stop working; worse, the entire server might stop working. Needless to say, this is an undesirable situation for Exchange Server.

If you open the EdgeTransport.Config.Exe file and browse through the file, you'll see the following keys:

QueueDatabasePath
QueueDatabaseLoggingPath
IPFilterDatabasePath
IPFilterDatabaseLoggingPath
TemporaryStoragePath

By default, these keys point to the location %ExchangeInstallPath%TransportRoles\data\, but by changing the values to, for example, D:\data\<variable>, another disk can be used.

Shadow Redundancy

There's one type of queue that always raises questions. At first look, there are always messages in this queue and they don't seem to disappear that quickly. *Shadow queues*, also referred to as *shadow redundancy*, are there for message redundancy: messages are stored in shadow queues until the next stop in the message path that moves toward delivering the message successfully and reporting the results. Only then is the message deleted from the shadow queue.

Imagine an Exchange 2013 Mailbox server in New York that's sending messages to the Internet, but has no internet connection of its own. There are also two Exchange 2013 Mailbox servers in Amsterdam, and Amsterdam has its own Internet connection. A network connection exists between the two locations.

1. The Exchange 2013 Mailbox server in New York sends an SMTP message to Exchange 2013 Mailbox server A in Amsterdam, AMS-EXCH02. As soon as the message is delivered in Amsterdam, it is stored in the shadow queue on the server in New York.

2. Exchange 2013 Mailbox server A in Amsterdam sends the message to server B in Amsterdam, AMS-EXCH01. As soon as the message is accepted, it is stored in the shadow queue on server A.

3. Server A knows the message was successfully delivered and reports back to the server in New York. At this moment the message can safely be deleted from the New York shadow queue since there still is a backup message, but now it's on server A.

4. Server B sends the message to the Edge Transport server in the perimeter network, and when delivered, server B reports back to server A, who can now delete the message from its shadow queue.

Sending a message from the Exchange server to the Internet is difficult, of course, since not all SMTP servers on the Internet support shadow queues. If not supported, the messages are automatically deleted from the sender's shadow queue after a period of time.

Shadow queue redundancy is built into Exchange 2013 when messages are in transit. If one server fails, for whatever reason, and the server is no longer available, the previous Exchange server in the message path can retry delivering the message via a different available path.

■ **Note**   The shadow queue function was available in Exchange Server 2010 as well.

Don't confuse the shadow queues with Exchange 2010's transport dumpster. While the transport dumpster also offers redundancy for SMTP messages, its primary purpose is to offer redundancy for messages that are delivered to mailboxes that are in a DAG. The transport dumpster evolved into Safety Net, which is explained a little later in this chapter.

Managing Queues

Most of Exchange 2013 Mailbox server's queues exist for only a limited time. When the Transport server cannot deliver a message, the message stays in the queue until the service can successfully deliver the message (it keeps trying), or until the message expires; the default message expiration time is two days.

These queues can be managed by using the Queue Viewer, which is a graphic tool, or by using the EMS. The Queue Viewer can be found in the toolbox, an MMC snap-in that's automatically installed during the installation of Exchange Server. Caution: The toolbox in Exchange 2013 has the same icon as the EMC in Exchange Server 2010, so don't let this fool you. Open the Exchange toolbox and select Queue Viewer under mail flow tools. The Queue Viewer shows the queues on the server currently operating, but if you select Connect to Server in the Actions pane, you can use it to view information on other Exchange 2013 Mailbox servers (see Figure 5-25).

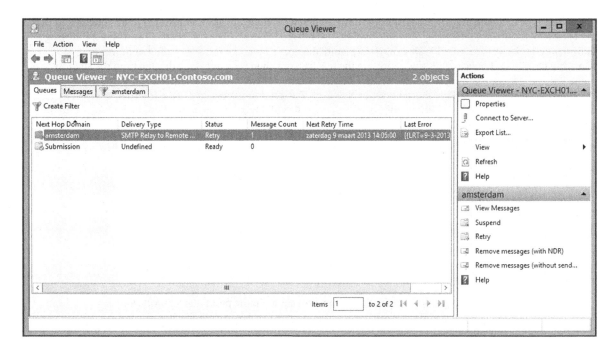

Figure 5-25. *A message is stuck in the queue on the New York server, destined for the Amsterdam server*

The Queue Viewer is an incredibly valuable tool for troubleshooting purposes. It shows messages that are in a queue, of course, but if you open the message, it also shows the reason why the messages cannot be delivered. The tool also gives you the option of suspending a queue or removing messages from a queue, either with or without generating a nondelivery report (NDR).

It is also possible to manage the queues using the EMS. This method is more complex, but it offers many more granular options. The basic command to get queue information is the Get-Queue cmdlet. The Get-Queue cmdlet will show the queues on the server where the cmdlet is executed (see Figure 5-26). Using the identity of the queue, you can get more information by using the Get-Queue -Identity NYC-EXCH01\6 cmdlet, for example. The actual error is not shown when using this cmdlet, but you can use the Get-Queue -Identity NYC-EXCH01\6 | FL cmdlet for all information regarding the queue, or the Get-Queue -Identity NYC-EXCH01\6 | select LastError to show the actual error message the transport service is experiencing.

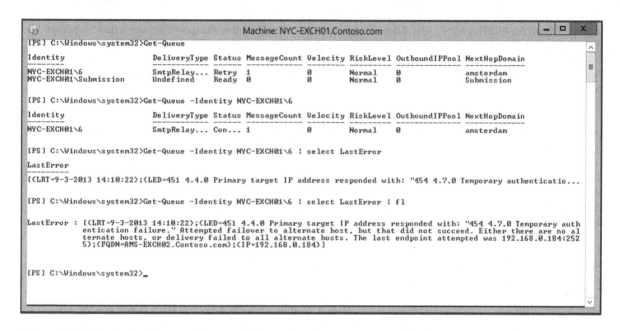

Figure 5-26. *Use the Get-Queue cmdlet to get information about messages stuck in the queue*

The Get-Queue cmdlet will only show results from the Exchange server where the cmdlet is executed. You can also use the Get-TransportService cmdlet to get a list of all Transport services running on all Exchange 2013 Mailbox servers, and pipe this output into the Get-Queue cmdlet: Get-TransportService | Get-Queue. This will show all queues on all Transport services in the organization.

■ **Note**   In the example in Figure 5-26, the message is not delivered owing to authentication problems. All servers are running in a Hyper-V environment, and you have to be careful with time synchronization complications. In the example, it turned out that some servers had major time differences because they were synchronizing against their Hyper-V host instead of against the PDC emulator. This situation sometimes also results in problems with the EMS (WinRM won't function correctly) or with the Server Manager.

When a message cannot be delivered, it will stay in the queue and it can stay here for up to two days, which is the default wait time. When this happens, there's no need for any concern; Exchange will keep trying to deliver the message. Also, the number of messages in a queue can vary over time; for example, you could have 20 to 30 messages in a queue for an Internet send connector. But the messages have to be delivered after some time, of course. If there's a steady increase in the number of messages in a queue, or if many queues are created and the messages get stuck in there, then it's time to dig deeper into the cause of the excessive queueing. (Chapter 6 will cover this more in detail.)

Safety Net

Safety Net is a new redundancy feature in Exchange 2013 for the Transport service and is the successor of the transport dumpster in Exchange Server 2007 and 2010. The transport dumpster was developed to provide message redundancy when these message were delivered to the mailbox. These messages were kept on the Hub Transport server, and when a database in a DAG failed for some reason and messages were not replicated to the passive copy, the missing messages were retransmitted to the passive copy. This would result in minimum data loss.

Safety Net provides the same function for Exchange 2013. As such, Safety Net stores in a queue the messages that were successfully delivered to the mailboxes. Safety Net is still associated with the Transport service, but now it stores information on the Mailbox server. The difference between Safety Net and the transport dumpster is that Safety Net does not require a DAG. It also stores copies of messages for Mailbox servers that are not DAG members.

Another major change is that Safety Net is redundant by itself; there's a primary Safety Net and a shadow Safety Net. The primary Safety Net exists on the Mailbox server where the message originates, the shadow Safety Net exists on the Mailbox server where the message is delivered. As soon as the message is delivered, it is stored in the Safety Net queue. Messages are kept in the Safety Net queue for 48 hours, which is the default length of time.

Safety Net and shadow redundancy are complementary. That is, shadow redundancy is responsible for messages in transit, while Safety Net is responsible for messages that have been delivered to mailboxes.

Messages can be resubmitted for delivery in case of: (1) activating a lagged copy of a mailbox database; or (2) after a failover of a mailbox database in a DAG. The cool thing is that Safety Net is a fully automated feature; there's no need for any manual action. All coordination is done by the Active Manager, who is also responsible for failover scenarios in the DAG.

When something untoward happens, the Active Manager requests a resubmission from Safety Net. For large organizations, these messages most likely exist on multiple Mailbox servers so (a lot of) duplicate messages can occur. Exchange 2013, however, has a mechanism that detects duplicate messages; it finds and elminates those duplicate message, preventing the recipient from receiving multiple copies. Unfortunately, resubmitted messages from Safety Net are also delivered to mail servers outside the Exchange organization. Since these servers don't have the duplicate-message-detection mechanism, external users can receive multiple identical messages.

When the primary Safety Net is not available, Active Manager tries requesting a resubmit for 12 hours. If unsuccessful after this time, Active Manager then contacts the other Mailbox servers and requests a resubmit of messages for the particular mailbox database. Either way, no messages should be lost during a failover, whether the failover is planned or not.

Edge Transport Server

As mentioned earlier, with the release of Exchange 2013 the Edge Transport server was no longer available, and it is unknown when the new Edge Transport server will be released. The good news, though, is that Exchange 2013 works perfectly well with the Exchange Server 2007 and 2010 Edge Transport servers.

The Edge Tranport server is designed for message hygiene—that is, anti-spam and anti-virus purposes. As such, the Edge Transport server is typically not a domain member but, rather, a stand-alone server installed in the company's perimeter network, as shown in Figure 5-27. This way, the Edge Transport server is the first line of defense when it comes to message security. You can have more than one Edge Transport server.

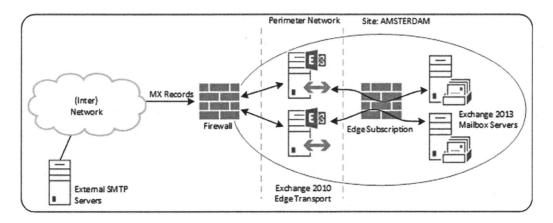

Figure 5-27. *The Edge Transport server is installed in the perimeter network*

So that the Edge Transport servers have up-to-date information from the internal network, they are synchronized with the Exchange 2013 Mailbox servers. The Exchange 2013 Mailbox servers push relevant information directly to the Edge Transport server. This is a push mechanism; the Edge Transport servers cannot pull information from the internal network, so even if they are compromised, they can never access the internal Active Directory information.

The synchronization is set up by subscribing the Edge Transport servers to the Exchange 2013 Mailbox servers. When the Exchange 2010 Edge Transport servers are fully installed and configured, a subscription file is created on each Edge Transport server, containing server-specific information. This subscription file is imported on the Exchange 2013 Mailbox server, at which point the synchronization can be started.

■ **Note**   An Edge Transport subscription file is created per Edge Transport server. So if you have four Edge Transport servers, you create and import four subscription files. Since the Exchange 2013 Mailbox servers are domain-joined servers, they can all use the Edge Transport servers, but the synchronization is Active Directory site bound.

Once the Edge Transport servers are up and running, you can create the subscriptions, as follows:

1. Log on to the Edge Transport server as a local administrator and open the EMS and enter the following command: `New-EdgeSubscription -FileName C:\Temp\Edge01.xml`.

2. A warning message is shown, basically saying the subscription file is valid for 1440 minutes (24 hours). If the subscription file is not processed within this time, a new subscription has to be created. Enter Yes to confirm the warning message and the subscription file will be created.

3. Copy the `Edge01.xml` subscription file to a directory on the local disk of the Exchange 2013 Mailbox server in the appropriate site. On the Exchange 2013 Mailbox server, open the EMS and enter the following commands:

```
New-EdgeSubscription -FileData ([byte[]]$(Get-Content -Path
"C:\Temp\edge01.xml"
-Encoding Byte -ReadCount 0)) -Site "Default-First-Site-Name"
-CreateInternetSendConnector $true
-CreateInboundSendConnector $true

Start-EdgeSynchronization
```

This will initiate the reading of the contents of the subscription file, import it, and bind it against the Active Directory site. Also, an Internet send connector and an inbound send connector are created. The second command starts the Edge synchronization process.

■ **Note**   The name resolution function on both the Edge Transport server and the Mailbox server must work correctly so that the servers can find each other on the network. The Exchange 2013 Mailbox server communicates with the Edge Transport server on TCP port 50636, so this port has to be open on the internal firewall in the outbound direction.

The easiest way to check for proper mail flow is to send a message to someone via the Internet. For example, when a user in New York called Dave sends an email for a colleague in Amsterdam to his Hotmail account, the message is sent from the New York site (NYC-EXCH01) to the Amsterdam site (AMS-EXCH01 or AMS-EXCH02); it is then sent to the Edge Transport server (smtphost.contoso.com) and the server sends the message to Hotmail. When the message is received in the Hotmail mailbox, the colleague can open it and check the message details. In this example, you can clearly follow the message path in the message header:

```
Received: from smtphost.contoso.com ([176.62.196.244]) by COLO-MC3-F29.COLO.hotmail.com with
Microsoft SMTPSVC(6.0.3790.4900);
Sun, 10 Mar 2013 06:17:21 -0700
Received: from AMS-EXCH02.Contoso.com (192.168.0.184) by smtphost.contoso.com
(192.168.0.186) with Microsoft SMTP Server (TLS) id 14.3.123.3; Sun, 10 Mar
2013 14:17:47 +0100
Received: from NYC-EXCH01.Contoso.com (192.168.10.192) by
AMS-EXCH02.Contoso.com (192.168.0.184) with Microsoft SMTP Server (TLS) id
15.0.620.23; Sun, 10 Mar 2013 14:22:39 +0100
```

When you log on to the Exchange 2010 Edge Transport server as a local administrator and open the EMC, you can check the information that's pushed from the Exchange 2013 Mailbox server. The accepted domains created on the Exchange 2013 environment, for example, are listed in the Accepted Domains tab (see Figure 5-28).

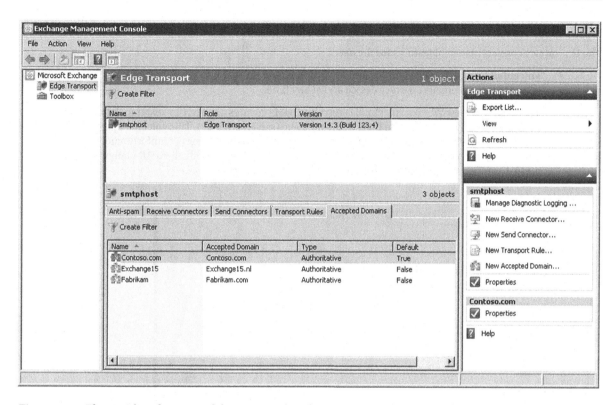

Figure 5-28. *The EMC lists the accepted domains on the Edge Transport server*

When the Send Connectors tab is selected, the Internet send connector is shown as well as the inbound send connector. (Chapter 6 will go more into detail about managing the Exchange Server 2010 Edge Transport server in combination with the Exchange 2013 Mailbox server.)

Unified Messaging

Unified messaging in Exchange Server combines voicemail features with email in one mailbox. For example, when an incoming phone call is not answered, the call can be routed to the Unified Messaging (UM) service, where a voicemail greeting is played after which the caller can leave a message. This message is recorded, converted to a standard MP3 file, and delivered to the recipient's mailbox. The user can listen to the voicemail whenever he wants, with whatever device he wants. This can be his workstation or his laptop, but also his smartphone or tablet, as long as the user has access to that mailbox and the device is capable of playing MP3 files.

Within the UM function it is not only possible to access information using a regular mail client but also, through the so-called Outlook Voice Access (OVA, sometimes also referred to as subscriber access), you can dial into the Exchange environment with a regular phone and use the keypad to navigate the various options.

UM Features

The UM service consists of several features for the users:

- **Voicemail** Complete voicemail system, tightly integrated into the user's mailbox, offering access to the voicemails on every device and at any time.

- **Voicemail Preview** When a voicemail is recorded, UM provides a speech-to-text translation, whereby the text is shown in the body of the message (see Figure 5-29). This voicemail preview is created only when there are enough resources available on the UM server; unfortunately, only a small subset of languages is supported. For an up-to-date list with all the UM languages and a download, check the Microsoft site `http://tinyurl.com/o6yhpxr`.

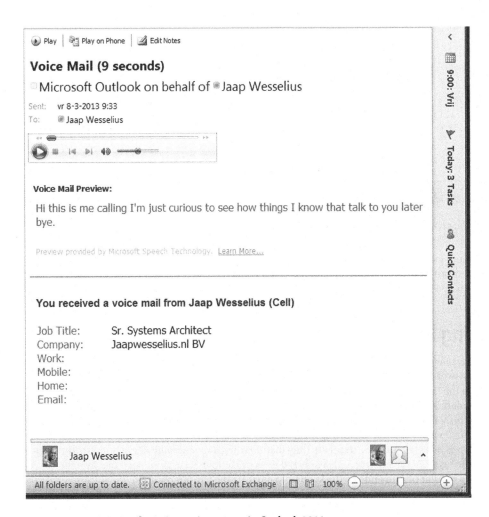

Figure 5-29. *Voicemail preview as it appears in Outlook 2010*

- **Outlook Voice Access** Use a normal phone to access the Exchange platform, not only the voicemail messages but also the entire mail platform. You can have your messages read by the system or you can change meeting requests when you're running late, and so on.

- **Play on Phone** An option that, after a voicemail is delivered, generates a new phone call to the originally called number and plays the message when the phone is answered.

- **Voicemail Form** When a voicemail is delivered to your inbox, a form is generated with the contact information (if in your Contacts folder), and there's a button for the Play on Phone option. When you click the Play on Phone button in your inbox the voicemail is sent to your phone, and you can listen it there for privacy purposes. Besides this, there's an Edit Notes feature for creating notes with the voicemail and storing this information in your inbox.

- **Call Answering** UM answers incoming calls, playing a welcome message and recording a message if left.

  You can create some rules to govern the answering of phone calls, including:

  - Leaving a voicemail message

  - Transferring to another recipient

  - Transferring to another recipient's voicemail

  - Transferring to an external phone number

- **Message Waiting Indicator** Standard for standard phone systems, the blinking "message waiting" indicator light is also available on the Exchange 2013 UM service.

- **Group Addressing** Access the Exchange service using a standard phone line and send a message (using the speech-to-text option) to a group of recipients located in your Contacts folder.

When you combine Exchange 2013 UM with a Microsoft Lync Server 2013 environment, especially when the Lync Server 2013 is equipped with a full-enterprise voice solution, you can build a consolidated voicemail system. Secured by the security model of Active Directory, it can be centrally managed, is available in multiple languages, and even has support for incoming faxes!

Part of this voicemail system is a so-called *auto attendant*, an automated system of all kinds of voice prompts. This service gives external users access to the voicemail system through a variety of commands in a customized menu.

UM Architecture

The separate UM server that was in Exchange Server 2007 and 2010 is is now part of the Exchange 2013 Mailbox server. This UM server consists of two separate functions:

- **Unified Messaging Call Router** Part of the Exchange 2013 Client Access service and responsible for receiving initial requests from the Private Branch Exchange (PBX) and for redirecting those requests to their appropriate Mailbox servers.

- **Unified Messaging Service** Part of the Exchange 2013 Mailbox server that's actually responsible for recording the messages and sending them to the mailbox service.

When an incoming call on the PBX is not answered, it is forwarded to the Exchange 2013 Client Access server. When the server receives the SIP INVITE for the incoming call, it first determines which mailbox the INVITE is for. The UM call router then redirects the INVITE to the Exchange 2013 Mailbox server that hosts the active copy of the mailbox database where the mailbox is located. The responsible Exchange 2013 Mailbox server sets up an RTP or SRTP connection with the VoIP gateway, the IP PBX, or the session border controller (SBC). The RTP or SRTP connection is used for the actual media traffic. The Exchange 2013 Client Access server doesn't do anything with media; it only accepts the incoming call and redirects the call to the Mailbox server.

■ **Note**   When multiple Exchange 2013 Client Access servers are used, a hardware load balancer (layer-4) can be employed in conjunction with UM. The VoIP gateway, the IP PBX, or the SBC should be configured to use the Exchange 2013 Client Access server or the load- balanced array of Client Access servers to point to.

As described above, when the RTP channel is set up, UM plays the welcome message; when needed, it processes the call using the call-answering rules, and the caller can leave a voicemail. The voicemail is recorded in an MP3 format and delivered to the recipient's mailbox. When possible, UM also processes the message with a speech-to-text converter, but only when enough resources are available.

When you're running Lync Server 2010 or Lync Server 2013, the architecture is a bit different. The SIP INVITE and the RTP or SRTP media channels are handled by the Lync front-end servers. From a Lync perspective, the Unified Messaging service is no different from an Exchange Server 2010 Unified Messaging server. Since the Exchange 2013 Client Access server's UM Call Router service and its Mailbox server UM service are added to the dial plan, the Exchange servers are automatically trusted. However, the Lync server still routes the call to the UM Call Router service, which redirects the call to the correct Mailbox server.

The UM services use a couple of important components that need to be configured:

- **PBX** The Private Branch Exchange (PBX) are what all internal telephones are connected to and from where all incoming phone calls are delivered by your telephone company; it routes the phone calls between telephones, and can be a traditional (legacy) phone system, but also can also be an OCS or a Lync Server system.

- **UM Dial Plan** Your existing PBX is a dial number plan consisting of each individual's unique extension number. A UM dial plan in Exchange Server 2013 contains the PBX dial plan.

- **UM IP Gateway** A device that connects your UM environment with your phone system. This can be an IP PBX (typically a single box) or a Lync Server system, or a combination of traditional PBX and separate IP gateway. In the latter scenario, the UM IP gateway is typically a hardware device.

- **UM Hunt Group** A set of extension numbers that are grouped together as a single unit. For example, the company's sales department might have a group number. When somebody dials that number, all of the telephones in this hunt group will start ringing.

Configuring UM

Unified Messaging has been around since the release of Exchange Server 2007. Up until the release of Lync Server 2010, however, there wasn't much interest in the UM service. That's changing now because of Lync Server 2010's functionality and ease of use, especially in conjunction with a SIP trunk for enterprise voice. In this scenario, the UM services are an extension of Lync functionality, offering a complete set of voicemail services. So, let's explore how to configure the UM services on the Exchange 2013 Mailbox server and the Client Access server in combination with Lync Server 2013. (For Lync Server 2010, the process is similar, so if that's what you're running, you should be able to follow this as well.)

Configuring the UM role in an environment that shares Exchange 2013 and Lync Server 2013 necessitates the following steps (assuming you have a fully functional Lync Server 2013 environment):

1. Configure the SSL certificates on the Exchange 2013 Mailbox servers and assign the UM service to the certificate.

2. Create a UM dial plan.

3. Create a UM IP gateway.

4. Configure the Lync Server.

5. Enable UM for a mailbox.

Configuring the SSL Certificates

The Lync Server 2013 front-end server and the Exchange Server 2013 UM service use Transport Layer Security (TLS) to communicate with each other. This means that a valid certificate needs to be installed on both servers. The Lync Server 2013 front-end server is already configured with a Unified Communications (UC) certifcate from the internal Certificate Authority (CA), so only the Exchange 2013 Mailbox server needs to be configured wih a valid certificate. There's no need to use a commercial third-party certificate for this; an SSL certificate from an internal Windows Active Directory PKI environment will do.

By default, the UM service and the UM Call Router service use TCP as their startup mode, so this has to be changed to TLS. This can done only by using the EMS with the following command on the Mailbox:

```
Get-UMService | Set-UMService -UMStartupMode TLS
```

And the following command on the Client Access server:

```
Set-UMCallRouterSettings -Server AMS-EXCH01 -UMStartupMode TLS
Set-UMCallRouterSettings -Server AMS-EXCH02 -UMStartupMode TLS
```

■ **Note** The Set-UMCallRouterSettings command doesn't seem to accept pipeline input, so the command has to be executed twice, once for every Exchange 2013 Client Access server.

When the startup mode of both the UM service and the UM Call Router service are changed to TLS, the certificate can be bound to the UM service. Then, after restarting both services, you can configure the UM services. If no certificate is bound to the services, they will not start.

Creating a UM Dial Plan

To create a new UM dial plan, use the EAC:

1. Log on to the EAC with an administrator account and in the left-hand menu, select Unified Messaging. In the UM dial plans section, click the + symbol to start the New UM Dial Plan page.

2. Give the new dial plan a name and enter the extension length (defaults at five characters). For Lync Server, select SIP URI for the type of dial plan; for VoIP security mode, select Secured; and for the region code, enter the digits for your country (e.g., 1 for United States, 31 Netherlands, 44 for UK, etc.), as shown in Figure 5-30.

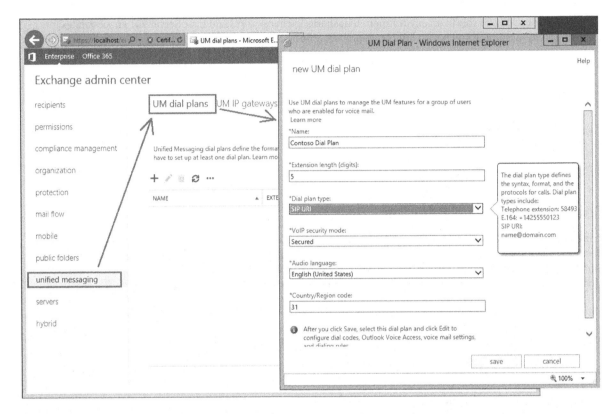

Figure 5-30. *The new UM dial plan wizard in the EAC*

3. Click Save to store the new UM dial plan.

Instead of using the EAC, it is possible to use the EMS; to do so, just enter the following command:

```
New-UMDialPlan –Name "Contoso Dial Plan" –UriType SipName –NumberOfDigitsInExtension 5
–VoIPSecurity Secured –CountryOrRegionCode 31
```

Creating the UM IP Gateway

The UM IP Gateway is responsible for traffic between the Lync Server 2013 mediation server and the Exchange 2013 Mailbox server. This UM IP Gateway is not created manually right now, but it is created by a (Microsoft-supplied) script in the "Configuring Lync Server" section later in this chapter.

UM Mailbox Policies

When a dial plan is created for the UM service, a default UM mailbox policy for this dial plan is created as well. The name for this policy is derived from the dial plan—for example, the name might be "Contoso Dial Plan Default Policy." In the window for the UM dial plans, just double-click the dial plan you created earlier and the UM mailbox policy will be shown in the dial plan properties (see Figure 5-31).

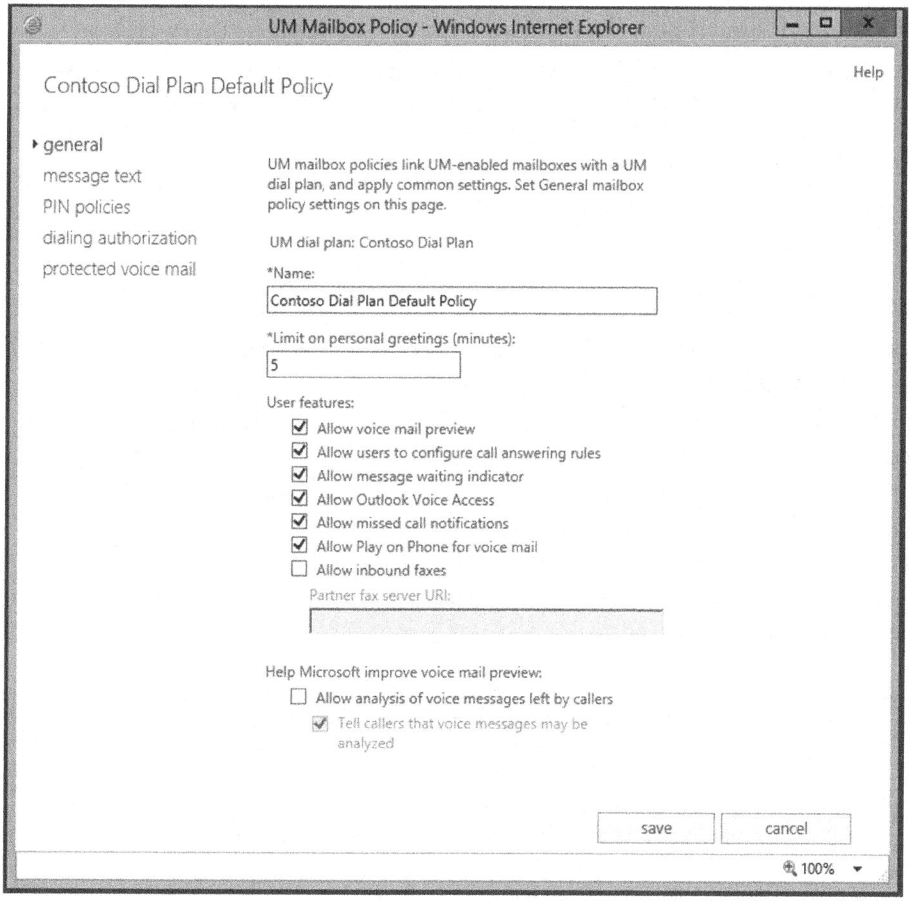

Figure 5-31. *The Contoso Dial Plan default policy*

With this UM mailbox policy, it is now possible to allow or disallow a specific feature, set PIN policies, change settings to the message text, or enable protected voice mail, for example.

Next, to assign the new dial plan to the UM services, both on the Client Access server (UM Call Router) and the Mailbox server, use an EMS window to enter the following commands:

```
Set-UMCallRouterSettings -DialPlans "Contoso Dial Plan" -Server AMS-EXCH01
Set-UMCallRouterSettings -DialPlans "Contoso Dial Plan" -Server AMS-EXCH02
Get-UMService | Set-UMService -DialPlans "Contoso Dial Plan"
```

The last step is to restart both the UM Call Router service and the UM service on the servers. On the Client Access servers, enter `Restart-Service MSExchangeUMCR`; On Mailbox servers, use: `Restart-Service MSExchangeUM`. When both roles are installed, then both commands have to be performed on the server.

Configuring Lync Server

To configure the UM service to be used with Lync Server 2013, Microsoft has a script that creates and configures all necessary components. This script is located in the Scripts directory: C:\Program Files\Microsoft\Exchange Server\V15\Scripts.

Begin by entering the following commands in the EMS:

```
CD $ExScripts
.\ExchUCUtil.ps1
```

This script does the following:

- Grants Lync Server permission to read Exchange UM Active Directory components—specifically, the SIP URI dial plan that was created in the first step.

- Creates a UM IP Gateway for each Lync Server pool that hosts users who will be enabled for Enterprise Voice.

- Creates an Exchange UM hunt group for each UM IP Gateway. The hunt group pilot identifier will be the name of the dial plan associated with the corresponding UM IP Gateway. The hunt group must specify the UM SIP dial plan used with the UM IP Gateway.

The output is shown in Figure 5-32. Clearly visible in the top half of the window is the creation of the UM IP Gateway, followed by the appropriate permissions.

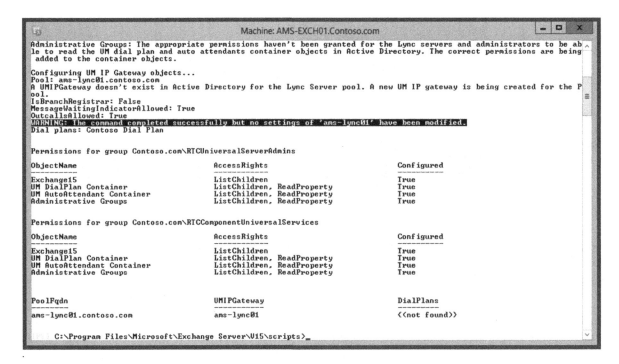

Figure 5-32. *Configuring the dial plan for use with Microsoft Lync Server 2013*

When the script has run, you'll see a new UM IP Gateway appear in the EAC (see Figure 5-33). Since this script not only creates the UM IP Gateway but also sets the necessary permissions, the UM IP Gateway was not created manually in the first step.

Figure 5-33. *The UM IP Gateway is created automatically*

The second step is to configure the Lync environment for use with Exchange 2013. Microsoft has another tool, called OcsUmUtil.exe, that can be found in C:\Program Files\Common Files\Microsoft Lync Server 2013\Support. This tool, supplied by Microsoft Lync 2013, reads the appropriate information from Active Directory regarding the dial plans and creates a new contact in Active Directory that will be used for subscriber access or for the auto attendant.

Perform these steps to configure the environment:

1. Navigate to the directory C:\Program Files\Common Files\Microsoft Lync Server 2013\Support and start the OcsUmUtil.exe utility. On the welcome screen, click Load Data to retrieve the appropriate information from Active Directory.

2. The Active Directory forest will be shown, including the SIP dial plans that are found. Click Add to create a new contact in Active Directory. It is possible to designate an organizational unit in Active Directory where the new contact will be stored. Fill in the appropriate values and click OK to store the new account in Active Directory (see Figure 5-34).

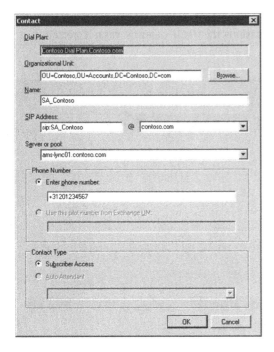

Figure 5-34. *Creating a contact in Active Directory for Lync Server 2013*

Enabling UM for a Mailbox

When Lync 2013 and Exchange 2013 UM are fully configured, it's time to UM-enable a mailbox.

1. Log on to the EAC with an administrator account. EAC automatically opens on the mailboxes page; select and open the mailbox you want to UM-enable.

2. Select the mailbox features in the left-hand navigation menu and click on Enable under the Phone and Voice Features option.

3. In the Enable UM Mailbox window, use the Browse button to select the UM mailbox policy that was automatically created during the creation of the dial plan—in our example, the Contoso Dial Plan Default Policy. Click Next to continue.

4. In the next window, enter the SIP address, like joe@contoso.com, and enter his extension number (see Figure 5-35). You can have an access PIN created automatically or can type a PIN manually. Click Finish to end the wizard.

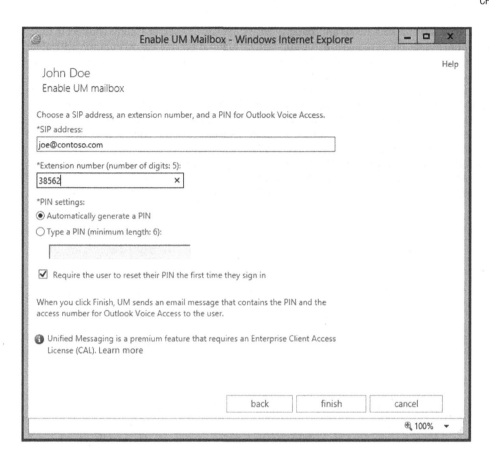

Figure 5-35. *UM-enabling John Doe from contoso.com*

John Doe's mailbox is now ready for use with Lync Server 2013 and Exchange 2013 UM. John can access his mailbox using the Lync client.

■ **Note** Unified Messaging is a feature that requires an enterprise Client Access License (eCAL).

Summary

The Exchange 2013 Mailbox server hosts almost all functions in an Exchange environment:

- **Mailbox Service** Responsible for storing all mail data in mailbox databases. This can be in mailboxes or in public folders stored in mailbox databases.

- **Transport Service** Responsible for routing SMTP messages, not only to and from the Internet but also within the Exchange 2013 Mailbox server or between various Exchange 2013 Mailbox servers.

- **Unified Messaging Service** Responsible for offering voicemail functions with mailboxes. This works great with Microsoft Lync server 2013, but also with other PBX systems.

The Exchange 2013 Mailbox server always needs an Exchange 2013 Client Access server. Clients connect to this, and the Client Access server proxies the client requests to the appropriate Mailbox servers. An exception is SIP traffic origination from the Lync server; this is redirected from the Client Access server to the appropriate Mailbox server. However, all processing takes place on the Exchange 2013 Mailbox server.

Exchange 2013 Mailbox servers can be single servers without any database redundancy, or they can be installed in a database availability group, or DAG. A DAG consists of a maximum of 16 Mailbox servers and can host multiple copies of mailbox databases. If one Mailbox server fails, other Mailbox servers in the DAG can take over its functions, offering a seamless experience for users. Combine this with the redundancy features in the Transport service—like shadow redundancy and Safety Net—and you get a serious, high-available messaging infrastructure.

The Unified Messaging service running on the Exchange 2013 Mailbox server provides voicemail functions. Incoming calls that are not answered are redirected to the Mailbox server, where the user's Mailbox receives and stdores a voicemail message. This function works relatively easy with Microsoft Lync Server 2010 or Lync Server 2013.

CHAPTER 6

■ ■ ■

Managing Exchange Server 2013

After installing Exchange Server 2013 and bringing it into production, it's time to manage your Exchange 2013 environment. You have to add new mailboxes, delete mailboxes, maybe add additional mailbox databases, or move mailbox databases to another location, just to name a few such tasks. Maybe you want to add additional services, like public folders, resource mailboxes, or linked mailboxes—or at one point, you may have to troubleshoot your Exchange Server 2013 environment.

In the previous chapters I described several ways of managing the various resources, and in this chapter I discuss these tools again, but in more depth, focusing on the tools themselves. The first part of the chapter discusses the multiple tools available to manage the Exchange 2013 environment. The second part covers the regular, day-to-day management tasks that can be handled in this environment. The chapter concludes with discussion of the installation of cumulative upgrades to Exchange Server.

The Management Tools

The following tools are available in Exchange Server 2013 for managing your Exchange 2013 environment:

- Exchange Management Shell (EMS)
- Exchange Admin Center (EAC)
- Exchange Toolbox
- Role Based Access Control (RBAC)

Let's get started with a discussion of each of these tools.

Exchange Management Shell (EMS)

The Exchange Management Shell (EMS) is the core of Exchange Server management. This is the place where you can configure everything—every little, tiny tidbit of Exchange Server. The EMS is not new; its first version appeared with Exchange Server 2007. But for anyone who's using Exchange Server 2007 and doesn't like the shell, and would prefer to stick to the GUI, here's news for you: the EMS is more important than ever before.

History of EMS

Windows Server 2008 was the first version of Windows that came with Windows PowerShell, version 1.0, and Exchange Server 2007 used this version of PowerShell. Then, Exchange Server 2010 used its successor, PowerShell 2.0. Now, PowerShell 2.0 was integrated with Windows Remote Management (WinRM), which made it possible to use PowerShell remotely via the standard HTTP protocol. To do this, all that was needed was a workstation or server with PowerShell 2.0 installed.

Windows Server 2012 comes with PowerShell 3.0 (which is bundled with WinRM 3.0), and so the EMS in Exchange 2013 is built on top of PowerShell 3.0. In a nutshell, EMS contains all kinds of Exchange-related commands (called *cmdlets*, pronounced com-MAND-lets), which are specific for the server role you're running in the Exchange Management Shell. The EMS can be recognized by the white characters on a black background. For readability purposes, however, EMS screenshots in this chapter show black characters on a white background.

■ **Note**   Although Exchange Server 2010 SP3 can be installed on Windows Server 2012, it is still using PowerShell 2.0. When installing Exchange Server 2010 SP3 on Windows Server 2012, the PowerShell 2.0 needs to be installed manually. Luckily, PowerShell 2.0 and PowerShell 3.0 can coexist happily on the same server.

An EMS command consists of two parts: a verb and a noun. The verb can be an instruction that needs to be executed, like Get, Set, New, Remove, Update, Enable, and Disable. The noun can be any Exchange-related object, like Server, Mailbox, Public Folder, Mailbox Database, Send or Receive Connector, Group, or Exchange Server. Here are some common examples of commands:

- Get-MailboxDatabase Retrieves a list of all mailbox databases in the Exchange organization.

- Get-Mailbox Retrieves a list of all mailboxes in the Exchange organization.

- Get-ExchangeServer Retrieves a list of all Exchange servers in the organization.

- Set-ClientAccessServer Sets properties on a specific Exchange Client Access server.

- New-DatabaseAvailabilityGroup Creates a new database availability group (DAG).

- Add-MailboxDatabaseCopy Creates a copy of a particular mailbox database in a database availability group.

- Disable-Mailbox Removes all Exchange-related properties from a user account but leaves the user account in Active Directory.

- Remove-Mailbox Removes the mailbox and removes the accompanying user object from Active Directory at the same time.

- Get-SendConnector Retrieves the properties of a particular send connector within the Exchange organization.

■ **Note**   In the EMS, you can retrieve a list of all available cmdlets by typing the Get-Command cmdlet.

The number of available cmdlets depends on the permissions that have been assigned to the user. The default Exchange administrator has a lot, but not all, of the cmdlets available; a help desk employee's available cmdlets should be restricted, of course. But not only can the availability of cmdlets be restricted but so can the available options for particular cmdlets. These restrictions are enforced by using the Role Based Access Control (RBAC), which is explained later on in this chapter.

Pipelining

A great feature of PowerShell and, consequently, of the Exchange Management Shell, is the pipelining function. This uses the output of one command as the input for a second command. It can drastically reduce the amount of work you need to do to accomplish relatively complex tasks, and it is more or less limited only by your own ingenuity.

For example, if you want to move all the mailboxes in a mailbox database (called DB01) to another mailbox database (called DB02), you can use the following command:

```
Get-Mailbox -Database DB01 | New-MoveRequest -TargetDatabase DB02
```

This is what happens in this example: `Get-Mailbox -Database DB01` retrieves a list of all mailboxes in this particular database. The output of this cmdlet is then used as the input of the second cmdlet, which is the request to move those mailboxes to the other database.

It's also possible to use more specific queries; for example, suppose you want to get a list of all mailboxes whose name starts with "John." You would use the command: `Get-Mailbox | where-object {$_.name -like "John*"}`. You can then use this result as the input for a request to move all of these mailboxes to another database:

```
Get-Mailbox | where-object {$_.name -like "John*"} | New-MoveRequest -TargetDatabase DB02
```

You can return only certain properties when using PowerShell commands by choosing the Select option in combination with the pipelining function. For example, to query for Peter's mailbox and return the name (alias, displayname), grant it permission, and archive the database, you can use the following command:

```
Get-Mailbox -Identity Michael | Select Name, Alias, DisplayName, GrantSendOnBehalfTo, ArchiveDatabase
```

You'll get an output like that shown in Figure 6-1.

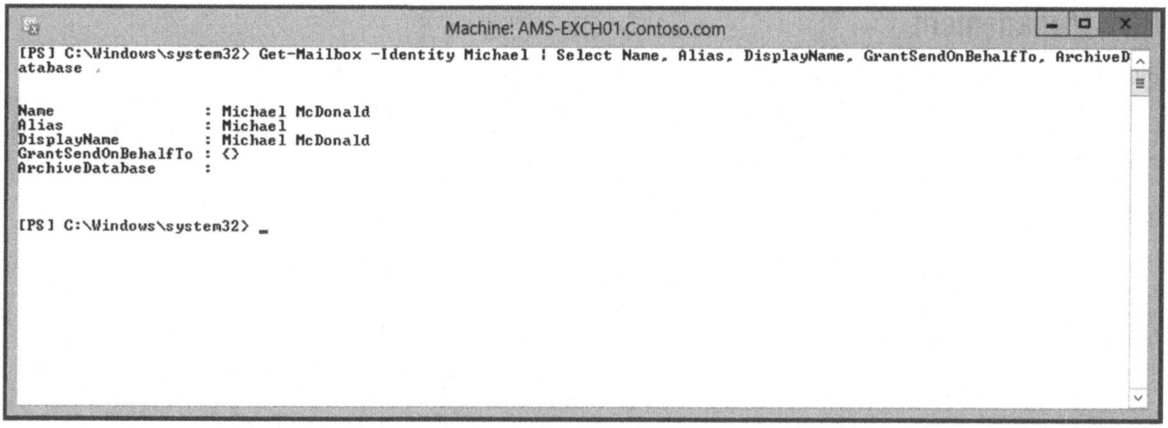

Figure 6-1. *Use the Select statement to return only particular properties in the Exchange Management Shell*

To make it a bit more readable, it is possible to use the Format-Table or FT option to show the information in a table style. An `-a` parameter (for -auto) will crop the output so it fits on the screen. This can be useful when multiple items are shown. The command in this example would be:

```
Get-Mailbox -Identity Michael | Select Name, Alias, DisplayName, GrantSendOnBehalfTo,
ArchiveDatabase | ft -a
```

You'll get an output like you see in Figure 6-2.

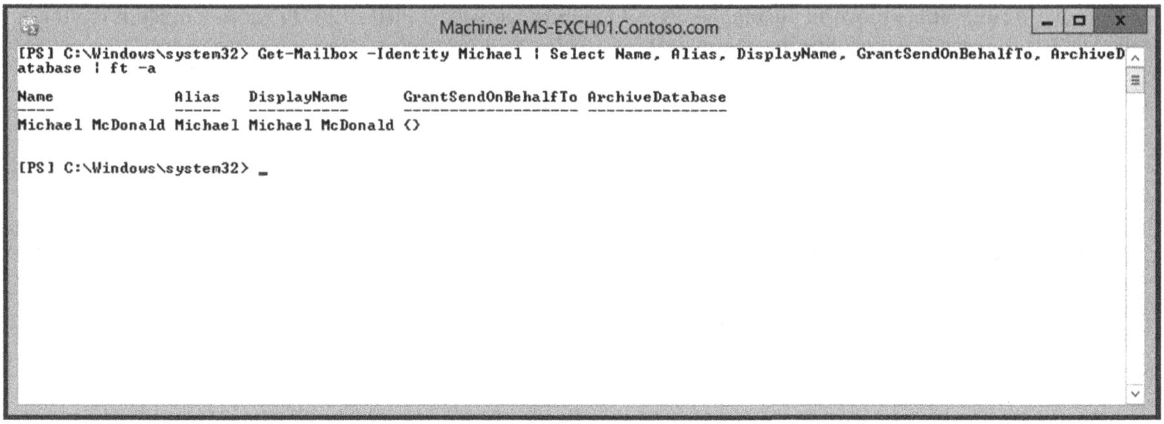

```
                              Machine: AMS-EXCH01.Contoso.com                    _  □  X
[PS] C:\Windows\system32> Get-Mailbox -Identity Michael | Select Name, Alias, DisplayName, GrantSendOnBehalfTo, ArchiveD
atabase | ft -a

Name            Alias    DisplayName      GrantSendOnBehalfTo ArchiveDatabase
----            -----    -----------      ------------------- ---------------
Michael McDonald Michael Michael McDonald ()


[PS] C:\Windows\system32> _
```

Figure 6-2. *The | ft and -a options give a more readable result*

It is obvious that the pipelining function gives you plenty of additional possibilities besides the standard commands. You have to keep in mind, though, that the object type of the first cmdlet must correspond to what the second cmdlet is expecting. If this is not the case, the pipeline function will not work.

Bulk Management

Bulk management can be very useful, particularly when you need to create a lot of mailboxes or are in some migration scenario. I have been using this in Unix to Exchange migration scenarios, for example. Suppose you have an organizational unit (OU) named "Sales" in Active Directory, where 100 user objects reside (without mailboxes, that is). The following command will create a mailbox for each user in this OU:

```
Get-User -OrganizationalUnit "sales" | Enable-Mailbox -Database DB01
```

When there are multiple OUs called "Sales," you have to specify the complete path of the OU:

```
Get-User -OrganizationalUnit "contoso.com/accounts/sales" | Enable-Mailbox -Database DB01
```

It's also possible to filter the output of the Get-User command with the -Filter parameter. For example, to mailbox-enable all users whose company attribute is set to "Fourth Coffee," enter the following command:

```
Get-User -Filter {Company -eq "Fourth Coffee"} | Enable-Mailbox -Database DB01
```

If you want to be even more specific—for example, to mailbox-enable all users whose company attribute is set to "Fourth Coffee" *and* whose department attribute is set to "Marketing," enter the following command:

```
Get-User -Filter {(Company -eq "Fourth Coffee") -AND (Department -eq "marketing")} | Enable-Mailbox
-Database DB01
```

In short, the following operations are available for the -Filter option:

- -and
- -or
- -not

- -eq (equals)

- -ne (does not equal)

- -lt (less than)

- -gt (greater than)

- -like (compare strings by using wildcard rules)

- -notlike (compare strings by using wildcard rules)

In some cases, you'll find it useful to import a list of users from a .CSV file. This list can be exported from another Active Directory, an HR (Human Resources) application, or any other LDAP directory. It is actually relatively easy to import a .CSV file using PowerShell; the only thing you need to be aware of is that the -Password option doesn't accept simple text string input. In a script, the input to this password field has to be converted to a secure string, as in the following:

```
$Database="DB01"
$UPN="FourthCoffee.com"
$users = import-csv $args[0]
function SecurePassword([string]$password)
{
$secure = New-Object System.Security.SecureString
$password.ToCharArray() | % { $secure.AppendChar($_) }
return $secure
}
ForEach ($user in $users)
{
$sp = SecurePassword $user.password
$upn = $user.FirstName + "@"+ $upn
$DisplayName = $user.FirstName + " "+ $user.LastName
New-Mailbox -Password $sp -Database $Database -UserPrincipalName $UPN -Name $DisplayName↵
-FirstName $user.FirstName -LastName $user.LastName -OrganizationalUnit $user.OU
}
```

On the first three lines, three parameters are set that are used during the actual creation of the user and the mailbox. The file is read in a ForEach loop, and the actual users and the mailboxes are created as this loop progresses.

The SecurePassword function converts the clear text password into a secured string that is used when the actual user is created. The .CSV file itself is formatted like this:

```
FirstName,LastName,Password,OU
Jaap,Wesselius,Pass1word,FourthCoffee
John,Lee,Pass1word, FourthCoffee
Michael,McDonald,Pass1word, FourthCoffee
John,Doe,Pass1word, FourthCoffee
```

To make this script usable, save the script file as Create_Users.ps1 in a directory like C:\scripts. You'll also need to save the .CSV output file as users.csv in the same directory. To actually use the script, open a PowerShell command prompt, navigate to the C:\scripts directory, and enter the following command:

```
.\create.ps1 users.csv.
```

Remote PowerShell

As in Exchange 2010, it is possible in Exchange 2013 to use a remote PowerShell as well, making it feasible to connect a local Windows PowerShell instance to an Exchange 2013 server at a remote location. The workstation doesn't have to be in the same domain; as long as the proper credentials and authentication method are used, it will work. With this kind of function, it's now as easy to manage your Exchange 2013 servers in another part of the building as those servers in a datacenter in another part of the country. Needless to say, if you are using a nondomain client for remote PowerShell, you cannot use Kerberos. You have to change authentication on the PowerShell Virtual Directory to Basic Authentication for this to happen.

When the Exchange Management Shell is opened, it will automatically connect to the Exchange 2013 server you're logged into. However, this is only true if you are logged into an Exchange server (Console or RDP) at the time. If you are on a management workstation, it will choose any Exchange server within your Active Directory site. Alternatively, by using the remote option it's possible to connect to a remote Exchange server at this stage.

To use remote PowerShell, you need to log on to a Windows server or workstation that has the Windows Management Framework 3.0 installed. The Management Framework consists of PowerShell 3.0 and Windows Remote Management (WinRM) 3.0. Also, make sure that the workstation (or server) supports remote signed scripts. Owing to security constraints, this is disabled by default. You can enable the support by opening an elevated Windows PowerShell command prompt and entering:

```
Set-ExecutionPolicy RemoteSigned
```

The next step is to create a session that will connect to the remote Exchange server. When the session is created, it can be imported into PowerShell:

```
$Session = New-PSSession -ConfigurationName Microsoft.Exchange -ConnectionUri
https://ams-exch01.contoso.com/PowerShell -Authentication Kerberos

Import-PSSession $Session
```

The PowerShell on the workstation will now connect to the remote Exchange server using a default SSL connection and, RBAC permitting, all Exchange cmdlets will be available. It's incredibly easy, as can be seen in Figure 6-3. To end the remote PowerShell session, just enter the command:

```
Remove-PSSession $session.
```

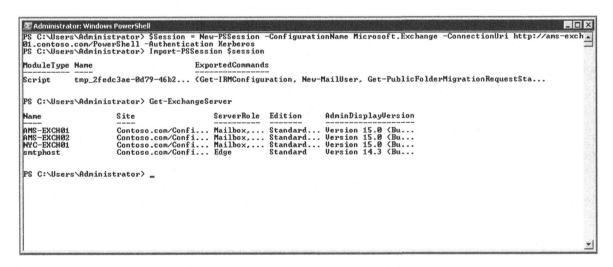

Figure 6-3. *Using Remote PowerShell on a local workstation to manage Exchange 2013*

Admittedly, the example in Figure 6-3 is from a Windows 7 workstation that's also a member of the same Active Directory domain. To connect to a remote Exchange 2013 server that's available over the Internet, multiple steps are required. The first step is to create a variable in the PowerShell command prompt that contains the username and password for the remote session $Credential = Get-Credential. A pop-up box will appear, requesting a username and password for the remote Exchange environment. Once you've filled in the credentials, the following command will create a new session that will set up a connection to the Exchange environment. The $Credential variable is used to pass the credentials to the Exchange environment, and then the session is imported into PowerShell. See Figure 6-4.

```
$Credential = Get-Credential

$Session = New-PSSession –ConfigurationName Microsoft.Exchange –ConnectionUri
https://webmail.contoso.com/PowerShell -Authentication Basic -Credential $Credential

Import-PSSession $Session
```

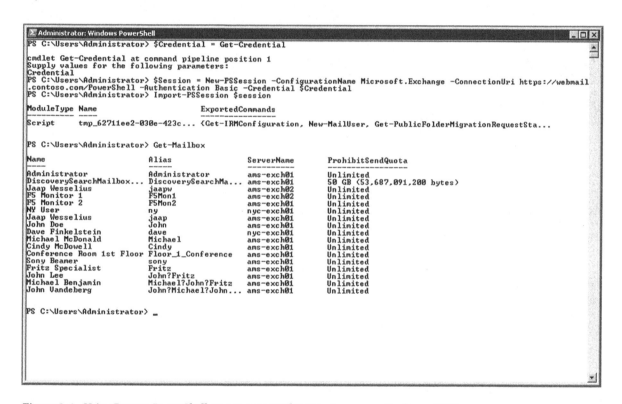

Figure 6-4. *Using Remote PowerShell on a remote workstation to manage Exchange 2013*

■ **Note**   If you want to connect to a remote Exchange 2013 server over the Internet, remember to enable Basic Authentication on the PowerShell virtual directory on the remote server, using the Exchange Management Shell and the Set-PowerShellVirtualDirectory command. When split-DNS is used, the authenication used for Internet connections can be used internally as well.

These examples were for the Active Directory domain administrator, who automatically has the remote management option enabled. To enable a non-domain administrator for remote management, just enter the `Set-User <username> -RemotePowerShellEnabled $True` command.

Reporting with Exchange Management Shell

The Exchange Management Shell can actually be very effective in creating reports. The EMS has quite a lot of powerful cmdlets, and with the pipelining option it is possible to create all kinds of reports. I'll give you a few examples.

The `Get-ExchangeServer` cmdlet will return a list of all Exchange 2010 servers in the organization (see Figure 6-5), like this:

```
Get-ExchangeServer | ft -a
```

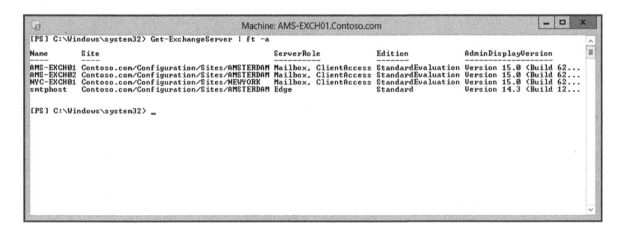

Figure 6-5. *The Get-ExchangeServer command returns all Exchange Servers in the organization*

With the `-Identity` option it is possible to retrieve the information for only one Exchange server, and when the `Get-ExchangeServer` cmdlet is used in a pipeline with the Format-List command, all the detailed information for the server in question is shown (see Figure 6-6).

```
Get-ExchangeServer -Identity AMS-EXCH01 | fl
```

Figure 6-6. *The Format-List option returns all available information*

To get detailed information about a particular mailbox (see Figure 6-7), the output of that mailbox's identity can be piped to the Format-List command:

```
Get-Mailbox -Identity John | fl
```

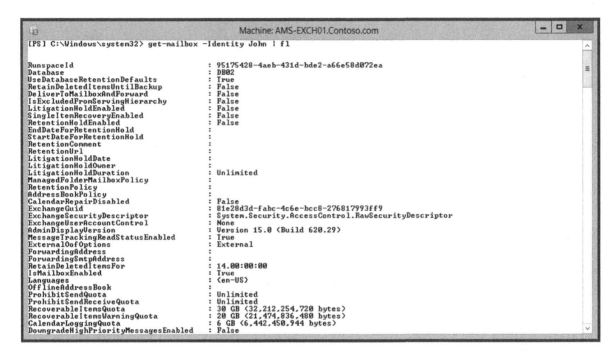

Figure 6-7. *Retrieving all properties from a mailbox. For practical reasons, only part of the output is shown here*

The Get-MailboxStatistics cmdlet retrieves detailed information about mailbox usage from an Exchange server; when combined with the Get-Mailbox command, you can obtain some specific information from user mailboxes (see Figure 6-8).

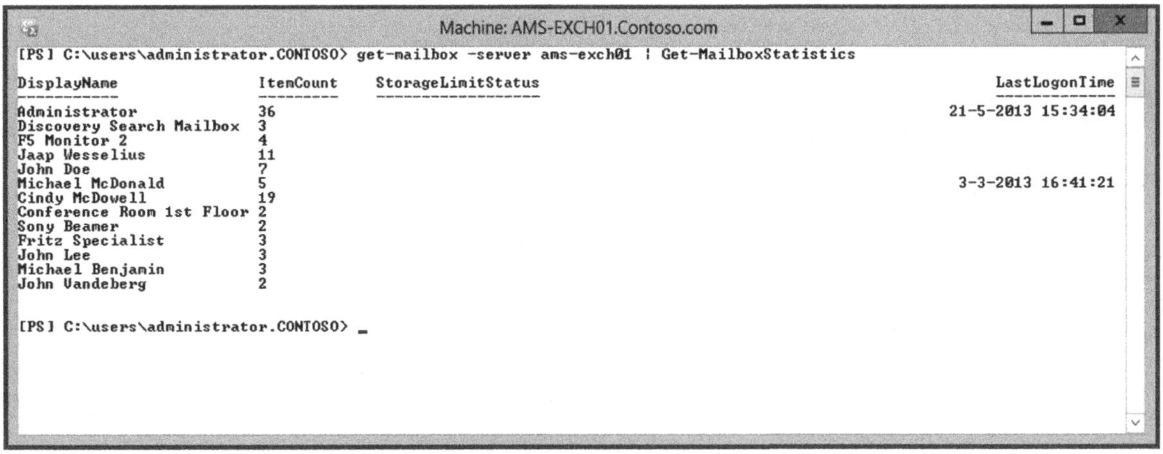

Figure 6-8. *Retrieve statistics from mailboxes using the Get-MailboxStatistics command*

So the Get-MailboxStatistics cmdlet gives lots of information about usage. To get some real reporting information, look to PowerShell for an option to convert its output to HTML. So, you enter the following command:

```
Get-Mailbox -Server AMS-EXCH01 | Get-MailboxStatistics | ConvertTo-HTML DisplayName > AMS-EXCH01.html
```

Nothing is logged to the screen, but an HTML file is created in the directory where the PowerShell is running. Use Internet Explorer to open the output file (see Figure 6-9).

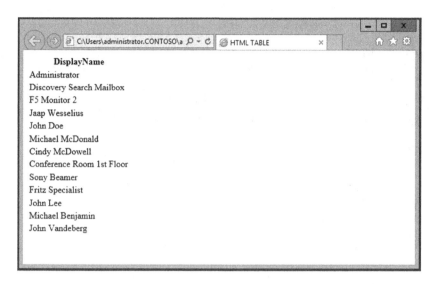

Figure 6-9. *Only the DisplayName property is shown*

Using just the DisplayName is not really useful, so let's add some more parameters:

```
Get-Mailbox -Server AMS-EXCH01 | Get-MailboxStatistics | ConvertTo-HTML DisplayName, ServerName, DatabaseName, ItemCount, TotalItemSize > MbxInfo.html
```

This will give the HMTL file, as shown in Figure 6-10.

DisplayName	ServerName	DatabaseName	ItemCount	TotalItemSize
Administrator	AMS-EXCH01	DB02	36	552.2 KB (565,449 bytes)
Discovery Search Mailbox	AMS-EXCH01	DB02	3	34.99 KB (35,831 bytes)
F5 Monitor 2	AMS-EXCH01	DB02	4	71.42 KB (73,134 bytes)
Jaap Wesselius	AMS-EXCH01	DB02	11	130.4 KB (133,578 bytes)
John Doe	AMS-EXCH01	DB02	7	110.7 KB (113,333 bytes)
Michael McDonald	AMS-EXCH01	DB02	5	78.07 KB (79,941 bytes)
Cindy McDowell	AMS-EXCH01	DB02	19	263.6 KB (269,969 bytes)
Conference Room 1st Floor	AMS-EXCH01	DB02	2	4.396 KB (4,501 bytes)
Sony Beamer	AMS-EXCH01	DB02	2	4.229 KB (4,331 bytes)
Fritz Specialist	AMS-EXCH01	DB01	3	28.16 KB (28,835 bytes)
John Lee	AMS-EXCH01	DB01	3	28.05 KB (28,724 bytes)
Michael Benjamin	AMS-EXCH01	DB01	3	28.26 KB (28,940 bytes)
John Vandeberg	AMS-EXCH01	DB01	2	3.071 KB (3,145 bytes)

Figure 6-10. *More information is shown in a pretty readable text*

■ **Note**   Instead of the ">" to flush information to disk, the pipeline option "|" in combination with the Out-File command can be used.

Now let's create a small script with some variables:

- $Now contains the date and time the script runs.

- $BodyStyle contains a value used to retrieve a stylesheet to customize the HMTL file.

- $MBXOutput contains the actual output from the Get-MailboxStatistics cmdlet.

Your script should look something like this:

```
$Now=Get-Date
$BodyStyle="<link rel='stylesheet' type='text/css' ↵
href= 'http://www.domain.com/styles/reporting.css' />"
$BodyStyle=$BodyStyle + "<title>Exchange 2013 Mailbox Reporting</title>"
$MBXOutput = Get-MailboxStatistics -Server ams-exch01 |
ConvertTo-HTML DisplayName, ServerName, DatabaseName, ItemCount, TotalItemSize
-Title "Mailbox Overview" -Head $BodyStyle
$MBXoutput = $MBXoutput -replace "<BODY>", "<BODY><div id='midden'> <h3>Report $($now)</h3>"
$MBXoutput = $MBXoutput -replace "</BODY>", "</DIV></BODY>"
$MBXoutput | Out-File MailboxInfo.html
```

Save this file as Mailbox_Reporting.ps1 and run the script. It will still show the output of the query, but now it'll be beautifully formatted according the CSS style sheet (see Figure 6-11). This method will allow you to create some really compelling reports.

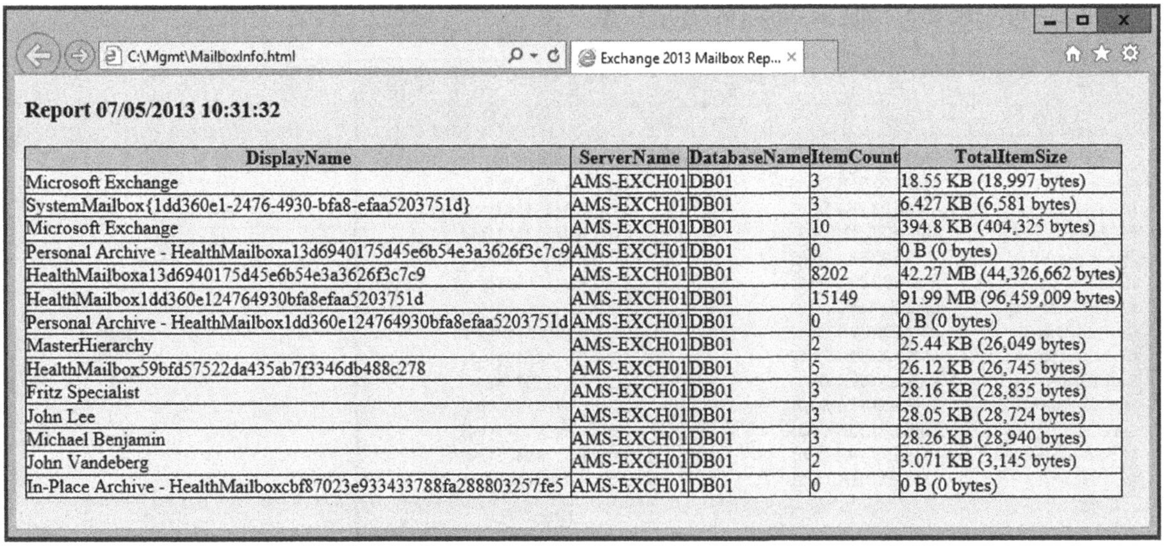

Figure 6-11. *Changing the layout using standard HTML CSS formatting*

To further automate the process, it's even possible to have these kinds of reports sent to you by using the Exchange 2013 server. Just create a new Message Object in PowerShell that holds all the message properties and create a new SMTP Client object that will actually send the message.

```
$Msg = new-object system.net.mail.MailMessage
$msg.IsBodyHtml = $True
$msg.Body = $MBXoutput
$msg.Subject = "Exchange 2013 Mailbox Information"
$msg.To.add("administrator@contoso.com")
$msg.From = "administrator@contoso.com"
$SmtpClient = new-object system.net.mail.smtpClient
$smtpclient.Host = 'localhost'
$smtpclient.Send($msg)
```

The body of the message is the $MBXoutput variable that was used in the previous example. If you run this script in an Exchange Management Shell, the output will automatically be mailed to the account mentioned in the script and it will show up in Microsoft Outlook, as shown in Figure 6-12.

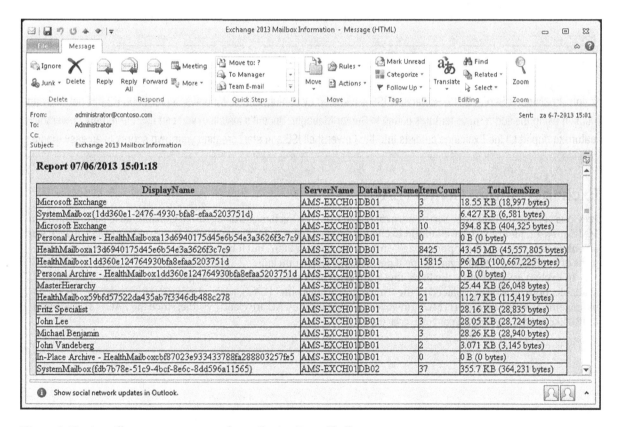

Figure 6-12. A mailbox report sent to you by mail using PowerShell

The last step is to create a Windows cmd file that calls the PowerShell script. This cmd file can be used when configuring the Windows Task Scheduler to run the script on a regular basis. The cmd file will look something like:

```
Powershell.exe -PSConsoleFile "C:\Program Files\Microsoft\Exchange Server\v15\bin\exshell.psc1"
-command ". 'C:\Mgmt\Mailbox_Reporting.ps1'"
```

Creating a mailbox report like the previous example might not be all that exciting, but with some more finetuning of the query it is possible to create a report of all mailboxes that were created in the last month:

```
$LastMonth = (Get-Date).AddDays(-30)
Get-Mailbox | where {$_.WhenCreated -gt $LastMonth} | select Name,Alias, Database,WhenCreated
```

Or, instead of querying for the mailboxes, it is possible to look for SMTP queue information on all Exchange 2013 Mailbox servers, like this:

```
Get-TransportService | Get-Queue | Select Identity,DeliveryType,Status, MessageCount,NextHopDomain,
LastRetryTime,NextRetryTime
```

Using creativity, you'll find it possible to develop the fanciest reporting options using PowerShell.

■ **Tip** Windows Server 2008 R2 and higher come with the PowerShell Integrated Scripting Environment (ISE). PowerShell ISE is a host application that can be used to run PowerShell commands, but it also is for writing, testing, and debugging PowerShell scripts. In Windows Server 2012, Powershell ISE is installed by default, but on Windows Server 2008 R2 it is not. You can install it using the add/remove features option in Server Manager. Once it's installed, you can use the remote Powershell feature to import all the Exchange cmdlets into the PowerShell ISE and start creating your own scripts in an easy manner.

Exchange Admin Center (EAC)

Previous versions of Exchange Server were managed from the Exchange Management Console, a GUI available as an MMC snap-in. Another GUI available in Exchange Server 2010 was the Exchange Control Panel, or ECP. The ECP was an enhanced version of the "options page" in Exchange Server 2007, but it had some interesting options to manage parts of the Exchange 2010 organization if permissions were sufficient.

In Exchange Server 2013, the Exchange Management Console and the Exchange Control Panel are no longer available; both have been replaced by the Exchange Admin Center (EAC), a brand-new GUI for Exchange 2013 management, fully based on HTML5. However, the roots of the EAC are clearly visible, since the EAC is accessible via a URL like https://webmail.contoso.com/ecp.

When the EAC is opened, a window like the one shown in Figure 6-13 appears:

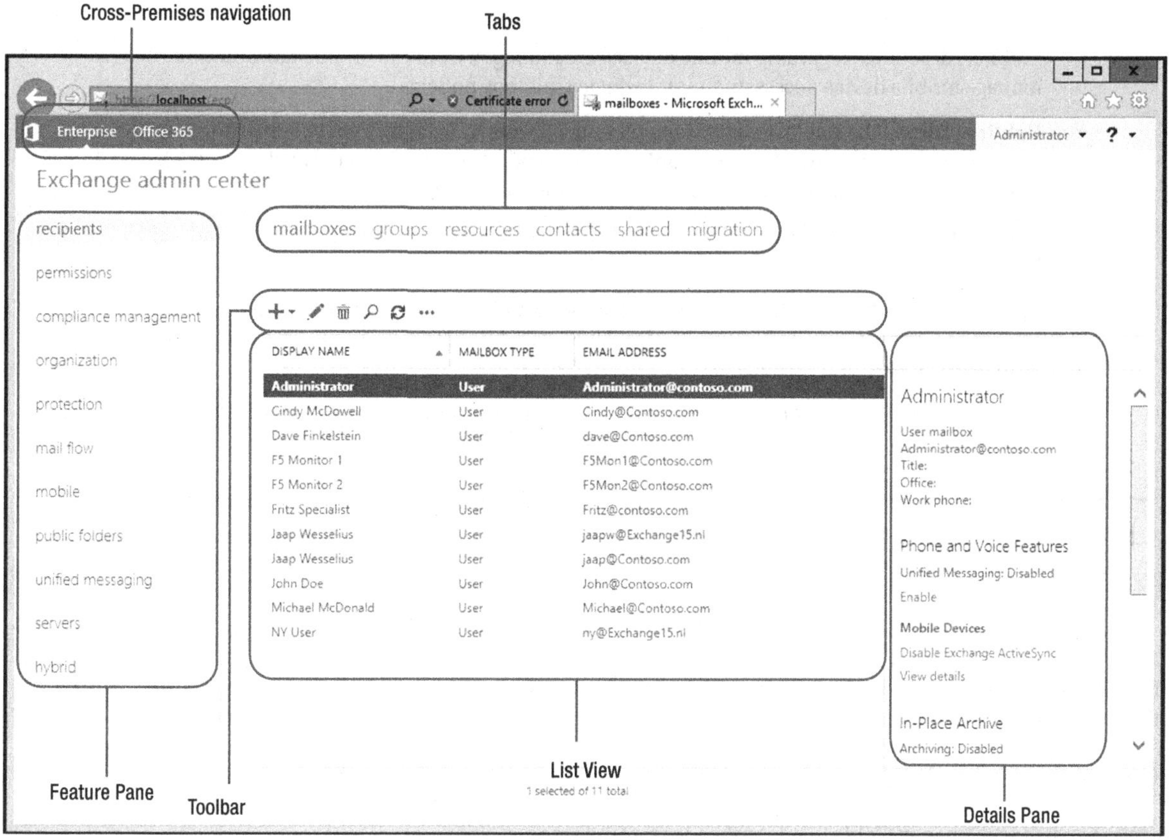

Figure 6-13. *The new Exchange Admin Center in Exchange 2013*

In the left-hand menu, there are various components of Exchange 2013 that can be managed in the EAC. The left-hand menu is also called the "Feature pane" and consists of the following options:

- **Recipients**. All recipients, like mailboxes, groups, contacts, shared mailboxes, and resource mailboxes, are managed from the Recipients option.

- **Permissions**. In the Permissions option, you can manage administrator roles, user roles, and Outlook Web App policies. The first two roles are explained in more detail in the RBAC section later in this chapter.

- **Compliance Management**. In the Compliance Management option, you can manage In-Place eDiscovery, In-Place Hold, auditing, data loss prevention (DLP), retention policies, retention tags, and journal rules.

- **Organization**. The Organization option is the highest level of configuration, and this is the place where you'll manage your Exchange organization, including federated sharing, Outlook Apps, and address lists.

- **Protection**. In the Protection option, you can manage the anti-malware protection for the Exchange 2013 organization.

- **Mail Flow**. The Mail Flow option contains all choices regarding the flow of messages, including rules, delivery reports, accepted domains, email address policies, and send and receive connectors.

- **Mobile**. All settings regarding mobile devices are managed from the Mobile tab. You can manage mobile device access and mobile device mailbox policies.

- **Public Folders**. The Public Folder Management Console in Exchange Server 2010 is replaced by this option in the EAC. From the Public Folders option you can manage Exchange 2013 public folders. Note that legacy public folders cannot be managed using the EAC.

- **Unified Messaging**. From the Unified Messaging option you can manage UM Dial Plans and UM IP Gateways.

- **Servers**. The Exchange 2013 servers, both Mailbox and Client Access server, can be managed from the Servers option. This also includes databases, database availability groups (DAGs), virtual directories, and certificates.

- **Hybrid**. Using the Hybrid option, it is possible to configure a hybrid organization—that is, connect your on-premises Exchange 2013 organization with an Office 365 tenant.

Note   Just like the EMS, the functions available in the EAC are limited by the permissions enforced by RBAC.

In previous versions of Exchange Server, all the configuration changes made using the Exchange Management Console were translated to EMS under the hood. In the EAC, this is no different, but unlike the previous version of Exchange Server, the actual commands can no longer be made visible. This is a widely heard complaint. At present, in Exchange 2013 CU3 this feature is not available, and it is unknown if future updates or service packs will contain the feature.

The tabs in the top-level menu are context sensitive. In other words, they change when a different option in the Feature pane is selected.

The toolbar can be compared to the Actions pane in the Exchange Server 2010 Management Console. All actions are associated with an icon. Table 6-1 describes each of the icons.

Table 6-1. *Available options (icons) in the EAC Toolbar*

Icon	Name	Description
✚	Add, New	Use this option to create a new object. Some of these icons have an associated down arrow you can click to show additional objects you can create. For example, in Recipients and then Mailboxes, clicking the down arrow displays User Mailbox and Linked Mailbox as additional options.
✎	Edit	You can use this option to edit an object.
🗑	Delete	Use this option to delete one or more objects.
🔍	Search	Use this option to query for a particular object.
⟳	Refresh	Use the icon to refresh the objects in the list view.
•••	More options	Use this icon to view more actions you can perform for that tab's objects. For example, in Recipients ➤ Mailboxes, clicking this icon shows the following options: Disable, Add/Remove Columns, Export Data to a CSV File, Connect a Mailbox, and Advanced Search.

(continued)

Table 6-1. (*continued*)

Icon	Name	Description
↑ ↓	Up and Down arrow	Use these icons to move an object's priority up or down. For example, in Mail Flow and then Email Address Policies, click the up arrow to raise the priority of an Email Address Policy. You can also use these arrows to navigate the public folder hierarchy, for example, and to move rules up or down in the list view.
📑	Copy	Use this icon to copy an object so you can make changes to it without changing the original object. For example, in Permissions and then Admin Roles, select a role from the list view, and then click this icon to create a new role group based on an existing one.
▬	Remove	Use this icon to remove an item from a list. For example, in the Public Folder Permissions dialog box, you can remove users from the list of users allowed to access the public folder by selecting the user and clicking this icon.

The list view in EAC is designed to remove limitations that existed in ECP. The ECP is capable of listing up to only 500 objects in one page at the same time, and if you want to view objects that aren't listed in the Details pane, you need to use Search and Filter options to find those specific objects. In Exchange 2013, the viewable limit from within the EAC list view is approximately 20,000 objects for on-premises deployments and 10,000 objects in Exchange Online. In addition, paging is included so you can page to the results. In the Recipients list view, you can also configure page size and export the data to a CSV file.

When you select an object from the list view, information about that object is displayed in the Details pane. In some cases (for example, with recipient objects), the Details pane includes quick management tasks. For example, if you navigate to Recipients and then Mailboxes, and select a mailbox from the list view, the Details pane displays an option to enable or disable the archive for that mailbox. The Details pane can also be used to bulk-edit several objects. Simply press the CTRL key, select the objects you want to bulk-edit, and use the options in the Details pane. For example, selecting multiple mailboxes allows you to bulk-update users' contact and organization information, custom attributes, mailbox quota, Outlook Web App settings, and more.

■ **Note** Supported browsers for the EAC are Internet Explorer 8 or later, Firefox 11 or later, Safari 5.1 or later, and Chrome 18 or later.

It is possible to completely turn off the EAC. In an EMS window, enter the following command to turn off EAC for a particular server:

```
Set-ECPVirtualDirectory -Identity "AMS-EXCH01\ecp (default web site)" -AdminEnabled $false
```

Exchange Toolbox

The Exchange Toolbox is the only MMC (Microsoft Management Console) snap-in that's left in Exchange 2013. The Exchange Toolbox contains the following three tools:

- Details Templates Editor
- Remote Connectivity Analyzer
- Queue Viewer

Details Templates Editor

A Details Template is a template file that's used by address lists—for example, in Microsoft Outlook. When a user opens the address book in Outlook and opens another user's properties, detailed information is shown. These pages can be edited using the Details Templates Editor. To change these pages, just open the template that needs to be changed and select the Edit option.

In Figure 6-14, two additional fields are shown as added to the General Properties page. When the address book in Outlook is opened and the properties are requested, the additional fields are shown as well.

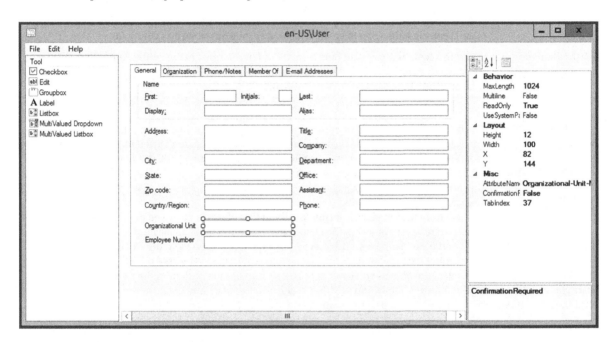

***Figure 6-14.** Adding additional fields in the user template*

In Figure 6-14, the address book template for Outlook in American English (en-US) is changed. If your company is using multiple languages, you will have to make the same change in the templates for the other languages.

Remote Connectivity Analyzer

The Remote Connectivity Analyzer in the toolbox is a link to an externally available analyzer tool offered by Microsoft. This tool is also directly accessible on the Internet; just open a browser and navigate to the following URL:
https://www.testexchangeconnectivity.com.

The Remote Connectivity Analyzer can be used to test your Exchange environment from the Internet—for example, how external clients access the environment. One of the most important benefits of using the Remote Connectivity Analyzer is testing the Autodiscover configuration of the Exchange environment. In the Remote Connectivity Analyzer, select Outlook Autodiscover under Microsoft Office Outlook Connectivity Tests. In the next window, enter your email address, domain\user name or UPN, and its password. Check the box for "I understand that I must use the credentials of a working account…" and in the verification box, enter the verification code and click Perform Test.

■ **Note**   For a successful Autodiscover test in the Remote Connectivity Analyzer, you need a mailbox with a normal email address, the Exchange 2013 Client Access server needs to be externally accessible, the Exchange 2013 environment needs to be configured for external access, and a third-party SSL certificate needs to be installed.

When the test is finished, the result is shown. Don't be alarmed when you see all kinds of red boxes with a cross in them, but you should see at least one or more green check boxes. When you seen a green check box with an exclamation mark on a yellow triangle in it, this typically indicates a warning (see Figure 6-15).

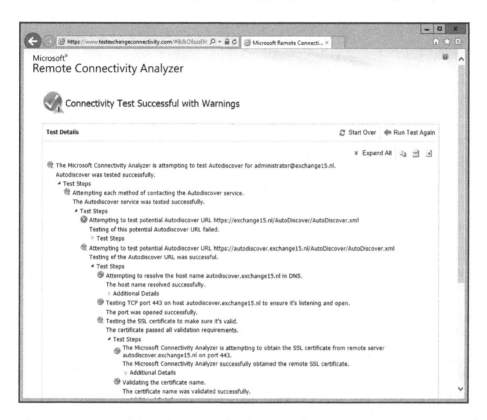

Figure 6-15.   *A successful Autodiscover test, but the SSL certificate test generates a warning about the intermediate certificate*

The Remote Connectivity Analyzer always shows detailed results of the actual tests. Most Exchange administrators panic when they see only the red boxes, but when you expand the various tests, the results are shown in greater detail, often with a pretty good explanation of the error being returned. The Remote Connectivity Analyzer is a great tool for troubleshooting external connectivity issues.

Queue Viewer

The Queue Viewer in the Exchange 2013 toolbox is a great way to quickly examine the SMTP queues on a particular Exchange 2013 Mailbox server. When you open the Queue Viewer, it automatically connects to the Transport service on the Mailbox server that it is running on, and it shows the queue information instantly (see Figure 6-16).

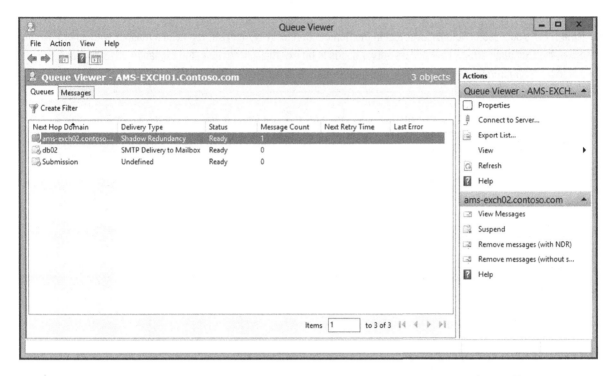

Figure 6-16. *The Queue Viewer shows queue information of the Transport service on a particular Mailbox server*

The number of messages in a queue are shown, as well as the next time the Transport service will try to resend the messages in the queue. When you double-click a queue, all messages in that queue are shown, including details on why the messages are not being sent.

In the Actions pane, another Mailbox server, or downlevel Hub Transport server, can be selected; there's also the option to remove messages from the queue, with or without sending a non-delivery report (NDR).

The Queue Viewer is a useful tool for troubleshooting SMTP-related problems on your Exchange 2013 Mailbox server.

Role Based Access Control (RBAC)

Role Based Access Control (RBAC) is not really a tool; rather, it's a framework on how to organize the permissions structure in Exchange 2013. Up to Exchange Server 2007, the delegation of control in Exchange Server relied on granting permissions to user or security groups and on setting access control lists (ACLs) to specific objects. However, this method was prone to error, and it could also happen that during an upgrade or installation of a service pack the permissions were lost.

In Exchange Server 2010, Microsoft introduced RBAC, a permissions framework that's been further developed in Exchange 2013. RBAC lets you control what administrators and users can do in your Exchange organization. At the same time, it lets you align the reponsibilities of users' daily jobs with their roles inside your Exchange organization. For example, suppose there's a role called help desk; with RBAC you can perfectly align that with the help desk department in your organization.

The RBAC consist of the following components:

- **Management role group** The management role group maps to a universal security group (USG) in Active Directory, and users or the administrator can be members of these security groups.

- **Management roles** Management roles are assigned to a management role group. A management role is a container for grouping management role entries. A management role entry can be a cmdlet or a script, so management role entries in a management role determine what an administrator or user can do.

- **Management role assignment** A management role assignment is the linchpin between a management role and a management role group.

- **Management role scope** A management role scope determines where the management role assignment is actually active—that is, where the user or administrator can perform his or her tasks.

- **Management role entry** A mangement role entry determines what the management role group (i.e., user or USG) can do and what cmdlets are available to the management role group.

Together these components in RBAC determine which user or administrator ("who") can do "what" management functions and "where" in Active Directory this management can be done (see Figure 6-17).

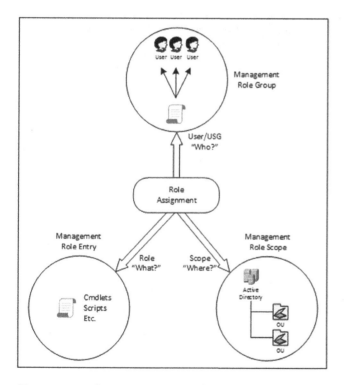

Figure 6-17. *Schematical overview of RBAC*

Out of the box, there are 12 management role groups available in Exchange Server 2013:

- Compliance management
- Delegated setup
- Discovery management
- Help desk
- Hygiene management
- Organization management
- Public folder management
- Recipient management
- Records management
- Server management
- UM management
- View-only organization management

To grant permission to a particular user, it's just a matter of adding this user to the appropriate role group. This can be achieved by using the EAC. Select Permissions in the Feature pane and select the Admin Roles tab. Select the appropriate role group and click the Edit icon in the toolbar to add a particular user to this role group (see Figure 6-18).

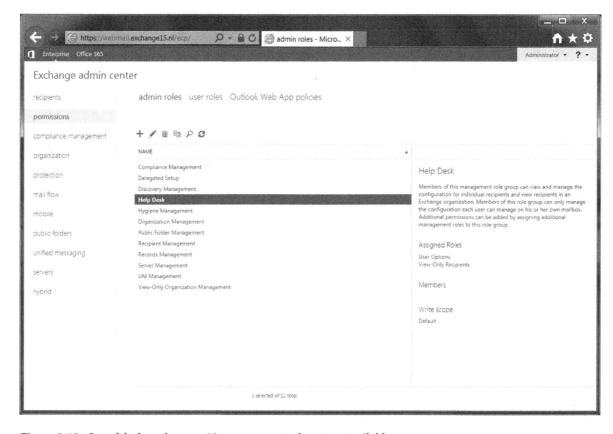

Figure 6-18. *Out of the box, there are 12 management role groups available*

Of course, it's also possible to use the EMS to add a particular user to a role group. To add a user named "John Smith" to a role group called "help desk," open the EMS and enter the following command:

```
Add-RoleGroupMember "Help Desk" -Member "John Smith"
```

Since role groups are mapped to universal security groups in Active Directory, you can find these USGs in the organizational unit called Microsoft Exchange Security Groups, which is in the Active Directory domain where Exchange 2013 is installed. If you've performed the previous example, you'll find the user John Smith as a member of the USG called "help desk" in the Active Directory Users and Computers MMC snap-in.

You might ask yourself: "Can I just add users to this or other security groups to achieve this result?" The answer is yes. You can add other users to these security groups. Only when you want to change very specific settings—for example, the possibility of importing and exporting mailboxes—you will have to use the native RBAC options.

Now that we've added the user John Smith to the role group "help desk," it is interesting to see what effect this has on the EAC, since the availability of management functions is limited by the role group entries as part of the "help desk" role group. When John Smith opens the EAC, he sees the features available, as shown in Figure 6-19.

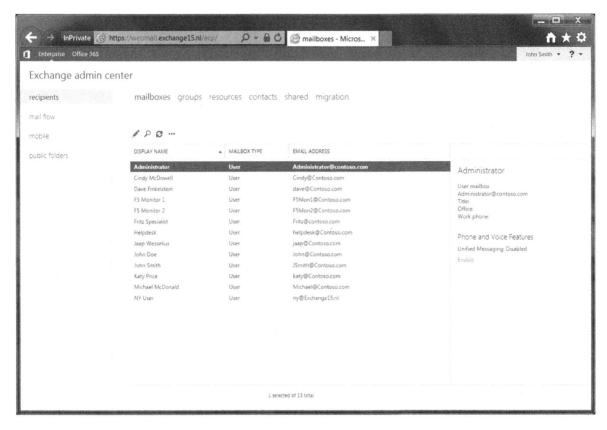

Figure 6-19. *Only a limited set of features is available to the role group "help desk"*

Out of the box, Exchange 2013 has only one role assignment policy: the Default Role Assignment Policy, which you can view using the Get-RoleAssignmentPolicy cmdlet:

```
[PS] C:\Windows\system32> Get-RoleAssignmentPolicy

RunspaceId        : a86badbc-76c2-4f76-be7c-a4e2f3044145
IsDefault         : True
Description       : This policy grants end users permissions to set their
                    Outlook Web App options and perform other self-
                    administration tasks.
RoleAssignments   : {MyTeamMailboxes-Default Role Assignment Policy,
                    MyDistributionGroupMembership-Default Role Assignment
                    Policy, My Marketplace Apps-Default Role Assignment Policy,
                    MyBaseOptins-Default Role Assignment Policy,
                    MyContactInformation-Default Role Assignment Policy,
                    MyTextMessaging-Default Role Assignment Policy,
                    MyVoiceMail-Default Role Assignment Policy}
AssignedRoles     : {MyTeamMailboxes, MyDistributionGroupMembership,
                    MyMarketplace Apps, MyBaseOptions, MyContactInformation,
                    MyTextMessaging, MyVoiceMail}
```

```
AdminDisplayName   :
ExchangeVersion    : 0.11 (14.0.509.0)
Name               : Default Role Assignment Policy
DistinguishedName  : CN=Default Role Assignment Policy,CN=Policies,CN=RBAC,
                     CN=Exchange15,CN=Microsoft Exchange,CN=Services,
                     CN=Configuration,DC=Contoso,DC=com
Identity           : Default Role Assignment Policy
Guid               : b4c756cc-d9b5-4593-b954-6962477b8287
ObjectCategory     : Contoso.com/Configuration/Schema/ms-Exch-RBAC-Policy
ObjectClass        : {top, msExchRBACPolicy}
WhenChanged        : 23-12-2012 17:55:41
WhenCreated        : 23-12-2012 17:55:41
WhenChangedUTC     : 23-12-2012 16:55:41
WhenCreatedUTC     : 23-12-2012 16:55:41
OrganizationId     :
OriginatingServer  : AMS-AD01.Contoso.com
IsValid            : True
ObjectState        : Changed


[PS] C:\Windows\system32>
```

This role assignment policy is assigned to all users by default, and it makes sure that the users can manage their own properties. The only other user who's a member of one of the role groups is the administrator who has installed Exchange 2013, who is a member of the "Organization Management" management role group.

It's not difficult to create your own management roles. Suppose you want to create a group "Contoso Recipient Admins" that needs to administer mailboxes in the Contoso OU. To do this, follow these steps:

1. Log on to the EAC as a domain administrator; in the Feature pane, select Permissions and then the Admin Roles tab (this one is selected by default).

2. In the toolbar, click the New icon to start the New Role Group wizard.

3. Enter the name "Contoso Recipient Admins" and enter a description when needed. For the write scope, select the organizational unit that needs to be managed—in this example, it is contoso.com/accounts/contoso.

4. In the Roles area, use the Add icon to add the Mail Recipient Creation and Mail Recipients role and click OK.

5. In the Members area, use the Add icon to add a user—for example, Michael McDonald—to the management role and click OK.

6. Click Save to finish the wizard and store the new management role in Active Directory.

Now when you open Active Directory and Computers, and check the Microsoft Exchange Security Groups OU, you'll notice that a new USG called "Contoso Recipiet Admins" has been created. When you open the USG and check the Members tab, you'll see that the user Michael McDonald is a member of this USG.

Suppose you log on to the EAC as the user Michael McDonald. You'll see a limited number of entries in the Features pane. If you open a mailbox that's *not* in the Contoso OU, all options are grayed out. This is because this user is not in your write scope. If you try to create a new mailbox and forget to select the Contoso OU, the actual creation will fail with an error message "Contoso.com/Users/Joe Blogs isn't within your current write scopes." You can't perform a save operation. Again, this is caused by the lack of permissions outside the Contoso OU. If you select the Contoso OU in the New User Mailbox wizard, the new mailbox will be created.

Management Tasks

This section will focus on the day-to-day management tasks for an Exchange 2013 administrator. Not all management tasks are explained in this chapter, however. Chapter 7 will focus on backup, restore, and disaster recovery in Exchange 2013. Chapter 8 will describe the monitoring of Exchange 2013, while Chapter 9 will cover troubleshooting of Exchange 2013.

Quite a number of administrative tasks can be performed using the EAC. Here, I won't explain stuff like "Log on as an administrator and open the EAC" but instead I'll start directly with something like "In EAC, select Mail Flow in the Feature pane." Also, when it comes to adminstrative tasks using the EMS, for the sake of simplicity I'll assume that you've opened the EMS with sufficient permissions.

Managing SSL Certificates

As explained in Chapter 4, the SSL certificates in Exchange 2013 are a very important aspect of server operations. The SSL certificate is responsible for encrypting HTTP traffic, which is used for Outlook Anywhere as well other web-related services like OWA/ECP, Exchange Web Services, ActiveSync, and Offline Address Book.

When installing an Exchange 2013 Client Access server, a self-signed SSL certificate is installed. In previous versions of Exchange Server, the life of the self-signed certificate was only one year, but in Exchange 2013 this life has been extended to five years.

Also, as explained in Chapter 4, it is not good practice to use the self-signed certificate on the Exchange 2013 Client Access server. Instead, you use an SSL certificate that's issued by the internal Active Directory Certificate Authority or use a third-party SSL certificate. The advantage of using a third-party certificate comes into play when using mobile devices. Mobile devices typically accept and trust most of the third-party certificates, and thus they work right out of the box. When using your own internal Active Directory Client Access certificate, you have to install the root certificate on the mobile device. For a couple of devices this is not a big deal, but when you're talking about hundreds of devices, it will become labor-intensive, of course.

A list of supported UC certificate partners can be found in knowledge base article KB929395 on the Microsoft web site: http://support.microsoft.com/kb/929395.

If you have a third-party UC certificate, most likely you'll receive an email from the vendor that your certificate will expire in (for example) 90 days. Renewing a certificate in Exchange 2013 is no different from creating a new certificate. So, using EAC or the EMS, you create a new certificate request file and this file is submitted to your certificate vendor. After validation, the certificate is returned, which you can install on the Exchange server. (This has been documented in Chapter 2, in the section on SSL certificates.)

Managing Mailbox Databases

As explained in Chapter 5, when you install an Exchange 2013 Mailbox server, a default mailbox database is also installed on a default location, such as C:\Program Files\Microsoft\Exchange Server\V15\Mailbox\Mailbox Database 9361956223. The number in the mailbox database name is randomly generated. Although this mailbox can be used for testing purposes, most likely it does not fit into your company's naming convention and it is likely stored in a wrong location.

Things you might want to do after the initial installation are:

- Rename the mailbox database to match your company's naming convention.

- Move the mailbox database and the accompanying log files to a more suitable location— for example, an external disk whether it be Direct Attached Storage (DAS) or some sort of SAN storage solution. Be aware that you can only do this *before* you create a DAG with additional mailbox database copies!

- Enable circular logging when you are using a DAG.

- Change quotas for the mailbox database or change the retention times for deleted items.

- Assign an Offline Address Book to a mailbox database.

Renaming a Mailbox Database

If you don't want the hassle of renaming a mailbox database and moving the mailbox database and the log files to another location, you can opt for creating a new mailbox database. However, renaming a mailbox database is not a big deal in EAC:

1. Select Servers in the Feature pane and select the Databases tab.

2. Select the mailbox database that needs to be renamed and select the Edit icon in the toolbar.

Renaming a mailbox database in the EMS is easy, too, and just a matter of one command:

```
Get-MailboxDatabase -Identity "Mailbox Database 9361956223" |
Set-MailboxDatabase -Name "Renamed Mailbox Database"
```

■ **Note**   In the previous example, the logical name of the mailbox database is renamed as they show up in EMS or in EAC. The actual EDB file or the directory on disk is not renamed. To rename these, you need to move the EDB file to another directory.

Moving the Mailbox Databases

It is strongly recommended that you move mailbox databases to a separate location, preferably a dedicated disk. In Exchange 2013, you can have up to four mailbox databases per disk. Unfortunately, it is not possible to move a mailbox database to a different location using the EAC, so the EMS should be used. To move a mailbox database named MDB01 and its log files to a different location, just enter the following command in EMS:

```
Move-DatabasePath -Identity MDB01 -EdbFilePath F:\MDB01\MD01.edb
-LogFolderPath F:\MDB01\LogFiles
```

An interesting option is the -ConfigurationOnly parameter. Normally when you use the Move-DatabasePath cmdlet, the mailbox database settings in Active Directory are changed and the mailbox database and its log files are moved to the assigned location. When the -ConfigurationOnly parameter is used, the settings are changed in Active Directory, but the actual file move does not occur. This can be very useful in a disaster-recovery scenario, where a particular mailbox database is recovered in another location and the Mailbox server needs to use this particular mailbox database. This will be explained in more detail in Chapter 7.

Enabling Circular Logging

As explained in Chapter 5 concerning mailbox database technology, circular logging is a technique whereby only a very limited number of log files are kept on the server. Normally, log files are kept until a backup has successfully run, but when circular logging is enabled, the log files are removed from the server once all the transactions have been successfully committed to the mailbox database.

In a single-server scenario, circular logging is not recommended because of its lack of recovery options, but in a DAG environment, circular logging poses less risk of loss. Recovery options are provided by the DAG itself, so if a mailbox database is lost, another server in the DAG takes over.

Circular logging can be enabled using the EAC as well as the EMS. To enable it via EAC, follow these steps:

1. Select Servers in the Feature pane and select the Databases tab.

2. In the list view, select the database you want circular logging to be enabled on and select the Edit icon in the toolbar.

3. In the mailbox database window, select the Maintenance option and check the Enable Circular Logging option.

4. Click Save to store the configuration and close the mailbox database window.

If you enable circular logging on a server that's not a DAG member, you'll get a warning message that the circular logging will become active only when the mailbox database is dismounted and mounted again. When the Mailbox server is a DAG member, the circular logging option is applied immediately and there's no need for remounting the mailbox database.

To enable circular logging on a mailbox database named MDB01 using EMS, enter the following command:

```
Set-MailboxDatabase -Identity -CircularLoggingEnabled:$TRUE
```

To disable the circular logging, it's just the other way around; in EAC, the option should be unchecked, and in EMS, the -CircularLoggingEnabled option should be set to $FALSE.

Changing Quota Settings

When a new mailbox database is installed, the default quotas are set on the mailbox database. Quotas are limits on the level of the mailbox database, and if they are not explicitly set, the mailbox database quotas are enforced on the mailboxes.

The following quota settings are set by default:

- **Issue Warning at 1.9 GB** This value determines when Exchange starts sending warning messages to the user about the fact that he's reaching his mailbox limit. By default this limit is 100MB lower than the next limit, whereby the user cannot send email anymore.

- **Prohibit Send at 2.0 GB** This value determines when the user cannot send email anymore.

- **Prohibit Send and Receive at 2.1 GB** This value determines when the user cannot send email but at the same time cannot receive email anymore. By default this value is 100MB higher than the previous limit—the Prohibit Send quota. Some customers prefer to leave this quota setting open, especially on mailboxes that receive email from customers, so as to prevent bouncing back email from customers.

While these settings are sufficient for the majority of users, they can be extended to a very large level. In Exchange 2013, a mailbox of 100GB is not a problem at all on a server level; the only thing you have to be aware of is that the storage sizing must be able to accommodate these large mailboxes.

The quota setting can be changed using the EAC and the EMS. Using EAC, follow these steps:

1. Select Servers in the Feature pane and then select the Databases tab.

2. In the list view, select the mailbox database you want to change and click the Edit icon in the toolbar.

3. In the mailbox database window, select the Limits option.

4. In the Details pane, you can now change the appropriate quota settings in GB. The Issue Warning is always the smallest value, the Prohibit Send and Receive quota is always the largest value, and the Issue Warning quota can never be larger than the Prohibit Send quota, for example.

5. Click Save to store the configuration and close the mailbox database window.

To change the quota settings in the EMS on a mailbox database MDB01, you can use the following command:

```
Set-MailboxDatabase -Identity MDB01 -IssueWarningQuota 4.9GB -ProhibitSendQuota 5GB
-ProhibitSendReceiveQuota 5.5GB
```

■ **Note** Having a 50 GB mailbox on an Exchange server is not a problem, but complications may arise on the Outlook client when running Outlook in cached mode. If so, Outlook will create an OST file that matches the size of the mailbox, so 50 GB of mail data will be downloaded to the client and stored on the local hard disk. When running a laptop with a 5400rpm hard drive, this for sure will give problems. A solution is to use an SSD disk in the laptop, or use Outlook 2013 where the size of the OST file can be controlled by the end user.

Exchange periodically sends warning messages to users who have almost hit their quota (the Issue Warning) or who have hit their quota and cannot send (the Prohibit Send) or have hit their quota and cannot send and receive (the Prohibit Send and Receive limit). The frequency of these warning messages is set using the QuotaNotificationSchedule property on a mailbox database, which you can check using EMS:

```
Get-MailboxDatabase -Identity db01 | fl Name,Quota*

Name                    : DB01
QuotaNotificationSchedule : {zo.01:00-zo.01:15, ma.01:00-ma.01:15,
di.01:00-di.01:15, wo.01:00-wo.01:15, do.01:00-do.01:15, vr.01:00-vr.01:15, za.01:00-za.01:15}
```

Mailboxes inherit their quotas from the mailbox database where they reside. It is possible to override these limits by setting the quotas directly on the mailbox. The quota can be higher or lower than the mailbox database setting.

Assigning an Offline Address Book

When a mailbox database is created, an Offline Address Book (OAB) is not assigned to it. In a typical environment this is not needed, but there are situations where you can put one set of mailboxes in one mailbox database and another set of mailboxes in another mailbox database, and you can assign a specific OAB to the mailbox databases, and thus to the mailboxes in these databases.

1. In the EAC, select Servers in the Feature pane and then select the Databases tab.

2. In the list view, select the mailbox database you want to change and click the Edit icon in the toolbar.

3. In the mailbox database window, select the Client Settings option.

4. Use the Browse button to select a particular OAB you want to assign to this mailbox database.

5. Click Save to store the configuration and close the mailbox database window.

This can also be achieved by using the EMS:

```
Set-MailboxDatabase -Identity MDB01 -OfflineAddressBook "Custom Department OAB"
```

Creating a New Mailbox Database

If you have a larger environment, then it's likely that you will need some additional mailbox databases besides the default mailbox database. When you have multiple mailbox databases you can spread your mailboxes across these mailbox databases. Even better, when provisioning mailboxes, you do not assign a mailbox database; Exchange itself will look for a mailbox database to host this new mailbox.

Follow these steps to create a new mailbox database using EAC:

1. Select Servers in the Feature pane and select the Databases tab.

2. Click the Add icon to start the New Mailbox Database wizard.

3. Enter the name of the new mailbox database and use the Browse button to select a mailbox server where you want to host the mailbox database.

4. Enter the full directory and name of the mailbox database in the Database File Path box and enter the full directory where the log files are stored. The mailbox database directory and the log files directory can be the same, although this is not recommended when using a single server. If you do choose this, the best option is to use separate disks for the mailbox database file and for the log files.

5. Click Save to store the information (see Figure 6-20) and have the mailbox database created and mounted.

Figure 6-20. *The New Mailbox Database wizard in the EAC*

When the mailbox database is created, you'll see a warning message that the Information Store needs to be restarted. This is because the assignment of server memory is done when the Information Store is started. Without restarting the Information Store, you can mount the new mailbox database but performance will be minimal owing to a lack of sufficient memory. Since you cannot restart the Information Store during business hours (I assume), you have to do this in the evening I'm afraid.

Of course, it is also possible to create a new mailbox database using the EMS; just enter the following command to create a new mailbox database called MDB03, running on Mailbox server AMS-EXCH02 and stored on the F:\ drive.

```
New-MailboxDatabase -Name MDB03 -Server AMS-EXCH02
-EdbFilePath F:\MDB03\MDB03.edb -LogFolderPath F:\MDB03\LogFiles

Mount-Database -Identity MDB03
```

■ **Note** When you create a new mailbox database, this information is stored in Active Directory. The information needs to be replicated across all domain controllers. It can happen that when creating a new mailbox database using the EMS, this information is not replicated across all domain controllers when you enter the Mount-Database command. If that happens, the Mount-Database command will fail and an error will be shown on the console. Nothing to worry about; just wait a couple of minutes and retry the Mount-Database command.

Deleting a Mailbox Database

For some reason, you may want to delete a mailbox database. Before a mailbox database can be deleted, however, all the mailboxes in it need to be either deleted or moved to another mailbox database. When the mailbox database is empty (and you've made a backup, just in case), you can remove it.

To delete a mailbox database using the EAC, follow these steps:

1. Select Servers in the Feature pane and select the Databases tab.

2. In the list view, select the mailbox database you want to delete and click the Delete icon in the toolbar.

3. In the warning message that is shown, click Yes to actually delete the mailbox database.

4. The list view is updated and another warning is shown saying that the specified mailbox database has been removed, but that the actual EDB and log files are not physically removed.

5. Open Windows Explorer, navigate to the location where the EDB and log files reside, and delete them from the disk.

It is also possible to remove the mailbox database from the Exchange environment using the EMS. When all the mailboxes are deleted or moved to another location, enter the following command:

```
Remove-MailboxDatabase -Identity MDB01 -Confirm:$false
```

Just as with the mailbox database removal using the EAC, you have to manually delete the physical files from the hard disk. However, there's a snag here that you will run into one day. Suppose you've moved all the mailboxes to another mailbox database and you want to delete the mailbox database. An error message is shown saying: "This mailbox database contains one or more mailboxes, mailbox plans, archive mailboxes, public folder mailboxes or arbitration mailboxes."

When you check again, the mailbox database looks empty because nothing shows up in EAC and nothing is shown when you enter a `Get-Mailbox -Database MDB01` command in ESM. This situation is caused by system mailboxes in this particular mailbox database, and these system mailboxes are not shown by default. They can only be shown in the ESM by using the `Get-Mailbox -Database MDB01 -Arbitration` command. To move these mailboxes to another mailbox database called MDB02, you can use the following command in ESM:

```
Get-Mailbox -Database MDB01 -Arbitration | New-MoveRequest
-TargetDatabase MDB02
```

When these system mailboxes are moved and the mailbox database is *really* empty, it is possible to remove the mailbox database.

Online Mailbox Database Maintenance

Maintenance is a broad term and describes several tasks. Described here are (1) the mailbox deleted items retention settings; and (2) online mailbox maintenance in the Exchange environment.

When items are removed from the mailbox database (messages, folders, mailboxes), they are not immediately deleted from the mailbox or the mailbox database; they they are kept in the background for a particular amount of time. This time is called the *deleted items retention time* and it is set by default to 14 days for individual mailbox items and 30 days for mailboxes.

The deleted items retention time can be set in the same window as the quota warnings:

1. In the EAC, select Servers in the Feature pane and then select the Databases tab.

2. In the list view, select the mailbox database you want to change and click the Edit icon in the toolbar.

3. In the mailbox database window, select the Limits option.

4. In the Details pane, you can now change the deleted items retention time for both mailboxes and individual mailbox items.

5. Click Save to store the configuration and close the mailbox database window.

■ **Note**   There's a checkbox for an option called Don't Permanently Delete Items until the Database is Backed Up. This is an important feature. Even when items are beyond the retention time, they are not deleted from the mailbox database if this mailbox database was not backed up during the retention time. Only if a valid backup is created, are the items deleted. This way you always have a way to recover information, even when it is physically deleted from the mailbox database. If this option is not checked, items beyond its retention time are always deleted.

So what actually happens? When a user deletes a message and purges it from the Deleted Items folder in his mailbox, or when an administrator deletes a mailbox, it is actually moved the dumpster. This is a special location in the mailbox database, not visible for users, where items are stored. These deleted items are stored there for as long as stipulated by the deleted items retention time.

Online mailbox maintenance is a process in Exchange Server that maintains the internal structure of the mailbox database and consists of two parts:

- **Content maintenance** Responsible for purging deleted items, purging indexes, purging deleted mailboxes, and checking for orphaned messages. This part focuses on content maintenance—that is, it is responsible for purging old content and keeping the mailbox database as accurate as possible.

- **ESE maintenance** Keeps track of all database pages and indexes inside the mailbox database and performs checksum checks of all individual pages inside the database. It reads all pages in the database and performs a checksum check on each page to see if the page is valid. Single-bit errors can be fixed on the fly by ESE maintenance. ESE maintenance also performs online defragmentation (also known as OLD) to optimize the internal structure of the mailbox database. Online defragmentation reads all pages and indexes in the database and reorganizes these pages. The idea behind this is to free up pages inside the database so new items can be written in the free space inside the database, preventing unnecessary growth of the database.

Content maintenance can finish in a couple of hours, even on the largest mailbox databases. By default, content maintenance runs from 1 am until 5 am on the Mailbox server. This timeframe can be changed, however, as a property of the mailbox database (see Figure 6-21).

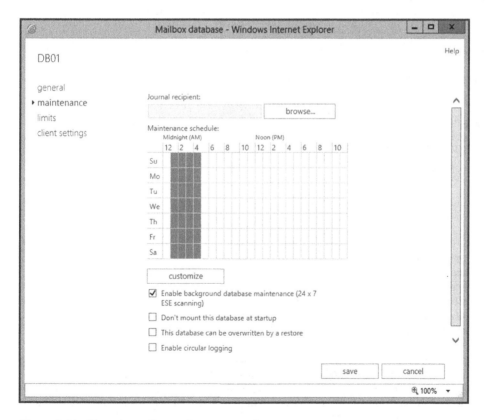

Figure 6-21. *Changing online maintenance settings*

Since ESE maintenance is far more I/O intensive, it needs more time. Therefore, the ESE maintenance runs 24 hours a day; this is also the default setting on a mailbox database, as shown in Figure 6-21, where the Enable Background Database Maintenance (24x7 ESE scanning) is checked. It is possible to uncheck this option, in which case ESE maintenance runs in the normal maintenance window.

The ESE maintenance is started when content maintenance is finished. For larger mailbox databases, this means that there's not sufficient time to scan all the pages inside the database. At 5 am (or whatever time is set) the maintenance is stopped, but it continues where it left off at the next maintenance interval. Despite this, not all pages will be checked, so the best option is to leave this checked to 24x7 maintenance.

■ **Note**   To prevent overwhelming the Mailbox server with checksum requests, and therefore possibly influencing client requests, ESE maintenance is a throttled process.

Managing Recipients

One of the most important parts of an Exchange server, at least from an end-user perspective, is the recipients—that is, the mailboxes, contacts, groups, public folders, and so on. Once provisioned, there's not much maintenance on the recipients, except for changing details, setting quotas, or maybe moving files to another location.

Managing Mailboxes

There are multiple types of mailboxes available in Exchange 2013:

- User mailboxes
- Lined mailboxes
- Resource (room or equipment) mailboxes
- Public folder mailboxes
- Site mailboxes

User Mailboxes

Mailboxes are the primary means of storing mail items. A mailbox is connected to a user, and the user is using a mail client like Outlook or a mobile client to read and send messages.

For a mailbox to be created, a new user needs to be created or the mailbox needs to be added to an existing user account in Active Directory. There's another option, however: a mailbox can be connected to a user account in Active Directory. This is called a *linked mailbox*. The Exchange organization is actually a resource forest, so for this link to be successful, a forest "trust" must exist between the forest where the user resides and the forest where the mailbox resides.

Mailboxes can be created using the EAC or the EMS, but also by using a script, as explained earlier in this chapter in the "Bulk Management" section, or a third party can be used to create mailboxes. Third-party solutions typically integrate with HR applications. When a new employee starts at the company, he is entered into the HR application; and using the third-party application, he automatically gets a user account in Active Directory and a mailbox in the Exchange organization.

Creating a mailbox in the EAC is easy:

1. When EAC is opened, it automatically starts in the Recipients option in the Feature pane and the Mailboxes tab.

2. In the toolbar, click the Add icon; right now you get the option to create a user mailbox or a linked mailbox. Select a user mailbox and the New User Mailbox wizard is shown.

3. Select the New User radio button and enter details such as the user's first name, initials, and last name, then use the Browse button to select an organizational unit in Active Directory where the user account will be stored (see Figure 6-22).

Figure 6-22. *Creating a new mailbox in EAC*

■ **Note** There are a couple of things you have to be aware of when creating a new mailbox this way. The user logon name (the left-hand side) is also known as the "alias" of the user. The default email address policy uses this alias for generating email addresses. It is also used for the old-style logon name (like CONTOSO\username). What is shown in Figure 6-22 is also known as the user principal name (UPN), which can be used for logging on to a workstation when the user is a member of a domain or to log on to OWA. Quite often it is identical to the user's email address.

---

4. Enter a password and select the option for "Require password change on next logon" if your security policy dictate so.

5. It is possible to set more options when you click on the Options link. By default, Exchange automatically selects the best location to store the new mailbox, but using the Browse button, you can manually select where to store the new mailbox.

6. Select the "Create an on-premises archive mailbox for this user" option when you want to create an archive mailbox, and use the Browse button again to select a mailbox database where the archive should be stored.

7. The last option is to select an Address Book Policy (ABP) if you've implemented one.

8. Click Save to store all information in Active Directory and create the new mailbox.

As you can see, only a limited set of properties can be selected during the creation of the mailbox. Once the mailbox is created, however, you can open to its properties and set all the properties that are needed. Useful information that can be set in this step are:

- Contact information
  - Street address
  - City of residence
  - Postal code or ZIP code
  - Work-, mobile, or home phone number
- Organization
  - Title
  - Department
  - Company
  - Manager
- Additional email addresses
- Mailbox features
  - Retention policy
  - Phone and voice features
  - Enabling available protocols (ActiveSync, OWA, IMAP/POP etc.)
  - Mail flow options and restrictions
- AdditionalgGroup membership
- Mailbox delegation

Creating a new mailbox using the EAC is easy, and is no problem when only a few mailboxes need to be started. When more mailboxes need to be created at one time, the EMS might be a more logical choice. To create a new mailbox with EMS, the following command can be used:

```
New-Mailbox -Name "Bruce Jackson" -Alias Bruce -UserPrincipalName BruceJ@contoso.com -SamAccountName
BruceJ -FirstName Bruce -LastName Jackson -ResetPasswordOnNextLogon $FALSE -Database DB01 -Password
(ConvertTo-SecureString 'Pass1word' -AsPlainText -Force)
```

■ **Note** The New-Mailbox command does not accept a user's password as plain text. The ConvertTo-SecureString converts a plain text password to a secure string.

Bulk management—that is, creating a lot of mailboxes using a script—was explained earlier in this chapter.

Additional properties cannot be set using the Set-Mailbox command, so the Set-User command has to be used to set additional properties:

```
Set-User -Identity BruceJ -Company Contoso -City Amsterdam -CountryOrRegion Netherlands -Department
Marketing -Manager "Cindy McDowell"
```

To add Bruce to the Contoso Employees and the Marketing Distribution Group, the following commands can be used in the EMS:

```
Add-DistributionGroupMember -Identity "Contoso Employees" -Member BruceJ
Add-DistributionGroupMember -Identity "Marketing" -Member BruceJ
```

It is also possible to mailbox-enable an existing user—a user who was created in Active Directory. For example, to mailbox-enable an Active Directory user called Kimmi Harrikiki in EAC, use the following steps:

1. In EAC, select Recipients in the Feature pane and then the Mailboxes tab.

2. To add the new mailbox, click the Add icon in the toolbar and select User Mailbox.

3. In the New User Mailbox, use the Browse button to select Kimmi Harrikiki. Since this is an existing user, the fields for First name and Last name are grayed out. However, don't forget to set the alias. This is easily overlooked since the Alias text box is listed above the user account.

4. You can select More Options to choose a mailbox database where the mailbox will be created, have an archive mailbox created, or establish an address book policy.

5. Click Save to store the information and create the new mailbox.

Of course, it is also possible to mailbox-enable an existing user in Active Directory by using the EMS; just use the following command:

```
Enable-Mailbox -Identity Kimi
```

Or, you can combine the Enable-Mailbox command with the Get-User command:

```
Get-User -Identity Kimi | Enable-Mailbox
```

As explained in the "Managing Mailbox Databases" section above, the quotas are set on a mailbox database level, but they can be overridden on a user level. Again, the EMS is a great way to achieve this since all three settings can be changed using one command:

```
Set-Mailbox -Identity Kimi -IssueWarningQuota 9.8GB -ProhibitSendQuota 10GB
-ProhibitSendReceiveQuota 10.2GB
```

When a new mailbox is created, it automatically receives the regional settings from the Exchange server. If you have an EN-US Exchange server, and you create a mailbox, it will automatically inherit these regional settings even if you're based somewhere else. This situation can be changed using the `Set-MailboxRegionalConfiguration` command in EMS. For example, to set the regional configuration to The Netherlands with the Western Europe Standard Time and include localization of the default folders in the mailbox, the following command can be used:

```
Set-MailboxRegionalConfiguration -Identity kimi -dateformat "d-M-yyyy"
-timezone "W. Europe Standard Time"  -timeformat "HH:mm" -Language "nl-NL"
-LocalizeDefaultFolderName:$true
```

Resource Mailboxes

A room mailbox and an equipment mailbox are like user mailboxes except that they do not represent a user account; rather, they are resources in the company. These resources can be a meeting room (room mailbox) or a beamer or, for example, a company car. These are the so-called "equipment" mailboxes, but the overall name for these kinds of non-user mailboxes is *resource mailboxes*.

The difference between a user mailbox and a resource mailbox is that resource mailboxes do not have accounts in Active Directory; their would-be accounts are disabled, since they don't represent standard users. Room and equipment mailboxes are not used for sending messages; instead they are for scheduling the resource in meeting requests. Therefore, a room mailbox and an equipment mailbox will automatically accept meeting or use requests when they do not conflict with other meeting or use requests; if there is a conflict, the request is declined. For administrative purposes, a user can be granted permission to manage the calendar of a room or equipment mailbox.

■ **Note**   Since a resource mailbox is not used for regular email traffic and no user logs on to the mailbox, it does not require a user license.

A room mailbox or an equipment mailbox can be created in either EAC or EMS. To create a room mailbox for a conference room on the ground level, for example, you can follow these steps to use EAC:

1. Select Recipients in the Feature pane and select the Resource tab.

2. Click the Add icon and select Room Mailbox to start the New Room Mailbox wizard.

3. Enter a name for the room mailbox, enter an email address, and use the Browse button to select an organizational unit for where you want to store the accompanying (disabled) user account. You can enter the location, phone number, and capacity of the room mailbox; this is the number of attendees that can attend a meeting in this meeting room (see Figure 6-23).

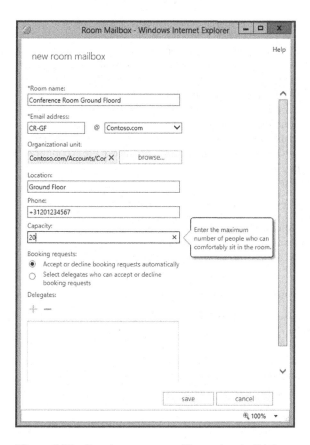

Figure 6-23. *Creating a room mailbox using the EAC*

4. By default, the room mailbox automatically accepts meeting requests when possible, but you can opt for delegates to accept or decline those meeting requests. If so, select Select Delegates radio button and pick who can accept or decline the booking requests, then add those delegates using the Add icon in the Delegates field.

5. Click Save to store this information and create the room mailbox.

Creating an equipment mailbox is similar; you just select Equipment Mailbox when using the Add icon in the toolbar.

To create a room mailbox in the EMS, you can use a command similar to this:

```
New-Mailbox -Name "Meeting Room 1st Floor" -Room -Alias MR-FirstFloor
-OrganizationalUnit contoso.com/accounts/contoso
-UserPrincipalName MR-FirstFloor@contoso.com -FirstName "Conference Room"
-LastName "First Floor"
```

The command to create a resource mailbox—for example, for a beamer—is similar, except that the -Room parameter is replaced with a -Equipment parameter:

```
New-Mailbox -Name "Panasonic Beamer" -Equipment -Alias Panasonic -OrganizationalUnit
contoso.com/accounts/contoso -UserPrincipalName Panasonic@contoso.com -FirstName Panasonic -LastName Beamer
```

Public Folder Mailboxes

As explained in Chapter 5, the public folders that were available in Exchange 2010 no longer exist in their own public folder database; they now are in a regular mailbox database. This way, a public folder can use the normal High Availability options as offered by the database availability group (DAG). For Outlook clients, there's no difference from previous versions of Exchange Server public folders; clients continue to identify the new public folders as "just" public folders.

As mentioned in Chapter 5 also, there are primary and secondary public folders. The first public folder mailbox that will be created is the primary Hierarchy mailbox, which contains a writeable copy of the Hierarchy. This is also the only writeable copy of the Hierarchy; if this is not available, the public folders are read-only. Therefore, it is important to safeguard this mailbox against outages using a DAG. Additional public folder mailboxes are secondary Hierarchy mailboxes and these contain read-only copies of the Hierarchy.

To create the first public folder mailbox in EAC, follow these steps:

1. Select Public Folders in the Feature pane and select the Public Folder Mailboxes tab.

2. Click the Add icon to start the New Public Folder Mailbox wizard. Enter a name for the mailbox and use the Browse button to select an organizational unit where the accompanying account in Active Directory will be created and a mailbox database where the public folder mailbox will be stored.

3. Click Save to store the information and create the public folder mailbox.

This first public folder mailbox will be shown in the list view as Primary Hierarchy. When you create a second public folder mailbox, it will be shown as Secondary Hierarchy.

By default, these public folder mailboxes are set to use the default quotas from the mailbox database, and these can be quite limiting for public folder usage. When selecting the public folder mailbox properties, you can customize the quotas and substitute your own settings. A typical size for a public folder mailbox would be 100GB. When the public folder mailbox reaches this limit, an additional public folder mailbox needs to be created.

To create a public folder mailbox using the EMS, you can use a command similar to this example:

```
New-Mailbox -PublicFolder -Name PF-Mailbox -Database MDB02
```

Site Mailboxes

Site mailboxes are new in Exchange 2013. They are a combination of a Sharepoint 2013 teamsite and an Exchange 2013 mailbox. From the end-user's perspective, only one client need be used—that is, an Outlook client. Site mailboxes are typically targeted to project members; email messages are stored in the Exchange 2013 mailbox, while documents are stored on the Sharepoint 2013 site. This content, however, can also be accessed using the normal Sharepoint site. This way, Sharepoint introduces document coauthoring and versioning to the solution, while Exchange synchronizes just enough metadata from Sharepoint to create a sufficient view in the Outlook client.

Site mailboxes rely on tight integration between Exchange 2013 and Sharepoint 2013. These site mailboxes are also managed from the Sharepoint 2013 server. More information regarding how to create and configure site mailboxes can be found on the Microsoft website at http://tinyurl.com/nqpbhqg.

Managing Groups

Distribution groups in Exchange 2013 are used as a way to send email messages to the groups' members. Exchange uses only universal groups for messaging purposes, since they can contain users from anywhere in the forest; their membership is published to the Global Address List (GAL).

There are two types of groups available:

- **Distribution groups** These groups are meant for grouping mailboxes together and sending email messages to all members by using just one recipient, the distribution group.

- **Security groups** These groups are used for grouping users together and granting permission to access particular resources, like file shares, other objects in Active Directory, and objects in other servers like SQL Server. Security groups are a so-called *security principal*. The good thing is that security groups can be used as distribution groups, which makes them useful. Important to note, however, is that security groups can be used as distribution groups but not the other way around. Distribution groups *cannot* be used as security groups!

Distribution groups are available in two versions:

- **Static distribution group** A static distribution group has its members set manually. Group membership is set during creation of the distribution group, and when new mailboxes are created they are added to the distribution group.

- **Dynamic distribution group** Membership in a dynamic distribution group is not set manually, but rather is determined by a query based on a property on the mailbox. For example, a dynamic distribution group called "Contoso - All Employees" could be based on mailboxes that have their company attribute set to "Contoso." When an email message is sent to the Contoso - All Employees distribution group, the Exchange server queries for all mailboxes with the company attribute set to Contos and sends a message to all these mailboxes.

Group Ownership

When a new distribution group is created, its administrator is automatically assigned ownership of the group. It is possible, however, to assign group ownership to another user, and the advantage of doing this is that when the new owner opens the distribution group in Outlook, he can manage the group himself and update membership if needed (see Figure 6-24).

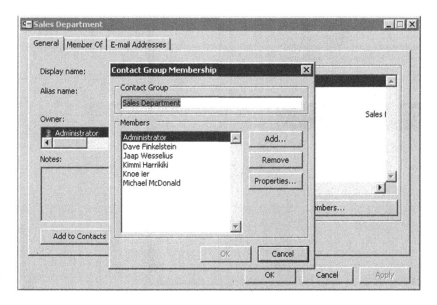

Figure 6-24. *Managing distribution group membership in Outlook*

A group owner can be assigned using the EAC when selecting the properties of the distribution group, or a group owner can be assigned using the EMS using the following command:

```
Set-DistributionGroup -Identity Sales -ManagedBy "Katy Price", Administrator
```

Personally, I think it's a good idea to add the administrator as a co-owner when reassigning ownership of a distribution group. If something happens and you as administrator need immediate access to a distribution group, you don't want to hassle with ownership issues.

Protected Groups

By default, a distribution group is an open group in that it will accept messages from all users in the organization. It is possible to restrict this arrangement, so that only assigned to this distribution group can send messages to the group. Other users who try to send messages to the group will get a non-delivery report (NDR). But before sending the message, the nongroup member will see a mailtip message that he's trying to send something to a restricted group!

Similar to this situation is the internal versus external senders. Again by default, a distribution group will accept messages only from users inside the organization. External users from other messaging platforms cannot send messages to a distribution group unless the distribution group is configured to do so. This is shown in Figure 6-25, where the security group HR Staff is set to receive messages only from senders inside the organization. In short, a sender from the Internet cannot send messages to this security group.

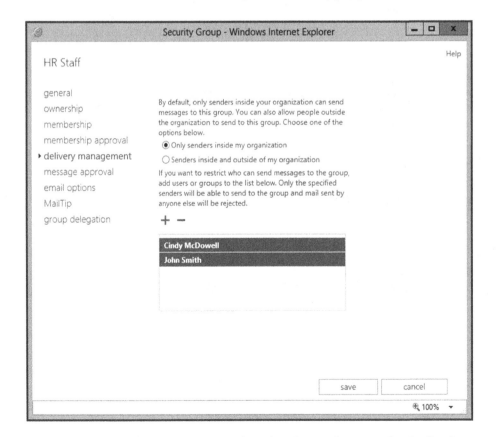

Figure 6-25. *A protected group has a limited number of users who can send to the distribution group*

User Managed Groups

In Exchange 2013, it is possible to create distribution groups where membership is managed by the users themselves. You don't want this to happen for company-related groups—for example, you don't want employees to leave or enter a group like "Contoso - All Employees"—but for subject-matter groups like "Exchange 2013 Special Interest Group," this flexibility can be useful.

Therefore, a distribution group can be:

- **Open** When a group is configured to be open, a user can join or leave this distribution group without any question. Only distribution groups can be open. If security groups were this type, it would present a major security breach—for example, when you use security groups to grant access to your mailbox.

- **Closed** When a group is configured to be closed, users can be added or removed only by the owner of the group. All requests to join or leave the group are rejected automatically.

- **Owner approval** When a group is configured as owner approval, all requests to join are sent to the owner of the group. The owner approves or rejects the membership request.

This categorization is shown in Figure 6-26, where the distribution group "Sales Department" is configured as open, both for join action and for leave action.

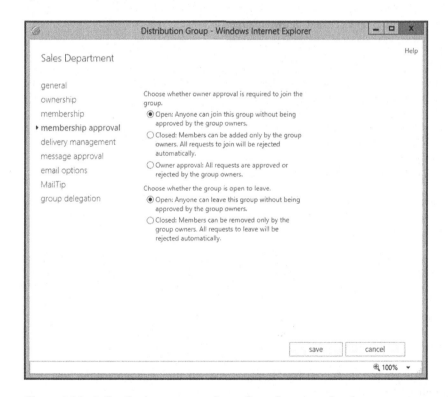

Figure 6-26. *A distribution group can be configured as open, closed, or owner approval*

It cannot be any surprise, but this designationcan be set using the EMS as well; try using:

```
Set-DistributionGroup -Identity Sales -MemberJoinRestriction Closed -MemberDepartRestriction Closed
```

In contrast to Figure 6-26, where the membership approval is set to open, we set the group membership to closed in the EMS example (Figure 6-25). In this latter case, membership can be changed only by the group's owner.

Creating a New Distribution Group

Creating new distribution groups is not a complex task, and it can be performed using the EAC or the EMS. I've seen customers with thousands and thousands of distribution groups that are sometimes as old as Active Directory in general. So, note that creating a new distribution group is one thing and maintaining it or even removing it when no longer needed is another thing. Administrators tend to forget to remove these old distribution groups, so this is something to keep in mind.

To create a new distribution group using the EAC, follow this procedure as an example:

1. In EAC, select Recipients in the Feature pane and select the Groups tab.

2. In the toolbar, click the Add icon and select Distribution Group to start the New Distribution Group wizard.

3. Enter a display name, alias, and if needed, a description. Use the Browse button to select an organizational unit where the group will be stored in Active Directory. As explained before, you can assign a user as the owner of the new group; by default, the owner of a group is also a member of the group, but this option can be deselected as well. It is also possible to designate if the group is open, closed, or owner approval.

4. Click Save to store all information in Active Directory and create the new distribution group.

Creating a dynamic distribution group is very similar to creating a static distribution group. When you click the Add icon in the toolbar, select Dynamic Distribution Group to start the New Dynamic Distribution Group wizard. This is similar to the earlier wizard, except it has the option to enter a rule. Membership in the dynamic distribution group is determined by these rules.

Just click Add a Rule, and in the drop-down box, select a property you want to query on. Enter a word or phrase that will be part of the rule. If you select Department and enter "Editors," the dynamic distribution group will contain all mailboxes that have "Editors" in their Department property.

As always, it is also possible to create a new distribution group using the EMS; enter the following command:

```
New-DistributionGroup -Name Support -DisplayName "Support Department"
-OrganizationalUnit contoso.com/accounts/contoso
-ManagedBy administrator, "john smith" -CopyOwnerToMember
```

If you want to create a room list, which is basically an address list but containing room-type resource mailboxes, it's just a matter of adding the -Roomlist parameter to the New-Distribution command.

To create a new dynamic distribution group using the EMS, you use another command:

```
New-DynamicDistributionGroup -Name Publishers -DisplayName "Contoso Publishers"
-IncludedRecipients AllRecipients -OrganizationalUnit contoso.com/accounts/contoso
-ConditionalDepartment Publishing
```

All users who have their department property in Active Directory populated with the value "Publishing" will automatically be part of this distribution group.

The advantage to using these dynamic distribution goups is obvious: no additional group membership maintenance. The only thing to consider is that these additional properties must be set when provisioning the users.

Creating a new security group is similar to creating a new distribution group. After clicking the Add icon in the toolbar, you select Security Group to start the New Security Group wizard. The values that are to be entered are the same as when you create a distribution group.

When creating a new security group through EMS, the parameter -Type Security needs to be added:

```
New-DistributionGroup -Name "Exchange Admins" -DisplayName "Exchange Admins"
-OrganizationalUnit contoso.com/accounts/contoso
-ManagedBy administrator, "Kimmi Harrikiki" -CopyOwnerToMember -Type Security
```

Mail-Enabling an Existing Security Group

If there are distribution groups or security groups already in Active Directory, and you want to have them available as distribution groups in Exchange, you can mail-enable them. When existing groups are mail-enabled, they can be managed as discussed earlier in this section.

In contrast to creating new distribution groups, mail-enabling of existing groups is performed only by using EMS with a command similar to this:

```
Get-Group -Identity Support | Enable-DistributionGroup -Alias Support
```

■ **Note** The existing group's scope needs to be Universal. If its scope is set to Global, an error message appears: "You can't mail-enable this group because it isn't a universal group. Only a universal group can be mail-enabled."

Managing Contacts and Mail-Enabled Users

Besides mailboxes and groups, there are two more types of recipients that cause confusion in an Exchange training session. When I ask for the difference between *mail*-enabled users and *mailbox*-enabled users, most students don't know the difference. Similarly, they don't recognize the difference between mail-enabled *users* and mail-enabled *contacts*. But, hey; that's why they attend the training—or read this book, of course.

- **Mail-enabled contact** A mail-enabled contact is a contact in the Global Address List (GAL), just like a business card you might have in the Rolodex on your desk. A mail-enabled contact has a first name, last name, display name, and internal and external email addresses. When selecting this contact from the GAL, an email will be sent to the contact's external email address—for example, JohnDoe@hotmail.com.

  A mail-enabled contact also has an internal email address composed of the contact's alias and the internal primary SMTP address. When a message is sent to this internal email address, the message is automatically routed to the contact's external email address—that is, JohnDoe@hotmail.com.

- **Mail-enabled user** A mail-enabled user has the same properties as a mail-enabled contact; t hat is, a first name, last name, display name, and internal and external email addresses. But a mail-enabled user does *not* have a mailbox on the Exchange server—only an external email address. This is the major difference between a normal mailbox-enabled user and a mail-enabled user. When a mail-enabled user is selected from the GAL in another user's Outlook, and this user sends a message to the mail-enabled user, the message is routed to the mail-enabled user's external email address.

The difference between the mail-enabled contact and mail-enabled user is that a mail-enabled user is, in fact, a security principal in Active Directory—that is, a regular user. This user can log on to Active Directory and can access all kinds of resources. The user only does not have a mailbox on the Exchange server; the user does have his own external email address, and that shows up in the GAL.

For example, there may be an external accountant visiting a company for a long period of time. The accountant can use the user account for accessing other resources on the internal network, like fileshares, printers, or maybe even financial applications, and therefore should be listed in the company's address list. The accountant should be able to receive email from other employees, but should not be able to send out email messages on behalf of the company by using the company's email domain.

An overview of the differences among various types of Active Directory accounts is listed in Table 6-2.

Table 6-2. *Overview of Active Directory accounts and email function*

Account Type	Uses Network Resources	Has Mailbox	Has external email address
User account	Yes	No	No
Mail-enabled user	Yes	No	Yes
Mailbox-enabled user	Yes	Yes	No
Contact	No	No	No
Mail-enabled contact	No	No	Yes

Creating a Mail-Enabled Contact

Mail-enabled contacts are easy to create in EAC. When selecting Recipients in the Feature pane and selecting the Contact tab, just click the Add icon and select Mail Contact. The wizard is straightforward and easy to use; just fill in the properties and click Save to store the information and create the mail-enabled contact. It's that simple.

To create a mail-enabled contact in EMS, you can use a command similar to this example:

```
New-MailContact -Name "John Williams" -FirstName John -LastName Williams -DisplayName
"John Williams" -OrganizationalUnit contoso.com/accounts/contoso -ExternalEmailAddress
"SMTP:JohnWilliams@hotmail.com"
```

Creating a Mail-Enabled User

Just like creating a mail-enabled contact, creating a mail-enabled user is not that difficult. Follow these steps to create one using the EAC:

1. Select Recipients in the Feature pane and select the Contact tab. In the toolbar, click the Add icon and select Mail User to start the New Mail User wizard.

2. Enter an alias and an external email address. The alias is used by the Exchange 2013 server, the external email address is the email address that's associated with the mail-enabled user account.

3. Independent of what you enter in step 2, it is possible to mail-enable an exisiting user account in Active Directory or to create a new account in Active Directory, in which case the mandatory properties need to be entered.

4. Select the New User radio button and fill in the fields for first name, last name, display name, and so on. Use the Browse button to select an organizational unit where the new user account will be stored. Enter a logon name for the user and enter a password (see Figure 6-27). Compared to creating a mailbox-enabled user, there are no more options to enter because there won't be any mailbox, of course.

Figure 6-27. *Creating a mail-enabled user in EAC*

5. Click Save to store the information in Active Directory and create the new mail-enabled user.

Creating a mail-enabled user in EMS is also possible; just use a command similar to this example:

```
New-MailUser -Name "Isaac Wesselius" -Alias Isaac -OrganizationalUnit contoso.com/accounts/contoso
-UserPrincipalName Isaac@contoso.com -FirstName Isaac -Initials M -LastName Wesselius -DisplayName
"Isaac Martinus Wesselius" -Password (ConvertTo-SecureString 'Pass1word' -AsPlainText -Force)
-ExternalEmailAddress "SMTP:IsaacMW@hotmail.com"
```

Both the mail-enabled user and the mail-enabled contact can be added to a distribution group. Both types of recipients will then receive messages that are sent to the distribution group. When a security group is used, it does not make sense from a permissions perspective to add a mail-enabled contact (a mail-enabled contact cannot access network resources anyhow), except for receiving messages, of course. A mail-enabled user, however, will inherit the permissions granted to the security group, so a mail-enabled contact can access these resources.

Managing Address Lists

In a typical organization, the default-available address lists in Exchange 2013 are sufficient. In Exchange 2013, it is possible to use multiple address lists and assign these address lists to mailboxes depending on their department, geographical location, business unit, and so on. A common example here is a university with various faculties where multiple address lists are created, one for each faculty. Another example is a multinational corporation that creates multiple address lists based on geographical location, like EMEA, US, or FAREAST. These address lists can be available for all users, but it's also possible to segregate the address lists through the use of Address Book Policies (ABP), a feature introduced in Exchange Server 2010 SP 2.

■ **Note** In Exchange Server 2007 and before, address list segregation was enforced by setting ACLs on the various objects in Active Directory and Exchange Server, a technique that was developed in Exchange Server 2000 but was still available, working and supported in Exchange Server 2007. But Exchange Server 2010 introduced the address book service running on the Client Access server, making it dangerous (and unsupported) to set ACLs on the various objects. This was the reason the address book policies were introduced in Exchange Server 2010 SP2.

Custom address lists in Exchange 2013 are created by means of special queries, just as done for dynamic distribution groups. A query determines in which address list a mailbox is shown, and this query can be based on a user's organization, department, or a custom attribute. Using a custom attribute when using Address Book Policies has the advantage that a user, or an Exchange administrator, cannot accidentally overwrite an attribute with a "wrong" value, causing unpredictable results from the ABP perspective.

For example, when a company called Fabrikam has its own address lists in Exchange, based on the user's company attribute, all Fabrikam users show up in the Fabrikam address lists. When somebody accidentally changes a user's company attribute, this user no longer shows up in the Fabrikam address List. Of course, this can happen when a custom attribute is changed as well, but changing a custom attribute cannot be seen as an accident;it is changed deliberately.

To create new address lists for all users—for example, in the Fabrikam OU in Active Directory, which have the value 'Fabrikam' in their Custom Attribute 1—you can follow these steps in EAC:

1. In EAC, select Organization in the Feature pane and select the Address Lists tab and click the Add icon to start the New Address List wizard.

2. In the wizard, enter a name for the new address list, like "Fabrikam All Users Address List" and select only "Users with Exchange Mailboxes" and click Add a Rule.

3. Create a rule based on Custom Attribute 1 and enter "Fabrikam" in the Specify Words or Phrases window, as shown in Figure 6-28.

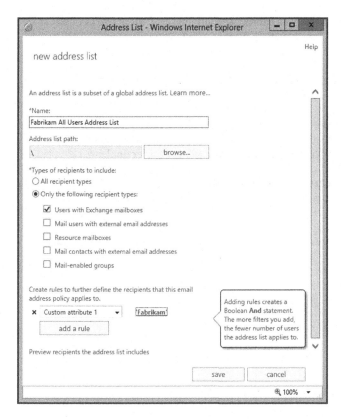

Figure 6-28. *Creating a new address list and using Custom Attribute 1 for filtering*

4. Use the Preview Recipients in the address list to check the results of the query created in the previous step.

5. If all is okay, click the Save button to store this in Active Directory and create the new address list.

6. To complete the example, repeat theses step to create the following additional address lists:

- Fabrikam All Rooms Address List

- Fabrikam All Groups Address List

- Fabrikam All Contacts Address List

- Fabrikam Offline Address Book

It is not possible to create a custom global address list for the Fabrikam Company, as in the above example, in EAC, so the EMS has to be used to create a dedicated Fabrikam GAL. Enter the following command in EMS to achieve this:

```
New-GlobalAddressList -Name "Fabrikam GAL" -RecipientFilter "((Alias -ne '`$NULL') -and
(CustomAttribute1 -eq 'Fabrikam'))"
```

An Offline Address Book (OAB) also cannot be created using the EAC, so the EMS needs to be used instead. To create a Fabrikam OAB where a rule is created for Custom Attribute 1 with the value "Fabrikam," and that will include all address lists created in the previous steps, you can use a command similar to this example:

```
New-OfflineAddressBook –Name "Fabrikam OAB" -AddressLists "Fabrikam GAL","Fabrikam All Users Address
List","Fabrikam All Rooms Address List","Fabrikam All Contacts Address List","Fabrikam All Groups
Address List"
```

Now that all required address lists are created, a new ABP can be established. The ABP for Fabrikam will accept the following address lists:

- Fabrikam All Users address list

- Fabrikam All Rooms address list

- Fabrikam All Contacts address list

- Fabrikam OAB

- Fabrikam GAL

To create a new ABP that will contain all these address lists, the OAB, and the GAL, you can use a command similar to this example:

```
New-AddressBookPolicy –Name "Fabrikam ABP" -GlobalAddressList "\Fabrikam GAL"
-OfflineAddressBook "\Fabrikam OAB" -RoomList "\Fabrikam All Rooms Address List" –AddressLists
"\Fabrikam All Users Address List","\Fabrikam All Groups Address List","\Fabrikam All Contacts
Address List"
```

At this moment, all Fabrikam address lists, the Fabrikam GAL, the Fabrikam OAB, and the Fabrikam ABP are done. The only thing left is to assign the Fabrikam ABP to the Fabrikam users. You can use the following command in EMS to assign the Fabrikam ABP to all users who have the Fabrikam value in their Custom Attribute 1:

```
Get-Mailbox | where {$_.customAttribute1 -eq "Fabrikam"} | Set-Mailbox -AddressBookPolicy↵
"Fabrikam ABP"
```

When a Fabrikam user logs on to Outlook and checks the available address lists, only the address lists supplied by the ABP are visible to this user (see Figure 6-29).

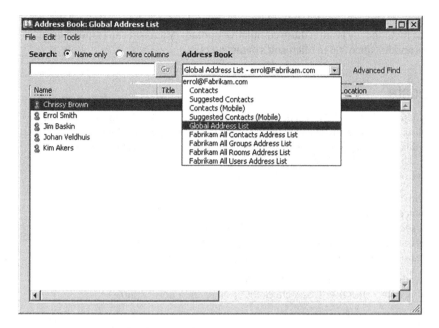

Figure 6-29. *The Fabrikam address lists show up in Outlook*

As you've seen, most of these options can be achieved only by using the EMS. Just the standard address lists can be created using the EAC. When you have to create multiple address lists, using the EMS can become interesting, since it will save you time, plus it is less prone to error. To create the Fabrikam All Users Address List using the EMS, you can use the following command:

```
New-AddressList -Name "Fabrikam All Users Address List" -Container "\"
-DisplayName "Fabrikam All Users Address List" -RecipientFilter "((Alias -ne '`$NULL') -and
(CustomAttribute1 -eq 'Fabrikam'))"
```

Patch Management

In early 2013, Microsoft announced a major change in the Exchange servicing model. Up until Exchange 2013, Microsoft released a service pack (SP) every 12 to 18 months. A service pack is a collection of fixes and patches and can also contain new features and functions for the product. For Exchange Server, the service pack is a full installation of the product, which means that you can download the service pack for Exchange Server 2010 and install the full product for this version.

Between service packs, Microsoft would release update rollups for Exchange Server on a regular basis, typically every three or four months. An update rollup also contains collections of fixes and patches but rarely new features or functions. For example, the Exchange Server 2010 SP 2 Update Rollup 4 contains new options for calendar and task-retention policies. But update rollups are version-specific, which means that they are released for, say, Exchange Server 2010 SP 1 or Exchange Server 2010 SP 2. Needless to say, these update rollups are not interchangeable. Also important to note is that an update rollup is not a full version of the product; it's just a collection of hot fixes. The sizing of Exchange Server update rollups is typically between 60 and 70GB.

To speed up the deployment process and to react quickly to customer demand and market changes, Microsoft has changed its service pack and update rollup strategies. Starting with Exchange Server 2013, Microsoft is releasing a cumulative update on a quarterly basis. The cumulative update is also a collection of fixes and patches for the given period, and it can contain some new features and functions, but the most important change is that it's a full product with normal setup application. Because of this setup application, Microsoft can make major changes in a cumulative update—even schema updates can be included. By issuing these cumulative updates, Microsoft can respond quickly to market demand, both on-premises and in Office 365 in Microsoft's datacenters.

Installing a Cumulative Update

As explained above, a cumulative update is a full product. It is possible to install Exchange 2013 from scratch using a cumulative update download, as well as to upgrade a previous release to the latest software level. Installing Exchange 2013 from a cumulative update download is no diffeeent from the procedure presented in Chapter 2, so I won't go into detail about doing that here.

Here's how to install a cumulative update to Exchange 2013:

1. Download the update from Microsoft and extract the download. Log in to the Exchange 2013 as an administrator account that's a member of the Enterprise Admins security group and the Schema Admins security group. Note: It is possible that a cumulative update will contain schema changes but the setup will take care of that. When logged on, navigate to the extracted cumulative update and start the graphic setup application setup.exe.

2. The setup application has the option of automatically checking for updates. Go ahead if you want to do this; otherwise, select the "Don't check for updates right now" radio button.

3. The setup application is initialized and the appropriate installation files are copied to the right location on the Exchange Server. After initializing, the upgrade window is shown; click Next to continue.

4. On the license agreement window, select the "I accept the terms in the license agreement" radio button and click Next to continue. The prerequisite check will automatically be started.

5. When blocking problems are found, they are reported in the prerequisite analysis window, including the steps needed to fix them. If nothing is found, click Install to start the actual upgrade. Note: If you have the Unified Messaging configured for use with different (i.e., non-US) language packs, the upgrade will fail. The additional language packs need to be uninstalled first, using the setup.exe /RemoveUMLanguagePack: <UmLanguagePackName> comand.

6. The upgrade is a multistep process, from changing the Active Directory to uninstalling the old binaries and installing the new binaries, to reconfiguring the services (see Figure 6-30). Except for changes made, for example, in the config files or customization to OWA, all old configuration settings should be preserved.

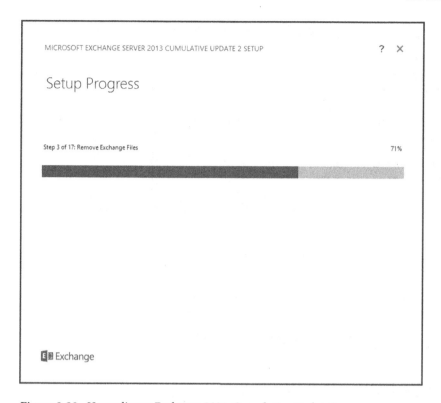

MICROSOFT EXCHANGE SERVER 2013 CUMULATIVE UPDATE 2 SETUP   ?   ✕

Setup Progress

Step 3 of 17: Remove Exchange Files   71%

E Exchange

Figure 6-30. Upgrading to Exchange 2013, Cumulative Update 1

7. After some time, the upgrade will be finished and a Setup Completed page will be shown. Reboot the server, and Exchange 2013 is up to date again. If you've had to remove the UM language pack in step 5, you have to reinstall the new UM language pack for the new cumulative update.

Unattended Installation of a Cumulative Update

It is possible to perform an unattended upgrade of a cumulative update. This action will break up the upgrade into multiple steps whereby the Active Directory partitions are upgraded and the actual Exchange Server software is installed. I won't go into too much detail about an unattended installation since that was covered in detail in Chapter 2, but the commands that need to be performed are as follows:

```
Setup.exe /PrepareSchema /IAcceptExchangeServerLicenseTerms

Setup.exe /PrepareAD  /IAcceptExchangeServerLicenseTerms

Setup.exe /PrepareDomain /IAcceptExchangeServerLicenseTerms

Setup.exe /mode:upgrade /IAcceptExchangeServerLicenseTerms
```

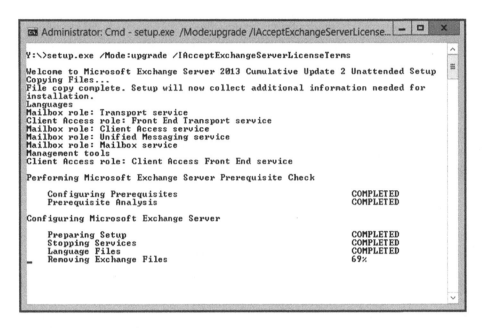

Figure 6-31. Installing Cumulative Update 2 on an existing Exchange 2013 server. Note the "removing Exchange Files" on the console

Exchange 2013 Maintenance Mode

If you have multiple Exchange 2013 Mailbox servers configured in a DAG, some additional management is needed when installing a cumulative update. Microsoft has introduced Maintenance Mode. In Maintenance Mode, the server you use to perform management tasks is removed from the service (it is not removed from the DAG, only from the service!) by moving all active mailbox databases off the server. Also, possible movements of mailbox databases from other Mailbox servers to this Mailbox server are blocked at that point. The Primary Active Manager (PAM) is moved to another Mailbox server, and possible movement back is blocked as well.

To place the Exchange 2013 Mailbox server in Maintenance Mode, Microsoft has supplied a script called StartDAGServerMaintenance.ps1, which can be found in the $ExScripts directory. So, when installing a cumulative update the steps are as follows:

1. Use the StartDAGServerMaintenance.ps1 script to place the DAG member in Maintenance Mode.

2. Install the cumulative update.

3. Use the StopDAGServerMaintenance.ps1 script to bring the DAG member back in production.

4. Use the RedistributeActiveDatabases.ps1 script to rebalance the active mailbox database copies across the DAG.

5. Repeat these steps on the other DAG members.

Although the setup application does not request a reboot, it's my personal experience that it doesn't do any harm to reboot the Exchange 2013 server once the cumulative update is installed. After the reboot, Exchange 2013 can be taken out of Maintenance Mode.

The DAG member is put into Maintenance Mode by using the following commands in EMS:

```
CD $ExScripts
.\StartDAGServerMaintenance.ps1 -Server AMS-EXCH01
```

When the DAG member is upgraded (and rebooted), it can be put back into normal operation using the following commands in EMS:

```
CD $ExScripts
.\StopDAGServerMaintenance.ps1 -Server AMS-EXCH01
```

The last step is to redistribute the mailbox databases across all the DAG members. Again, the RedistributeActiveDatabases.ps1 script can be found in the $ExScripts directory so you can use the following command in EMS:

```
CD $ExScripts
.\RedistributeActiveDatabases.ps1 -DagName DAG01 -BalanceDbsByActivationPreference
-Confirm:$False
```

This redistributes the active mailbox databases across the DAG based on their activation preference.

Summary

In this chapter, I explained some of the basics of managing your Exchange 2013 environment. This involves using the following:

- **Exchange Admin Center** (EAC) The new graphic UI, fully based on HTML5 and the successor of the Exchange Management Console in Exchange Server 2010. Although it works fine for most of the administrative tasks, not all tasks can be performed using the EAC, as shown in this chapter.

- **Exchange Management Shell** (EMS) The EMS is running on top of PowerShell 3.0 in Windows Server 2012 (which is an additional download when running Exchange 2013 on Windows Server 2008 R2), and can be used for all configuration changes in Exchange 2013. When you're working with Exchange Server for a longer period, you'll see that you get more familiar with EMS.

- **Toolbox** The toolbox is literally an MMC left over from the past, which contains only a link to the Remote Connectivity Analyzer (RCA), the Queue Viewer, and the Template Details editor.

When it comes to overall management tasks, I have covered the management of mailbox databases with all of the various options and the management of recipients, like mailboxes, groups, and contacts—and related to this, the address lists and the Address Book Policy.

I did not cover backup and restore, tasks that are for sure part of day-to-day management, but that's because the next chapter is all about backup, restore, and disaster recovery.

Monitoring and troubleshooting are not covered in this chapter either, as these topics are discussed in Chapter 8 and Chapter 9.

■ ■ ■

## CHAPTER 7

Backup, Restore, and Disaster Recovery in Exchange Server 2013

One of the things a typical Exchange Server administrator doesn't want to talk about is restoring information or disaster recovery, because it can be so very difficult in Exchange 2013. The first part, backing up data, is not that difficult; you just install a backup application and have it run on a regular basis. So far, no need to worry.

But what happens if a mailbox database crashes and you've got complaining users? What do you do then? What's a good time to start looking at tools like ESEUTIL? Or, when do you decide to restore a mailbox database from your backup?

Even worse, what happens when an entire Exchange 2013 server crashes and is completely lost? Do you rebuild the server? Restore it from backup? Or, maybe rely on snapshot technology, which you've been told is a good thing?

In this chapter we're going to explore backup technologies in Exchange 2013; in particular, we'll cover:

- **Streaming backups** Although discontinued in Exchange 2010, and no longer supported for backing up data, streaming gives a good overview of what's actually happening under the hood. The streaming technology is also used when copying mailbox databases in a DAG (see Chapter 5).

- **VSS backups** Volume Shadowcopy Service, sometimes also referred to as "snapshot backup." We'll explore the default Windows Server Backup (WSB) and a low-level tool called DiskShadow, which shows you what's happening when creating a VSS backup.

Besides backup, in this chapter we'll discuss restore technologies; for example, how to:

- Restore your mailbox database to its original location— basically a traditional mailbox database restore.

- Restore you mailbox database to an alternative location and discover the possibilities there for using a recovery database and a dial-tone recovery.

When your Exchange 2013 server crashes dramatically, it's time to recover your Exchange Server 2013, and we're going to explore your options there as well. In short, we're going to rebuild and recover the entire Exchange 2013 server, but we'll also have a look at rebuilding and recovering a mailbox database.

The last topic that's explored in this chapter is a new technology introduced in Exchange 2010 (so it's not so entirely new), which is called *Exchange Native Data Protection*. This is also sometimes referred to as a "backupless" Exchange environment. This backupless thing scares a lot of IT administrators, but in fact it is possible to recover from all major outages without having a backup. The only thing you have to do is evaluate the requirements for implementing this Exchange Native Data Protection solution to determine if it fits your needs.

Let's get started.

Backing up Exchange 2013

Backing up Exchange 2013 is a process of storing your valuable Exchange server data like the mailbox databases, which contain the actual mailboxes, on another media. This media, in turn, can be stored on another location that can be a safeguard if you face the loss of an entire location.

But not only mailbox databases need to be backed up; you can also backup information like your Transport log files or Protocol log files, SSL certificates, or maybe the entire Exchange 2013 server.

Before we dive into backing up Exchange 2013, especially the mailbox databases, though, we have to take a closer look at the mailbox databases themselves and the database internals. Only this way can you fully understand what's happening when a backup of a mailbox database is created; this knowledge is necessary to successfully recover a mailbox database after a failure.

A Refresher on Mailbox Database Technologies

In Chapter 5, I explained the internals of the mailbox database, but for the backup technology, let's do a refresher. The mailbox database is a transactional database, but it is not a relational database, as in a SQL server. The mailbox database in Exchange 2013 is a balanced tree, or B+ tree.

ESE - The Database Engine

The database engine used in Exchange Server is the Extensible Storage Engine, or ESE—lso, known as a JET blue database. JET stands for Joint Engine Technology, a database initiative from Microsoft that appeared long ago. ESE doesn't use a relational database technology, but it has its own, highly optimized technology.

A relational database is a predefined database with columns and rows, much like a Microsoft Excel spreadsheet. The columns are objects like Name, Address, ZIP code, Phone number, and so on, and the rows are the records in the database.

A balanced tree database is a database in which all data is stored in leaves. At the root level, there are only pointers, which point to internal pages that contain pointers to the leaves (see Figure 7-1). As mentioned, the leaves contain the actual data. In Exchange 2013, each page is 32KB. If 5MB of messaging data needs to be stored in the mailbox database, it is cut into more than 160 individual pages—without the overhead, that is.

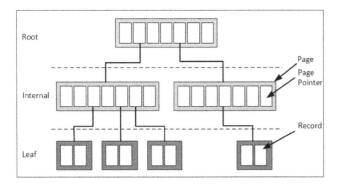

Figure 7-1. *A balanced tree database has a root level with pointers, an internal layer with pointers and pages, and a bottom level with leaves that contain data*

The tree as shown in Figure 7-1 is a balanced tree. Exchange Server, however, uses a modified structure where all the pages contain a pointer to the previous page and a pointer to the next page. This is referred to as a B+ tree.

The database technology used in Exchange Server is the ESE (Extensible Storage Engine), and it has been very much optimized over the years. Database pages are sequentially numbered, starting with 1 at the very beginning, when the mailbox database is created, going up until the end of time. In all my years working as an Exchange consultant (since Exchange Server 5.0 in 1997), I've never seen any problems with this.

■ **Note** ESE was previously referred as Joint Engine Technology (JET) Blue. JET Blue is not the same as the version of JET found in Access (referred to as JET Red).

One of the functions of ESE is to balance the tree. It's not hard to imagine that when lots of data is added to the database, the tree becomes unbalanced. When this happens, though, ESE reorganizes the tree by splitting and merging the pointer pages.

When a page becomes full, ESE splits the page into two adjacent pages. If this happens, an additional key is put into the secondary key's parent page. This happens on a continuous basis, until the parent pages become full as well. If that happens, the parent page is split also and the new secondary page's parent page is updated with a new key.

It can happen that the fullness reaches to the root level, and then the root level needs to be split. If this happens, an additional layer of pages is inserted into the tree and B-tree now has four layers instead of three. A balanced tree with four layers is shown in Figure 7-2. Obviously, a four-layer tree has many more leaves containing data.

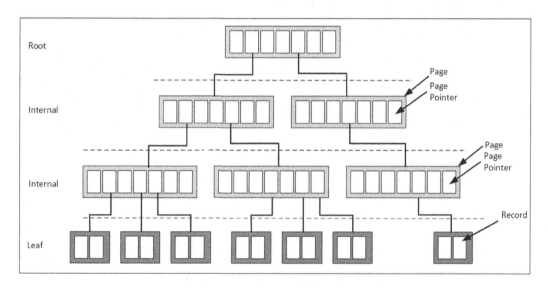

Figure 7-2. *A B-tree with four layers, which can contain much more data*

If data is removed from the mailbox database, the leaves are emptied and the parent pages become available as well. When too many adjacent parent pages become available, ESE can merge those pages in the tree. Eventually, when lots and lots of merges happen, even up to the root level, ESE can remove an entire layer of pages, thereby shrinking the tree. Note that this happens *inside* the database. The tree can shrink, but the size of the database will never shrink! ESE pages are freed up and filled as a continuous process; once freed, they are reorganized as explained in Chapter 6 regarding Online Defragmentation (OLD).

To read data from a particular leaf, ESE starts at the root level and follows the tree down to the leaf. To reach the data, only three or four read actions are needed. Since most of the pages and pointers are stored in memory, this happens extremely fast—even in a 250GB database, for example. ESE stores over 1,600 page pointers in a 32KB page, making it possible to create a tree with a minimal number of parent/child levels.

Where Is My Data?

Mail data on the Mailbox server can be found in three different locations:

- Mailbox database
- Transaction log files
- Server memory

All processing—that is, the creation of transactions—takes place in the server memory, in particular in the log buffers, the ESE cache (this is where the pages reside), and the version store. The Version Store is a small part in memory, tied to the ESE cache, that's used by ESE to keep track of all transactions while they are created. When something goes wrong with a transaction, ESE can create a new transaction and keep track of the various versions of these transactions, hence the name.

The log buffers, each 1MB in size, contain the contents of a log file that's currently being created. When transactions are created, they are stored in a particular log buffer, and this log buffer represents a log file that belongs to a certain mailbox database.

When a log buffer is filled with transactions, the entire log buffer is flushed to disk (i.e., written to a log file), the log file is closed, and a new one is created. At this point, no changes are made to the mailbox database and all pages are kept in memory. This mechanism is called *write ahead logging,* so the data in the log files is always ahead of the data in the mailbox database. A graphic represenation of this techology can be seen in Figure 7-3.

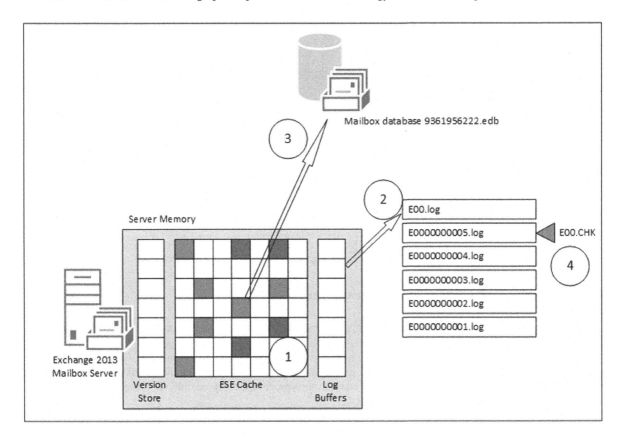

Figure 7-3. *The mailbox database, server memory, and log files*

The *checkpoint file* keeps track of which pages are already flushed to the mailbox database. All pages older than the checkpoint file are flushed to the mailbox database, all pages newer than the checkpoint file remain in the ESE cache. Note that all transactions are stored in the log files, and thus are safe. If the server crashes, memory content is lost but all the transactions are secure in those log files. The only data that gets lost when the server crashes is the content in the current log buffers.

The log files are sequentially numbered; when a mailbox is created, the number starts with with E0000000001.log. It's important to note that the numbering is in hexadecimal format. The name of the log file can be split into two parts:

- **The prefix** This is the first three characters of the name—in this example, E00. Every mailbox database has its own, unique set of log files, and the prefix is what differentiates them from each other. The first mailbox database has prefix E00, while mailbox database number 100 has prefix E99. In contrast to the sequential numbering of the transaction log files, which is in hexadecimal notation, the prefix is in decimal notation.

- **The number** An eight-character hexidecimal number that's generated sequentially, starting with 0x00000001 and theoretically ending with 0xffffffff. This hexidecimal number is not only used in the filename of the log file; it is also used inside the log file as a sequence number. In ESE terms, it is called the *lGeneration number*.

The log file that's currently in use—that is, the log file where the contents of the log buffer will be flushed to—is a log file called E00.log (or any other prefix, of course). You might see a log file called E00TEMP.log occasionally; that's a log file that's pre-created by ESE. When the log buffers are flushed to the log file (i.e., E00.log), the log file is stored with a filename based on the prefix and its lGeneration number; in Figure 7-3, this would be E0000000006.log. The E00TEMP.log will then be renamed E00.log to save time during this processing of the log file.

The third important file is the *checkpoint file,* mentioned briefly above. This is a very small file (8KB) that keeps track of which transactions are already flushed to the mailbox database. Remember that, because of the write-ahead mechanism, all transactions are already flushed to the log files, but that flushing to the mailbox database happens later. The checkpoint file, which points to transactions somewhere in the log files, keeps track of this. When a transaction is flushed from server memory to the mailbox database, the checkpoint file is moved forward. But there's always data that's *not* in the mailbox database; instead, it is flushed to the log files (where it is safeguarded against server failure). This can be seen in Figure 7-4.

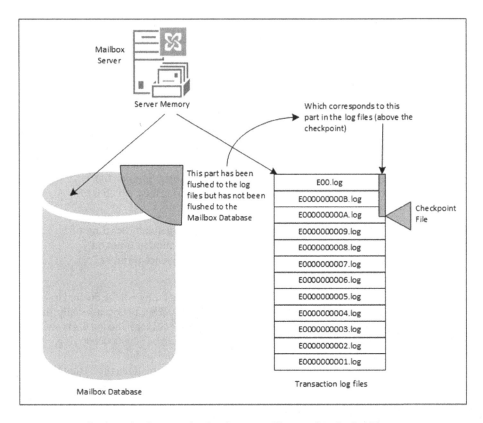

Figure 7-4. *The data that's not in the database is safely stored in the log files*

Mailbox Database File Information

Information regarding the mailbox database is stored in the *header* of the mailbox database. The first page of the mailbox database contains the header and the second page contains a copy of the header, which should be identical, of course.

You can read the header of the mailbox database by using the ESEUTIL tool with the /MH option, followed by the name of the mailbox database. All kinds of (internal) information can be retrieved from the mailbox database, such as:

- **The signature** This is the internal identifier of the database, composed of the date and time the database was created, followed by a unique, random number.

- **The state** The state of the database can be either *clean* if the database was shutdown properly (and all data is written from server memory) or *dirty*. The latter is the case if the database was running ("open") at the time of viewing. Since a running mailbox database cannot be viewed using ESEUTIL, this is the case with a backup restored from backup media, or a mailbox database where the Information Store has crashed (or was killed).

- **Log required** This is populated if the database is in a dirty state and tells which log files are required to bring the database into a consistent (clean) state. It refers to the amount of data that's stored in the log files but was not committed to the database, and thus corresponds to the checkpoint depth.

- **Last ObjID** This is the number of B+ trees in the database; see Figure 7-1.

- **Last consistent** (1), **last attached** (2), and **last detached** (3) This tells when the database was in a clean shutdown the last time (1), when the database was last mounted (2), and when it was last dismounted (3). Mounting a database is sometimes called "attaching to the log stream."

- **Log signature** This shows the internal identifier of the corresponding log files. The log files not only have their name as shown in Windows Explorer but, under the hood, they also have their unique identifier, just like the mailbox database. This way, ESE can differentiate between an E00.log from server 1 and an E00.log from server 2. Or even worse, it can differentiate E00.log versions from the same Exchange server when the Exchange administrator has been messing around!

- **Previous full backup** This is information regarding the last full backup, including the log file information.

To retrieve this information using ESEUTIL, the mailbox database has to be offline (dismounted) or restored from a backup to an alternative location. (This will be covered later in this chapter.) Use the following command to read the header information:

```
ESEUTIL /MH db01.edb
```

This generates output such as the following (but not all information is shown here, for readability purposes):

```
Extensible Storage Engine Utilities for Microsoft(R) Exchange Server
Version 15.00
Copyright (C) Microsoft Corporation. All Rights Reserved.

Initiating FILE DUMP mode...
        Database: db01.edb

Fields:
        File Type: Database
     DB Signature: Create time:12/23/2012 18:32:24.362 Rand:4071177377 Computer:
            State: Dirty Shutdown
     Log Required: 6169-6169 (0x1819-0x1819)
       Last Objid: 35405
  Last Consistent: (0x1818,A1,88)  07/23/2013 22:32:25.612
      Last Attach: (0x1819,2,268)  07/23/2013 22:35:54.412
      Last Detach: (0x0,0,0)  00/00/1900 00:00:00.000
    Last ReAttach: (0x1818,2,0)  07/23/2013 21:04:44.445
    Log Signature: Create time:12/23/2012 18:32:24.268 Rand:2709814512 Computer:

Previous Full Backup:
        Log Gen: 6163-6163 (0x1813-0x1813) - OSSnapshot
           Mark: (0x1815,C9,94)
           Mark: 07/23/2013 20:58:52.781

Operation completed successfully in 0.16 seconds.
```

Obviously, this output is from a mailbox database that was created eight months ago (from the time of this writing). It is in a dirty shutdown mode because the Information Store was crashed (deliberately). The log file required to get this mailbox database in a consistent state is number 6169 (which corresponds to file E0000001819.log). This is where things become confusing, since decimal and hexadecimal notations are used to reference the same log file.

Header information from the corresponding file is interesting to have a close look at, again using the ESEUTIL tool, but now with the /ML option:

```
ESEUTIL /ML E000000181A.log
```

The output is something like the following (again, some information is deleted for better readability):

```
Extensible Storage Engine Utilities for Microsoft(R) Exchange Server
Version 15.00
Copyright (C) Microsoft Corporation. All Rights Reserved.

Initiating FILE DUMP mode...

        Base name: E00
        Log file: E000000181A.log
        lGeneration: 6170 (0x181A)
        Checkpoint: (0x1819,FFFF,FFFF)
        creation time: 07/23/2013 22:32:32.773
        Signature: Create time:12/23/2012 18:32:24.268 Rand:2709814512 Computer:
        Env SystemPath: F:\DB01\LogFiles\
        Env LogFilePath: F:\DB01\LogFiles\
        Checkpoint at log creation time: (0x1819,1,0)
        1 F:\DB01\DB01.edb
                dbtime: 10213675 (0-10213675)
                objidLast: 35405
                Signature: Create time:12/23/2012 18:32:24.362 Rand:4071177377 Computer:
                MaxDbSize: 0 pages
                Last Attach: (0x1819,2,268)
                Last Consistent: (0x1818,A1,88)

        Last Lgpos: (0x181a,FF,0)

Number of database page references:  972

Operation completed successfully in 0.125 seconds.
```

You'll notice that both signatures (database signature and log signature) are identical, so these form a pair. Of course, the log file was created very recently, but in this header information you'll also find information regarding the position of the checkpoint file. Additionally, there's file information about the location of the log files, the checkpoint file itself, and the mailbox database file. This particular log file is referencing 972 database pages, as explained in the beginning of this chapter.

The last part to have a closer look at is the checkpoint file. As we now know, it references a page in the log file. To look at the header information of the checkpoint file, this command is used:

```
ESEUTIL /MK E00.CHK
```

This generates output like the following (some information is deleted here, as well):

```
Extensible Storage Engine Utilities for Microsoft(R) Exchange Server
Version 15.00
Copyright (C) Microsoft Corporation. All Rights Reserved.

Initiating FILE DUMP mode...
      Checkpoint file: e00.chk

      Signature: Create time:12/23/2012 18:32:24.268 Rand:2709814512 Computer:
    1 F:\DB01\DB01.edb LogOff VerOn RW
      dbtime: 10214635 (0-10214635)
      objidLast: 35405
      Signature: Create time:12/23/2012 18:32:24.362 Rand:4071177377 Computer:
      MaxDbSize: 0 pages
      Last Attach: (0x1819,2,268)
      Last Consistent: (0x1818,A1,88)

Operation completed successfully in 0.31 seconds.
```

This checkpoint file was created during creation of the mailbox database, as can be derived from the signature of the mailbox database. If you examine these examples closely, you'll find that the three files are very closely related.

Checkpoint Depth

In the previous examples, most information was already written from server memory to the mailbox database. You can check this by looking at the location of the checkpoint file, which is close to the last log files.

The amount of data that's still in server memory and not flushed to the mailbox database, and thus the amount of data "above" the checkpoint in Figure 7-3, is called the *checkpoint depth*. In Exchange 2013, the checkpoint depth can be 100MB; this means that 100MB of data can be located in server memory but hasn't been flushed to the mailbox database, and so it is safely stored in the log files. When looking at Figure 7-4, you'll see that this means there are a maximum of 100 log files located "above" the checkpoint file.

The checkpoint depth is per database; each database has its own set of log files, its own checkpoint file, and thus its own checkpoint depth. This means when you have, for example, five mailbox databases, you can have 5 × 100 log files, or 500MB of mailbox data in server memory that's not been flushed to the mailbox database (but that is stored in the transaction log files, though!).

Why is this important to know? There are two reasons you want to know this:

- Exchange Server uses this technique for recovery purposes, either in combination with restoring a mailbox database from a backup or by using the ESEUTIL tool.

- Mailbox data is very dynamic, as data can be in server memory, in the mailbox database, or in the transaction log files. The backup application needs to be aware of this process so it can interact with the Exchange server while creating the backup. Needless to say, a regular file-level backup is not going to work when you are backing up mailbox databases.

Backup Technologies

Before diving into the snapshot technology used for creating backups, let's discuss briefly the "old" backup technology in Exchange Server—the streaming backup. This way, I hope you can get a better understanding of what happens during the creation of a backup.

Streaming Backup

Up until Windows Server 2003, the operating system offered a backup API that made it possible to create a streaming backup. When it comes to Exchange Server, Exchange 2007 was the last version that was able to use streaming backups when running on Windows Server 2003.

A *streaming backup* is a backup mechanism whereby all database pages are read sequentially directly from disk, checked for consistency, and written to a backup location. That backup location can be another disk or a tape library. The NTBackup running on Windows Server 2003 was a utility able to create streaming backups of Exchange mailbox databases.

When a streaming backup is started, the first action is to freeze the checkpoint file. This way, the backup application knows which data is already written to the mailbox database, and thus which log files can safely be deleted from the disk when the backup successfully finishes.

The next action is to sequentially read all the database pages, check them for consistency, and write them to a backup location. When an inconsistent (i.e., corrupt) page is found, the backup is halted and an error is raised.

When the backup application has finished reading all database pages, the header of the mailbox database containing information regarding the backup is updated, the log files below the checkpoint file are purged, and then Exchange Server continues to work normally.

This method used to work fine, since mailbox databases in the old days weren't that big; but when the databases started to grow, those backup applications weren't capable anymore of creating decent backups in a normal time period. It was important to have the backup finished before the users came into the office the next morning, since creating backups was resource-intensive and that could have a negative impact on the server's performance. Also, a backup is typically created overnight, but the mailbox database online maintenance and online defragmentation were also running overnight, causing resource demand conflicts.

Though this streaming technology is no longer used for backup purposes, it is still used by the Exchange 2013 Mailbox server to create additional mailbox database copies in the DAG. When you create a copy of that mailbox database, the original mailbox database is streamed from the originating server to the target server.

Nowadays, backup technology is built into VSS backups, sometimes referred to as "snapshot backups."

■ **Note**   In the old days of Exchange Server there were third-party backup solutions capable of creating a so-called brick-level backup. These backups used MAPI to log on to individual mailboxes, making it possible to backup all mailbox items individually. The advantage, of course, is that when there's a crash, restoration of individual mailbox items is possible, a solution that's widely asked for. The problem is that brick-level backups are awfully slow. When using small mailbox databases, you can overcome this, but over time even these small mailbox databases become too big for brick-level backups. Another drawback of brick-level backups is that the transaction log files are not purged when the backup is completed.

VSS Backup

Windows Server 2003 was the first Microsoft operating system capable of creating snapshot backups using the VSS framework. Exchange Server 2007 was the first version capable of using the VSS technology, and VSS backups have been used in Exchange Server ever since.

There are two kinds of snapshot backups:

- **Clone** (full copy or split mirror) In this scenario, a complete copy, or "mirror," is maintained until an application or administrator effectively "breaks" the mirror. From this point on, the original and the clone are fully independent of each other. The mirror copy is effectively frozen in time.

- **Copy on Write** (differential copy) A shadow copy is created that is different from a full copy of the original data, made before the original data is overwritten. Effectively, the backup copy consists of the data in the shadow copy combined with the data on the original location. Both need to be available to reconstruct the original data.

VSS stands for Volume Shadow Copy Service, and it consists of the VSS service, requestors, writers, and providers. The central part is the VSS running on the computer. It is responsible for coordinating all activities concerning the backup and restores.

The *requestor* typically is the backup application. This can be the default out-of-the-box Windows Server backup, or it can be any third-party backup solution or a Windows tool like DiskShadow.

The *writer* is the application-specific part of VSS. Writers exist for Microsoft Exchange, Active Directory, IIS, NTFS, SQL Server, and so on. The Exchange Writer is responsible for coordinating all Exchange-related activities, such as flushing all data to the mailbox database, freezing the mailbox database during the VSS snapshot, and so on.

In Exchange 2010, the writer consisted of actually two writers: one inside the Microsoft Information Store (`store.exe`) and one inside the Microsoft Exchange Replication service (`MSExchangeRepl.exe`). In Exchange 2013, the functions of the Information Store writer have been moved to the Microsoft Exchange Replication service, thereby forming one new writer, called Exchange Writer. This new Exchange Writer is used by Exchange-aware backup applications, which include out-of-the-box Windows Server Backup, to create snapshot backups of both the active copy and the passive copies of a mailbox database.

The *provider* is the part of VSS that works with storage. It can be the Windows providers, which can create copy-on-write snapshots of a disk, or a vendor-specific hardware provider.

As stated above, the VSS is at the core of everything, as can be seen in Figure 7-5. The arrows show the communication paths within the VSS solution.

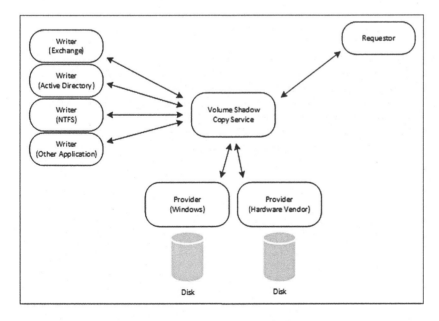

Figure 7-5. *VSS with the requestor, writers, and providers*

For a VSS backup to be created, the following steps occur sequentially:

1. The backup application or requestor sends a command to the VSS to make a shadow copy of the mailbox database.

2. The VSS sends a command to the Exchange Writer to prepare for a snapshot backup.

3. The VSS then sends a command to the appropriate provider to create a shadow copy of the mailbox database. The storage provider can be a hardware storage provider (provided by the hardware vendor) or the default Windows storage provider.

4. The Exchange Writer temporarily stops, or quiesces, the mailbox database and puts it into read-only mode; all data in server memory is then flushed to the mailbox database. Also, a log file rollover is performed to make sure that all data will be in the backup set. This holds for a couple of seconds for the snapshot to be created (in the next step). All write IOs are queued at this point.

5. The shadow copy is created.

6. The VSS releases the Exchange Server to resume ordinary operations, and all queued write IOs are completed.

7. The VSS queries the Exchange Writer to confirm that the write IOs were successfully held during the snapshot creation. If the write operations were not successfully held, there could be a potentially inconsistent shadow copy. If this is the case, the shadow copy is deleted and the requestor is notified of the failed snapshot.

8. If the snapshot was successful, the requestor verifies the integrity of the backup set (the clone). If the clone integrity is good, the requestor informs Exchange Server that the snapshot was successful. The snapshot can now be transferred to a backup device.

9. When all data is succesfully moved to the backup device, the requestor informs VSS that the backup was successful and that the log files can be purged.

In contrast to the streaming backup, where consistency is checked by ESE, it is not the responsibility of the backup application to actually perform the consistency check. That is, the Exchange Writer itself does not perform this check.

Steps 1 throught 6 usually take between 10 and 15 seconds. Note that this is the time to create the actual snapshot, and it does not include the time needed to write all the data to the backup device. Depending on the size of the mailbox database, this step can take up to several hours to complete.

If you're working with an earlier version of Exchange Server, you might be familiar with a VSS administrative tool called VSSADMIN. You can use VSSADMIN to quickly check the various components in the VSS infrastructure. For example, to list all the VSS writers on a server, simply use the VSSADMIN List Writers command in a command prompt window. For Exchange Server 2013, the output will be something like that shown in Figure 7-6.

Figure 7-6. *A list of VSS writers on an Exchange 2013 server*

Similarly, you can list the VSS providers, existing shadow copies, or the volumes eligible for creating shadow copies. VSSADMIN, however, was replaced by a new administrative tool called DiskShadow, which is more powerfull than VSSADMIN and as such will return more detailed information about the VSS infrastructure. It is even possible to create backups using DiskShadow, something to be discussed later in this chapter.

Backing up a Mailbox Database

For backing up your mailbox databases, there are various applications available. Which one you use is a matter of personal experience (or maybe your company has a license for some applications), but the most important factor is that the application be "Exchange aware." Windows Server 2008 R2 and later versions ship with Windows Server Backup (WSB), which is capable of backing up Exchange 2013 mailbox databases. It's a pretty simple and limited backup application, but is used quite often. A low-level tool you can use for backing up your Exchange 2010 mailbox databases is DiskShadow, but I wouldn't recommend it for daily use, since it is quite complex. Let's discuss both applications.

Windows Server Backup

Exchange 2013 contains a VSS plug-in that can be used with WSB. Although WSB has limited functionality, it can be used to create backups and restore them if needed, and is used quite often. Another advantage of WSB is that it's free and comes with Windows Server 2008 R2 and Windows Server 2012.

WSB can be installed using the Add Roles and Features wizard in Server Manager for Windows Server 2012, as shown in Figure 7-7.

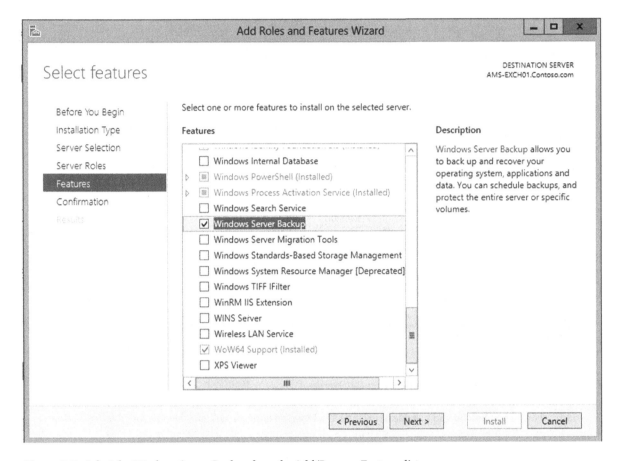

Figure 7-7. Select the Windows Server Backup from the Add/Remove Features list

To create a backup of your Exchange 2013 databases, use the following steps:

1. In the Administrative Tools section, select Windows Server Backup. This is an MMC snap-in. In the Actions pane, select Backup Once.

2. In the Backup Options page, select Different Options and click Next to continue.

3. In this example we want only to backup the mailbox database, so select the Custom option and click Next to continue.

4. Our mailbox database is located on disk F; use the Add Items button to select this disk.

5. To change the type of backup that's being created, click the Advanced Settings button, select the VSS Settings tab, and select the VSS Full Backup radio button. Click OK to return to the previous page and click Next to continue.

■ **Note** By default, Windows Server Backup will create a copy backup instead of a full backup. This is understandable, since it will not interfere with a normal backup cycle when using another backup solution and you want to test using WSB. If you want to make a regular backup using WSB, make sure you change this setting. This is a common pitfall with WSB.

---

6. Windows Server Backup has the option to backup to a remote share or to a local disk, whichever you prefer. On our server there's an additional backup disk (disk X), so select Local Drives and click Next to continue.

7. In the Backup Destination drop-down box, select the disk where the backup needs to be stored; on our server this would be disk X. Click Next to continue.

8. The selection is now complete. Click Backup to start the actual backup process.

The backup will now start with the creation of the VSS snapshot, and will perform a consistency check of the mailbox data, as shown in Figure 7-8. Be aware that this can be visible for a small amount of time, especially when the mailbox database is not that large and the consistency check takes only a few seconds. This is the only visual indication you have that an Exchange-aware backup is running.

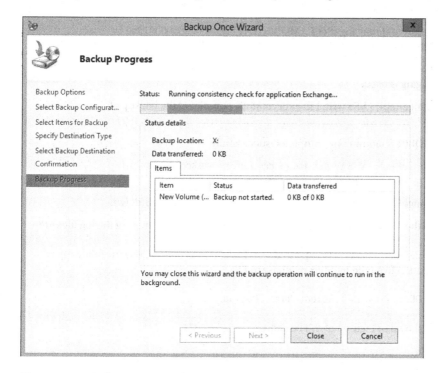

Figure 7-8. *Windows Server Backup automatically checks for database consistency*

When the consistency check is finished successfully, the data is backed up to the backup location, and after a while (which can take a couple of hours if you have a large mailbox database), the backup is completed.

9. Click the Close button to return to the initial Windows Server Backup MMC snap-in.

If you check the Application Log in the Event Viewer, you'll see the following entries:

- Event ID 2021 (MSExchangeRepl) - Successfully collected metadata document in preparation for backup.

- Event ID 2110 (MSExchangeRepl) - Successfully prepared for a full or a copy backup of database MDB01.

- Event ID 2023 (MSExchangeRepl) - VSS Writer successfully prepared for backup.

- Event ID 2005 (ESE) - Shadow copy instance started.

- Event ID 2025 (MSExchangeRepl) - VSS successfully prepared for a snapshot.

- Event ID 2001 (ESE) - MDB01 Shadow copy freeze started.

- Event ID 2027 (MSExchangeRepl) - VSS Writer instance has successfully frozen the databases.

- Event ID 2003 (ESE) - MDB01 Shadow copy freeze ended.

- Event ID 2029 (MSExchangeRepl) - VSS Writer instance has successfully thawed the databases.

- Event ID 2035 (MSExchangeRepl) - VSS Writer has successfully processed the post-snapshot event.

- Event ID 2021 (MSExchangeRepl) - VSS Writer has successfully collected the metadata document in preparation for backup.

- Event ID 224 (ESE) - MDB01: deleting log files F:\MDB01\Log Files\E0000000001.log to F:\MDB01\Log Files\E000000002B.log

- Event ID 225 (ESE) - MDB01: No log files can be truncated will be logged instead of Event ID 224 when circular logging is used.

- Event ID 2046 (MSExchangeRepl) - VSS writer has successfully completed the backup of database MDB01.

- Event ID 2006 (ESE) - MDB01 Shadow copy completed successfully.

- Event ID 2033 (MSExchangeRepl) - VSS Writer has successfully processed the backup completion event.

- Event ID 2037 (MSExchangeRepl) - VSS Writer backup has been successfully shutdown.

When you check the location of the log files using Windows Explorer, you'll notice that most of the log files are indeed purged.

The information in the mailbox database itself is also updated with backup information. Use the following command to retrieve backup information from the mailbox database in ESM:

```
Get-MailboxDatabase -Identity MDB01 -Status | Select Name,*backup*
```

The information similar to that shown in Figure 7-9 will be shown.

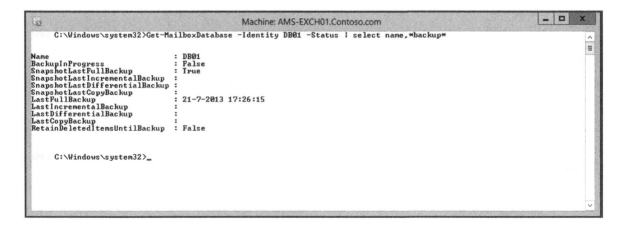

Figure 7-9. *Checking the backup status using the EMS*

You can also use the ESEUTIL /MH DB01.edb command to check the header for backup information; if so, you'll see something like this:

```
Previous Full Backup:
      Log Gen: 6163-6163 (0x1813-0x1813) - OSSnapshot
         Mark: (0x1815,C9,94)
         Mark: 07/21/2013 17:26:15.781
```

■ **Note**   It is only possible to check the header information of a mailbox database when the database is dismounted. If the database is mounted, an error saying "the file is in use" is shown.

You might ask yourself why this information is written under Previous Full Backup, while the entry under Current Full Backup is empty. The reason is that when you create a backup, the entry Current Full Backup is written with information regarding the backup as it runs. When the backup is finished, the entries are moved from the Current Full Backup section to the Previous Full Backup section and the Current Full Backup is emptied. When a backup is restored to disk and you check the header information after a restore, you can always identify the database as a backup that's restored instead of a "normal" mailbox database since it will show Previous Full Backup.

Using DiskShadow to Create Backups

As mentioned, DiskShadow is a VSS management tool you can use to manage your VSS infrastructure at a low level. DiskShadow lets you check your writers, providers, shadow copies, and so on much as with VSSADMIN, but you'll get more detail. You can also use DiskShadow to create VSS snapshots on a low level, which is a great way to demonstrate what exactly happens during VSS backup creation.

DiskShadow can be used in interactive mode, but it can also be used in scripting mode, where it accepts input from a text file.

For example, in our earlier Contoso environment, there were two Exchange 2013 multi-role servers at the Amsterdam site, and these were configured in a DAG. Each server has one active mailbox database and one passive mailbox database. The mailbox databases are located on drive F: (DB01) and driver G: (DB02).

When employing DiskShadow to create a VSS backup, the following input file can be used:

```
SET verbose on
SET context persistent

# Exclude other writers on Exchange Server
# Can be retrieved using VSSADMIN List Writers
Writer Exclude {d61d61c8-d73a-4eee-8cdd-f6f9786b7124}
Writer Exclude {75dfb225-e2e4-4d39-9ac9-ffaff65ddf06}
Writer Exclude {0bada1de-01a9-4625-8278-69e735f39dd2}
Writer Exclude {e8132975-6f93-4464-a53e-1050253ae220}
Writer Exclude {be000cbe-11fe-4426-9c58-531aa6355fc4}
Writer Exclude {1072ae1c-e5a7-4ea1-9e4a-6f7964656570}
Writer Exclude {afbab4a2-367d-4d15-a586-71dbb18f8485}
Writer Exclude {4dc3bdd4-ab48-4d07-adb0-3bee2926fd7f}
Writer Exclude {542da469-d3e1-473c-9f4f-7847f01fc64f}
Writer Exclude {4969d978-be47-48b0-b100-f328f07ac1e0}
Writer Exclude {a6ad56c2-b509-4e6c-bb19-49d8f43532f0}
Writer Exclude {2a40fd15-dfca-4aa8-a654-1f8c654603f6}
```

```
Writer Exclude {7e47b561-971a-46e6-96b9-696eeaa53b2a}
Writer Exclude {41e12264-35d8-479b-8e5c-9b23d1dad37e}
Writer Exclude {59b1f0cf-90ef-465f-9609-6ca8b2938366}

# Exchange writer is required
Writer Verify {76fe1ac4-15f7-4bcd-987e-8e1acb462fb7}

# Take the actual snapshot
begin backup
add volume F: alias VSS_Backup_F
add volume G: alias VSS_Backup_G

create

# Expose the snapshot as additional drive S:
expose %VSS_Backup_F% S:
expose %VSS_Backup_G% T:

End backup
```

The first two entries are to set verbose logging on and to set the context to persistent so information won't be lost.

Then, all VSS writers on the Exchange servers are disabled except the VSS Exchange Writer. The GUIDs of the VSS writers can be retrieved by using the VSSADMIN List Writers command.

Volumes F: and G: are used for creating the VSS snapshots, and an alias VSS_Backup_F and VSS_Backup_G is assigned. (I just used these names but you can use any readable name you like.)

At this point the actual snapshot is created using the CREATE command. In Windows, this is a copy-on-write snapshot where the snapshot information is written on the same disk and on the mailbox database (i.e., drive F: and drive G:), but it's not visible for a regular user or administrator. (All the steps as explained in the previous section are performed here, and all the events are recorded in the event log as well.) This step usually takes between 15 and 30 seconds, depending on the hardware that's used for the Exchange server.

When the snapshot is created, it is exposed using the EXPOSE command. This way it is visible as a regular disk to the operating system, and thus accessible, as shown in Figure 7-10.

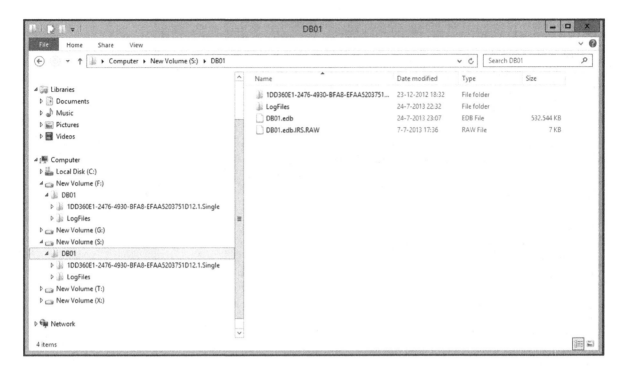

***Figure 7-10.** The VSS snapshots are published as additional drives in Windows*

When the backup in DiskShadow is ended using the End Backup command, a request is sent to ESE to purge any log files that are no longer needed for recovery purposes. If the VSS snaphost was created on a single Exchange server, or a DAG member with active copies of the mailbox database, then the request is processed locally. If the snapshot was created against a passive copy of a mailbox database, the request is automatically sent to the Mailbox server that is hosting the active copy of the mailbox database. The log files are purged on that particular Mailbox server, and the truncation itself is replicated to the Mailbox servers hosting the passive copies of the mailbox database. This means that you no longer need to know which mailbox database in a DAG you backup; the appropriate log files are automatically purged.

This is the pure VSS snapshot function: a snapshot of the mailbox database is created, and its log files are purged (when successful, of course). But remember that the mailbox database has not been checked for consistency, nor has it been backed up to a safe location. To check the consistency of a mailbox database, use the ESEUTIL tool again, but now with the /k switch:

```
ESEUTIL /K db01.edb
```

This command will read all the pages in the database and check the consistency of all those pages, as shown in Figure 7-11.

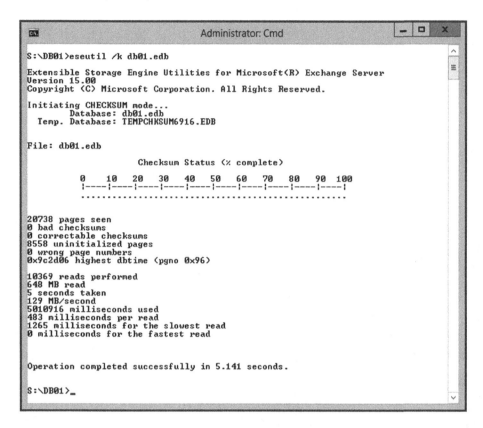

Figure 7-11. *Checking the database consistency using the ESEUTIL tool*

The final step in a backup, then, would be to copy the mailbox database snapshots from the published locations (drive S: and drive T:) to another safe location using, for example, Explorer. Once done, you have successfully created a full backup manually.

■ **Note**   Don't forget to remove the exposed VSS snapshots using the UNEXPOSE command in DiskShadow, and remove the actual VSS shadow copies using the DELETE SHADOWS command.

Backup of Other Configuration Information

The previous section discussed how to back up mailbox databases in Exchange 2013, since this is the most important aspect of an Exchange server's role.

There are a couple more things that need to be backed up, either in a regular backup sequence or maybe after configuration changes; for example:

- Log files (not transaction log files). Exchange 2013 logs quite a lot of information in log files—for instance, in IIS log files located C:\inetpub\logs\logfiles, which contain logging from all HTTPS-based clients like Outlook Web App, Exchange Web Services, Autodiscover, Outlook Anywhere, and ActiveSync.

- SMTP Transport Protocol logs, located in `C:\Program Files\Microsoft\Exchange Server\ V15\TransportRoles\Logs\ Hub\ProtocolLog`. These are disabled by default, but when enabled these might be included in a daily backup routine.

- Message tracking information, located in `C:\Program Files\Microsoft\Exchange Server\ V15\TransportRoles\ Logs\MessageTracking`.

- Depending on the (legal) backup requirements of your company, it might be necessary to back up the entire logging directory in `C:\Program Files\Microsoft\Exchange Server\V15\Logging`.

- CONFIG files—for example, Transport configuration files located in `C:\Program Files\ Microsoft\Exchange Server\V15\Bin`. This file is used to relocate the SMTP message database and log files to another location. No need to include this in a daily backup sequence, but necessary to back up after configuration changes.

- SSL certificate, especially on the Exchange 2013 Client Access server. No need to back up this on a daily basis, but back up after the initial installation of the certificate. It is needed when rebuilding a Client Access server, or maybe adding an additional Client Access server. Make sure that when you create a backup of your SSL certificate you also include the private key in the certificate backup. If not, it's still useless when rebuilding your Client Access server.

- System State or entire server. Depending on your disaster recovery plan you might want to back up the server's System State, or maybe the entire server, for rebuilding purposes. We'll get back to this later in this chapter.

When using server virtualization, it is an option to back up the entire virtual machine using a backup solution. Veeam, for example, is a third-party vendor that offers backup solutions in a virtual environment. Veeam can back up the VMs, and using the Hyper-V Integration Components, the VSS backup information is sent to the operating system inside the VM. This way the virtual machine is also aware that a snapshot is made.

Restoring Exchange Server 2013

Backing up your Exchange 2013 environment does make sense, but restoring the backup is even more important. In all my years as an Exchange consultant, I have regularly met customers who thought that their backup solution was fine, but they did not have any idea how to restore. The worst way to find out, however, is during a disaster, when you must restore information while you have hundreds of users and managers complaining. Most likely, the restoration will fail at this moment because of the lack of experience.

In this part of the chapter I focus on restoring mailbox databases, since these are where all the data is. In the next part, I will focus on restoring the Exchange servers as part of the disaster recovery operation.

There are two options for restoring mailbox databases:

- **Restore the mailbox database to its original location** In this scenario, the original mailbox database is taken offline and is overwritten by the mailbox database in the backup set. Since all information is also stored in the log files, the information processed by the Exchange server since the last backup was created will automatically be replayed by the Exchange server. If all goes well, no information, or almost no information, will be lost and the mailbox database will be in the same state as before.

- **Restore the mailbox database to another location** In this scenario, the mailbox database from the backup set is restored to another location, most likely a dedicated restore disk on your Exchange 2013 server. When restored to another location, the original mailbox database can continue running and thus continue servicing client requests. A recovery mailbox database can be used as well. This is a special mailbox database, not visible for regular clients (only for the Exchange administrator), that can be used to restore only a particular mailbox; you can move this mailbox into the production mailbox database or export it to a PST file.

Restoring a Mailbox Database to Its Original Location

A lot of interesting technologies are used to make the mailbox database backup process as smooth as possible without interupting any users. Restoring a mailbox database to its original location is, on the other hand, very straightforward.

The mailbox database has to be taken offline, and thus users will face some downtime because the Exchange service is not available anymore. The mailbox database is then restored from the backup set, additional log files are replayed automatically, and the mailbox database can then be mounted again. Nothing fancy when restoring a mailbox database.

In the previous section, WSB was used to back up the mailbox database so you have to use WSB again to restore the mailbox database. For testing purposes, you can log on to the mailbox before the restore and send some messages around to see if these are actually replayed after the backup is restored. To restore a previous backup using WSB, you can use these guidelines:

1. Log on to the Exchange 2013 Mailbox server and dismount the mailbox database.

2. Log in to the EAC as an administrator. In the Feature pane, select Servers and then select the Databases tab.

3. Select the mailbox database you want to restore (and you dismounted in step 1), and open its properties. In the navigation menu, select Maintenance and check the "This database can be overwritten by a restore" checkbox, as shown in Figure 7-12.

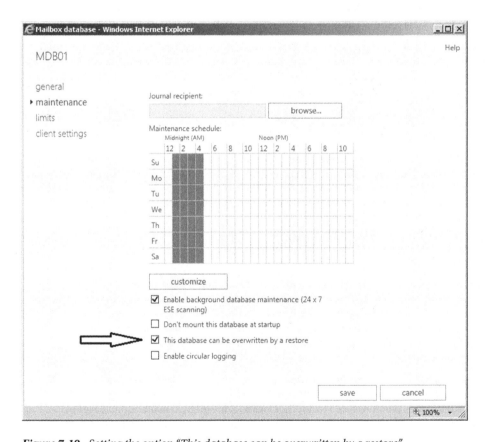

Figure 7-12. *Setting the option "This database can be overwritten by a restore"*

4. Open WSB and in the Actions pane, select Recover.

5. In the Recovery wizard that starts, select where the backup is located. This can be on a disk attached to the server itself or it can be a remote location. Select the appropriate option and click Next to continue.

6. In the Select Backup Date window, select the backup set you want to restore to this server. Once selected, click Next to continue.

7. The Select Recovery Type window is very important. WSB is Exchange-aware and thus an Exchange backup is an Application backup. This way, the backup is restored as the Exchange Writer would like it to be. If you select Volumes, for example, the backup is restored as an ordinary file backup and this is useless from an Exchange perspective. Select Applications and click Next to continue.

8. In the Select Application window, make sure Exchange is selected and click Next to continue.

▓ **Note** This option is only available when the mailbox database is not located on the system drive and boot drive, typically drive C:\. That is, it's only available when the mailbox database is on a separate drive.

9. Since the backup will be restored to its original location, select the Recover to Original Location option and click Next to continue.

10. In the Confirmation window, WSB will show the backup set that was selected. If this is correct, click Recover to start the restore process.

11. The restore operation will run in the background so it is safe to close WSB at this point.

What happens during the restore process is that the mailbox database and the log files that are in the backup set are restored to the original location. After the initial restore of the individual files, the mailbox database is still in an inconsistent (i.e., dirty shutdown) state. Exchange will try to start a recovery process with the log files that are also restored from the backup set.

When finished, any additional log files that are written to disk after the previous backup was taken are replayed into the mailbox database as well, so no mail data will be lost when restoring a mailbox database from backup.

▓ **Note** Exchange Server has always been very sensitive when it comes to transaction log files and with replaying these into the mailbox database. In the "A Refresher on Mailbox Database Technology" section earlier in this chapter, I explained the ESE internals and so it should be clear that Exchange Server is 100 percent dependent on all transaction log files. If only one log file is missing, the replay of the log files will fail. Therefore, you should never delete any of the log files manually; or do so only if you're 150 percent sure of what you're doing, or if Microsoft support instructs you to do so!

During the restore process, several events are written to the event log, indicating the progress of the restore or if any problems have arisen during the restore operation:

- **Event ID 4347** (MSExchangeRepl) Exchange Replication Service VSS Writer will restore a backup set to database MDB01\EXCH01, which is the same database from which the backup was originally taken.

- **Event ID 4367** (MSExchangeRepl) Exchange Replication Service VSS Writer successfully restored the backup set. In order to bring the restored databases to a clean-shutdown state, database recovery will be performed using the information in the restore environment document MDB01\EXCH01.

- **Event ID 4370** (MSExchangeRepl) Exchange Replication Service VSS Writer will perform database recovery on database MDB01.edb as part of the restore process for MDB01\EXCH01, followed by a number of events from ESE, indicating the recovery steps for the restored mailbox database.

- **Event ID 40008** (MSExchangeIS) Mount completed successfully for database <<GUID>>.

- **Event ID 3156** (MSExchangeRepl) Active Manager successfully mounted database MDB01 on server EXCH01.contoso.com

- **Event ID 737** (Backup) The operation to recover component(s) d7f01671-c9c7-46d6-abac-00fd27e1ebf2 has completed successfully at 2013-07-25T14:52:38.059000000Z.

If you log on to your mailbox and check any messages that were send after the last backup was taken, you'll see that these are still available in the mailbox and thus successfully recovered.

Restoring a Mailbox Database to Another Location

Restoring a mailbox database to its original location is only useful when the original mailbox database is lost, for whatever reason. In a normal production situation you don't want to dismount your mailbox database for restoring purposes unless there's no other option. Restoring to its original location means you have to dismount the mailbox database, resulting in an outage for users.

Restoring a backup to another location has the advantage of leaving the original mailbox mounted and then users can continue to work. When using this method there's no risk in accidentally overwriting the mailbox database with a database that's restored, since the original database is still mounted and thus reports as "file in use." Restoring the mailbox database to another location does not differ much from restoring to its original location.

The Restore Process

If you want to restore to another location, follow these guidelines:

1. Log on to the Exchange 2013 Mailbox server, open WSB, and in the Actions pane, select Recover.

2. In the Recovery wizard that starts, select where the backup is located. This can be on a disk attached to the server itself or it can be a remote location. Select the appropriate option here and click Next to continue.

3. In the Select Backup Date window, select the backup set you want to restore to this server. Once selected, click Next to continue.

4. The Select Recovery Type window is very important. WSB is Exchange-aware and thus an Exchange backup is an Application backup. This way, the backup is restored as the Exchange Writer would like it to be. If you select Volumes, for example, the backup will be restored as an ordinary file backup and this is useless from an Exchange perspective. Select Applications and click Next to continue.

5. In the Select Application window, make sure Exchange is selected and click Next to continue.

6. Since the backup will be restored to another location, select the Recover to Another Location option, and use the Browse button to select a disk and directory where you want to restore the mailbox database. Typically a dedicated restore LUN is used for this purpose. In our example, we use G:\RestoreDB to restore the mailbox database from backup.

7. The selection is shown in the confirmation window. If all is okay, then click the Restore button to start the recover process.

8. Since only the mailbox database and its log files are restored from backup, the process finishes much faster than when restoring to its original location. In this process, no additional recovery steps are performed so you have to do this manually.

The mailbox database and the accompanying log files are now restored from the backup set. The file location is also restored, so now there's a mailbox database DB01 located in G:\RestoreDB\F_\MDB01 and the log files are stored in G:\RestoreDB\F_\MDB01\LogFiles. This file is taken from a running copy of the mailbox database and thus the mailbox database is in a dirty shutdown state. You can check this using the ESEUTIL /MH command, which would produce something like this:

```
     State: Dirty Shutdown
Log Required: 82-84 (0x52-0x54)
```

To bring this database back into a consistent state the mailbox database has to be recovered—something that can be achieved using the ESEUTIL tool with the /R option for recovery and the /l and /s options for the file locations of the log files and the system file (i.e., the checkpoint file).

```
ESEUTIL /R E00 /lG:\RestoreDB\F_\MDB01\Logfiles /sG:\RestoreDB\F_\MDB01\Logfiles
```

This is shown in Figure 7-13.

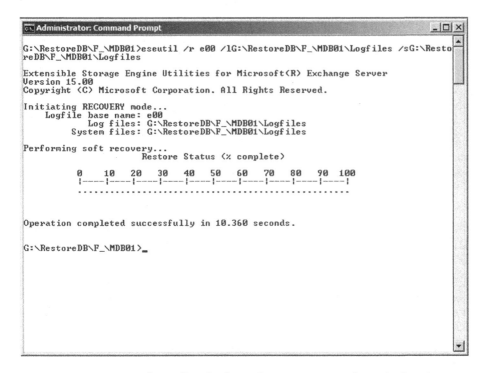

Figure 7-13. Recovering the mailbox database after a restore to an alternative location

Now when you check the database again using the ESEUTIL /MH command, the database will be in a clean shutdown state and ready to use.

Recovery Database

A recovery database in Exchange 2013 is a special mailbox database, invisible for normal users, where you can mount a normal database restored from backup. This means that you will have one normal mailbox database MDB01 running in its original location and one recovery mailbox MDB01 running in recovery mode.

Creating a recovery mailbox database is not very different from creating a regular mailbox database, but it can be managed only by using EMS. When creating the recovery mailbox database, you have to use the -Recovery switch to tell Exchange that a recovery mailbox database is created.

To create a recovery mailbox database using the database we've restored in the previous section, an EMS command like this would be used:

```
New-MailboxDatabase -Name "MDB01 Recovery" -Recovery -Server EXCH01 -EdbFilePath
G:\RestoreDB\F_\MDB01\MDB01.edb -LogFolderPath G:\RestoreDB\F_\MDB01\LogFiles
```

When the recovery mailbox database is created, it can be mounted, again only using the EMS since the recovery mailbox database is not visible in EAC (at least not up to Exchange Server 2013 CU2).

Now that the recovery mailbox database is up and running, you can view what's inside this database. An ordinary `Get-Mailbox` command is not going work, since this is targeted against normal mailbox database, but the `Get-MailboxStatistics` command does work against a recovery mailbox database. Just use the following command to retrieve mailbox data from the recovery mailbox database:

```
Get-MailboxStatistics -Database "MDB01 Recovery" | select DisplayName,ItemCount | ft -a
```

Figure 7-14 shows the output from this command.

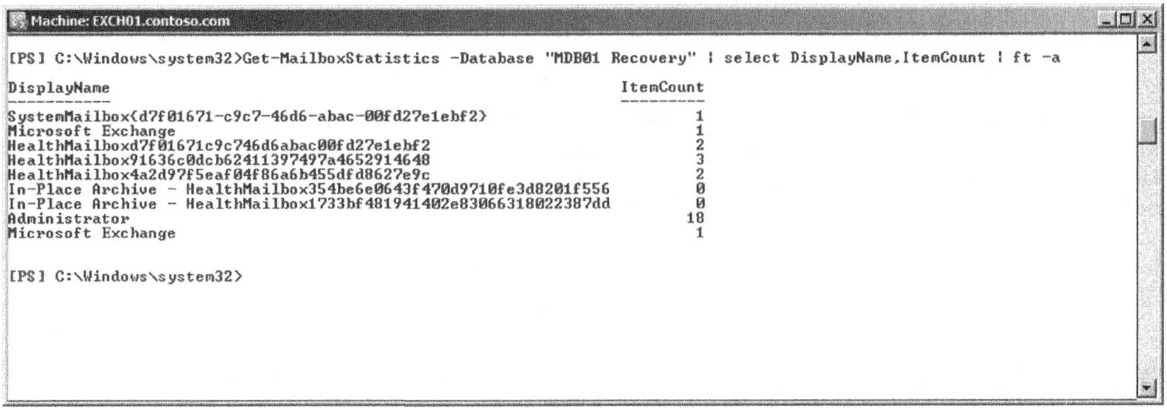

Figure 7-14. Using the Get-MailboxStatistics command to view what's inside the recovery mailbox database

This information can be used to restore mailbox content from the recovery mailbox database into the normal production mailbox database using the `New-MailboxRestoreRequest` command in the EMS.

To retrieve mailbox content from the administrator mailbox inside the recovery mailbox database into the normal administrator mailbox, you can use the following command:

```
New-MailboxRestoreRequest -SourceDatabase "MDB01 Recovery" -SourceStoreMailbox Administrator
-TargetMailbox administrator
```

The content will be imported into the normal mailbox, but content will not be overwritten. If items already exist in the target mailbox, an additional copy of the item will be created so no information gets lost.

■ **Note** If you're uncertain what will happen during a command like the `New-MailboxRestoreRequest`, you can always use the `-Whatif` option. The command will be the same, but it won't be executed. The results, however, will be shown on the console. If you're satisfied with the results, you can then rerun the command but without the `-Whatif` option.

The example above will restore the entire mailbox from the recovery mailbox database, but it is possible to use a more granular approach. For instance, you can use the `-IncludeFolders` option to specify the folder in the mailbox that needs to be restored. To include the contents from the inbox, the option `-IncludeFolders "Inbox/*"` can be used; or in case of restoring only the Deleted Items folder, the option -IncludeFolders "DeletedItems/*" can be used. For example:

```
New-MailboxRestoreRequest -SourceDatabase "MDB01 Recovery" -SourceStoreMailbox Administrator
-TargetMailbox administrator -IncludeFolders "DeletedItems/*"
```

■ **Note**   There's a dependency here on the regional settings of the mailbox. In English, you have an "inbox" while in Dutch the same folder is called *Postvak in* or in Spanish it is *bandeja de entrada*. You have to be aware of the regional setting of the mailbox when performing this command.

For certain purposes, it is possible to restore mailbox content from the mailbox in the recovery mailbox database to another mailbox that's not the original mailbox—for example, a legal mailbox. Suppose there's a mailbox called Legal and this mailbox is used to gather information from a mailbox from a backup. A command similar to this can be used:

```
New-MailboxRestoreRequest -SourceDatabase "MDB01 Recovery" -SourceStoreMailbox Administrator
-TargetMailbox legal -TargetRootFolder "Recovery Items"
```

Dial-tone Recovery

A recovery database is also used in a process called *dial-tone recovery*. In this recovery scenario, you get the users back online as quickly as possible after a mailbox database crash, and you work on mailbox database recovery in the background.

Suppose a mailbox database has crashed beyond repair, but you need to get users back online immediately. In this case you can remove all corrupted files from the disk and mount the mailbox database again. Since Exchange does not find any mailbox database files, it will create a new mailbox database and new log files (after showing a warning message).

Users who had their mailboxes in the crashed mailbox database can now start their mail client, and new mailboxes will automatically be created in the new mailbox database. Of course, it is empty, but users are online again. They can send mail but, more important, they can receive mail again. The last thing you want to have happen is for external customers to send email to your organization and receive error messages like "Mailbox info@contoso.com is not available."

Since users are online, they can continue to function and you can work in the background on restoring the last mailbox database backup to a recovery mailbox database. When the mailbox database is restored and all remaining log files are replayed into the recovered mailbox database, you can swap the two mailbox databases. The recovered mailbox database will be moved to the production location while the newly created mailbox database, which now also has items in it, will be moved to the recovery mailbox database location.

The trick you will perform now is to mount the newly created mailbox database as a recovery mailbox database and move the new content, using the New-MailboxRestoreRequest command as explained in the previous section, into the restored mailbox database. Once finished, you will have the mailbox database up and running again, without losing any data.

The good part here is that you can restore the mailbox database from a backup, but your users are able to log on again and continue sending and receiving email. Yes, at that moment they won't have their "old" mailbox content available (not only email items but also the temporary mailbox doesn't contain any information or additional permissions), but at least they are online during the restore procedures.

> ■ **Note**   Some third-party backup applications use a granular restore technology, whereby it is possible to restore individual items directly from the VSS backup. What happens is that the VSS backup is completely indexed after the backup, indexing all individual email messages. These messages can then be restored directly from the backup, where the MAPI CDO is used for storing directly into the mailbox. While this works very well, it is not an official Microsoft-supported solution.

Disaster Recovery with Exchange Server 2013

The previous section discussed mailbox database technologies: how they work, how to back them up, and how to restore them. It is possible to restore a mailbox database to its original location or to an alternative location. In the last scenario, it was possible to create a recovery mailbox database, restore data from this recovery mailbox database, or use it in a dial-tone scenario.

But what happens if an entire server is lost and it is beyond repair? Then you need to rely on your disaster recovery skills.

Rebuilding the Exchange Server

When the Exchange 2013 Mailbox server is lost, it needs to be rebuilt and the services, configuration, and data need to be restored. Earlier in this chapter I described where all the information is stored that's needed to rebuild an Exchange 2013 server; for example:

- Mailbox data is stored in the mailbox database, which should be on additional disks. If you're in luck, these are still safe after losing your Exchange server.

- Configuration data is sometimes stored in config files, located somewhere in the `C:\Program Files\Microsoft\Exchange Server` directory.

- All kinds of log files are also stored in the `C:\Program Files\Microsoft\Exchange Server` directory.

- SSL certificates are stored somewhere safe.

- Server configuration is stored in Active Directory.

Now, assuming that you've take care of the first four bullets, the last bullet about Active Directory is interesting. All configuration data that's not in the config files is stored in Active Directory, and that can be used when rebuilding the Exchange 2013 Mailbox server. But instead of entering all the details manually during setup, this information will be retrieved from Active Directory during installation.

Rule number 1 in a crisis situation: don't panic and don't destroy any data. Not from disks and not from Active Directory, since this action will be used against you at some point!

To successfully rebuild an Exchange 2013 server, you can use the following steps.

1. Reset the Computer Account. When the server has crashed beyond repair and you have to rebuild your server, DO NOT REMOVE the Computer object from Active Directory. Instead, reset the Computer object in Active Directory:

   a. To reset the Computer object, log on to a Domain Controller, or any other member server that has the Active Directory tools installed, and open the Active Directory and Computers MMC snap-in.

   b. Locate the Computer object, right-click it, and select Reset Account (see Figure 7-15). This will reset the Computer object so you can join a new Windows Server (using the same name) to Active Directory.

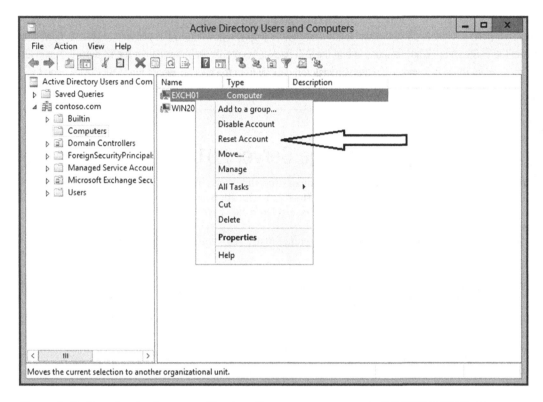

Figure 7-15. *Resetting the Computer object in a disaster recovery scenario. DO NOT DELETE this computer account!*

2. Install a new Windows server with the same specifications as the "old" Exchange 2013 server. Use the same operating system and bring it up to date with the same hot fixes and service packs as were applied to the old Exchange 2013 server. Very important: *use the same server name* as the old Exchange 2013 server. So, when the old server name was EXCH01, the new server name needs to be EXCH01 as well.

3. Join the new server, using the original name, to the Active Directory domain. When joined, reboot the server and log on to the new server as a Domain administrator.

4. When logged on as a Domain administrator, install the prerequisite software. This is explained in Chapter 2, but as a friendly reminder this is the prerequisite software when using a Windows Server 2012 server:

```
Import-Module ServerManager
Install-WindowsFeature AS-HTTP-Activation, Desktop-Experience, NET-Framework-45-Features,
RPC-over-HTTP-proxy, RSAT-Clustering, RSAT-Clustering-CmdInterface, Web-Mgmt-Console,
WAS-Process-Model, Web-Asp-Net45, Web-Basic-Auth, Web-Client-Auth, Web-Digest-Auth,
Web-Dir-Browsing, Web-Dyn-Compression, Web-Http-Errors, Web-Http-Logging, Web-Http-Redirect,
Web-Http-Tracing, Web-ISAPI-Ext, Web-ISAPI-Filter, Web-Lgcy-Mgmt-Console, Web-Metabase,
Web-Mgmt-Console, Web-Mgmt-Service, Web-Net-Ext45, Web-Request-Monitor, Web-Server,
Web-Stat-Compression, Web-Static-Content, Web-Windows-Auth, Web-WMI,
Windows-Identity-Foundation
```

The following prerequisite software need to be installed as well:

- Microsoft Unified Communications Managed API 4.0, Core Runtime 64-bit - http://go.microsoft.com/fwlink/p/?linkId=258269

- Microsoft Office 2010 Filter Pack 64 bit - http://go.microsoft.com/fwlink/p/?linkID=191548

- Microsoft Office 2010 Filter Pack SP1 64 bit - http://go.microsoft.com/fwlink/p/?LinkId=254043

■ **Note** It looks strange, but the Filter Pack components used here are really version 2010.

5. When the server is fully up to date, the (external) disks containing the "old" mailbox databases must be accessible to the new Exchange 2013 server. The setup application will look for these disks; this is one kind of information that is stored in Active Directory as part of the Exchange 2013 Server object. If you omit this step, the setup application will halt and will generate a couple of errors on the console, such as those shown in Figure 7-16.

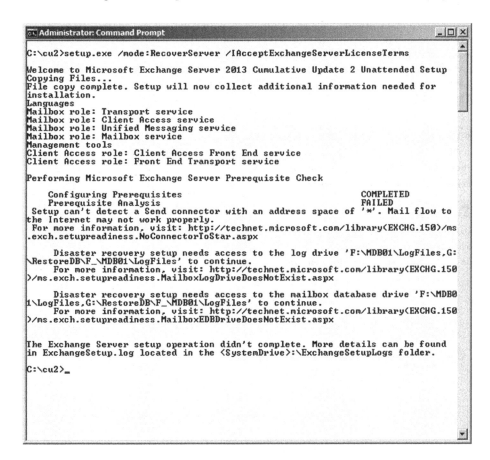

Figure 7-16. *When the original disks are not available, the setup application will halt during the RecoverServer operation*

6. When the disks are connected and configured with the previous drive letters, the Exchange 2013 server can be recovered. To do this, open a command prompt, navigate to the installation media, and enter the following command:

    ```
    Setup.exe /mode:RecoverServer /IAcceptExchangeServerLicenseTerms
    ```

    This will install Exchange 2013, and all the configuration information that's normally entered in the setup application is now retrieved from Active Directory.

7. When the setup application is finished and the server is reinstalled, reboot the server.

After rebooting, you can check the mailbox databases that were on the (external) disk drives; they should be good, although dismounted. When you mount the mailbox databases on the recovered server, you're good to log in to your mailbox using OWA. The last steps are to restore additional items like the SSL certificate, additional config files, or other log files, as explained earlier in this chapter (in the "Backup of Other Configuration Information" section).

When done, your server has been unavailable for some time, but it is now restored to its original location. If you're unhappy with the down time, you should continue reading the "Database Availability Group" section in Chapter 5, which explains how to avoid or minimize downtime.

ESEUTIL and Corrupted Databases

Although rare these days, it can happen that you end up with a corrupted mailbox database and no backup of your mailbox database. In this case, you have to rely on tools that can repair your mailbox database. ESEUTIL is such a tool and it comes with Exchange Server; you can use ESEUTIL to repair a corrupted mailbox database.

When a mailbox database is corrupted, that means it has corrupted pages in it and most likely it will not mount. When you perform an integrity check on the mailbox database using ESEUTIL /G, it will report that the mailbox database is corrupted (see Figure 7-17).

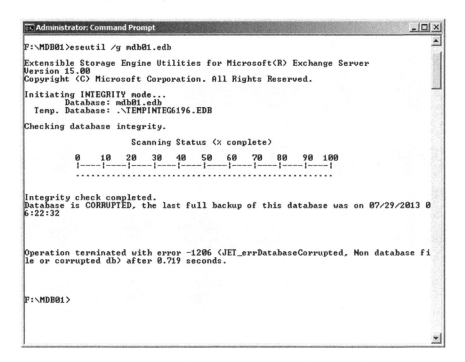

Figure 7-17. ESEUTIL reports that the mailbox database is corrupted

ESEUTIL also has an option to repair a mailbox database, but it is a very destructive way of repairing. What it does is open the mailbox database and check all the pages in the database. When a page is found to contain corrupted pointers (i.e., pointers to other pages containing data), it will remove these pointers from the page. The result is that no pages contain invalid pointers anymore, but the data that was referenced using those pages is automatically lost. It is not possible to predict which pages and pointers are corrupted, and thus it's not possible to anticipate what data you will be missing. Unfortunately, your users will find out in the end.

You can start a repair with ESEUTIL /P MDB01.edb. A warning message is shown saying that you should only run Repair on damaged or corrupted databases. The caution is that Repair will not apply information in the transaction log files to the database and may cause information to be lost. And it will ask you if you want to continue.

If you do, click the OK button to continue. ESEUTIL will perform a consistency check first, then scan the database and repair any damaged information that it found (see Figure 7-18).

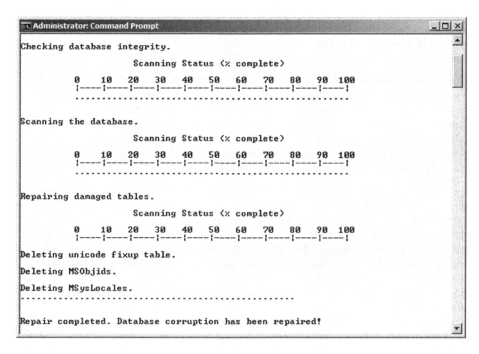

Figure 7-18. *ESEUTIL /P does several checks before repairing damaged information*

One question that always pops up is how long it actually takes for a mailbox database repair to be completed. As a rule of thumb, I use 10GB per hour for processing. So, if you have a 250GB mailbox database you have to repair, it will take approximately 25 hours to complete. There's no need to panic when you don't see any dots moving on the console; ESEUTIL just needs its time to do its work.

This is the reason Microsoft recommends not using large mailbox databases (i.e., larger than 200GB) when a DAG is not used. If you're using a 500GB mailbox database in a single Mailbox server environment, and you run into a situation like this, you will have a hard time ensuring service delivery (which should be documented in the SLA).

■ **Note**   It is my personal experience that it's best not to use a large mailbox database when using a single Mailbox server. Although Microsoft recommends a maximum size of 200GB for a mailbox database in such a scenario, I think it's still too large. When you run into problems and have to start repairing your mailbox database, it will take too much time to do so. Stay on the safe side and keep your mailbox database between 50GB and 75GB. When more space is needed, just create additional mailbox databases.

It is recommended that you create a new mailbox database after a corrupted mailbox database has been repaired. This can be done in two ways:

- Create a new mailbox database on the Exchange server and move all the mailboxes from the old and repaired mailbox database to the new mailbox database. Once they are moved, the old mailbox database can be removed. Do not forget to create a new backup of the new mailbox database when done.

- Use ESEUTIL /D to perform an offline defragmentation. The net effect of this is that a new mailbox database is created with the old name. When you use ESEUTIL /D to perform an offline defragmentation, it will create a new mailbox database file next to the old mailbox database file. Then it will read all information from the old file and merge it into the new file. This way not only is a new file created but also new indices, new tables, new pointers, and so on, so basically you end up with a new mailbox database. When the copy process is complete, the old (and previously corrupted) mailbox database will be deleted.

In the Exchange 5.5 days, it was a best practice to run ESEUTIL /D on a biweekly or monthly basis to be running with relatively fresh mailbox databases. Considering the quality and stability of ESE in those days, this made perfect sense. But Exchange and ESE have come a long way, and now it doesn't make much sense to run this on a regular basis.

The only time you should run this is when you have moved a large number of mailboxes (and thus a lot of data) from one mailbox database to another mailbox database. This will result in large amounts of white space inside the mailbox database, which won't be reclaimed by online defragmentation (OLD) as part of online maintenance. Yes, this will restructure the data inside the mailbox database, but it won't shrink the mailbox database.

If you are in a situation like this and you do not have a DAG, you can use ESEUTIL /D to offline defragment the mailbox database to reclaim this white space.

■ **Note**   Offline defragmentation is what its name implies—an offline process. During this, the mailbox database is not available for users. It is hard to predict how long it will take for an offline defrag to finish. A good rule of thumb is 10GB per hour, depending on the amount of database inside the mailbox database that needs to be moved. If you have a 200GB mailbox database with 150GB of white space, you have to move 50GB of data, which can take up to 5 hours to complete.

File Recovery Tools

This is not really a native Exchange server topic, but it is interesting enough to mention, viewed from a disaster recovery perspective.

There are situations when you do have a mailbox database file and you are in urgent need of data inside this mailbox database file, but you don't have an Exchange server available to perform these kinds of recovery services. In this case, a file recovery tool can be helpful. Several tools are available, but the most well known is called PowerControls, from Kroll Ontrack.

These tools let you open the mailbox database file (the EDB file), regardless of whether they are in a clean shutdown state or are taken from a backup and thus in a dirty shutdown state. Either way, you don't need an Exchange server for opening the EDB file.

You can connect to a source, which in Figure 7-19 is a mailbox database taken from a backup. This is shown in the top pane. You can also connect to a target, which can be a PST file or a live Exchange 2013 server. It is possible to connect to all folders in a mailbox; even the `Recoverable Items` folder is available.

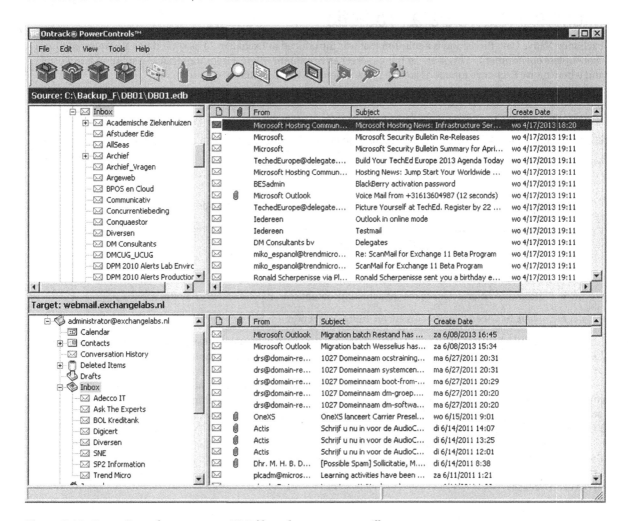

Figure 7-19. *PowerControls can open an EDB file and connect to a mailbox*

Messages can be exported to MSG, TXT, or EML files, but can also be exported to a PST file. Besides exporting to one of these files, items from the source mailbox database files can be moved to a live mailbox when the tool is connected to an Exchange 2013 server.

The tool is using MAPI under the hood, so Outlook needs to be installed on the server and there must be a working Outlook profile on the recover server to make sure that the tool can connect to the Exchange 2013 server.

A recovery tool like Kroll Ontrack PowerControl can be an interesting addition to your toolbox of restore or disaster recovery solutions.

■ **Note**   Opening a mailbox database directly by a recovery tool is not supported by Microsoft, nor is a direct restore by this tool using the MAPI interfaces.

Exchange Native Data Protection

Exchange Native Data Protection is a solution that was introduced in Exchange 2010, sometimes also referred to as a "backupless environment." This is an Exchange server environment where a traditional backup solution is not used, and where native Exchange functions are the replacement—when possible, of course.

■ **Note**   In some market segments, such as legal, finance or healthcare, there are (legal) requirements that dictate how to create regular backups, keep them for a certain amount of time, and/or store them on a separate location. For these, Exchange Native Data Protection is not a solution.

Exchange Native Data Protection should be able to help you in scenarios where:

- Users have unintentionally deleted items from their mailboxes and need them urgently.

- You need to restore items from a user's mailbox for legal purposes.

- A mailbox was deleted unintentionally.

- Hardware failures caused loss of a mailbox database or maybe loss of an entire server.

- There has been failure or loss of an entire datacenter.

Exchange 2013 has a lot of built-in features that can take care of some of these items; for example, deleted items retention, In-Place Hold, Single Item Recovery, archive mailboxes, retention policies, and database availability group (DAG).

Using these features, it is possible to create an environment where a traditional backup is not used, but where the disasters mentioned earlier would be fully covered. The advantage of this arrangement is that the total cost of ownership (TCO) of a full-fledged Exchange 2013 environment is most likely lower than that of a regular Exchange 2013 environment with a traditional backup solution.

Microsoft recommends evaluating your various requirements and the available options to decide whether this is a viable solution for your organization. For more information, visit the Microsoft Exchange team site on http://blogs.technet.com/b/omers/archive/2010/11/05/designing-a-backup-less-exchange-2010-architecture.aspx.

Deleted Items Retention

When users delete items from their mailboxes, the items are not visible for the users anymore, but they are still in the users' mailboxes. They are stored in hiddens folders in their mailboxes, which is part of the so-called dumpster.

Deleted items are kept in the Recoverable Items folder for a time called the *deleted item retention period*. By default, the retention time for deleted items is 14 days and for a deleted mailbox, it is 30 days. This means that after these times, the items are deleted from the server. Deleted item retention is a property of the mailbox datatabase and can be set using EAC (see Figure 7-20).

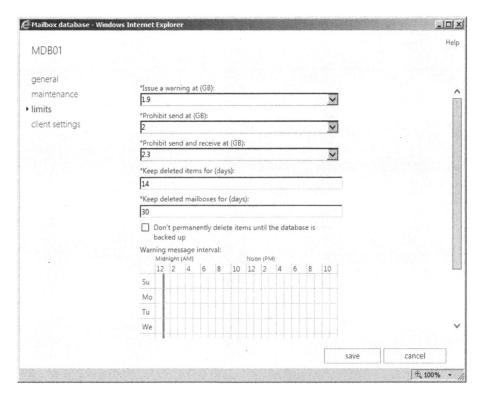

Figure 7-20. *Deleted items retention is a property on a mailbox database*

The deleted item retention period can also be set using the ESM. It is a parameter of the mailbox database called DeletedItemRetention, and is specified as a time span: dd.hh:mm:ss. To set the deleted item retention time to 60 days, for example, you can use the following command:

```
Set-MailboxDatabase -Identity MDB01 -DeletedItemRetention 60.00:00:00
```

To set the deleted item retention time for mailboxes, the same command is used but with the MailboxRetention option. For example, to change the deleted item retention time for mailboxes to seven days, you can use the following command:

```
Set-MailboxDatabase -Identity MDB01 -MailboxRetention 7.00:00:00
```

Within this deleted items retention time, users can recover deleted items themselves in Outlook. In Outlook 2013, select the Folders tab and then click the Recover Deleted Items button. A new window will pop up showing all messages that are not in the Deleted Items folder but can still be recovered from the Recoverable Items folder (see Figure 7-21).

Figure 7-21. *End users can recover deleted items*

In Outlook Web App, the deleted items can be recovered as well. In the OWA navigation pane, right-click the Deleted Items folder and select the Recover Deleted Items option.

When the user permanently deletes a message (i.e., purges the `Deleted Items` folder), the message can no longer te recovered—not even by administrators—unless the Single Item Recovery is enabled. This will be covered later in this section.

In-Place Hold

Although you now know it is possible to stretch the deleted item retention period, it is not really a good idea to stretch this time to a couple of years; doing so would have a disastrous effect on the size of the mailbox database. So Exchange 2010 came up with a new feature called Litigation Hold, which was then replaced by In-Place Hold in Exchange 2013. With In-Place Hold, you have the possibility to:

- Place user mailboxes on hold and preserve mailbox content immutably.

- Preserve deleted ttems; that is, items that can be deleted manually by the user or by an automated process like Messaging Records Management (MRM).

- Search for and retain items matching specified criteria.

- Preserve items indefinitely or for a specific duration.

- Keep In-Place Hold transparent from the user by not having to suspend MRM.

- Enable In-Place eDiscovery searches of items placed on hold.

In short, items will be on hold in a user's mailbox without the user knowing it.

Litigation Hold allowed you to put all items on hold for an indefinite amount of time.In-Place Hold is more granular, with the following parameters being able to be be specified:

- **What to hold** It is possible to specify which items to put on hold by using parameters such as keywords, recipients, senders, start and end dates, and the type of items such as messages, calender items, and so forth.

- **How long to hold** Besides specifying what to hold, there's the option to specify how long these items should be on hold.

■ **Note** With In-Place Hold, the previous indefinite hold is still possible.

To place a mailbox on In-Place Hold, you need to have specific permissions. These permissions are granted to users who are members of the Discovery Management RBAC group or users who are assigned the Legal Hold and Mailbox Search management roles.

You can create an In-Place Hold by using either the EAC or EMS. When using the EAC, you follow these steps:

1. Select Compliance Management in the Feature pane, and then select In-Place eDiscovery and Hold tab. In the toolbar, click the New icon.

2. In the New In-Place eDiscover and Hold wizard, enter a name and a description for the new hold you're creating. Click Next to continue.

3. The next window lets you decide if you want to search all mailboxes or only specific mailboxes. Assuming the latter, select the Specify Mailboxes to Search radio button and use the Add (+) button to select a mailbox that needs to be added to the new search. Select the mailbox, use the Add button, and click OK to return to the previous window. This mailbox should now be listed in the Results pane. Click Next to continue.

4. By default, the setting for mailbox content is set to Include All Mailbox Content, but it is also possible to enter keywords, a start and end date, and specific recipients or senders. Make you own choice and click Next to continue.

5. To activate the In-Place Hold, check the Place Content Matching the Search Query in Selected Mailboxes on Hold option and select if you want to hold the items indefinitely (default setting) or specify the number of days to hold items relative to their received date, whichever you need.

6. Click Finish to store the new In-Place Hold and activate it.

■ **Note** In-Place Hold is a premium feature that requires an Enterprise Client Access License (CAL). You only need the Enterprise CAL for mailboxes that use this feature.

To create a new In-Place Hold using the EMS, you can use the following command:

```
New-MailboxSearch "In-place hold Joe Jackson Mailbox" -SourceMailboxes "joe@contoso.com"
-InPlaceHoldEnabled $true
```

When a new mailbox search is created using the EMS, an informational warning message is shown saying that the new Mailbox server won't be effective immediately and that it can take up to 60 minutes before becoming active (see Figure 7-22).

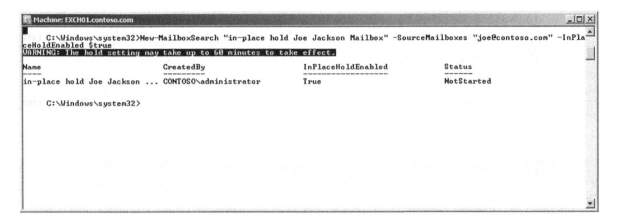

Figure 7-22. *Creating a new mailbox search using the EMS. Note the warning message*

All items in Joe's mailbox will now be on hold for an indefinite period. When Joe deletes items and purges his deleted items manually, they will be stored. If Joe receives a message and deliberately makes changes to this message, the original and the changed messages will both be kept. It is a good practice to monitor the deleted items quota in the mailboxes for which you have enabled In-Place Hold.

■ **Note** This will work only for mailboxes on Exchange 2013. For mailboxes stored on an Exchange 2010 Mailbox server, the corresponding cmdlet has to be used on an Exchange 2010 server.

Single Item Recovery

Single Item Recovery is a feature that was introduced in Exchange 2010 and is still available in Exchange 2013.

When a message is deleted from a mailbox, it is stored in the Recoverable Items folder of that mailbox. Items stay in this folder until the deleted items retention period expires. Only then is it fully removed from the Exchange server by the server's online maintenance. When a user permanently deletes a message, it is removed immediately from the Recoverable Items folder and the user is no longer able to recover that message; not even the administrator is able to recover it. One exception, however, is when the mailbox is on In-Place Hold. Then, deleted items are retained until the In-Place Hold is removed.

To be able to recover these deleted items when they have been permanently deleted by the user, you can enable Single Item Recovery on the mailbox. When enabled, permanently deleted messages are retained in the Recoverable Items folder until the deleted item retention period is passed and then the message is fully removed from the Recoverable Items folder.

Single Item Recovery can be enabled only with the EMS and using the following command:

```
Set-Mailbox -Identity "April Summers" -SingleItemRecoveryEnabled $true
```

For mailboxes that have Single Item Recovery, it is also possible to set a different deleted item retention time, using the -RetainDeletedItemsFor option:

```
Set-Mailbox -Identity "Kim Akers" -SingleItemRecoveryEnabled $true -RetainDeletedItemsFor 30
```

Recovering items when Single Item Recovery is enabled consists of two steps:

1. Search for the missing items and recover them.

2. Restore the recovered items.

Searching for deleted items in mailboxes that have Single Item Recovery enabled or mailboxes that are on In-Place Hold is part of the InPlace eDiscovery. As such, you need special permission to search for these deleted items or search in these mailboxes. This makes sense, since you're looking in somebody else's potentially private information. With the permission stipulation in place, it is impossible to "accidentally" search others' mailboxes. Permission is granted to members of the Discovery Management RBAC Role Group.

The process for searching for missing items is similar to that for putting a mailbox on In-Place Hold. In EAC, follow these steps:

1. Select Compliance Management in the Feature pane and select the In-Place eDiscovery and Hold tab. In the toolbar, click the New icon.

2. In the New In-Place eDiscover and Hold wizard, enter a name and a description for the new hold you're creating. Click Next to continue.

3. The next window lets you choose if you want to search all mailboxes or only specific mailboxes. Assuming the latter, select the Specify Mailboxes to Search radio button and use the Add (+) button to select a mailbox that needs to be added to the new search. Select the mailbox, use the Add button, and click OK to return to the previous window. This mailbox should now be listed in the Results pane. Click Next to continue.

4. In the Search Query window, you can define the query that needs to be used. Enter the keywords, start and end dates, recipient and sender, and the item type, like email, meeting, notes, and so forth. Select the options you need and click Next to continue.

5. If needed, you can opt to place the content matching the Search Query on hold. It can be on hold indefinitely or for a certain number of days. Click Finish to continue.

The search is not executed immediately, but an estimate of the search results is shown in the Details pane, including the number of items returned by the search and its size (see Figure 7-23).

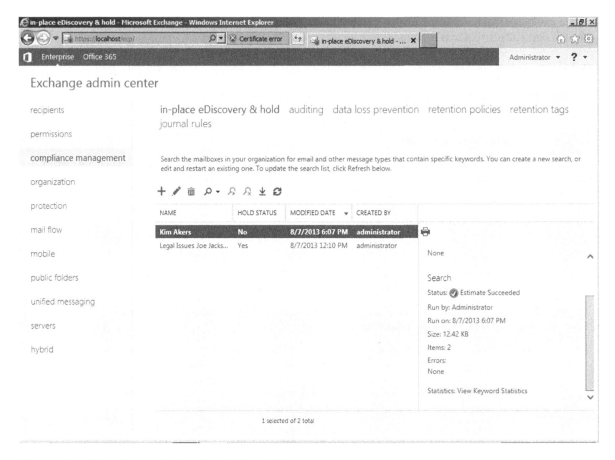

Figure 7-23. *The estimate of results of an In-Place eDiscovery*

6. When the results are satisfactory, the search can be executed. Click the down arrow next to the search icon and select the Copy Search Results option. You can select which options can be enabled, such as:

- Include unsearchable items

- Enable de-duplication

- Enable full logging

- Send me mail when the copy is completed

7. The last action is to select where the search will store its results; typically this is the Discovery Search Mailbox. Click Copy to start copying the search results to the Discovery Search Mailbox.

Members of the Discovery Search RBAC Role Group are automatically assigned Full Access permission to the Discovery Search Mailbox. When you open the Discovery Search Mailbox, either in Outlook or in OWA, you should see a folder with the name you specified in the eDiscovery wizard. This is where the search results are stored (see Figure 7-24).

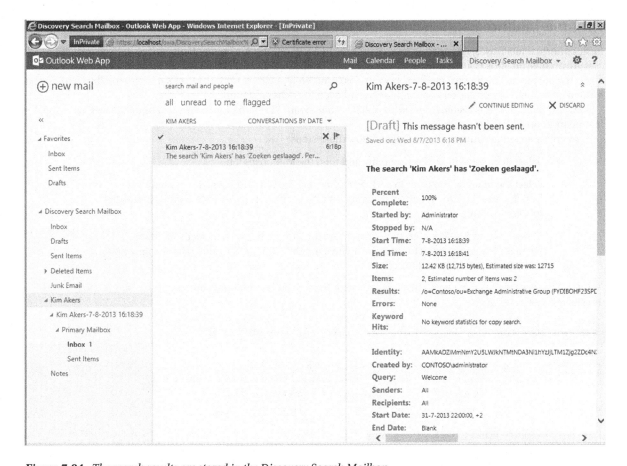

Figure 7-24. *The search results are stored in the Discovery Search Mailbox*

When the results are stored in the Discovery Search Mailbox, it is possible to export those results to the user's mailbox using the Search-Mailbox command:

```
Search-Mailbox "Discovery Search Mailbox" -SearchQuery "Welcome" -TargetMailbox "Kim Akers"
-TargetFolder "Recovered Messages" -LogLevel Full -DeleteContent
```

This command will move the items from the search results into the user's mailbox in a folder called Recovered Messages. When done, the items in the Discovery Search Mailbox are deleted.

Using New-MailboxExportRequest, it is also possible to export the results to a PST file. The same prerequisites apply as when using a "normal" export request. The MRS will process the request, so the PST file needs to be stored to a fileshare where the Exchange Trusted Subsystem USG has permission for full access.

For example, the following command will start a new export request of the folder called Kim Akers in the Discovery Search Mailbox, where the subject of the items is "Welcome," and will store the PST file on a fileshare called HelpDeskPst on a server called AMS-FS01:

```
New-MailboxExportRequest -Mailbox "Discovery Search Mailbox" -SourceRootFolder "Kim Akers"
-ContentFilter {Subject -eq "Welcome"} -FilePath \\AMS-FS01\HelpDeskPst\KimAkersRecovery.pst
```

Archive Mailboxes

Besides normal mailboxes, there are archive mailboxes in Exchange 2013, a concept introduced in Exchange 2010.

An archive mailbox is just a normal mailbox, but it's connected to a user as a secondary mailbox and is used for archiving purposes. The archive mailbox, however, is completely separate from the user's primary mailbox and can be located on additional storage, on a separate server, or even in Exchange Online.

An archive mailbox is visible from Outlook 2007 Professioanl Plus and higher, and also from Outlook Web App; it appears as an additional mailbox in the client.

To create an archive mailbox in EAC, just follow these steps:

1. Select Recipients in the Feature pane and then the Mailboxes tab.

2. Select the mailbox you want to add the archive mailbox to, and scroll down in the Details pane until you reach In-Place Archive. In the Details pane, click Enable, just under In-Place Archive.

3. In the Create an In-Place Archive wizard, use the Browse button to select a mailbox database where you want to store the archive mailbox. Click OK to store all the information and have the archive mailbox created.

It is also possible to create an archive mailbox with EMS, using a command similar to this example (the results are shown in Figure 7-25):

```
Enable-Mailbox -Identity Joe@contoso.com -Archive -ArchiveDatabase MDB01
```

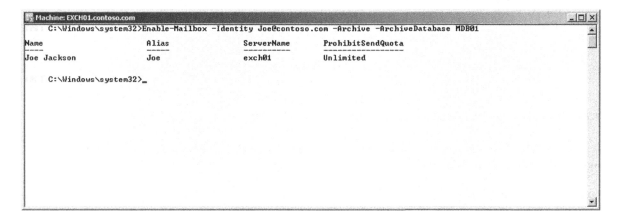

Figure 7-25. *Creating an archive mailbox using EMS*

■ **Note**   In-Place Archiving is a premium feature and requires an Exchange Enterprise Client Access License (CAL).

By default, an archive mailbox has an archive quota of 100GB and an archive quota warning at 90GB. This means that a warning message will be sent to the user when the archive reaches 90GB, but this is sufficient to store tons of information.

■ **Note** Achive mailboxes are a perfect "PST killer." By nature, PST files are stored on the user's workstation or laptop, where they are not backed up and are prone to getting lost when the laptop is stored. Storing PST files on a network share is not supported and can give erratic results in Outlook. Also, a backup application can skip these files when they are still open in Outlook. But when they are moved to archive mailboxes, they are stored safely, available for the user and backed up frequently. It's a perfect solution for getting rid of your PST files.

The user can manually move data to the archive mailbox, but an administrator can also import data into that archive mailbox. The New-MailboxImportRequest command can be used to import PST files from a fileshare directly into an archive mailbox. To achieve this in EMS, use a command similar to this example:

```
New-MailboxImportRequest -Mailbox Joe@contoso.com -FilePath \\AMS-FS01\PSTFiles\Archive2011.pst
-IsArchive
```

Another way to automatically move data from the user's mailbox into the archive mailbox is by using retention policies.

Retention Policies

Over the years, the amount of information stored in mailboxes has kept growing and growing. To deal with this, Microsoft introduced messaging records management (MRM) in Exchange 2007. The implementation of MRM was by means of managed folders, which are folders created by an Exchange administrator. On top of these managed folders, the Exchange administrator had to create rules that govern certain actions against items in the folders, such as marking them as past retention or to permanently delete. Users were able to store information in these managed folders, and after a retention time set by the administrator, the information would be processed.

In addition to using MRM to manage amounts of information, and thus meet larger storage requirements, MRM can be used to:

- **Meet business requirements** Depending on your organization's messaging policies, you may need to retain important email messages for a certain period. It is not uncommon that HR information with resumes of nonhired people are kept for only six months, or information regarding business strategy or transactions is kept for only a certain amount of time. When items are stored for a limited time in Exchange 2013, the items are not set to read-only so that users are able to delete these items if they want to.

- **Meet legal and regulatory requirements** Many organizations have a legal or regulatory requirement to store messages for a designated period and to remove messages older than that time. Storing messages longer than necessary may increase your organization's legal or financial risks.

- **Increase user productivity** The amount of information, or the ever-increasing amount of information, has a negative impact on productivity. For example, consider those newletters that are kept for ages but never read. Using MRM, it is possible to remove these after a certain amount of time, thereby reducing the clutter in a user's mailbox and increasing the productivity.

MRM version 2 was introduced in Exchange 2010 and included the personal archive and retention tags and retention policies, a concept further developed in Exchange 2013.

As an Exchange administrator, you can choose the tags that can be assigned to items in a mailbox. There are various types of tags available:

- A default policy tag (DPT)

- Personal tags applied to folders or individual items by the user

- Retention policy tags (RPT) assigned to specific folders to expire items in those folders

Retention policy tags can be created for the folders listed in Table 7-1.

Table 7-1. *Folder in a Mailbox that Can Have RPTs Applied*

Folder Name	Details
Calendar	Default folder used to store meeting dates and appointments.
Conversation History	Created by Microsoft Lync (when implementend); although not treated as a default folder by Outlook, it's regarded as a special folder by Exchange and can have RPTs applied.
Deleted Items	Default folder used to store items deleted from other folders in the mailbox. Outlook and Outlook Web App users can manually empty this folder. Users can also configure Outlook to empty the folder upon closing Outlook.
Drafts	Default folder used to store draft messages that haven't been sent by the user. Outlook Web App also uses this folder to save messages that were sent by the user but not submitted to the Hub Transport server.
Inbox	Default folder used to store messages delivered to a mailbox.
Journal	Default folder for actions selected by the user. These actions are automatically recorded by Outlook and placed in a timeline view.
Junk Email	Default folder used to save messages marked as junk email by the content filter on an Exchange server or by the anti-spam filter in Outlook.
Notes	Contains notes created by users in Outlook.
Outbox	Default folder used to temporarily store sent messages until processed by a Hub Transport server. Messages usually remain in this folder for a brief period so it isn't necessary to create an RPT for this folder.
RSS Feeds	Default folder containing RSS feeds.
Recoverable Items	Hidden folder in the Non-IPM sub-tree. It contains the Deletions, Versions, Purges, and Audits sub-folders. Retention tags for this folder move items from the Recoverable Items folder in the user's primary mailbox to the Recoverable Items folder in the user's archive mailbox. You can assign only the Move To Archive retention action to tags for this folder.
Sent Items	Default folder used to store messages that have been sent.
Sync Issues	Contains synchronization logs.
Tasks	Default folder used to store tasks.

You can create a DPT that will move all items in a mailbox to the personal archive in 180 days, but create personal tags that will keep items in the mailbox for one or two years. These personal tags can be assigned by the user to items and will override the DPT.

Additionally, it is possible to create RPTs that will mark messages as past retention after a certain number of years or when legal or company requirements dictate, then permanently remove those items. Another RPT can be applied to the junk email folder in the mailbox that will permanently remove items after, for example, seven days.

When creating an RPT, you can specify the following actions to be taken when the retention time expires:

- **Move to Archive** Items are moved to the archive mailbox. Naming in the archive mailbox will be identical, so when a folder named Finance exists in the primary mailbox, it will automatically be created as such in the archive mailbox.

- **Delete and allow recovery** Items are deleted, but kept in the Recoverable Items folder.

- **Permanently Delete** Items are permanently deleted (and not stored in the Recoverable Items folder) and cannot be recovered. When the In-Place Hold is set on a mailbox, the item is kept in the Recoverable Items. If Single Item Recovery is enabled for a mailbox, the item will be kept in the Recoverable Items until the deleted item retention time for this mailbox database or the Single Item Recovery setting is reached.

- **Mark as past retention** Messages are marked as past retention. Outlook and OWA will show this message with a notification string "This item has expired."

To apply the retention tags to a mailbox, they must be added to a retention policy, and this retention policy is applied to the mailbox. A mailbox can have only one retention policy applied, but a retention policy can have multiple retention tags.

By default, 11 retention policy tags are created (in Exchange 2013 CU2) and two retention policies are created. One retention policy is for the arbitration mailboxes, the other retention policy is applied to mailboxes that have an archive mailbox.

■ **Note**   The EMS shows 11 retention policy tags and two retention policies. For some reason, EAC only shows 10 retention policy tags and one retention policy.

Table 7-2 shows the default retention policy tags that are used in the default retention policy.

Table 7-2. *The Default Retention Policy and its Retention Policy Tags*

Name	Type	Retention Time	Retention Action
Default 2 years move to archive	DPT	730	Move to archive
Personal 1 year move to archive	Personal Tag	365	Move to archive
Personal 5 year move to archive	Personal Tag	1,825	Move to archive
Personal never move to archive	Personal Tag	N/A	N/A
Recoverable items 14 days move to archive	Recoverable Items folder	14	Move to archive
1 week delete	Personal Tag	7	Delete and allow recovery
1 month delete	Personal Tag	30	Delete and allow recovery

(continued)

Table 7-2. (*continued*)

Name	Type	Retention Time	Retention Action
6 months delete	Personal Tag	180	Delete and allow recovery
1 year delete	Personal Tag	365	Delete and allow recovery
5 years delete	Personal Tag	1,825	Delete and allow recovery
Never delete	Personal Tag	N/A	N/A

The Managed Folder Assistant is a service running on the Mailbox server that's responsible for processing the mailboxes with retention policies indicated. It applies the retention policy by inspecting items in the mailbox and determines whether they are subject to retention. It then stamps the items subject to retention with the appropriate retention tags and takes the specified retention action when items are past their retention age.

The Managed Folder Assistant is a throttled service. This means that it is running 24 hours a day, but it does not have full control over system resources to prevent depletion of resources.

■ **Note**   The Managed Folder Assistant doesn't take any action on messages that aren't subject to retention.

When moving items from one folder in the inbox to another folder in the inbox, the items inherit the retention policy tag that has been applied to the target folder.

The default 11 retention policy tags are most likely sufficient for 99 percent of all Exchange 2013 implementations, but if you want to create additional RPTs you can use the EAC:

1. Select Compliance Management in the Feature pane and then the Retention Tags tab. The default RPTs are listed here.

2. To create a new RPT, click the New icon and select the type of tag you want to create—for example, applied by users to items and folders (personal).

3. The New Tag wizard appears. Enter a name for the new tag, select a retention action (what will happen when the retention time expires) and the retention period, and enter a comment (see Figure 7-26). Click Save to store the new tag.

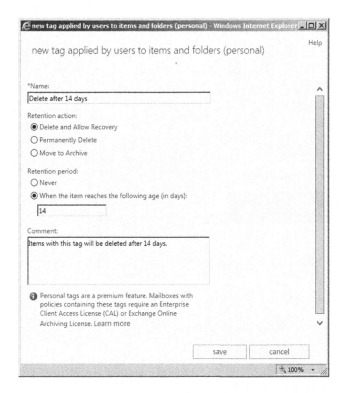

Figure 7-26. *Creating a new retention policy tag*

To create the same RPT with the EMS, you can use the following command:

```
New-RetentionPolicyTag -Name "Delete after 14 days" -Type Personal -RetentionAction
DeleteAndAllowRecovery -AgeLimitForRetention 14 -Comment "Items with this tag will be deleted
after 14 days"
```

The EAC can be used to create a new retention policy as well. Suppose you want to create a new policy called "My Exchange 2013 Policy" and assign the default policy tag "Default 2 years move to archive" and the RPT we just created; you would use the following procedure:

1. Select Compliance Management in the Feature pane and then the Retention Policies tab. The default policy is listed here.

2. Click the New icon to start the New Retention Policy wizard.

3. Enter the name for the new Policy (My Exchange 2013 Policy) and use the Add icon to select the default retention policy tag (the newly created personal retention policy tag); see Figure 7-27. Click Save to store the new retention policy.

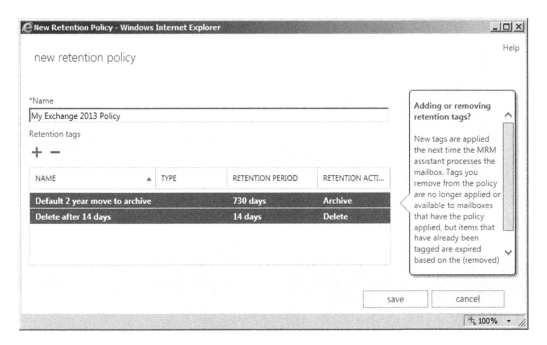

Figure 7-27. Creating a new retention policy in EAC

To create this retention policy using EMS, use the following command:

```
New-RetentionPolicy "My Exchange 2013 Policy" -RetentionPolicyTagLinks "Default 2 years move to
archive","Delete after 14 days"
```

To assign this retention policy to a mailbox in EAC, open the mailbox and navigate to its Mailbox Features in the Feature pane. In the Retention Policy drop-down box, select the new retention policy.

To assign this retention policy to a mailbox in EMS, use the following command as an example:

```
Set-Mailbox -Identity joe@contoso.com -RetentionPolicy "My Exchange 2013 Policy"
```

■ **Note** Personal tags are a premium feature. Mailboxes with retention policies require an Enterprise Client Access License.

Database Availability Group

Chapter 5 talked about the database availability group, or DAG, and how a DAG can be used to improve the uptime of an Exchange 2010 installation. In this part, we revisit the DAG, but now it's to see what it can do for a backupless environment.

A DAG is a logical grouping of Exchange 2013 Mailbox servers that are used to host multiple copies of mailbox databases. One Mailbox server in a DAG holds an active copy of a mailbox database; this is the mailbox database that's used by clients. One or more Mailbox servers in a DAG hold a passive copy of a mailbox database, and these passive clients are not used by any clients; they are only for redundancy purposes. One exception can be a backup application that uses a passive copy to create backups.

Figure 7-28 illustrates how redundancy works with a DAG. Clients like Outlook use a load balancer to connect to an Exchange 2013 Client Access server where they are authenticated. After authentication, the request is proxied to the Mailbox server holding the active copy of the mailbox database. On this Mailbox server, the data is retrieved from the mailbox and returned to the client. The most important part of this to remember is that all mail processing is taking place on the Mailbox server holding the *active* copy of the mailbox database.

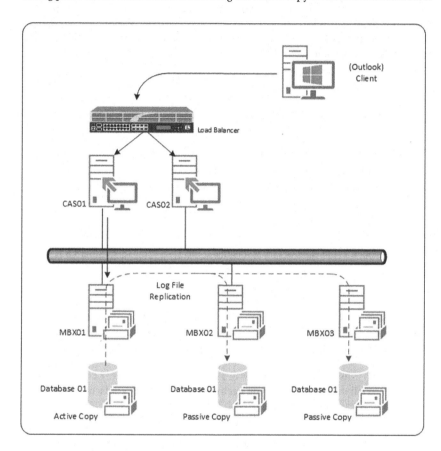

Figure 7-28. *The DAG makes sure your mailbox databases are redundant*

As we've seen earlier in this chapter, mailbox data is in the Mailbox server's memory, the transaction log file, or the mailbox database. During processing, new transaction files are created; once they are stored on the server's hard disk, they are sent to the Mailbox server holding a passive copy of that mailbox database. At minimum, there's one passive copy of the mailbox database, but more passive copies can be used as well.

In a DAG, there's always one active copy of the mailbox database and replication always takes place from this active copy to all the passive copies. So how do the passive copies get on the other Mailbox servers? This is a process called *seeding*. It's the actual copying of the mailbox database from the server holding the active copy to another Mailbox server. Seeding a mailbox database is not an NTFS copy; instead, a technique called *streaming* is used—very similar to the streaming backup technology explained earlier in this chapter. When streaming, the active mailbox copy is read (database) page by page. When the page is read, its checksum is checked; when it's okay, the page is sent to the other Mailbox server, where it is stored. This way the new passive copy is always identical to the active copy of the mailbox database and it's 100 percent consistent.

What happens when a Mailbox server fails? Clients are connected to the Client Access server and continue to be so. Referring back to Figure 7-27, we see that when the mailbox database on Mailbox server MBX01 fails, the passive copy of the mailbox database on server MBX02 is automatically activated. The Client Access server now connects to this Mailbox server within seconds. Clients do notice a small disturbance; in the taskbar, a balloon will pop up saying "Connection lost," followed shortly by a balloon saying "Connection restored."

So, if a mailbox database is lost, the service continues to run even when the mailbox database is beyond repair. When a disk containing one or more mailbox databases is lost, though, you have to replace the disk and manually perform a reseed of the mailbox database to the new disk. Depending on the size of the mailbox database, this can take a considerable amount of time, but since the users can continue to work with another copy of the mailbox database, this is no big deal.

■ **Note** Multiple mailbox databases in a DAG have another advantage. When a Mailbox server encounters a corrupted page, a process called *page patching* is started. A special marker is placed in the current transaction log file, which is then closed and replicated to another Mailbox server holding a passive copy of the mailbox database. When this Mailbox server encounters the marker, it tries to retrieve a copy of the patch (which should be fine on the passive copy) and returns the healthy page to the first Mailbox server. This places the page in its cache buffer, where it is then written into one of the log files and eventually written into the mailbox database.

When this happens, the header of the mailbox database file is updated as well. There's a special entry called "patch count" for this with the number of patches applied. It is possible to check this using the ESEUTIL /MH command. When the patches are applied and the database header is updated, the mailbox database is repaired.

When using a DAG, you achieve higher availability because of the multiple mailbox databases and replication technology, but it doesn't prevent human failures, such as the accidental deletion of mailbox content or even of a mailbox itself. As far as Exchange is concerned, these kinds of deletions are legitimate actions and thus are replicated across all mailbox databases.

A DAG does, however, protect you against hardware failures, like server failure, controller failure or a hard disk failure, resulting in physical database corruption. It does not protect you against logical corruption of a mailbox database. Though logical corruption of a mailbox database is very rare, it can lead to data loss.

There are two types of logical corruption:

- **Database logical corruption** In this case, the checksum of a page in the mailbox database is correct but the data inside the page is wrong. This can happen when ESE tries to write a page to disk (and ESE gets a success message back from disk), but the page isn't actually written to disk or is written to the wrong location. This is also referred to as a "lost flush." A common cause is that an NFS volume is used instead of block-level storage.

- **Store logical corruption** Data inside a page is added, modified, deleted, and so on in an unexpected way, usually caused by a third-party application. From an Exchange Server point of view, this is not really corruption, as the database pages contain valid operations, but the user still experiences this as message corruption in his or her mailbox.

Among other solutions like In-Place Hold, which was explained earlier, a means to help guard against logical corruption is using a lagged copy in the DAG.

Lagged Copies

A *lagged copy* is a passive mailbox database copy, but one that has a lag time in replaying the log files into the mailbox database. This lag time can be anywhere between one second and 14 days. The lagged copy of a mailbox database can be in the same (Active Directory) site as the active copy of the mailbox database, but it can also be located in another, remote (Active Directory) site for offsite storage.

■ **Note**   Lagged copies are not a high-availability solution, as outlined in Chapter 5, but are a disaster-recovery solution. Manual intervention is needed to activate a lagged copy, and when you're using a 14-day lag time, that means you need a substantial amount of time to replay the log files and activate the lagged mailbox copy.

In a DAG, the log files are replicated from the Mailbox server holding the active copy of the mailbox database to the Mailbox servers holding the passive copies of the mailbox database. This is no different for lagged copies.

Normal passive copies of the mailbox database inspect the log file that was received, and at some point the log file is read and the information is replayed into the passive copy of the mailbox database. Just like the active copy of the mailbox database, there can be some delay in replaying—in other words, there is a certain checkpoint depth.

For lagged copies, however, the log files are not replayed into the passive copy of the mailbox database during the time, as specified in the lag time. When the lag time is two hours, this is not a big deal; but when the lag time is seven days, it means that seven days of log files will be stored on the Mailbox server holding the passive copy. Consequently, you have to take this into account when it comes to your storage design, since seven days of log files can consume a considerable amount of storage space. The Exchange 2013 Server Role Requirements Calculator can do this math for you.

As stated, a lagged copy is not part of a high-availability solution but is part of a disaster-recovery solution. The lagged copy is not activated automatically; it is activated manually. When a lagged copy is activated, the log files that are stored during the lag time need to be replayed into the passive copy first. When the lag time is set to seven days, this can take quite some time to finish.

When creating a lagged copy, there are two choices:

- There are already copies of a mailbox database running and the only thing you have to do is add the lag time.

- You want to create an additional copy of a mailbox database and include the lag time during creation of that additional copy.

To create an additional copy of a mailbox database and add the lag time during creation, you follow these steps in EAC:

1.   Select Servers in the Feature pane, and select the Databases tab. Select the mailbox database you want to create an additional copy of. Click the More icon and select Add Database Copy.

2.   In the Add Mailbox Database Copy wizard, use the Browse button to select a server that will host the additional copy of the mailbox database. Click on More Options to show the option for the replay lag time (see Figure 7-29). Note that this replay lag time can only be set in days. Enter a lag time and click Save to continue.

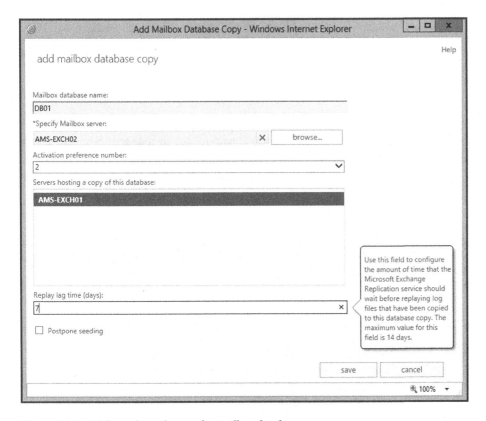

Figure 7-29. Adding a lagged copy of a mailbox database

For a more granular setting of the replay lag time, use EMS. To create an additional copy and set the replay lag time to four days, seven hours, and 36 minutes, for example, you can use the following:

```
Add-MailboxDatabaseCopy -Identity DB01 -MailboxServer AMS-EXCH02 -ReplayLagTime 00:10:00
-TruncationLagTime 4.7:36:00 -ActivationPreference 2
```

When you already have a copy of a mailbox database and want to add a replay lag time to this copy, the steps in EAC are very similar to when you create an additional copy:

1. Select Servers in the Feature pane, and select the Databases tab. Select the mailbox database that you want to change. At the bottom of the Actions pane there's information regarding the copy of the mailbox database—for example, DB02\AMS-EXCH02. Under this option, select View Details.

2. In the Edit Database Copy window, scroll down and at the bottom of the windows you can add the lag time (see Figure 7-30). Again, the only lag time is in days, so it's not very granular.

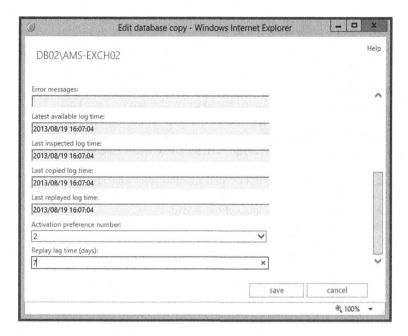

Figure 7-30. *Adding lag time to an existing mailbox database copy*

To add a replay lag time to an existing copy of a mailbox database using EMS, you can use the following example:

```
Set-MailboxDatabaseCopy -id DB01\AMS-EXCH01 -ReplayLagTime 7.0:0:0
```

■ **Note**   For redunancy purposes in transport, the SafeteNet feature is used. To prevent unwanted data loss, the SafetyNetHoldTime should be higher than the replay lag time of the mailbox database copy. The `Set-TransportConfig` cmdlet can be used to set this using the `-SafetyNetHoldTime` option.

When you have a lagged copy of a mailbox database, the log files from the active copy of the mailbox database are continuously sent to the passive copies, including the lagged copy. On the Mailbox server holding the lagged copy of the mailbox database, the log files are kept in a queue until the lag time expires. If a lag time of seven days is used, this can become a tremendous amount of data. You can check the number of log files in the Replay Queue using the `Get-MailboxDatabase | Get-MailboxDatabaseCopyStatus` command in EMS. This will show the mailbox database, its status, the copy queue length, and the replay queue length. The copy queue length should be close to zero (although it can increase occasionally), but the replay queue will show the number of log files waiting for the lag time to expire. So don't be alarmed when you see a high number of log files in this queue!

Another option that's only settable using EMS is the `TruncationLagTime` option. This is the lag time that the Microsoft Exchange Replication service should wait after replaying the information into the passive copy of the mailbox database before the log file is actually deleted. The minimum value of the TruncationLagTime is 0 seconds, the maximum value is 14 days.

Having lagged copies is only one part of the story; recovering from a lagged copy is another part. This is covered in the "Point in Time (PIT) Recovery" section later in this chapter.

Circular Logging

As explained in Chapter 5 about the Mailbox server, using circular logging on a production Mailbox server is, generally speaking, not a good idea since this will block log file replay during recovery. You can restore from a backup without the proper log files, but you cannot recover to a newer point in time, since this information is missing.

When a DAG is configured in your Exchange 2013 environment, things are a bit different. Since there are multiple copies of a mailbox database, there's no need to restore from a backup. In case of a failure, another copy of the mailbox database takes over and continues servicing the user requests.

If there are no legal requirements to create backups, it is possible to use only the Mailbox servers running in a DAG. When one mailbox database fails, another one takes over without the need for an Exchange administrator to restore a mailbox database from backup.

But one of the functions of a backup is to purge log files that are not needed anymore after a backup was taken. To overcome this, circular Logging can be enabled within the DAG. Circular logging in a DAG isn't a function of ESE as in a normal scenario, but it is performed by the Microsoft Exchange Replication service.

Circular logging in a DAG is called *continuous replication circular logging* (CRCL). There's a major difference with the default circular logging as used by ESE. In a normal circular logging scenario, log files are deleted once the data in the files is stored in the mailbox database. When using CRCL, however, the log files are deleted only when they have been replicated to the passive copies of the mailbox database. The Microsoft Exchange Replication service communicates using RPC with each other to determine the status of the replication and which log files can be safely deleted.

The following must be true for log files to be deleted:

- CRCL must be enabled.
- The log file is below the checkpoint.
- Other copies of the mailbox database agree with the deletion.
- The log file has been inspected by all lagged copies of the mailbox database.

Log files are also deleted on Mailbox servers holding a lagged copy of the mailbox database. For this to happen, the following must be true:

- The log file is below the checkpoint.
- The log file is older than the combined value of the replay lag time and the truncation lag time.
- The log file is already deleted on the active copy of the mailbox database.

So when using CRCL, you should always be safe, able to recover from a mailbox database failure with minimum loss of data.

Point-in-Time (PIT) Recovery

When using a lagged copy of a mailbox database, it is possible to return to a specific point in time between the active copy of the mailbox database and the replay lag time of the lagged copy of a mailbox database. This means that it is possible to recover to an exact point in time between 0 seconds and a maximum of 14 days ago.

The technology behind point-in-time (PIT) recovery is that all information stored in log files is replayed into the lagged copy of the mailbox database—up to the exact moment you want to recover to.

■ **Note** Although a very rare occasion, this technique can be used to recover from a logical mailbox database corruption.

The steps to recover to a certain PIT are:

1. Suspend the replication to the lagged copy of the mailbox database.

2. Determine the last log file you want to replay into the mailbox database. This is the PIT you want to recover to.

3. Use ESEUTIL to replay the log files into the lagged copy of the mailbox database.

4. Use this copy of the mailbox database for recovery purposes.

A PIT recovery cannot be performed by the EAC, so the EMS is the only option you have here. To suspend the replication of the lagged copy of the mailbox database, use an EMS command similar to this:

```
Suspend-MailboxDatabaseCopy DB01\AMS-EXCH02 -SuspendComment "Activate lagged copy of DB01 on Server
AMS-EXCH02" -Confirm:$false
```

Determine which log file you want to use for recovery purposes. All log files that are more recent than the chosen one should be moved to a different location to prevent accidental replay of information.

Before replaying the log files, you need to remove the checkpoint file. Replaying the log files starts at the location of the checkpoint file; by removing the checkpoint file, replay starts automatically at the oldest available log file. If information found in these log files is already in the mailbox database, then that's no problem; it will just be skipped. At one point, though, information inside the log files that's not in the mailbox database will be replayed into the mailbox database until the last available log file is replayed. Then, the replaying stops and the mailbox database is closed, as in a clean shutdown state. The mailbox database is available for any recovery purpose you have in mind—for example, a recovery database.

When the checkpoint file is deleted, you open a command prompt, navigate to the location where the lagged copy is stored, and enter a command similar to this example:

```
ESEUTIL /R E00 /LF:\DB01\Logfiles /D /I
```

The E00 prefix is the prefix used by this lagged copy, the /L option is used to point to the location of the log files, and the /S option is used to point to the location of the system file. /D is used to point to the location of the mailbox database, but in this example it is the current directory. The /I option is used to ignore any missing attachments into the log files that need to go into the mailbox database. All options should have values that correspond to your environment, of course.

Summary

In this chapter I explained about backup, restore, and disaster recovery. I especially tried to indicate how the three work together. The last part of this chapter explained the Microsoft Exchange Native Data Protection, sometimes referred to as a "backupless environment."

Exchange 2013 uses snapshot technology provided by the Virtual Shadowcopy Services (VSS). The out-of-the-box tool Windows Server Backup is able to create VSS backups of the mailbox database. New to Exchange 2013 is the fact that Windows Server Backup can back up passive copies of a mailbox database—something that was not possible to do before.

Mailbox databases can be restored from a backup on the original location, but a recovery mailbox database can be used as well where the mailbox is restored to a different location, after which all kinds of recovery actions can be taken.

The ultimate disaster recovery is when an entire server is lost. It is possible to rebuild a new but identical Exchange 2013 server using the setup application with the `/Mode:RecoverServer` option. This will retrieve all information from Active Directory.

The Exchange Native Data Protection is a set of technologies that can be used to overcome all kinds of disasters, ranging from messages that are accidentally deleted to additional copies of a mailbox database stored in another location. When designed properly, there are situations where a traditional backup is not needed anymore but, of course, this fully depends on your organizational needs and requirements.

The next chapter is about monitoring Exchange 2013—something that's needed as well, and quite a lot of times is forgotten because the typical administrator is too busy. But when monitoring is not performed properly, there's always a risk encountering disaster and the subsequent recovery scenarios.

CHAPTER 8

■ ■ ■

Monitoring Exchange Server 2013

Regularly monitoring your Exchange 2013 environment is a very important part of managing an Exchange Server environment. Regular monitoring gives you an idea of how the service is running and provides a warning of upcoming issues or bottlenecks. Unfortunately, most Exchange administrators start monitoring their environments when it's too late—that is, when end users begin complaining or after they have raised a support call at Microsoft.

In the early days, monitoring an Exchange server was nothing more than checking that its particular service was running—for example, as with the Information Store. If it was running, then everything was supposed to be okay. If users were not able to connect, then it was not an Exchange problem. That the service was running was the only thing that mattered.

Things have changed dramatically, however. Microsoft is now operating Exchange Server in their datacenters for Office 365 and Exchange Online. One of the goals in doing so was to reduce the number of support incidents to an absolute minimum. When you have a huge number of servers running, as in the case of Office 365, there's no other choice other than to handle it this way. Thus, Exchange 2013 now has this magical "self-healing" feature by which it is constantly monitoring itself and, when needed, will take appropriate action. This new feature is called Managed Availability, and it is one of the great improvements that came with Exchange 2013. We'll get back to this feature later on in this chapter.

But to return to the idea of monitoring itself, you should know that proper monitoring of your Exchange environment has a number of advantages:

- It gives you good insights into the functioning of your Exchange environment. If you monitor on a regular basis, you can create a baseline by which you can compare performance when problems arise.

- It provides a basis for trend analysis, which you can use to timely identify capacity issues. For example, when monitoring the amount of disk space on your Exchange servers, you can identify any unusual mailbox growth and predict when you will need additional space. And you'll get a better response when you go to management 12 months in advance with a request for that additional disk space. This, overall, is the preferred method of managing capacity.

Monitoring your Exchange environment involves a number of manual tools, like the Event Viewer, Performance Monitor, and Exchange Management Shell, as well as automated tools like the new Managed Availability service and the System Center Operations Manager. I've divided the discussion of these tools into major categories of performance, availability, workload, and systems monitoring, but let's begin with a couple of ad hoc monitoring tools.

Ad Hoc Monitoring Tools

There a number of tools available for monitoring your Exchange environment on an ad hoc basis, like the Event Viewer, the Performance Monitor MMC snap-in, and the Queue Viewer. Besides giving an inside view of the behavior of the Exchange 2013 servers, these tools allow you to begin troubleshooting those Exchange 2013 servers. As such, this chapter is closely related to Chapter 9, which covers troubleshooting of the Exchange environment.

Event Viewer

The Event Viewer will be available as long as Microsoft Windows is available. This is an MMC snap-in, used to view the event logs that are available on every server. Event logs can be separated into many different log categories.

Windows Logs

These are the default logs used by Windows and applications running on top of Windows. The windows logs themselves contain four separate logs:

- *Application event log* This is the log file where applications can store application-specific messages. These can be informational messages, warning messages, error messages, or critical messages. Exchange 2013 is an application that extensively uses the application event log, and as such is a very useful source of information.

- *Security log* This log file is used by Windows to store security-related events, such as the successful logon of accounts.

- *Setup log* This log file is used by the setup application for various applications to store information regarding the installation of those applications. Installation of Windows roles or features is also logged in the setup log.

- *System log* This log file is used by Windows to log all system-related events. These entries can be events from services running on the server.

- *Forwarded events* When Exchange is out of the box, this log file is empty, but it can be configured to accept events from other servers so as to create an aggregate view of multiple Windows servers.

Applications and Services Logs

These are an interesting feature. These files contain additional logs from hardware or from applications and services like Internet Explorer, the MSExchange Management, and the Windows PowerShell—that is, applications and services that have a very close relationship with the operating system.

- *MSExchange Management log* The Exchange Management Shell (EMS) runs on top of the Windows PowerShell. All commands that are run in EMS are logged in the MSExchange Management log. This log file can be very valuable in detecting issues or problems that prevent EMS from running properly.

- *Windows PowerShell log* This log file contains PowerShell commands that are executed on the Windows server.

- *Microsoft log* This event log is known as the "crimson channel event log," an event channel that Exchange 2013 relies on heavily. This will be explained later in this chapter.

The application event log contains a lot of interesting information when it comes to Exchange Server. This is true not only true for Exchange 2013 but also for older versions of Exchange Server; they have all written their events to the application event log. Informational events are general events written to the application event log in order to record general information about the well-being of the Exchange server.

As an example, Exchange 2013 regularly logs information about the Active Directory environment—specifically, the domain controllers that the Exchange server has access to. As we've seen in Chapter 1, Exchange 2013 relies heavily on Active Directory, so proper access to a domain controller is crucial for an Exchange server. This information is logged in the application event log as follows:

```
Log Name:        Application
Source:          MSExchange ADAccess
Date:            8-10-2013 11:21:29
Event ID:        2080
Task Category:   Topology
Level:           Information
Keywords:        Classic
User:            N/A
Computer:        AMS-EXCH01.Contoso.com
Description:
        Process Microsoft.Exchange.Directory.TopologyService.exe (PID=2188). Exchange Active
Directory Provider has discovered the following servers with the following characteristics:
(Server name | Roles | Enabled | Reachability | Synchronized | GC capable | PDC | SACL right |
Critical Data | Netlogon | OS Version)
In-site:
AMS-AD01.Contoso.com    CDG 1 7 7 1 0 1 1 7 1
Out-of-site:
NYC-AD01.Contoso.com    CDG 1 7 7 1 0 1 1 7 1
```

What does this entry specifically tell us? It tells us that the Topology service that's running on the Exchange server has discovered two domain controllers in this environment:

- AMS-AD01.Contoso.com. This domain controller is located in the same Active Directory site as where the Exchange server resides.

- NYC-AD01.Contoso.com. This domain controller is located in a site different from where this Exchange server is located. Because the domain controller is in another Active Directory site, the Exchange server will not use this domain controller.

Each domain controller has its own view on Active Directory, which is described by the string right after the name of the domain controller; in this example, it is CDG 1 7 7 1 0 1 1 7 1.

It's quite cryptic, but a description of each entry is given in the same entry, where it says: Server name | Roles | Enabled | Reachability | Synchronized | GC capable | PDC | SACL right | Critical Data | Netlogon | OS Version. Some of the characteristics speak for themselves, but here's a brief explanation:

- Server name: The name of the domain controller being discovered.

- Roles: The roles a domain controller can have, which are Configuration Domain Controller (C), regular Domain Controller (D), or Global Catalog server (G). When a hyphen (-) appears, it means that one particular role cannot be found on this domain controller.

- Reachability: How the Exchange server can reach the domain controller over the network via a regular TCP port:

  - 0x1 means the server is reachable as a Global Catalog server (via port 3268).

  - 0x2 means it is reachable as a regular Domain Controller (via port 389).

  - 0x4 means it is reachable as a Configuration Domain Controller (via also port 389).

Multiple functions are added, so if a domain controller is reachable on all three roles, the end result will be 7 (1 + 2 + 4). An Exchange server should typically see and reach all roles of a domain controller. Since a firewall is not supported between an Exchange 2013 server and a domain controller, a value of 7 should be expected here.

- Synchronized: This value shows if the role is synchronized with other domain controllers in the network. It follows the reachability columns, and therefore a value of 7 should be considered normal.

- GC capable: This tells us if this servers is a Global Catalog server or not.

- PDC: This tells us if this domain controller holds the PDC Emulator role (value 0x1) or not (value 0x0). There is only one domain controller in the entire organization holding the PDC Emulator role.

- SACL right: This column tells us whether DSAccess has the correct permissions to read the SACL (part of nTSecurityDescriptor) against that directory service.

- Critical Data: This tells us whether the server found its own Computer object in the configuration container of the domain controller listed in Server Name column. If you find a zero here, you most likely face an Active Directory replication issue.

- Netlogon Check: This shows whether DSAccess successfully connected to a domain controller's Net Logon service.

- OS Version: This column tells us if the correct version (minimal) of Operating System is used at the domain controller. If it's Windows 2003 SP1 or higher, it lists 0x1 here; otherwise it will list 0x0. Therefore, it should read 0x1.

Plenty of other entries are logged in the application event log as well, and these are there for informational purposes. *Warning messages*, shown with a yellow exclamation mark, show potential issues that might need attention, but sometimes Exchange 2013 is able to solve these problems automatically. *Error messages* are shown with a red exclamation mark and do need attention. They should be resolved, although immediate action is not always necessary. For example, when Exchange 2013 is not licensed, whether you have a trial license or are still in the 120 days grace period, Event ID 8198 is logged as an error message:

```
Log Name:       Application
Source:         Microsoft-Windows-Security-SPP
Date:           8-10-2013 17:12:25
Event ID:       8198
Task Category:  None
Level:          Error
Keywords:       Classic
User:           N/A
Computer:       EXCH02.wesselius.local
Description:
License Activation (slui.exe) failed with the following error code:
hr=0x8007232B
Command-line arguments:
RuleId=eeba1977-569e-4571-b639-7623d8bfecc0;Action=AutoActivate;AppId=55c92734-d682-4d71-983e-
d6ec3f16059f;SkuId=d3643d60-0c42-412d-a7d6-52e6635327f6; NotificationInterval=1440;Trigger=UserLogo
n;SessionId=2
```

Exchange 2013 continuously logs information in the application event log. Checking this event log will give you more information regarding the functioning of your server, and you'll notice if there are any emerging problems.

■ **Note** In all my years as an Exchange consultant I've never seen an Exchange server that was completely free of warning messages and error messages in the application event log. Even worse, if you start investigating these messages using Google or Bing, you'll encounter official Microsoft knowledge-base articles that say things like "this error message can be safely ignored." You need to rely on your troubleshooting skills, of course, but there's no such thing as an "errorless Exchange server;" Exchange will happily survive these error messages in the application event log.

Crimson Channel

In Windows Server 2008, a new type of event log was introduced: the *crimson channel event log*. This is a special event log where applications like Exchange can write certain types of events. At the same time, other services running on the same server can subscribe to the crimson channel to consume those entries.

The crimson channel can be found in the Event Viewer tool in the Applications and Services Logs, located in the Microsoft/Exchange folder (see Figure 8-1).

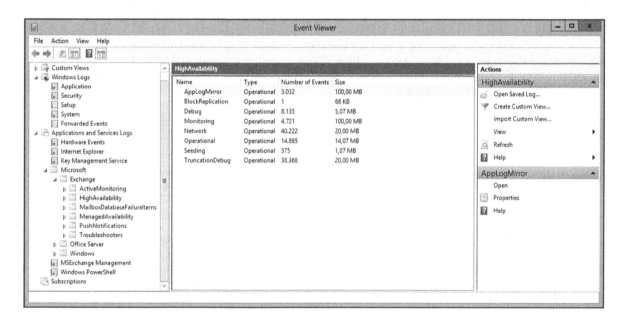

Figure 8-1. *The crimson channel for Exchange Server 2013*

Using a solution like the crimson channel, it is possible for one service or application to log certain events while another server reacts on those events. The new Managed Availability service in Exchange 2013 works according to this principle (more about Managed Availability later in this chapter).

The Applications and Services Logs category includes four subtypes:

- *Admin logs* Events logged here are interesting for troubleshooting purposes.

- *Operational logs* Events logged here are for more experienced system administrators, since they require (a lot) more interpretation.

- *Analytic logs* These logs are hidden and disabled by default, but events logged here trace a problem. Normally, lots of events are written to this log.

- *Debug logs* These logs are used by the developers of an application (i.e., Exchange 2013) for troubleshooting purposes.

For Exchange 2013, the following crimson channels are available:

- ActiveMonitoring

- HighAvailability

- MailboxDatabaseFailureItems

- ManagedAvailability

- PushNotifications

- Troubleshooters

The HighAvailability channel contains information that is related to the startup and shutdown of the Microsoft Exchange Replication service and the components that run inside the Exchange Replication service, such as Active Manager and the Volume Shadow Copy Service (VSS) writer. This channel is also used by Active Manager to log events related to the role monitoring and database actions, such as mounting and dismounting of mailbox databases or the truncations of transaction log files. Also, events coming from the underlying failover clustering software are written in this channel.

For example, the AppLogmirror log in the HighAvailability channel shows all kinds of intersting information regarding the redundancy of mailbox databases within a database availability group (DAG). Exchange is constantly monitoring the redundancy of its mailbox databases, and the results are written in this crimson channel. When all is well, Event ID 1104 is written (see Figure 8-2).

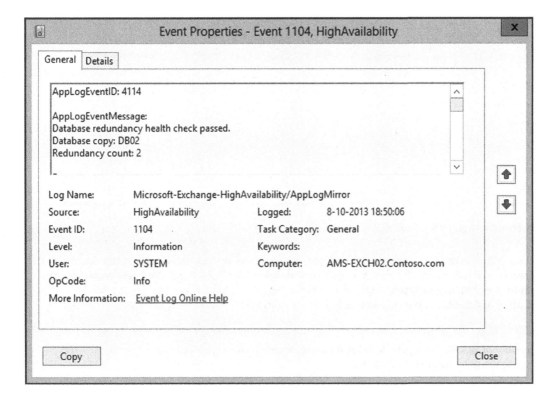

Figure 8-2. Mailbox database redundancy written in the crimson channel

It's not visible in Figure 8-2, but there's a lot more information regarding the mailbox database copies when you scroll down; for instance, you'll find the lowest available log file present, volume information where the mailbox database copies are stored, (free) disk space information, backup information, and Content Index information.

When running in maintenance mode—for example, when installing a new cumulative update—the server is not operating a passive copy and the DAG, and thus the availability is running in a degraded state. If this is the case, Event ID 1106 is logged in the AppLogMirror log in the HighAvailability crimson channel, saying that the database availability health check failed and that the availability is reduced (see Figure 8-3).

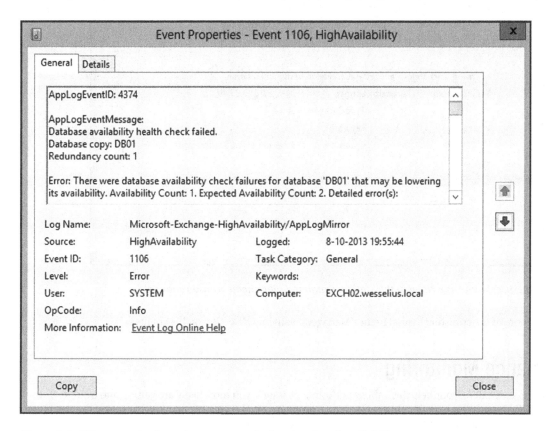

Figure 8-3. When running in maintenance mode, there's reduced availability

The MailboxDatabaseFailureItems channel is used to store events that are related to failures in a replicated mailbox database. When an Exchange 2013 Mailbox server is abruptly turned off (in this example, deliberately of course), this unexpected shutdown is written into the Operational log of the MailboxDatabaseFailureItems crimson channel (see Figure 8-4).

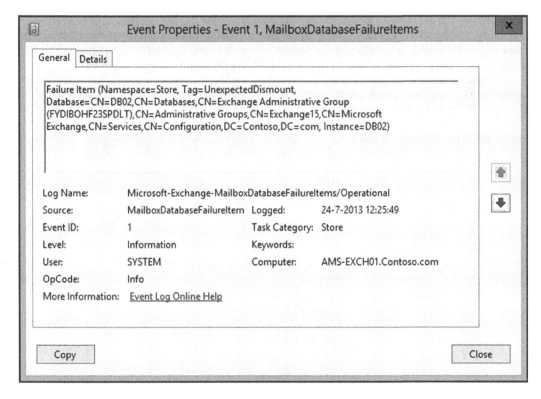

Figure 8-4. Unexpect failure as written in the MailboxDatabaseFailureItems crimson channel

We'll see more of the crimson channel in the "Managed Availability" section of this chapter.

Performance Monitoring

When end users start calling your help desk about performance issues, you most likely are getting into trouble. But how do you know the server is experiencing performance problems? When you log on to the console of the Exchange server and it is responding sluggishly, you know there's something wrong. But a sluggish response is not exactly something that can be precisely monitored. What to do?

Task Manager

The Task Manager of Windows will give you a good first glance at the performance of an Exchange server. To open the Task Manager, right-click the taskbar and select Task Manager.

When you select the Performance tab, there are multiple options available:

- *CPU* This will give a quick overview of the CPU utilization of the server. Don't be alarmed when it spikes to 80 percent, but when the CPU utilization is constantly over 80 percent, this is a good indication that the server is having performance problems.

- *Memory* Selecting this option will show you the amount of memory being used by the server. The total amount of memory is shown as well as the amount of memory in use and what is available. Note that the committed bytes of memory can be larger than the physical amount of memory; this is because of virtual memory, which can be temporarily stored on disk when it is not being used.

- *Ethernet* For every network card (NIC) that's available in your Exchange server, there's an additional NIC option shown. Network speeds for Send and Received are shown, including the adapter name, the connection type, and the IPv4 and IPv6 addresses.

This tool gives you a quick overview of the performance of your Exchange server. Also available in Task Manager is the Resource Monitor, which gives you yet more information. To open it, just click on Open Resource Monitor at the bottom of the Task Manager.

The Resource Monitor, shown in Figure 8-5, also provides a brief overview of what's happening in your Exchange server, but it also includes information on the hard disk—something that's not available in Task Manager. Interesting to see is the separation into the various processes on the server; you'll be able to determine immediately which process is consuming the most resources. The Overview tab offers a brief survey of all different subjects; the tabs for CPU, Memory, Disk, and Network give an overview of these components.

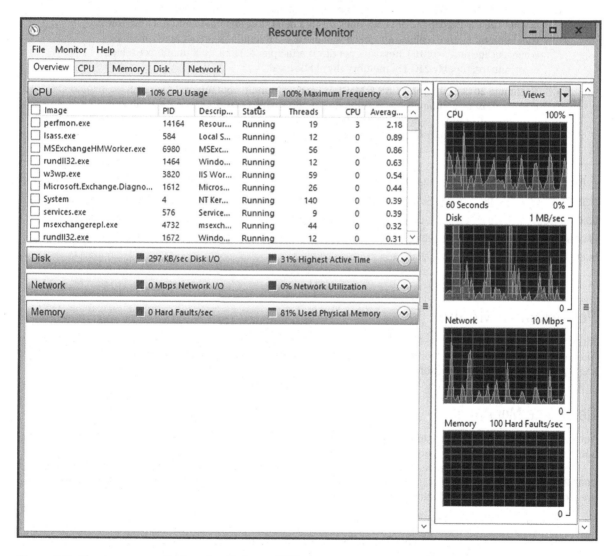

Figure 8-5. *The resource monitoring of an Exchange 2013 server*

Memory and disk have a close relationship in an Exchange server. The more memory an Exchange server has, the more mailbox data it can keep in memory. As a result, you'll see fewer disk I/O (Input/Output) operations when there's sufficient memory. On the other hand, if the server lacks enough memory, you'll see a dramatic increase in disk I/O. If the latter is the case, most likely you'll observe an increase in CPU usage as well, because the CPU needs to coordinate all traffic flowing through the Exchange server.

This chapter isn't about sizing and design, but for memory requirements, the following rules of thumb can be used:

- **Exchange 2013 CAS only** The absolute, bare minimum for memory on an Exchange 2013 CAS-only server is 4GB. This is more a marketing statement than a technical requirement. The technical memory requirement for a CAS-only would be 2GB base memory plus 2GB per processor core. If a 4GB processor core server is used, you end up with a 10GB memory requirement for an Exchange 2013 CAS-only server.

- **Exchange 2013 Mailbox only** The minimum for an Exchange 2013 MBX server is 8GB, but like the the Exchange 2013 CAS-only, this is a marketing statement and not a technical requirement. A more realistic approach is to use a 24GB requirement per active mailbox when a usage profile of 100 messages per day is anticipated. For a 1,000-mailbox Exchange environment, roughly 24GB of memory should be used.

- **Exchange 2013 multi-role (CAS & Mailbox) server** A multi-role server, where CAS and Mailbox are combined, has a minimum requirement of 8GB memory. If a multi-role Exchange 2013 server is used, the numbers can be added on top of each other, so that a 4GB processor/1,000-mailbox server would have roughly 24GB + 10GB = 34GB of memory.

■ **Note** These numbers are just rule of thumb, not detailed technical design guidelines. For more information regarding sizing, check the Ask the Perf Guy: Sizing Exchange 2013 Deployments whitepaper on the Microsoft website, which can be downloaded at `http://tinyurl.com/bmdj3l6`. If you want to make a detailed design, I recommend using the Exchange 2013 Server Role Requirements Calculator, which can be downloaded from the Exchange Product Group teamsite at `http://tinyurl.com/a2ozxlk`.

Performance Monitor

All objects, including the Exchange 2013 object, have performance monitors that can be used for checking on usage. The tool for this is Performance Monitor, or Perfmon. The Performance Monitor can display data in real time and it can log data for longer term monitoring.

Real-Time Monitoring

You can use Performance Monitor to view performance data in real time, which means you can open the tool, select some counters, and monitor the performance on the spot.

You can open the Performance Monitor by typing `perfmon.msc` on the Start ➤ Run menu (in Windows Server 2008 R2) or by typing `perfmon.msc` in the Search window on Windows Server 2012. You'll see the following sections, shown in Figure 8-8, in the Navigation pane on the left-hand side:

- *Monitoring Tools* This shows the real-time results.

- *Data Collector Sets* This contains the logging option, where you can create custom sets of objects that need to be monitored.

- *Reports* Reports are constantly generated and stored on the local hard disk of the Exchange 2013 server in C:\Program Files\Microsoft\Exchange Server\V15\Logging\Diagnostics \DailyPerformanceLogs. From there, these log files are used by the Managed Availability service for constant checking of the server's performance.

To start the monitoring, select Performance Monitor in the Navigation pane (as shown in Figure 8-6) and click on the plus (+) icon in the Results pane. A new window is shown where you can select the server that you want to monitor. This can be the local computer you're logged on to, but it can also be a remote Exchange server. In the scroll-down box below the computer name, you can select the object that you want to monitor. I haven't counted them, but on a typical Exchange 2013 server there are hundreds of objects that can be selected.

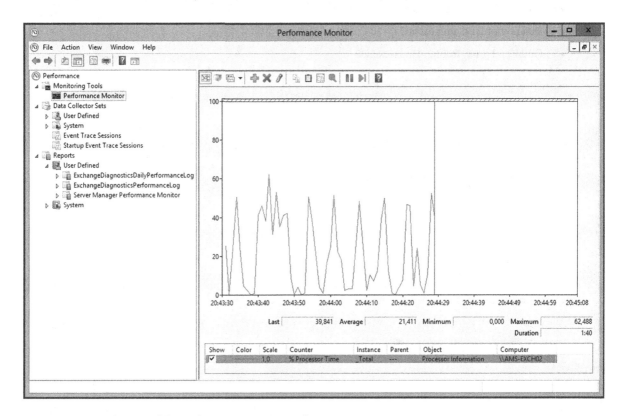

Figure 8-6. *Initial screen of the Performance Monitor tool*

Each object on a Windows Server, and thus on an Exchange server, can be monitored; the objects can be:

- Logical Disk
- Memory
- MSExchange Active Manager
- MSExchange Database
- MSExchange Replication Server
- MSExchangeFrontEndTransport SmtpReceive
- Network adapter

- Physical Disk

- Processor

Just to name a few . . .

An object can have one or multiple instances that can be monitored. For example, the MSExchangeFrontEnd Transport SmtpReceive object has the following available instance options, also shown in Figure 8-7:

- _total

- <All instances>

- Client frontend ams-exch02

- Default frontend ams-exch02

- Outbound proxy frontend ams-exch02

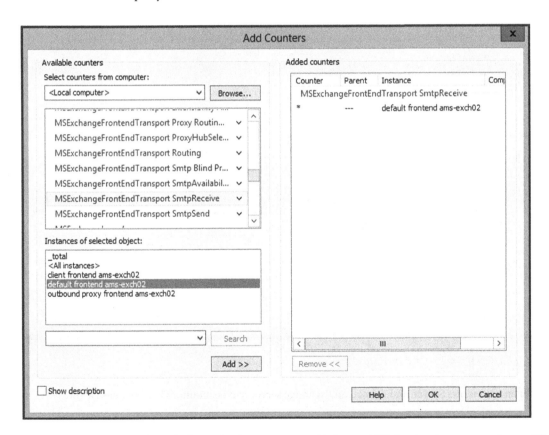

Figure 8-7. *Monitoring the Default Receive Connector on an Exchange 2013 front-end server running on Windows Server 2012*

■ **Note**   The entire object, including all counters, can be selected, as shown in Figure 8-7. All counters on this particular object will be shown in this case. When you click on the arrow button, all counters on this object are shown and then the individual counters can be selected for monitoring.

What are interesting objects to monitor, one might ask? Personally, I always start monitoring the Physical Disk object, just to see how the disk is performing. A disk that cannot keep up with the demand will always result in a slow-responding server and also with complaining users. Counters of a Physical Disk object that can be monitored are:

- *% Disk Time* The "% Disk Time" counter is nothing more than the "Avg. Disk Queue Length" counter multiplied by 100. It is the same value displayed in a different scale.

- *Disk Reads/sec* An average disk is capable of handling 100 I/O operations per second at maximum, so this value should give you a quick overview of how busy a particular disk is.

- *Disk Writes/sec* The same applies here as with the previous bullet.

- *Average Disk sec/Read* This value should be below 20 milliseconds. It is allowed to show spikes to a higher value, but on average it should be below 20 msec.

- *Average Disk sec/Write* The same applies here as with the previous bullet.

- *Average Disk Read Queue Length* This value shows how many read actions are queued for the disk to process. On average, it should be below two per spindle. If you're using a JBOD solution, then it should be below two, but if you're using a RAID set, it can be higher. A RAID-10 set, for example, with 10 disks (5 disks in a mirro) should show a maximum value of 10 for this counter. The disk controller, on the other hand, has a serious impact here as well. For detailed information, consult your hardware vendor.

- *Average Disk Write Queue Length* The same applies here as with the previous bullet.

■ **Note**   In Performance Monitor, there are two disk objects: the Physical Disk and the Logical Disk. The Physical Disk object is a representation of the actual, physical spindle. A Logical Disk object is a representation of a drive letter. A disk in a server can hold multiple volumes, each representing a Logical Disk object in Performance Monitor.

Another interesting counter to have a look at is the MSExchangeTransport SMTPReceive, and then specifically the Default Receive Connector. This counter shows you all kinds of detailed information regarding the number of messages received on the Default Receive Connector on this Exchange 2013 Mailbox server. Counters to examine for problems are Messages Received/sec, Message Byte Received/sec, Average Bytes/message, and Bytes Received/sec. These counters will give you a good estimate of the load generated on your server by incoming SMTP messages.

Performance Monitor Logging

Real-time monitoring of performance data is good for a quick overview of how the Exchange 2013 server is doing, but unless you have nothing else to do besides watching a console, logging the performance data might be a better use of your time.

You can use the Performance Monitor tool to capture and log performance data to a log file on disk. This log file can then be read at a later time. You can also select a particular timeframe for the monitoring. To achieve this, you have to create a User Defined Data Collector Set, following these steps:

1. Log on to an Exchange 2013 server and start the Performance Monitor tool. In the Navigation pane, expand Data Collector Sets, right-click User Defined, select New, and then select Data Collector Set.

2. In the Create New Data Collector Set wizard, enter a descriptive name like My Exchange 2013 Logging, and select the Create Manually (Advanced) radio button. Click Next to continue.

3. In the next window, check the Performance Counter checkbox and click Next to continue.

4. In the next window, you can add the performance counters you want to log. Your choices depend on the situation and requirements, but for informational logging, the following counters are good candidates:

    - MSExchange Database

    - MSExchange Autodiscover

    - MSExchange ActiveSync

    - MSExchange OWA

    - MSExchange EWS

    - MSExchange Transport Receive Connector

    - MSExchange Transport Send Connector

    - Physical Disk

    - Processor

    - RPC/HTTP proxy

5. Change the sample interval to something useful for longer term logging. A 15-second interval gives you much information, but when logging for 24 hours, 48 hours, or maybe a week, the size of the log file will become unmanageable. I use a 1- or 2-minute interval for logging. Click Next to continue.

6. By default, the log files are stored on the system drive with the Data Collector Set name appended. In this example, this would be `%systemdrive%\PerfLogs\Admin\My Exchange 2013 Logging`. Click Next to continue.

7. The last window is to set the permissions under which the data is logged. You can leave this <default> and click Finish to create a Data Collector Set and close the wizard.

The new Data Collector Set will now show up in the User Defined section. Right-click the Data Collector Set and select Start to begin the actual logging. Logging is a background process, so it's safe to log off and log back on to the server when you want to check your logging results after 24 or 48 hours.

When the logging has been stopped after a given period of time, you can use Performance Monitor again. But instead of using real-time data, you can import the data from the log file that was collected earlier and as shown in Figure 8-8. At the same time, you can use the slider to set the time period of the data you want to analyze; the window results of a 24-hour logging are shown in Figure 8-9.

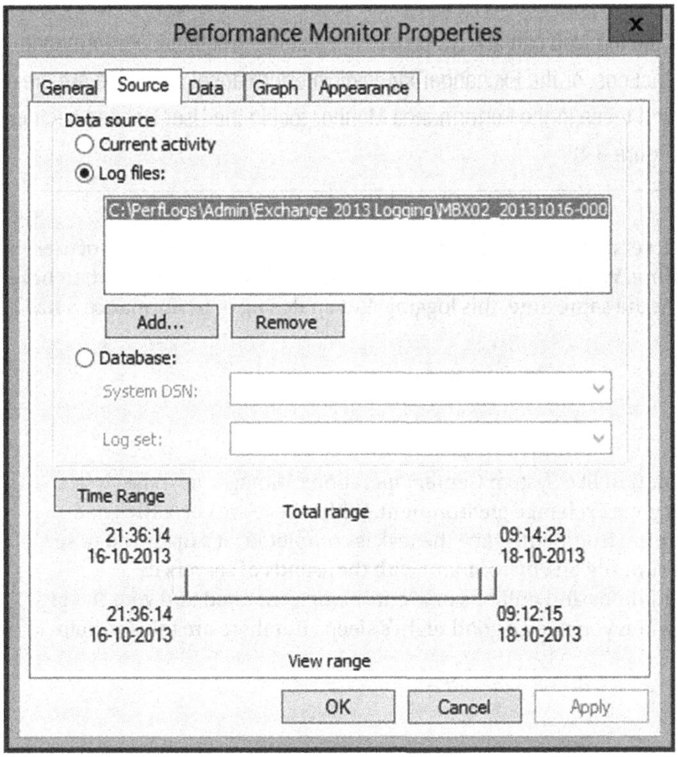

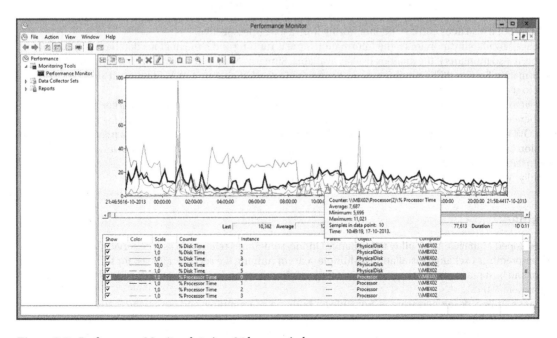

Figure 8-8. *Importing data from a Performance Monitor log file*

Figure 8-9. *Performance Monitor data in a 24 hour period*

▪ **Note**   If you are not sure which counters you should log, you can always decide to open the predefined Performance Monitor log files, ExchangeDiagnosticsDailyPerformancLogs, or the ExchangeDiagnosticsPerformanceLog, which are created by the Exchange Diagnostics Service. You can find these in the Performance Monitor tool in the User Defined section of the Data Collector Sets. These are also shown in Figure 8-8.

It's good practice to monitor your Exchange servers this way on a regular basis, so as to get an overview of their performance and to establish a performance baseline. When performance problems arise later on, you will then have a good reference for how performance should be. At the same time, this logging and analyzing of performance data will help you in monitoring your disk capacity.

Managed Availability

In the past, you could use a separate monitoring solution like System Center Operations Manager or some (less sophisticated) solution based on SNMP to monitor your Exchange environment. While these are certainly good solutions, their only task is to monitor the Exchange environment. Once the task is completed, it's up to you to see any problems and solve them. Imagine that you're running an environment with thousands of servers in a high-availability environment. This will result in millions and millions of events being generated and your having to take action on a continuous basis; that's no fun when you need a good night's sleep. But there are tools to help you avoid this situation.

End-to-End Monitoring

This is where Managed Availability comes into play. Managed Availability is a new service in Exchange 2013 that constantly monitors the Exchange servers and takes appropriate action when needed, without any system administrator intervention. Managed Availability not only monitors the various services within an Exchange server for their availability but it also does end-to-end monitoring from a user's perspective.

So, Managed Availability monitors if the Information Store is running and if the mailbox database is mounted; at the same time, it also monitors if the mailbox itself is available. Simiarly, Managed Availability not only checks if the Internet Information Server (IIS) is running and is offering the Outlook Web App (OWA) function, it also tries to log in to a mailbox to see if the OWA service is actually available.

This service represents a huge difference from past versions of Exchange Server and their earlier monitoring solutions, where the only monitoring was to determine if the web server was up and running. If a logon page was shown, then OWA was supposed to be running fine. Likewise, SMTP monitoring in the past was a matter of setting up a Telnet session on port 25 so you would get a banner showing the service as up and running; however, there was no monitoring to determine if a messages could actually be delivered.

Thankfully, Managed Availability is cloud trained, user focused, and recovery oriented.

Cloud Trained

Microsoft developed Managed Availability in Exchange Online, sometimes referred to as "the service," and brought it back to the on-premises Exchange installations. Multiple years of running the services allowed for the incorporation of experience and best practices from operations in a large environment and with a diverse, worldwide client base running operations 24/7.

In Exchange Online, developers were responsible for building, maintaining, and improving Managed Availability. Those developers also handled escalations in Exchange Online that allowed them to take feedback, not only for the software they were coding but also for improvements in the monitoring process itself. The developers were paged in the middle of the night when problems escalated, so they had to focus on improving Managed Availability.

This service is included in the Exchange 2013 product and installed out of the box by default; no additional configuration is needed. At the same time, Microsoft has the ability to make changes and improvements to Managed Availability every time a Cumulative Update is released.

User Focused

Managed Availability is based on end-user experience. Listening on port 443 for OWA or on port 25 for SMTP does not guarantee successful message delivery. Managed Availability, however, performs monitoring checks for the following:

- *Availability*. Is the service being monitored actually accessible and available?

- *Latency*. Is the service working with an acceptable degree of latency?

- *Error*. When accessing the service, are there any errors logged?

These items result in a Customer Touch Point—a test that ensures the availability of the service; it responds at or below an acceptable latency and returns no error when performing these operations.

Recovery Oriented

Managed Availability protects the user experience through a series of recovery actions. It's basically the recognition that problems may arise, but the user experience should not be impacted. An example of Managed Availability's monitoring of OWA is as follows:

1. The monitor attempts to submit a message via OWA and an error is returned.

2. The responder is notified and tries to restart the OWA application pool.

3. The monitor attempts to verify OWA and checks if it's healty. When healthy, the monitor again attempts to submit a message and again an error is returned.

4. The responder now moves the active mailbox database to another Mailbox server.

5. The monitor attempts to verify OWA and checks for health status. When healthy, the monitor attempts to submit a message and now receives a success.

Managed Availability is implemented through the new Microsoft Exchange Health Manager Service running on the Exchange 2013 server. How does the Health Manager Service gets its information? Through a series of new crimson channels. As described earlier, a crimson channel is a channel where applications can store certain events, and these events can be consumed by other applications or services. In this case, various Exchange components write the events to a crimson channel and the Health Manager Service consumes those events to monitor the service and take appropriate actions.

The configuration files that are used by Managed Availability are XML files supplied by Microsoft and stored on the local hard drive on C:\Program Files\Microsoft\Exchange Server\V15\Bin\Monitoring\Config (see Figure 8-10).

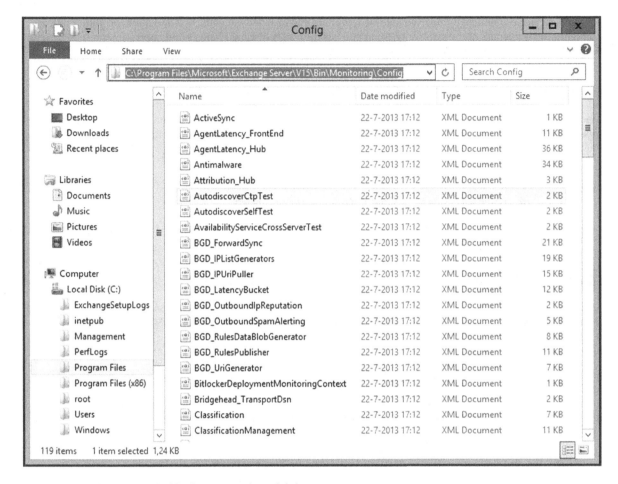

Figure 8-10. *The XML config files for Managed Availability*

■ **Note**   While it is interesting to check out these XML files, it's not a good idea to modify them—not even when you know 120 percent of what you're doing. You will most likely see unexptected results and Managed Availability will do things you don't want, like rebooting servers that have no problems, only because you incorrectly changed some configuration file.

You have to be careful. When you look at the SmtpProbes_Frontend.xml, for example, you'll see the following in the WorkContext:

```
<WorkContext>
  <SmtpServer>127.0.0.1</SmtpServer>
  <Port>25</Port>
  <HeloDomain>InboundProxyProbe</HeloDomain>
  <MailFrom Username="inboundproxy@contoso.com" />
  <MailTo Select="All" />
  <Data AddAttributions="false">X-Exchange-Probe-Drop-Message:FrontEnd-CAT-250&#x
```

```
000D;&#x000A;Subject:Inbound proxy probe</Data>
  <ExpectedConnectionLostPoint>None</ExpectedConnectionLostPoint>
</WorkContext>
```

Above all, this tells us that the Health Service is using port 25 on IP address 127.0.0.1 to check the Front-End proxy function on the Exchange 2013 C AS. At the same time, you know that if, for whatever reason, you have to unbind LOCALHOST from 127.0.0.1 in the server's configuration, you'll get unwanted complications. So you have to take special care when making changes to the server configuration!

The Architecture of Managed Availability

Managed Availability consists of three different components (illustrated in Figure 8-11):

Probe engine

Monitor

Responder engine

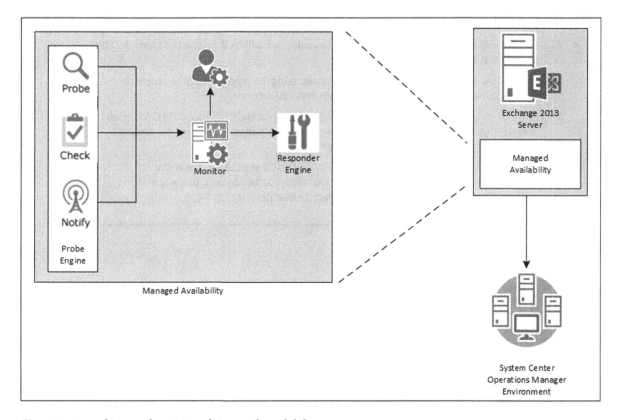

Figure 8-11. *Architectural overview of Managed Availability*

The probe engine consists of three different components:

- **Probe** Determines the success of a particular service or component from an end-user perspective. A probe performs an end-to-end test, also known as a *synthetic transaction*. One probe may perform a portion of a stack, such as checking if a web service is actually running, while another probe tests the full stack—that is, it sees if any successful data is returned. Each component team in the Exchange Product Group is responsible for building its own probe.

- **Check** Monitors end-user activity and looks for trends within the Exchange server that might indicate (known) issues. A check is implemented against performance counters where thresholds can be monitored. A check is a passive monitoring mechanism.

- **Notify** Processes notifications from the system that are known to be issues in an Exchange 2013 server. These are general notifications and they do not automatically mean they have originated from a probe. The notifier makes it possible to take immediate action when needed, instead of waiting for a probe to signal that something is wrong.

The monitor receives data from one or more probes. The feedback from a probe determines if a monitor is healthy or not. If a monitor is using multiple probes, but one probe returns unhealthy feedback, the entire monitor is considered unhealthy. Based on the frequency of the probe feedback, the monitor decides whether a responder should be triggered.

In Figure 8-12, it is clear that a monitor works at different levels. The levels illustrated in the figure include:

1. *Mailbox self-test (MST)* This first check makes sure the mailbox database is accessible. The mailbox self-test runs every 5 minutes.

2. *Protocol self-test (PST)* This second test is for assessing the protocol used to access the mailbox database. The protocol self-test runs every 20 seconds.

3. *Proxy self-test (PrST)* This third test is actually running on the Exchange 2013 CAS server to make sure that requests are proxied correctly to the Mailbox server. Like the protocol self-test, this proxy self-test runs every 20 seconds.

4. *Customer touch point (CTP)* This is an end-to-end test that validates the entire accessability of the mailbox, starting at the Exchange 2013 CAS down to the actual mailbox. The customer touch point runs every 20 minutes.

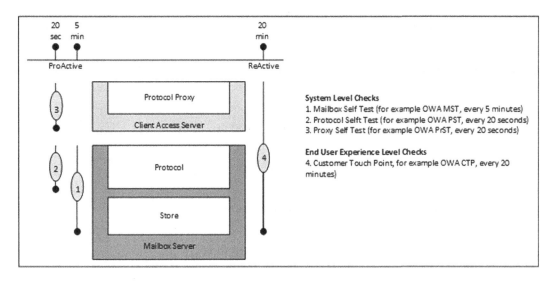

Figure 8-12. Monitoring occurs at different layers

The advantage of this multi-layer approach is that it is possible to check various components using different probes, and to respond in different ways using the responder. Thus, a responder is a component that responds with a predefined acount when a monitor turns unhealthy. The following responders are available:

1. *Restart responder* This responder terminates and recycles a particular service.

2. *Reset AppPool responder* This responder can recycle the IIS application pool.

3. *Failover responder* This responder can take an Exchange 2013 Mailbox server out of service by failing all the mailbox databases on this Mailbox server over to other Mailbox servers.

4. *Bugcheck responder* This responder can bugcheck a particular server—that is, it will restart with a "blue screen."

5. *Offline responder* This responder can take a protocol running on an Exchange 2013 server out of service. Especially when if you're using a load balancer, this is important. When the Offline responder kicks in and a protocol component is shut down, the load balancer will notice and disable the Exchange 2013 CAS (or this particular protocol), so it stops servicing client requests.

6. *Escalate responder* This responder can escalate an issue to another application, like System Center 2012 Operations Manager. It is an indication that human intervention is required.

The responder sequence is stopped when the associated monitor becomes healthy again. Responders can also be throttled. Imagine that you have three Exchange 2013 Mailbox servers in a DAG. You don't want two different responders (each on a Mailbox server) to bugcheck this particular Mailbox server, since it will result in a complete outage of the DAG. When two Mailbox servers are bugchecked, then the remaining Mailbox server loses quorum and shuts down the DAG, which of course will result in downtime for all users.

Exchange 2013 CAS and Managed Availability

In theory, this monitoring is nice, but how does it work in a production environment? When looking at the Exchange 2013 CAS protocols, Managed Availability dynamically generates a file called healthcheck.htm. Since this file is dynamically generated to test a particular protocol, you will not find it anywhere on the Exchange 2013 CAS's hard disk.

This is a very basic HTM file and the only thing is does is to return a 200 OK code plus the name of the server. You can easily open the file using a browser. It doesn't reveal much information, but when it returns the information as shown in Figure 8-13, you know your server is fine from an OWA protocol perspective.

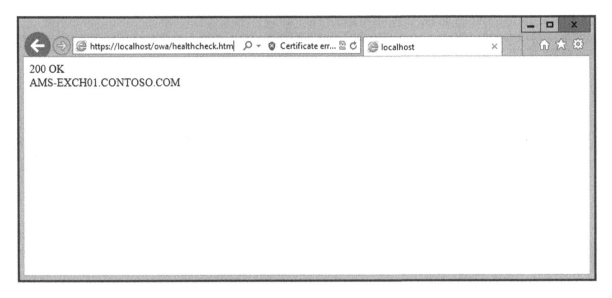

Figure 8-13. *A dynamically generated file for health checking by a probe*

All other protcols, like ECP, EWS, Autodiscover, and Outlook Anywhere, have their own `healthcheck.htm` files when the server is running fine. A hardware load balancer as shown in Figure 8-14 can use this information as well. The when load balancer checks for this file, and a 200 OK is returned, the load balancer knows that the respective protocol is doing fine. If an error is returned, the load balancer knows there's something wrong and it should take this protocol out of service.

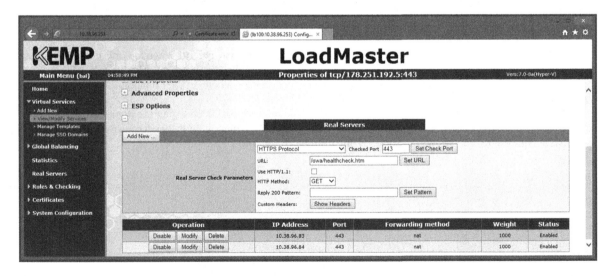

Figure 8-14. *The load balancer is using the healthcheck.htm file for checking availability*

■ **Note**   This is only a protocol check and doesn't say anything if a user can actually log in or not.

What can you do with this information? The Offline responder, for example, can be invoked to place a node in maintenance mode— say, when you're patching your servers or updating to the latest cumulative update. To accomplish this, you have to change the Server Component State of an Exchange server. The Server Component State of an Exchange server can be requested using the Get-ServerComponentState command in EMS like this:

```
Get-ServerComponentState -Identity AMS-EXCH01
```

This command will show the state of all server components on the console, as displayed in Figure 8-15.

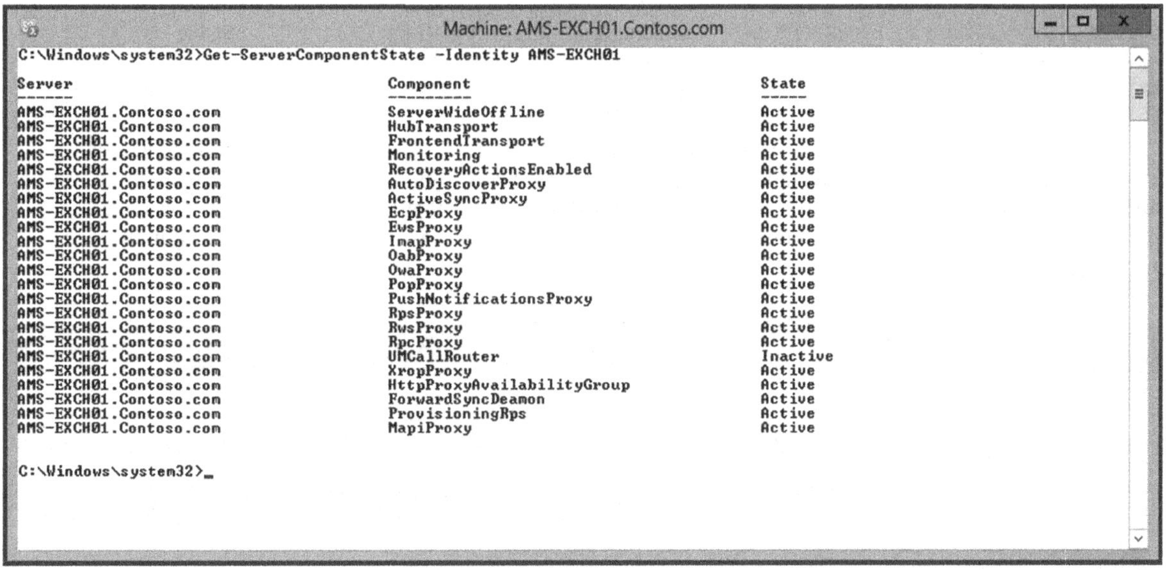

Figure 8-15. Requesting the component state of an Exchange 2013 server

The items listed in Figure 8-15 are all components on the Exchange 2013 server AMS-EXCH01, which is a multi-role server—that is, with both the CAS and a Mailbox server installed on it. The components are not the individual services running on the Exchange server, but they are an abstraction layer that mimics the individual services. For example, in Figure 8-15 you can see the Hub Transport component. In this case, the Hub Transport component represents all services running on the Mailbox server, as explained in Chapter 5.

The components that reside on an Exchange 2013 CAS are the ones with "Proxy" in their name, with UMCallRouter and FrontEndTransport as an exception (also components of the Exchange 2013 CAS). The HubTransport is a component that belongs to the Mailbox server role, while Monitoring and RecoveryActionsEnabled belong to both roles.

When a component is shut down, the requester acts as a label on the actual shutdown. There are five types of requesters defined:

- HealthAPI
- Maintenance
- Sidelined
- Functional
- Deployment

Since these act as labels, you can use them when you want to shut down a component manually. To do this, you can use the Set-ServerComponentState command in EMS:

```
Set-ServerComponentState -Identity AMS-EXCH01 -Component OWAProxy -State Inactive -Requester
Maintenance
```

When this command is run and you check the state of the components using the Get-ServerComponentState -Identity AMS-EXCH01 –Component OWAProxy command in EMS, you'll see on the console that the OWA component is actually inactive:

Server	Component	State
AMS-EXCH01.Contoso.com	OwaProxy	Inactive

When you open a browser and navigate to https://localhost/owa/healthcheck.htm, you'll observe that an error message is generated. The load balancer will notice that the OWA component is no longer available and will automatically disable this server. You can see this in the load balancer configuration, since the inactive server is marked in red (the top Real Servers number in Figure 8-16, which appears as a different shade of gray in the printed book).

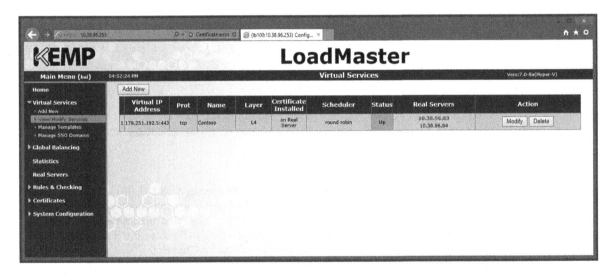

Figure 8-16. *The load balancer detects that OWA is not available on the Exchange 2013 CAS*

■ **Note**   All server components change their status immediately, with the exception of the Hub Transport and the FrontEnd Transport components. When these components are disabled in EMS, they continue to run until the service is restarted. This can be confusing when you are not aware of this situation; you will think you disabled the component (actually you did!) but it continues working. However, Managed Availability will notice this inconsistency and force a restart of the service after some time.

The component state is stored in two places:

- **Active Directory** In Active Directory, they are stored in a property of the Exchange server object in the Configuration partition. You can find this server object in:

```
CN=Servers, CN=Exchange Administrative Group (FYDIBOHF23SPDLT), CN=Administrative Groups,
CN=Contoso, CN=Microsoft Exchange, CN=Services, CN=Configuration, DC=Contoso, DC=COM.
```

The value in Active Directory is used when performing Set-ServerComponentState commands against a remote server.

- Local Registry When checking the registry, you have to check:

```
HKEY_LOCAL_MACHINE\Software\Microsoft\ExchangeServer\v15\ServerComponentStates
```

and then the component you want to check. This can be seen in Figure 8-17.

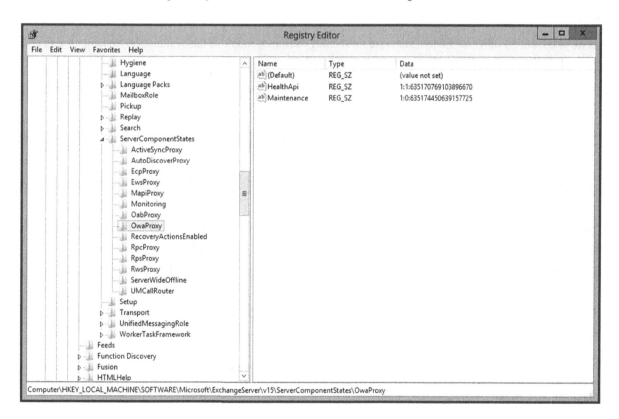

Figure 8-17. *The Server Component state is stored in the Registry of the Exchange 2013 server*

When the work on the Exchange 2013 server is finished, the components can be activated again in EMS using the following command:

```
Set-ServerComponentState -Identity AMS-EXCH01 -Component OWAProxy -State Active -Requester
Maintenance
```

If you check the server component state using the `Get-ServerComponentState` command in EMS, you'll see that it is active again:

```
Server                          Component                         State
------                          ---------                         -----
AMS-EXCH01.Contoso.com          OwaProxy                          Active
```

When you check the load balancer, you'll see that the Exchange 2013 server is back online again.

Monitoring by Using the Exchange Management Shell

In addition to all kinds of manual tools you can use to monitor your Exchange environment, the Exchange Management Shell (EMS) can be very helpful, especially for determining server health, queue monitoring, and replicating mailbox databases.

Server Health

As we've seen in the previous section, Managed Availability constantly monitors the health of the Exchange server and when needed takes appropriate action. However, not all parts of the Exchange servers can be fixed automatically.

To get an overview of the health of components in the Exchange server, you can use the `Get-ServerHealth` and `Get-HealthReport` commands in EMS. This command results in a complete list of all components on the Exchange server, and if all goes well these components will show up as healthy, as can be seen in Figure 8-18.

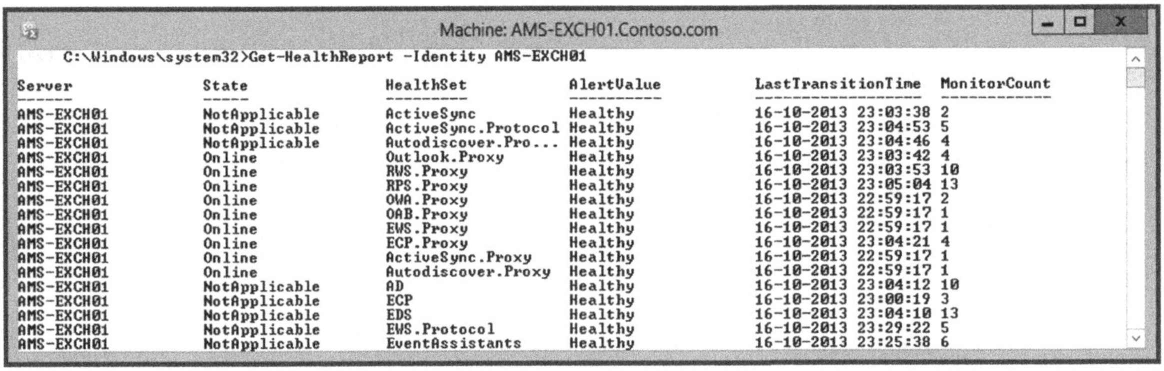

Machine: AMS-EXCH01.Contoso.com

C:\Windows\system32>Get-HealthReport -Identity AMS-EXCH01

Server	State	HealthSet	AlertValue	LastTransitionTime	MonitorCount
AMS-EXCH01	NotApplicable	ActiveSync	Healthy	16-10-2013 23:03:38	2
AMS-EXCH01	NotApplicable	ActiveSync.Protocol	Healthy	16-10-2013 23:04:53	5
AMS-EXCH01	NotApplicable	Autodiscover.Pro...	Healthy	16-10-2013 23:04:46	4
AMS-EXCH01	Online	Outlook.Proxy	Healthy	16-10-2013 23:03:42	4
AMS-EXCH01	Online	RWS.Proxy	Healthy	16-10-2013 23:03:53	10
AMS-EXCH01	Online	RPS.Proxy	Healthy	16-10-2013 23:05:04	13
AMS-EXCH01	Online	OWA.Proxy	Healthy	16-10-2013 22:59:17	2
AMS-EXCH01	Online	OAB.Proxy	Healthy	16-10-2013 22:59:17	1
AMS-EXCH01	Online	EWS.Proxy	Healthy	16-10-2013 22:59:17	1
AMS-EXCH01	Online	ECP.Proxy	Healthy	16-10-2013 23:04:21	4
AMS-EXCH01	Online	ActiveSync.Proxy	Healthy	16-10-2013 22:59:17	1
AMS-EXCH01	Online	Autodiscover.Proxy	Healthy	16-10-2013 22:59:17	1
AMS-EXCH01	NotApplicable	AD	Healthy	16-10-2013 23:04:12	10
AMS-EXCH01	NotApplicable	ECP	Healthy	16-10-2013 23:00:19	3
AMS-EXCH01	NotApplicable	EDS	Healthy	16-10-2013 23:04:10	13
AMS-EXCH01	NotApplicable	EWS.Protocol	Healthy	16-10-2013 23:29:22	5
AMS-EXCH01	NotApplicable	EventAssistants	Healthy	16-10-2013 23:25:38	6

Figure 8-18. *Use the Get-HealthReport command to get the health status of all components*

It is also possible to drill down into the health of a component using the `Get-ServerHealth` command, and this command takes the `-HealthSet` as a parameter. To drill down into the health of OWA, for example, you can use the following command:

```
Get-ServerHealth - Identity AMS-EXCH01 -HealthSet OWA.Proxy
```

The command shows the different monitors and their statuses related to OWA, as can be seen in Figure 8-19.

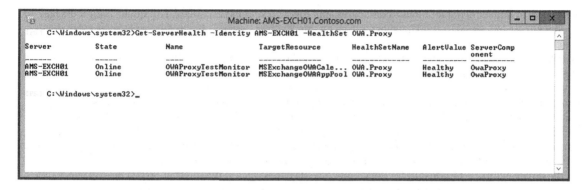

Figure 8-19. Use the Get-ServerHealth command to drill down into a specific Component

These commands are nice for informational purposes, but they can show their real value when you have to troubleshoot components, as will be discussed in the next chapter.

Queue Monitoring

The SMTP queues should be monitored on a regular basis. The Transport service running on the Mailbox server is using SMTP queues, both inbound and outbound, to store messages temporarily before they are actually delivered. Delivery can be in a local mailbox or to another SMTP server, either internal or external.

In previous versions of Exchange Server, there was the toolbox in the Exchange Management Console. The toolbox still exists in Exchange 2013, but it is very limited now. Luckily, the Queue Viewer is still available. You can open Queue Viewer by opening the Exchange Toolbox from the Start menu, and then selecting Queue Viewer under Mail Flow Tools.

When the Queue Viewer is opened, you get an overview of all queues on this particular server. In Figure 8-20, you can see the queues for two Exchange 2010 Edge Transport servers (which are synchronized with this Exchange 2013 Mailbox server) in shadow redundancy and a queue for the SMTP Connector being used by the Edge Transport server.

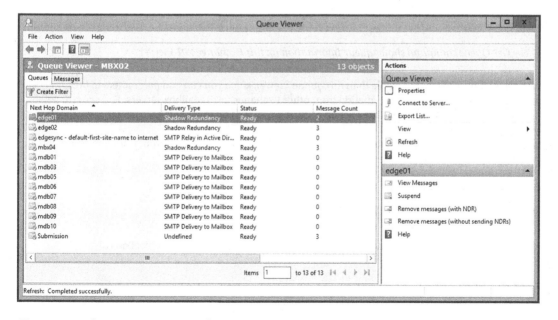

Figure 8-20. The Queue Viewer in Exchange Server 2013

There are multiple queues for mailbox databases, and there's a submission queue. This queue is for messages in transit that are not processed by the Transport service on this Mailbox server. This situation was explained in detail in Chapter 5.

It is good practice to open Queue Viewer every now and then to determine how the queues are actually behaving. During normal operations you'll see the queues increasing and decreasing, and that's okay. An SMTP queue can show a serious number of messages in the queue—for example, when the remote server is not available because of maintenance. As longs as the queues decrease after some time, it's not a big deal. What also happens is that an Exchange server receives spam for nonexisting users. This results in an NDR (nondelivery report) typically to a nonexisting domain. These NDRs usually end up in the queue for 48 hours, before they are deleted.

In Figure 8-20, an Edge Transport server is used and all outbound SMTP messages are sent to this Edge Transport server. Unless the Edge Transport server is not available, you won't see too many messages in the queue. The Edge Transport server, in turn, is responsible for delivering the SMTP messages to the Internet, so you have to check this queue as well. Queues are dynamically created, so that after a message is deliverd, they exist in the queue for another 10 minutes before they're removed from the server.

It is also possible to use EMS to retrieve queue information from the Transport service using the Get-Queue command, as shown in Figure 8-21.

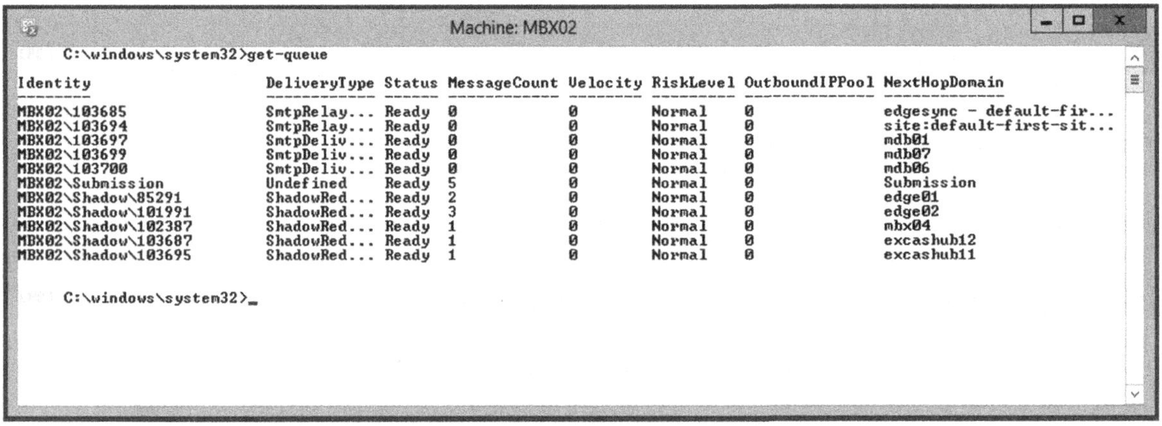

Figure 8-21. The Get-Queue command shows queue information on this Exchange 2013 server

The Get-Queue command is more flexible than the Queue Viewer, since you can add parameters to the command, use filtering, or obtain queue information from other Exchange 2013 Mailbox servers. For a complete overview of the Get-Queue command, check the Exchange 2013 help pages on Microsoft TechNet on http://tinyurl.com/q42yxns.

As explained in Chapter 6, you can "chain" multiple commands in EMS to use the output from one command as the input for another command; for example:

```
Get-TransportService | Get-Queue
```

or

```
Get-TransportService| Get-Queue | Select Identity, Status, MessageCount, NextHopDomain,
LastRetryTime, NextRetryTime
```

This command will list all Transport services on all Exchange 2013 Mailbox servers in the organization, and use this as the input for the Get-Queue command. In turn, this command will return all queues on these servers, but will show only the identity, status, number of messages in the queue, next domain the queue is destined for, and the times the queue has been trying to deliver or will try to deliver the message.

When you follow the guidelines as detailed in Chapter 6 concerning mailbox reporting, you'll end up with something like this:

```
$BodyStyle  = "<style>"
$BodyStyle = $BodyStyle + "BODY{background-color:peachpuff;}"
$BodyStyle = $BodyStyle + "TABLE{border-width: 1px;border-style: solid;
border-color: black;border-collapse: collapse;}"
$BodyStyle = $BodyStyle + "TH{border-width: 1px;padding: 0px;
border-style: solid;border-color: black;background-color:thistle}"
$BodyStyle = $BodyStyle + "TD{border-width: 1px;padding: 0px;
border-style: solid;border-color: black;background-color:PaleGoldenrod}"
$BodyStyle = $BodyStyle + "</style>"
Get-TransportService | Get-Queue | Select Identity, DeliveryType, Status, MessageCount,
NextHopDomain, LastRetryTime, NextRetryTime | ConvertTo-Html -head $BodyStyle | Out-File
C:\Temp\QueueInfo.html
```

When the above is stored in a PowerShell script—for example, c:\temp\queue.ps1–you can run it and get the output you want. Further, you can combine this result with the .NET message functions and send the output in an HTML formatted message.

```
$Msg = new-object system.net.mail.MailMessage
$msg.IsBodyHtml = $True
$msg.Body = $Queue
$msg.Subject = "Hub Transport Queue Information"
$msg.To.add("postmaster@contoso.com")
$msg.From = "postmaster@contoso.com"
$SmtpClient = new-object system.net.mail.smtpClient
$smtpclient.Host = '<your SMTP relay server>'
$smtpclient.Send($msg)
```

The $Queue variable contains the data that was collected using the Get-Queue command. The $Queue variable is populated as follows:

```
$Queue = Get-TransportService | Get-Queue | Select
Identity,DeliveryType,Status,MessageCount,NextHopDomain,LastRetryTime, NextRetryTime |
ConvertTo-Html -head $BodyStyle
```

When this is all stored in the queue.ps1 file, you can fire this off using the following command and, in turn, can schedule this to run frequently so that you get an overview of all queues delivered right to your own mailbox on the regular basis:

```
Powershell.exe -PSConsoleFile  "C:\Program Files\Microsoft\Exchange Server\v15\bin\exshell.psc1"
-command ". 'C:\Temp\queue.ps1'"
```

Monitoring the queues is just one aspect. When something goes wrong and the queues start to build up, you have to troubleshoot your Exchange environment to determine why those messages are not being delivered. This troubleshooting will be discussed in more detail in Chapter 9.

Mailbox Database Replication

Mailbox database replication is a key service for determining if the servers are performing as expecting. When the performance of an Exchange 2013 server or related service degrades, you'll see the replication queues start growing. There are two types of queues available for mailbox database replication:

- **Copy queue** This is the queue where transaction log files reside before they are replicated (over the network) to other Mailbox servers holding passive copies of a mailbox database.

- **Replay queue** This queue resides on the Mailbox server holding a passive copy of the mailbox database. It holds transaction log files that are received from the active mailbox database copy but haven't yet been replayed into the passive mailbox database copy.

Both queues fluctuate constantly, and it's no big deal when they are momentarily increasing as long as they start decreasing in minutes.

■ **Note** When you have lagged copies in your DAG, especially when the lag time is long, you can expect a large number of items in the replay queues. If so, there's no need to worry since this is expected behavior.

You can monitor the replication queues in EMS using the `Get-MailboxDatabaseCopyStatus` command:

- To monitor all copies of a particular *mailbox database*, you can use the following command: `Get-MailboxDatabaseCopyStatus -Identity DB1 | Format-List`

- To monitor all mailbox database copies on a given *server*, you can use the following command: `Get-MailboxDatabaseCopyStatus -Server MBX1 | Format-List`

- To monitor the *status and network information* for a given mailbox database on a given server, you can use the following command: `Get-MailboxDatabaseCopyStatus -Identity DB3\ MBX3 -ConnectionStatus | Format-List`

■ **Note** The syntax of the Identity of the mailbox database copy looks a bit odd, but it is the name of the mailbox database located on the Mailbox server holding the passive copy. In this case, it is mailbox database DB3 located on Mailbox server MBX3, thus DB3\MBX3.

- To monitor the *copy status* of a given mailbox database on a given server, you can use the following command: `Get-MailboxDatabaseCopyStatus -Identity DB1\MBX2 | Format-List`

I often combine the `Get-MailboxDatabaseCopyStatus` command with the `Get-MailboxDatabase` command to get a quick overview of all mailbox databases, their passive copies, and the status of the replication queues (see Figure 8-22). To do this, use the following command:`Get-MailboxDatabase | Get-MailboxDatabaseCopyStatus`.

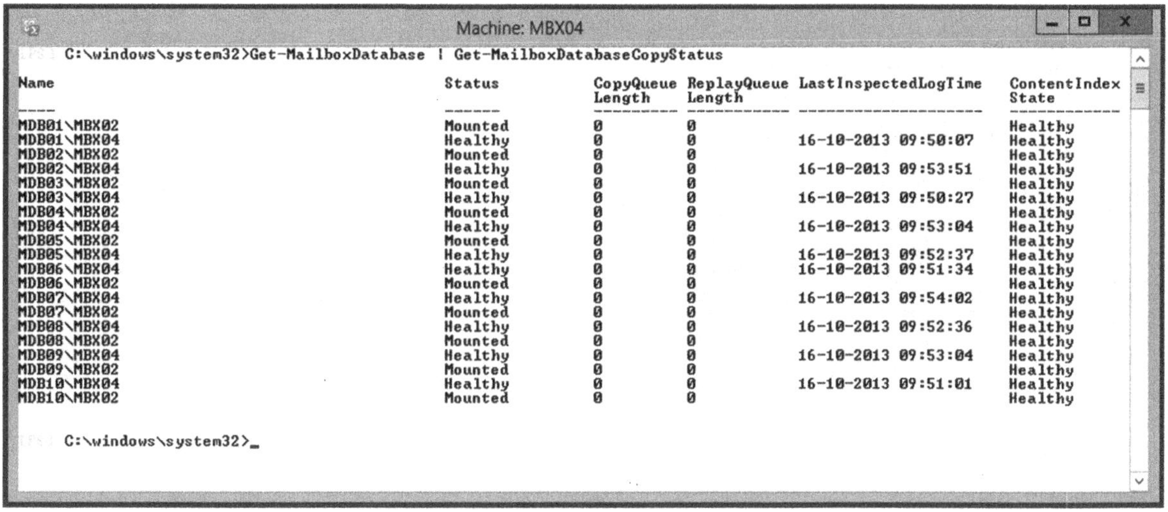

```
Machine: MBX04
C:\windows\system32>Get-MailboxDatabase | Get-MailboxDatabaseCopyStatus

Name                 Status     CopyQueue ReplayQueue LastInspectedLogTime   ContentIndex
                                Length    Length                             State
----                 ------     --------- ----------- --------------------   ------------
MDB01\MBX02          Mounted    0         0                                  Healthy
MDB01\MBX04          Healthy    0         0           16-10-2013 09:50:07    Healthy
MDB02\MBX02          Mounted    0         0                                  Healthy
MDB02\MBX04          Healthy    0         0           16-10-2013 09:53:51    Healthy
MDB03\MBX02          Mounted    0         0                                  Healthy
MDB03\MBX04          Healthy    0         0           16-10-2013 09:50:27    Healthy
MDB04\MBX02          Mounted    0         0                                  Healthy
MDB04\MBX04          Healthy    0         0           16-10-2013 09:53:04    Healthy
MDB05\MBX02          Mounted    0         0                                  Healthy
MDB05\MBX04          Healthy    0         0           16-10-2013 09:52:37    Healthy
MDB06\MBX04          Healthy    0         0           16-10-2013 09:51:34    Healthy
MDB06\MBX02          Mounted    0         0                                  Healthy
MDB07\MBX04          Healthy    0         0           16-10-2013 09:54:02    Healthy
MDB07\MBX02          Mounted    0         0                                  Healthy
MDB08\MBX04          Healthy    0         0           16-10-2013 09:52:36    Healthy
MDB08\MBX02          Mounted    0         0                                  Healthy
MDB09\MBX04          Healthy    0         0           16-10-2013 09:53:04    Healthy
MDB09\MBX02          Mounted    0         0                                  Healthy
MDB10\MBX04          Healthy    0         0           16-10-2013 09:51:01    Healthy
MDB10\MBX02          Mounted    0         0                                  Healthy

C:\windows\system32>_
```

Figure 8-22. *Monitoring the status of mailbox database copies*

■ **Note** When you are moving mailboxes from one Mailbox server to another Mailbox server, a lot of transaction log files are generated. It is quite common that, under these circumstances, replication cannot keep up with demand and you will see a dramatic increase in the replication queues. Things can get even worse when you are using circular logging in a DAG, since the log files will be purged only when the transaction log files are replayed into the mailbox database and all the DAG members agree on purging the log files. When there are too many log files, replication will slow down, the disk holding the log files will fill up, and the mailbox database can potentially dismount. The only way to avoid this situation is to throttle down the mailbox moves so that replication can keep up with demand.

Another way in EMS to check for mailbox replication is to use the `Test-ReplicationHealth` command. This command tests the continuous replication, the availability of the Active Manager, the status of the underlying failover cluster components, the cluster quorum, and the underlying network infrastructure. To use this command against server AMS-EXCH01, you can use the following command:

```
Test-ReplicationHealth -Identity AMS-EXCH01
```

The output of this command is shown in Figure 8-23.

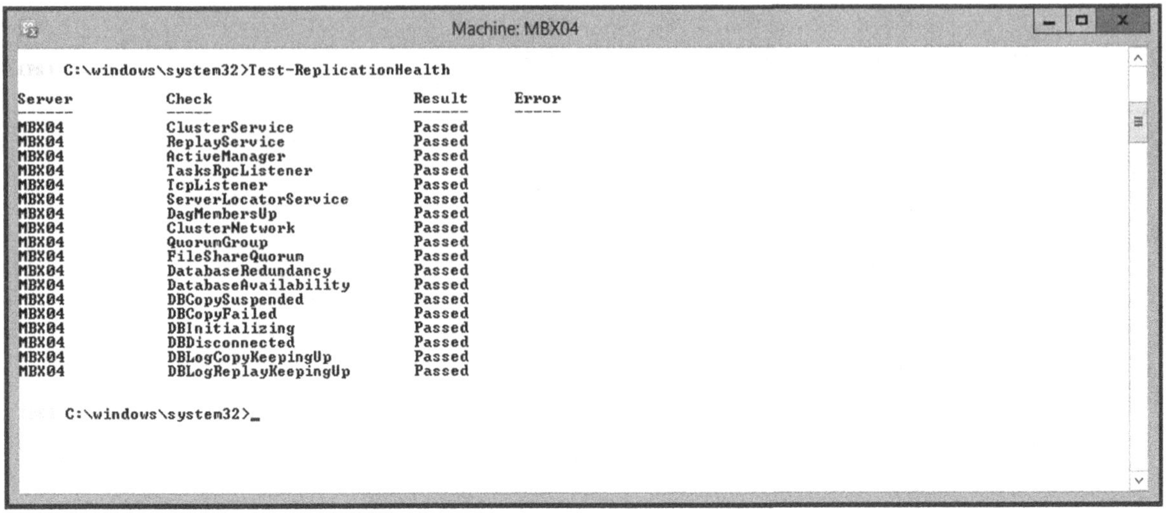

Figure 8-23. *The Test-ReplicationHealth command checks the entire replication stack*

Microsoft has written two health metric scripts, which are located in the C:\Program Files\Microsoft\Exchange Server\v15\Scripts directory that gathers information about mailbox databases in a DAG. These scripts are:

- CollectOverMetrics.ps1
- CollectReplicationMetrics.ps1

The CollectOverMetrics.ps1 script reads DAG member event logs to gather information regarding mailbox database operations for a specific time period. Database operations can be mounting, dismounting, database moves, or failovers. The script can generate an HTML file as well as a CSV file for later processing in Microsoft Excel, for example.

To show information in a DAG called DAG01, and all mailbox databases in this DAG, you can navigate to the scripts directory and use a command similar to the following:

```
.\CollectOverMetrics.ps1 -DatabaseAvailabilityGroup DAG01 -Database:"DB*" -GenerateHTMLReport
-ShowHTMLReport
```

The CollectReplicationMetric.ps1 is a more advanced script, since it gathers information in real time while the script is running. Also, it gathers information from performance monitor counters related to mailbox database replication. The script can be run to:

- Collect data and generate a report (CollectAndReport, the default setting)
- Collect data and store it (CollectOnly)
- Generate a report from earlier stored data (ProcessOnly)

The scripts start PowerShell jobs that gather all information and, as such, it is a time- and resource-consuming task. The final stage of the script, when all data is processed to generate a report, can also be time and resource intensive. To gather one hour of performance data from a DAG using a one-minute interval and generate a report, the following command can be used:

```
.\CollectReplicationMetrics.ps1 -DagName DAG1 -Duration "01:00:00" -Frequency "00:01:00"
-ReportPath
```

To read data from all files called CounterData* and generate a report, the following command can be used:

```
.\CollectReplicationMetrics.ps1 -SummariseFiles (dir CounterData*) -Mode ProcessOnly -ReportPath
```

Note Do not forget to navigate to the scripts directory before entering this command.

Not directly related to monitoring an Exchange server is the RedistributeActiveDatabases.ps1 script. It can happen, especially after a failover, that the mailbox databases are not properly distributed among the Mailbox servers. For example, in such a scenario, one Mailbox server may be hosting only active copies of mailbox databases while another Mailbox server is hosting only passive copies. To redistribute the mailbox database copies over the available Mailbox servers, you can use the following command:

```
.\RedistributeActiveDatabases.ps1 -DagName DAG1 -BalanceDbsByActivationPreference
-ShowFinalDatabaseDistribution
```

This command will distribute all mailbox databases by their activation preference, which was set during creation of the mailbox database copies. If you have a multi-site DAG, you can use the -BalanceDbsBySiteAndActivationPreference parameter. This will balance the mailbox databases to their most preferred copy, but also try to balance mailbox databases within each Active Directory site.

Workload Management

An Exchange workload is an Exchange Server feature, protocol, or service within an Exchange server that has been explicitly purposed for Exchange system resource management. Examples of Exchange workloads are:

- Outlook Web App
- Exchange ActiveSync
- Outlook Anywhere
- Moving mailboxes
- Mailbox assistents

Basically anything that consumes system resources on an Exchange server is an Exchange workload and can somehow be managed. There are two ways to manage Exchange workloads:

1. *Monitoring the health of system resources* This is what we have been discussing earlier in this chapter.

2. *Controlling how resources are consumed* In Exchange 2010, this was referred to as "throttling." This feature has been expanded in Exchange 2013.

Managing Workloads by Monitoring System Resources

When you manage Exchange workloads by monitoring the Exchange system resources, you are able to optimize resource utilization and thus manage user expectations when it comes to the performance of the Exchange environment.

Workloads and Performance

When an Exchange server starts to suffer owing to high load, Exchange Server begins to slow down low-priority tasks or workloads on the server. This way, Exchange Server can spread the load across multiple services within the servers and restore the resources to a healthy state without negatively impacting the user's experience.

Exchange Server constantly monitors the following resources within the servers:

- CPU usage

- Mailbox database RPC latency

- Mailbox database replication health

- Content indexing age as of last notification

- Content indexing retry queue size

Besides regular services, Exchange workloads can include background services or asynchronous services like the Exchange Mailbox Replication service, the Calendar Synchronization workload, and the Exchange Mailbox Assistance service.

By monitoring the resources in an Exchange server, it is also possible to throttle those resources. For instance, when an Exchange server's performance starts to degrade, the Exchange workloads that rely on this specific service are throttled down so that Exchange Server can work on a backlog efficiently (if one exists, of course) and get back to a healthy state. This throttling allows users to work with an Exchange server without noticing any performance degradation. The throttling is sometimes referred to "shaving the peaks" in Exchange performance. The other way around is also possible. When performance permits, workloads are allowed to speed up in their resource usage; this is sometimes referred to as "filling the valleys."

Workload Classifications

Exchange workloads are assigned a classification, and the following classifications can be assigned to a workload:

- Urgent

- Customer Expection

- Internal Maintenance

- Discretionary

When resource health shows signs of performance degradation, a workload in a higher classification is given preference over a workload with a lower classification. Take a look at the local Exchange server CPU. When it is running at high usage, workloads classified as Internal Maintenance can continue to run while workloads classified as Discretionary can be temporarily stopped. Table 8-1 shows all Exchange 2013 workloads, with a description of each workload and its default classification.

Table 8-1. *Exchange Workloads and The ir Classifications*

Workload Policy Name	Description	Workload Classification
MailboxReplication ServiceHighPriority	Mailbox replication service, high priority	Urgent
EAS	Exchange ActiveSync	Customer Expection
JunkEmailOptionsCommitter-Assistant	Junk email	Customer Expection
PowerShellBackSync	Windows PowerShell BackSync operations	Customer Expection
PowerShellForwardSync	Windows PowerShell FwdSync operations	Customer Expection
PublicFolderMailboxSync	Public Folder Mailbox synchronization	Customer Expection
TeamMailboxSync-	Site Mailbox synchronization	Customer Expection
Transport	Transport mailflow	Customer Expection
CalendarRepairAssistant	Calendar Repair Assistant	Internal Maintenance
CalendarSyncAssistant	Calendar Synchronization Assistant	Internal Maintenance
ContactLinkingAssistant	Contact Linking Assistant	Internal Maintenance
DirectoryProcessorAssistant	Directory Processore Assistant	Internal Maintenance
Domt	Address Book	Internal Maintenance
ELCAssistant	Managed Folder Assistant	Internal Maintenance
EWS	Exchange Web Services	Internal Maintenance
IMAP	IMAP4	Internal Maintenance
MOMT	RPC Client Access	Internal Maintenance
OABGeneratorAssistant	Offline Address Book generation assistant	Internal Maintenance
OrgContactsSyncAssistant	Organizational contacts Synchronization Assistant	Internal Maintenance
OWA	Outlook Web App	Internal Maintenance
OWAVoice	Outlook Web App voice access	Internal Maintenance
PeopleRelevanceAssistant	People Relevance Assistant	Internal Maintenance
POP	POP3	Internal Maintenance
PowerShell	PowerShell work not included in other workloads	Internal Maintenance
PowerShellGalSync	Powershell work for GAL synchronization	Internal Maintenance
PowerShellLowPriority WorkFlow	Non-time-sensitive PowerShell work	Internal Maintenance
PushNotificationService	Push Notification service	Internal Maintenance
SharingPolicyAssistant	Sharing Policy Assistant	Internal Maintenance
SiteMailboxAssistant	Site Mailbox Assistant	Internal Maintenance
StoreMaintenanceAssistant	Store Maintenance	Internal Maintenance

(continued)

Table 8-1. (*continued*)

Workload Policy Name	Description	Workload Classification
TopNAssistant	Top N Words Assistant	Internal Maintenance
TransportSync	Transport synchronization	Internal Maintenance
UMReportingAssistant	Unified Messaging Reporting Assistant	Internal Maintenance
InferenceDataCollection Assistant	Inference Data Collection Assistant	Discretionary
InferenceTrainingAssistant	Inference Training Assistant	Discretionary
MailboxReplicationService	Mailbox Replication service	Discretionary
PowerShellDiscretionary WorkFlow	Non-time sensitive PowerShell work	Discretionary
PublicFolderAssistant	Public Folder Assistant	Discretionary

Now why is this good to know? Because the various workload policies give you a good overview of the classifications and their priorities. For example, Exchange ActiveSync (EAS) in Table 8-1 has a classification of Customer Expectation, while Exchange Web Services (EWS) and MOMT (RPC Client Access) have classifications of Internal Maintenance. This indicates that when an Exchange server is under pressure, it will assign more system resources to EAS, giving priority over those used by EWS and MOMT. EAS in this case continues to run better than EWA and MOMT.

Policies, classifications, and monitoring are nice to do, but you need predefined values to compare these against. Thresholds are values that define the state of a particular resource. For example, a certain service might use CPU resources that could be between 0 and 100 percent; a threshold can be set on 80 percent to avoid that service from consuming too many CPU resources. This means that when this service reaches its threshold—that is, 80 percent—certain action needs to be taken, such as throttling the service so it doesn't consume more than 80 percent of the available CPU resources.

Workloads have thresholds similar to services, and these thresholds define the state of those particular resources. For example, a workload can have a state of Critical when it is consuming way too many resources and it needs to be stopped to preserve server health.

The following thresholds are available for Exchange workloads:

- *Critical* Workload must be stopped when resource use is above this threshold.

- *Overloaded* Workload must be throttled when resource use is above this threshold.

- *Underloaded* Workload can be speeded up when resource use is below this threshold.

■ **Note**   When a workload is Underloaded and/or below Overloaded, then performance isn't throttled.

Workload Management Policy Settings

Out of the box, Exchange 2013 comes with a default set of workload management policy settings that are sufficient for most scenarios. It is possible, though, to change these default settings, and that can be done for the entire Exchange organization or just on a per server basis.

To make workload management policy changes for the entire organization, you have to create a new workload management policy and apply it to the GlobalOverrideWorkloadManagementPolicy policy. Using the applied GlobalOverrideWorkloadManagementPolicy, then, will override all the default settings. For example, to create a new workload management policy for ActiveSync with a classification of Discretionary (useful when iPhone and iPad users bring too much load to your Exchange servers), you can use the following command in EMS:

```
New-WorkloadPolicy OrgActiveSyncWorkloadPolicy -Workload EAS -WorkloadClassification
Discretionary -WorkloadManagementPolicy GlobalOverrideWorkloadManagementPolicy
```

If you want to check whether this workload policy is actually created, you can use the Get-WorkloadPolicy and filter on the name of the new workoad policy, like this:

```
Get-WorkloadPolicy | where {$_.Name -like "*ActiveSync*"}
```

Both commands can be seen in Figure 8-24.

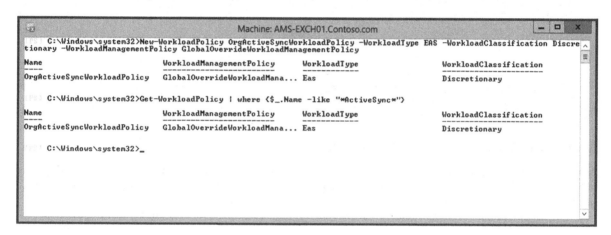

Figure 8-24. *Creating and checking a new workload policy in EMS*

Creating a new workload policy on a per server basis is a little bit more work and consists of the following steps:

1. Create a new workload management policy for a specific server.

2. Create a new workload policy that defines the workload type and its classification, and assign it to the workload management policy that was created in the previous step.

3. Apply the new workload management policy to a specific server.

For example, in our test environment, we have two Exchange 2013 (multi-role) servers in an Active Directory site called AMSTERDAM and one Exchange 2010 (multi-role) server in an Active Directory site called NEWYORK. To create a new workload policy for POP3 usage that's only applied to the Exchange 2013 server in NEWYORK, you can use the following commands in EMS:

```
New-WorkloadManagementPolicy NewYorkWorkloadManagementPolicy

New-WorkloadPolicy -Name NewYorkPOP3WorkloadPolicy -WorkloadType POP -WorkloadClassification
Discretionary -WorkloadManagementPolicy NewYorkWorkloadManagementPolicy

Get-ExchangeServer -Identity NYC-EXCH01 | Set-ExchangeServer -WorkloadManagementPolicy
NewYorkWorkloadManagementPolicy
```

The results of running these commands can be seen in Figure 8-25.

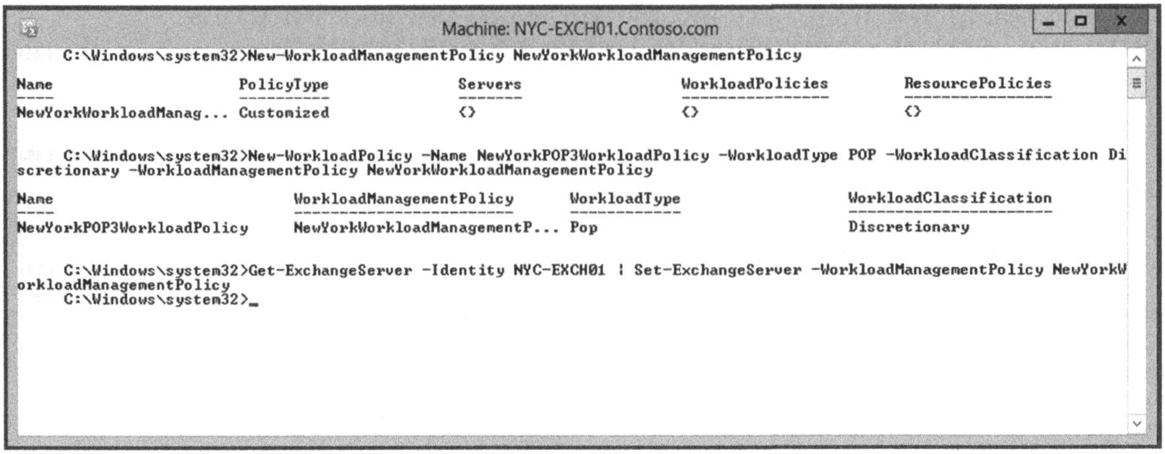

Figure 8-25. *Creating a new workload policy for the NEWYORK Exchange 2013 server*

Managing Workloads for Individual Users

In addition to throttling workloads and services, it is possible in Exchange 2013 to throttle performance on an individual basis. By doing so, you can control resource usage per individual and thereby prevent one user from negatively affecting server performance.

User throttling in this instance allows you to increase resource usage for small amounts of time. On the other hand, locking out a user who consumes very large amounts of system resources is infrequent. Instead of locking out that user, and thereby denying the useraccess to the Exchange service, you throttle the user's usage and delay the processes for a small amount of time.

Users are assigned a "usage budget" that grants a certain amount of system resource usage. When users are consuming these system resources, this usage is subtracted from their budget, or allotment. When their budget is empty, the users are temporarily locked out so that the budget can recharge.

Here are some characteristics of the way Exchange controls the resources for individual users:

- **Maximum usage** When a user consumes a large amount of system resources and hits the threshold, the user is temporarily locked out. If this happens, the user can start using system resources again when his budget is recharged. This happens very infrequently, though.

- **Traffic shaping** When a user's usage reaches the threshold over a period of time, usage is delayed for a short time. This happens well in advance of having any performance impact; in fact, traffic shaping has less impact than a lockout, since the use blockage is limited.

- **Recharge rate** This manages the user's resource consumption via a budget system and the rate of recharge can be set. For example, a value of 600,000 milliseconds means that the budget is recharged with 10 minutes per hour of usage.

- **Burst allowance** Users can use large amounts of resources, but only for a very limited time without experiencing throttling.

There's only one throttling policy available in an Exchange organization, but most of the time this is sufficient. You can check the default throttling policy by using the Get-ThrottlingPolicy command in EMS. To display all throttling policy settings related to Exchange ActiveSync (EAS), you can use the following command in EMS: Get-ThrottlingPolicy | select name,*EAS*.

When using this command, the default throttling policy is read from the Exchange organization, but only the settings related to Exchange ActiveSync are shown, as can be seen in Figure 8-26.

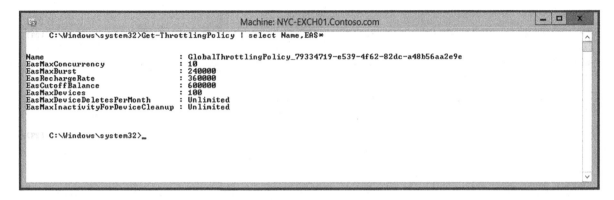

Figure 8-26. *Throttling policy settings for Exchange ActiveSync*

■ **Note** Exchange 2013 comes with its predefined throttling policy, which is different from the default throttling policy in Exchange 2010. In a coexistence scenario with Exchange 2010 and Exchange 2013, the throttling policy of Exchange 2013 is applied only to mailboxes on an Exchange 2013 Mailbox server. Mailboxes still running on an Exchange 2010 Mailbox server have the Exchange 2010 throttling policy applied to them.

New in Exchange 2013 is the concept of "scoping" when using a throttling policy. The default throttling policy has a Global scope, hence its name `GlobalThrottlingPolicy_<<some GUID>>` (see Figure 8-26). This Global throttling policy can be seen as a baseline when it comes to user throttling, and generally speaking, there's no need to change this. In fact, because the default throttling policy has a Global scope, Microsoft recommends not changing this default policy.

However, you can create a new throttling policy with a scope of Organization or Regular. This way, the default throttling policy always remains intact, but it also prevents a customized default throttling policy to be overwritten in the future, when you might be upgrading with a new Cumulative Update.

When you create a new throttling policy with an Organization scope, you have only to set the new throttling settings that are different from those in the default policy. The Organization throttling policy is also applied to all mailboxes in the Exchange organization. If you want to set a throttling policy for specific users, you can create a new throttling policy with a Regular scope. Only the changes to the policy have to be set in this Regular throttling policy; all other settings aree inherited from the default throttling policy or the Organization throttling policy.

By default, all throttling policy settings related to PowerShell are set to Unlimited, with the exception of the number of concurrent sessions, which is set to 18. For example, to create a new Regular policy that can be set to help desk staff who have a throttled number of PowerShell sessions, you can use the following command in EMS:

```
New-ThrottlingPolicy -Name ITStaffPowerShell -PowerShellMaxDestructiveCmdlets 10
-PowerShellMaxDestructiveCmdletsTimePeriod 60 -PowerShellMaxConcurrency 6
-PowerShellMaxCmdletQueueDepth 12 -ThrottlingPolicyScope Regular
```

To assign this throttling policy to a help desk employee called Beau, you would use the following command in EMS:

```
Get-Mailbox -Identity Beau | Set-Mailbox -ThrottlingPolicy ITStaffPowerShell
```

Both commands are shown in Figure 8-27:

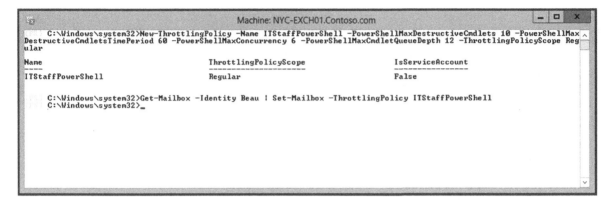

Figure 8-27. *Creating a throttling policy with a scope setting of Regular*

Remember that only the PowerShell settings come from the Regular throttling policy; all other settings are inherited from the default throttling policy.

■ **Note** In my experience, I've never had to change the throttling policies, neither in Exchange 2010 nor in Exchange 2013. My recommendation is not to add additional throttling policies but wait for users to complain about performance and then start investigating the need for additional throttling policies.

System Center Operations Manager

In the prior sections of this chapter I explained the use of several monitoring tools that you can you keep an eye on your Exchange 2013 servers. While all of these are useful and have their own usage scenarios, they have one thing in common: they are all manual tools, with the exception of Managed Availability. This means that you have to check the event log manually, you have to manually run all kinds of commands or scripts in EMS, and you have to monitor your Exchange server in the Performance Monitor tool.This is all doable if you have only one server, but if you have multiple Exchange 2013 servers, these tasks can becoming annoying; likely you will spend all day checking the Event Viewer or running PowerShell commands in EMS.

Another option is to use a tool that does all this work for you: System Center Operations Manager (SCOM). Full coverage of System Center Operations Manager is outside the scope of this book, and there are available plenty of good references about System Center Operations Manager. Here, I'll cover some basics of System Center Operations Manager, since it can be a helpful tool in a larger Exchange environment.

Introduction to Operations Manager

The Microsoft solution for a complex Exchange environment is System Center Operations Manager (SCOM), or just Operations Manager, 2012 R2, which is part of the System Center 2012 R2 suite. Using Operations Manager, you can monitor servers, services, devices, and operations for many computers from a single console, as shown in Figure 8-28.

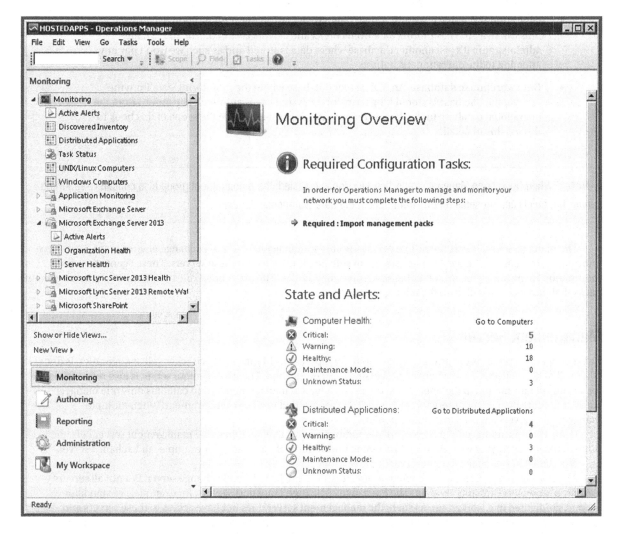

Figure 8-28. *System Center Operations Manager console*

Operations Manager can tell you which monitored objects are not healthy, send alerts when problems are identified, and provide information to help you identify the cause of a problem and possible solutions. As the systems administrator, you configure what will be monitored by selecting the computers and devices and by importing management packs that monitor for specific features and applications.

To decide which objects to monitor and what to monitor for, however, you need to understand the features that constitute the Operations Manager infrastructure and how Operations Manager works.

Operations Manager Infrastructure

Operations Manager is running in a so-called management group, which is the basic unit of management functionality. A management group consists of the following:

- **Management server** The core of the Operations Manager infrastructure, this is the server where all monitoring information is processed. The management server is also the server that's responsible for communicating with the databaser server.

345

- **Operational database** An SQL Server database where all the configuration data is stored, plus where all the monitoring data from clients and servers is stored. For an Exchange administrator, it's just another database where data is stored and as such we won't pay any attention to the operational database.

- **Data warehouse database** An SQL Server database where the monitoring data from the operational database is stored long term for analysis. Data is automatically moved from the operational database to the data warehouse database. It is outside the scope of this book to discuss this in detail.

■ **Note** When Operations Manager's reporting function is installed, the management group also contains a reporting server that builds and presents reports from data in the data warehouse database.

The management server is the primary access point for management of the Exchange environment. To retrieve information from the Exchange 2013 servers, agent software is installed on these servers. These agents then send information to the management server based on predefined rules. The predefined rules are found in the management packs that have been installed on the management server.

Management Server

The management server is the primary access point for Operations Manager. This is where all configuration is done, where all data is collected, and where all processing is accomplished. The management server is also responsible for storing all information in the operational database. A typical management group contains only one management server, but more management servers can be added when needed in a large environment. When multiple management servers are used, a resource pool needs to be created.

Using multiple management servers creates redundancy, of course. When one management server fails, the other management server will take over. Processing information of an object—for example, an Exchange server—is only performed by one management server at a given time.

A management server is part of an Active Directory domain, just like an Exchange server. But not all servers are part of an Active Directory domain. The Exchange 2010 Edge Transport servers, for example, are standalone servers, configured in a workgroup. As such, the management server does not have access to these servers and needs a different approach to get authenticated. This is achieved by using certificates, typically issued by an internal Certificate Authority, so that the management server in the Active Directory domain trusts the Edge Transport servers and vice versa.

For a large number of nondomain-joined servers—approximately 10 or more servers—an Operations Manager gateway server can be used to act for the member servers. In a typical Exchange 2013 environment, only a few Edge Transport servers are used, so the authentication method using certificates is sufficient.

The Agents

The management server communicates with clients like the Exchange servers. This communication is achieved by means of an agent. The agent is a small application installed on the Exchange server and that runs as a service. Responsible for gathering data from the Exchange server, the agent compares it to predefined data and sends that result to the management server. Every agent reports to a management server in a management group, and this management server is referred to as the agent's primary management server.

Agents watch data sources on the monitored computer and collect information according to the configuration that is sent to it from its management server. The agent also calculates the health state of the monitored computer and the objects on that monitored computer, and reports back to the management server. When the health of a monitored object changes or other criteria are met, the agent can generate an alert. This alert lets the Operators Manager know that something requires attention. Thus, the agent provides an up-to-date picture of the health of the device and all the applications that it hosts.

Management Packs

The agents are the primary means of communication between the management server and the managed Exchange servers. The actual workflow that the Operations Manager runs is defined by these management packs. Therefore, the management packs determine information that the agent collects and returns to the management server.

The Exchange Server management pack contains the rules and monitors that collect and evaluate events and operations that are so important to ensuring the health and efficiency of the Exchange Server application. Management packs are available for almost all Microsoft server applications. Besides this, a lot of third-party vendors offer management packs for Operations Manager.

The agent is installed on an Exchange server and is initiated from a management server, so the agent knows which management server to communicate with. After installation, the management server sends an initial configuration to the agent. This initial configuration includes object discoveries from the management pack. That is, the management pack defines the types of objects, such as applications, and the features that will be monitored on those computers that have been discovered by Operations Manager. Agents then send data to the management server that identifies those instances of objects discovered on the computer. The management server responds to the agents by sending the elements of the management pack that apply to the discovered objects for each computer, such as rules and monitors.

To clarify, a rule defines the events and performance data to collect from the computers and what to do with that information. A simple way to think about rules is as If/Then statements. For example, an Exchange 2013 management pack might contain rules such as the following:

- If an event indicating that Exchange is shutting down appears in the event log, create an alert.

- If sending message to a particular domain fails and a queue starts to build up, collect the event that indicates this failure.

As these examples show, rules can create alerts and collect events or performance data, which the agent sends to the management server. Rules can also run scripts, such as allowing a rule to attempt to restart a failed application.

Discovered objects have a health state, which is reflected in the Operations console as green (successful or healthy), yellow (warning), or red (critical or unhealthy). Monitors define the health states for particular aspects of the monitored objects. For example, a monitor for disk drive capacity might define green as less than 85 percent full, yellow as over 85 percent full, and red as over 90 percent full. A monitor can be configured to generate an alert when a change occurs in the state of the object.

SCOM works closely with Managed Availability, so problems that Managed Availability cannot solve, or that need to be escalated, are handed over to Operations Manager.

Working with Operations Manager

For sake of simplicity, I will assume you already have Operations Manager up and running, and that you've installed the Exchange 2013 servers. Using the Operations Manager console, you can install the agents on the various Exchange servers.

After the initial configuration, you won't see much information until you install the Exchange 2013 management pack, which you can download from http://tinyurl.com/kjx2xdu. Installing a management pack is a two-step process. First, you extract the management pack, and then you import the management pack.

In the Operations Manager console, you can see all the active alerts becasue they appear on the main screen. The Exchange 2013 events are collected automatically and shown on the console as well. One drawback of Operations Manager is that it shows a tremendous amount of information, and it's easy to get overwhelmed by the number of alerts you will see on the console. Alas, it is not possible to give a guideline for trimming the number of alerts generated; events that are considered important for one organization can be completely irrelevant for another, so it comes down to your own operational environment.

Earlier I discussed Managed Availability and explained how it integrates with operations manager. This is clearly visible in the Operations Manager console. When you scroll down to the Microsoft Exchange 2013 folder, you'll see the following:

- *Active alerts* These are events that occur on the Exchange 2013 servers and that bubble up to the management server; they are processed there.

- *Organization health* This is a health overview for the Exchange 2013 environment. Figure 8-29 shows the organizational health, with information regarding the Active Directory site and the database availability group.

Figure 8-29. *The Exchange Server organization's healthstatus, with information from Managed Availability*

- *Server health* This is a health overview but it is organized per server. It also shows information that comes from the Managed Availability services running on the various Exchange servers.

Operations Manager in conjunction with Exchange Server is a dynamic system. Problems can occur on an Exchange 2013 server, but they can be solved automatically. For example, a mail queue can suddenly increase because an Exchange server cannot deliver SMTP messages in a timely manner. This raises an alert in Operations Manager, as can be seen in Figure 8-30.

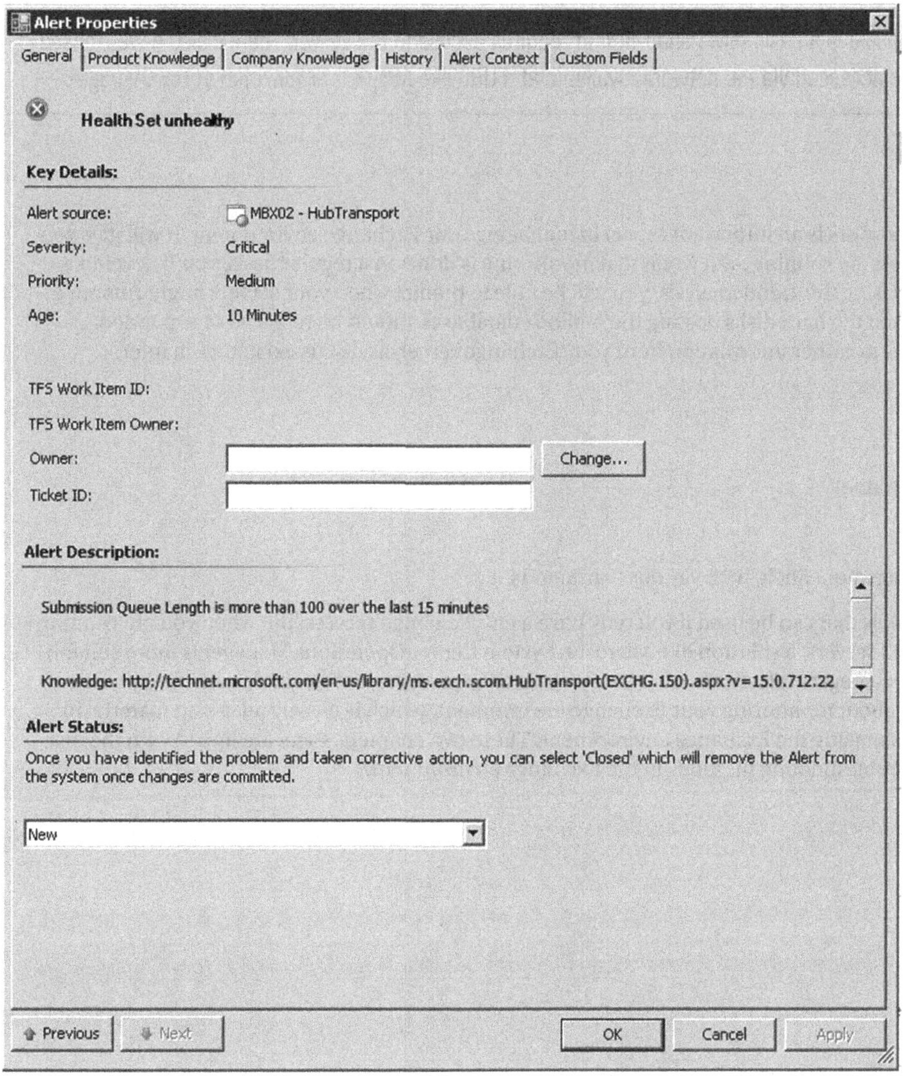

Figure 8-30. *An alert in Operations Manager when a queue is increasing*

But when the burden in SMTP is solved, the queue is automatically emptied and the event can be closed, without the system administrator's taking any action. Because of this, information in the Operations Manager console can contain stale information. For example, suppose the Mailbox Transport service on an Exchange 2013 Mailbox server shows an alert regarding its health. As a warning, the following can be seen in this alert when it is opened:

```
States of all monitors within the health set:
Note: Data may be stale. To get current data, run: Get-ServerHealth -Identity 'MBX02' -HealthSet
'MailboxTransport'
```

So when you see alerts appear in the Operations Manager console, it's always good to double-check the alert on the Exchange 2013 server itself.

■ **Note** The operations console is a basic MMC snap-in that requires access to the server. There's also a web-based console available that can be accessed via the network, available at a URL like `https://fqdn/OperationsManager`.

Summary

Monitoring your Exchange servers is an important aspect of managing your Exchange environment. It will give you insights into how your servers are running, and when that monitoring is done on a regular basis, you'll develop a baseline for trend analysis. Using this trend analysis, you will be able to predict when your servers might run out of resources—for example, when the hard disks hosting the mailbox databases should be replaced or expanded.

There are multiple ways to gather information from your Exchange server, as discussed in this chapter:

- Task Manager

- Event Viewer

- Performance Monitor

- Queue Viewer

- Exchange Management Shell, with various commands

These are all manual tools that can be used if you only have a few Exchange servers. But when you are running an entire farm of Exchange 2013 servers, a solution like Microsoft System Center Operations Manager is more suitable, since it makes it possible to aggregate information from all your Exchange servers into a single console.

Thus, this chapter was about monitoring your Exchange environment, which is closely related to material in Chapter 6, which covered managing the Exchange environment. These two chapters, then, are linked with the next chapter, which describes troubleshooting methods in the Exchange environment.

CHAPTER 9

■ ■ ■

Troubleshooting Exchange 2013

The previous chapter discussed the monitoring of your Exchange 2013 servers. As mentioned, it is good practice to monitor your Exchange 2013 servers on a regular basis to proactively gather information regarding the well-being of those servers.

Unfortunately, it happens every now and then that one of your Exchange 2013 servers does not do what you expect it to do. It doesn't send messages or it doesn't receive messages, users get erratic messages when connecting to the Exchange server, they cannot connect at all, or even worse, some clients can connect while other cannot connect. Then, it's time to start troubleshooting your Exchange 2013 environment.

There are multiple tools available to do this. They include internal tools out-of-the-box or external tools on the Internet, like the Microsoft Remote Connectivity Analyzer. But also important in this respect are your own troubleshooting skills. You have to figure out what's wrong and why, and use the proper tools you have to pinpoint the problems. In this chapter, I give some rough guidelines for where to start looking for answers.

For taking proper troubleshooting steps, you need to have extensive knowledge of messaging services. It is important that you not only know your Exchange 2013 environment but also that you understand things about Active Directory and internal DNS, as the latter are features closely related to Exchange 2013. You also need to know how messaging on the Internet works, how it interacts with public DNS, and so on. And it's also often a matter of experience that you need to have or to build. Only then can you figure out if the error messages as explained by end users are actually caused by your Exchange servers or by the email servers used by the external recipients.

I cannot explain all the steps you need to know in this regard without writing a book several thousand pages long. However, I try here to explain the fundamental and most common troubleshooting steps. As you'll see, this chapter on troubleshooting goes hand in hand with the previous chapter on monitoring.

Troubleshooting Tools

There are several free tools available that you need to know about and that will become handy when you have to troubleshoot your Exchange 2013 servers. I discuss a few of the more interesting tools here. There are other tools, particularly third-party commercial tools, but researching and explaining them is beyond the scope of this chapter.

First, let's briefly review the available tools, then I will cover each of them in more detail.

Exchange Toolbox

As explained in Chapter 6, the Exchange 2013 Toolbox is installed automatically in the Start screen during installation of Exchange 2013. The toolbox holds the following tools:

- **Details Templates Editor** This is not a troubleshooting tool and won't be discussed in this chapter.

- **Remote Connectivity Analayzer** (RCA) This is a Microsoft tool that's available on the Internet. When you click the link in the toolbox, you will automatically be redirected to the www.testexchangeconnectivity.com website. This tool was briefly discussed in Chapter 6, but I go into more depth on the RCA in this chapter when I discuss several components of Exchange server troubleshooting.

- **Queue Viewer** This is a great graphic tool you can use to quickly examine if messages are stuck in your Exchange 2013 server. It is also briefly discussed in Chapter 6, but I cover it in more detail in the "SMTP Transport Routing Issues" section later in this chapter.

■ **Note** If you have been working with previous versions of Exchange Server, you know that the toolbox was more extensive in previous versions. Unfortunately, some of those tools have been discontinued but some of the functions, like message tracking, are available via the Exchange Management Shell (EMS).

Exchange Management Shell

By now you know that the EMS is a very powerful tool, not only for managing and monitoring your Exchange 2013 servers but also for troubleshooting purposes. Microsoft supplies a wide range of test commands in Exchange 2013, like:

- `Test-ReplicationHealth`

- `Test-Mailflow`

- `Test-MapiConnectivity`

- `Test-OutlookConnectivity`

- `Test-OutlookWebServices`

- `Test-SenderID`

There are many more troubleshooting commands available. The list is too extensive to explain them all here, but I cover a few of them later in this chapter. However, all of the EMS commands are discussed in the Microsoft documentation, which can be found on the Microsoft TechNet site; this information is also available in a downloadable help file: http://tinyurl.com/9ksaxll. It's possible to download this file and install it on your Exchange Server or workstation, so you'll always have the information on hand. You have to download the updates manually, though, since the file is not updated with Windows Update. This option is extremely useful when working with EMS.

■ **Note** When troubleshooting Exchange 2013, your favorite search engine will be your friend, of course. A lot of problems have already been discussed and answered in the Microsoft Exchange forums that are hosted on the Microsoft TechNet site: `http://tinyurl.com/pa4j4zk`. The Microsoft forums are monitored by Microsoft support staff. This is not always a guarantee for success, but it certainly helps. Other forums that contain valuable information are the Petri IT Knowledge base (`http://tinyurl.com/q59j97p`) and the MSExchange.org forums (`http://forums.msexchange.org/`).

Notepad++

At one point during any troubleshooting you will have to start looking at log files. These are regular text files that you can open with the default application Notepad. Since Notepad doesn't work with all layouts, this can be a real pain.

A very valuable tool I always use on any Exchange server is Notepad++, which can be downloaded from `www.notepad-plus-plus.org`. This tool can open large log files much faster than the default Notepad application, but it also uses a good layout that can be useful when working with XML files, as can be seen in Figure 9-1.

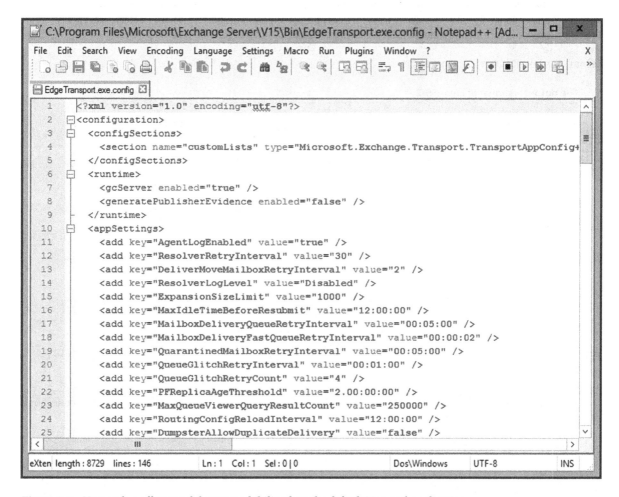

Figure 9-1. Notepad++ offers much better readability than the default Notepad application

Telnet Client

A "must have" tool for every syadmin is the Telnet client. This is part of Windows, but it needs to be installed manually using the Add Roles and Features option in Windows Server Manager.

With Telnet client you can test if servers are listening on specific ports, thereby determining if the corresponding services on those servers are running. For example, you can use Telnet client to test if a server is listening on:

- Port 25, to check if the SMTP service on the server is running and accepting normal SMTP connections.

- Port 587, to check if the SMTP service on the server is running and accepting connections for SMTP submission (as used by SMTP clients)

- Port 443, to check if the IIS server (needed for OWA) is running on that server

- Port 110/143, to check if if the server is accepting connection for POP3 and IMAP4.

- Port 50636, to check if the Edge Transport server is accepting connections for Edge Synchronization.

Thus, the Telnet client is a great tool to quickly check if the (remote) server is accepting connection. For example, to check if an Exchange 2013 Client Access server is accepting connection on port 25, so as to determine if the Transport service is running, you can use the following command from a regular command prompt:

```
Telnet ams-exch01.contoso.com 25
```

The output is shown in Figure 9-2.

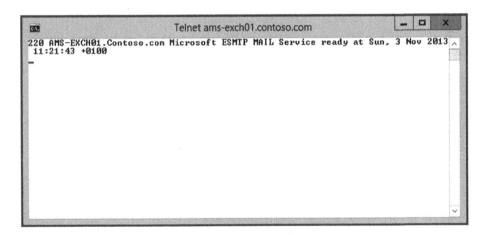

Figure 9-2. *Using the Telnet client to check if server is accepting connections—in this example, the SMTP Transport service on port 25*

I discuss the Telnet client in more detail at other points in this chapter, with the appropriate input to troubleshoot various components of Exchange 2013.

NSLookup

NSLookup is a standard DNS checking tool that's widely used for troubleshooting DNS issues. NSLookup is a default tool, and it is installed with Windows Server.

NSLookup can be run as a single command from a command prompt, or it can be run in interactive mode. It is a great tool for querying public DNS; and when it comes to messaging platforms, it can retrieve information regarding the MX records of domains.

To query the MX records of our ongoing example, the contoso.com domain, by using NSLookup, you open a command prompt and enter the following command:

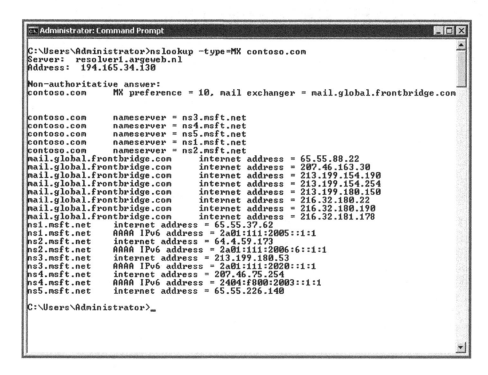

Figure 9-3. *NSLookup -type=MX shows the MX records for a particular domain*

```
nslookup -type=MX contoso.com
```

This command will return the MX records to the console, as shown in Figure 9-3.

■ **Note** The options in the nslookup command seem to be case-sensitive. Entering -type=MX will show results as displayed in Figure 9-3, but entering -Type=MX will result in an error.

As you can see in Figure 9-3, the domain contoso.com is owned by Microsoft, and its MX records point to a Microsoft environment. Also both IPv4 and IPv6 are used by these mail servers.

Now, you combine this with the Telnet client, as explained in the previous section. You can then use the MX record, as shown in Figure 9-3, as input for the Telnet client to see if this mail server is actually accepting connections. To test this, open a command prompt and enter the following command:

```
Telnet mail.global.frontbridge.com 25
```

As shown in Figure 9-4, you'll see that it accepts connections, so you can assume that the mail server on the contoso.com domain is up and running.

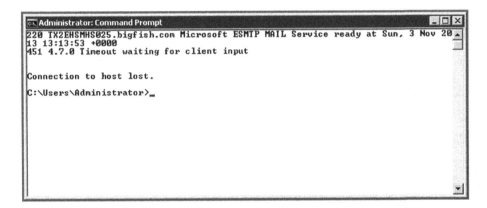

Figure 9-4. *The* contoso.com *mail server is accepting connections on port 25*

Don't get confused by the error message, as shown in Figure 9-4. When the mail server doesn't get any input after a short amount of time, it automatically disconnects the client.

For a complete list of the NSLookup commands, check the knowledgebase article 200525 on the Microsoft support website: http://support.microsoft.com/kb/200525.

Besides the default NSLookup tools, there are free tools available on the Internet. For example, the Network Tools website is found on www.network-tools.com; this web-based toolset can do the same jobs as NSLookup, and even a lot more, like:

- Ping a host
- Perform lookups
- Perform network traces
- Check spam blacklists
- Show HTTP headers

The Network-Tools.com website is shown in Figure 9-5.

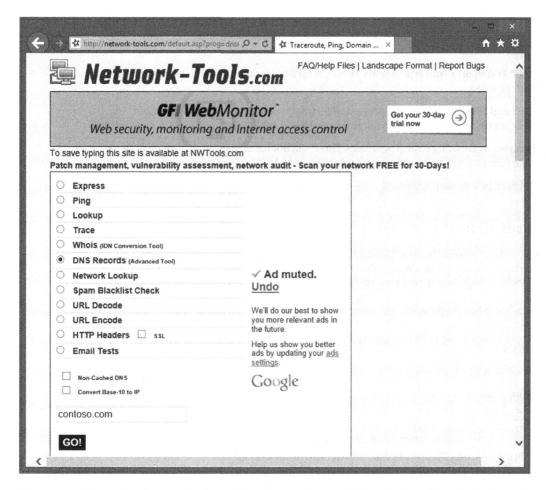

Figure 9-5. *Network-Tools.com is a free web-based networking tool for retrieving all kinds of information*

The only "bad" thing about free web tools is that ads normally show up on these sites; otherwise, they are a great addition for a sysadmin's toolbox.

Analyzing the Problems

When a user calls you with a problem, you as Exchange administrator have to start troubleshooting. The first thing you have to find out is whether it's a problem with your Exchange server or with the mail server for the intended recipient. Mail can be delivered to the recipient's mail server, but when the mailbox is not available, your user will be confronted with an error message. It's not *his* problem if it's your Exchange server or the intended recipient's mail server.

Here are few of the most common scenarios in Exchange 2013 that will cause warnings or issues:

- **Autodiscover issues** Autodiscover itself will not generate any warnings or errors, but your users will report problems such as the Out-of-Office Assistant not working, or being unable to see the availability of coworkers when planning a meeting. These matters are tightly related to the next bulleted item.

- **Certificate warnings** These are shown on the user's desktop. The result is that the Outlook client will not connect or parts of the Outlook functionality, like configuring Out-of-Office, are not working.

- **SMTP Transport routing problems** These prevent the sending or receiving of messages to or from the Internet.

- **POP3 and IMAP4 issues** These prevent users from receiving messages. Some CRM applications use POP3 for retrieving email, and these applications will not function correctly.

- **Database Availability Group problems** These will not harm immediately, but will cause major complications when the mailbox database of a Mailbox server failover occurs.

Let's look at each of these in more detail.

Autodiscover Issues

Autodiscover is used by Outlook clients to configure their Outlook profiles; this is explained in detail in Chapter 4. What most people don't know is that the Autodiscover process is repeated once every hour, to check if there are any changes in the Exchange Server environment. If there are changes, these are automatically reflected in the Outlook profile.

Autodiscover also retrieves information regarding the web services that are offered by the Exchange 2013 Client Access server; for example:

- Outlook Web App URL

- Out-of-Office URL

- Offline Address Book URL

- Availability Service URL

So, when Autodiscover fails during normal operation, Outlook is not able to get this information and thus will fail. The irritating part, however, is that normal messaging operations continue to work in most cases. And when it's the other way around, when users call the help desk with problems such as not being able to schedule meetings or not being able to set their Out-of-Office using Outlook, most likely it is also an Autodiscover issue. If they experience problems like these, suggest they try using OWA and they will likely be successful.

There are two possible causes for Autodiscover issues:

1. The virtual directories are not set correctly on the Exchange 2013 CASs. Especially if you have a load-balanced array of Exchange 2013 CASs, configuring the virtual directories is extremely important. At the same time, doing so is prone to error, so you have to be careful here. The scripts as explained in Chapter 2 can help you configure the virtual directory appropriately.

2. Since the web-based services offered by the Exchange 2013 CAS are encrypted by default, they use an SSL certificate. If there's something wrong with this SSL certificate, the Autodiscover service won't work and the appropriate settings won't be available to the Outlook client, either. Besides, the user will be confronted with certificate warnings.

Certificate Warnings

A common cause of headaches in Exchange 2013 implementations is certificate warnings, both in Outlook Web App and in Outlook. And not only is the certificate warning a reason for concern; other web-based services offered by the Exchange 2013 CAS won't work, either.

When an Exchange 2013 CAS is installed, it is automatically configured with a self-signed certificate, and this certificate has the NetBIOS name of the server as its Common Name (CN). The Fully Qualified Domain Name (FQDN) of the server is then added to the Subject Alternate Names (SAN) field. The problem arises in the self-signed part of the certificate, since this certificate is not trusted by any computer! It is for testing purposes and that's it. It should never be used for production purposes.

When you open the browser and navigate to the Exchange 2013 CAS, `https://ams-exch01.contoso.com/owa` in our example, you get a certificate warning. When you click on the Certificate Error icon next to the address bar, the full error is shown, as can be seen in Figure 9-6.

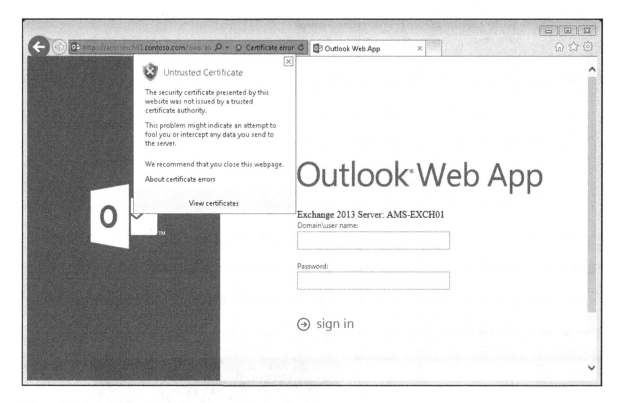

Figure 9-6. *The certificate warning shown in Internet Explorer*

In OWA, it's easy to ignore the certificate error and continue logging on without any problems. Except for that certificate warning, you can continue testing.

Microsoft Outlook is a different story, though. When the self-signed certificate is installed on a fresh Exchange 2013 CAS, and you want to start testing Microsoft Outlook for the first time, it just doesn't want to finish the Autodiscover phase, as shown in Figure 9-7.

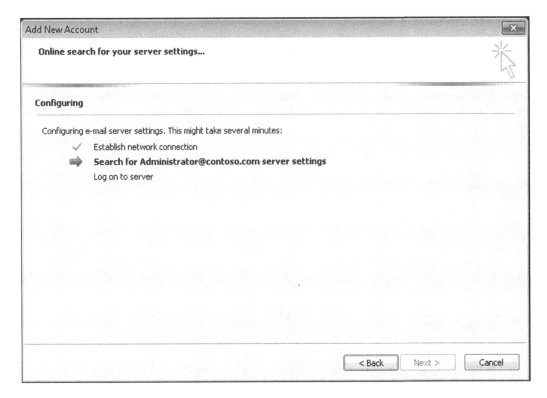

Figure 9-7. When connecting for the first time, Outlook will not finish the Autodiscover phase

If you configure the Outlook profile manually and try to connect, you'll see a cryptic error message saying that there's a problem with the proxy server's security certificate and that Outlook is unable to connect to the proxy server, as can be seen in Figure 9-8.

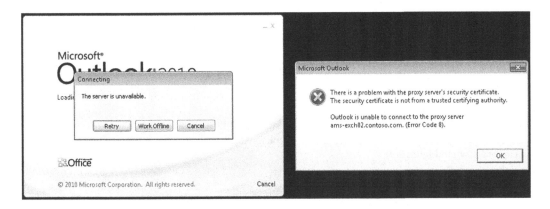

Figure 9-8. Outlook shows an error when using the self-signed certificate

■ **Note**   The warning message on the right in Figure 9-8 is normally on top of the Microsoft Oulook splash screen. For demonstration purposes, it is dragged here somewhat to the right.

When you click OK, you'll see the Connecting window with the Retry, Work Offline, and Cancel buttons. In short, Outlook will not connect using the self-signed certificate.

■ **Note**   In previous versions of Exchange Server, it was possible to bypass this by not using Outlook Anywhere and using direct MAPI instead. But since direct MAPI is not supported in Exchange 2013 and only supports Outlook Anywhere, the Outlook client just won't connect.

As explained in Chapter 4, you'll need a Unified Communications SSL certificate with at least the external name of Exchange 2013 CAS in it, and the Autodiscover FQDN, such as:

- `webmail.contoso.com`
- `autodiscover.contoso.com`

Microsoft recommends you use a split-DNS scenario in which your Exchange 2013 CAS uses the same FQDN internally and externally. If this is the case, only these two FQDNs are used. If you don't use a split-DNS scenario, you have to add the server FQDN or the internal load-balanced FQDN to the server names list in the SSL certificate, as in the following:

- `webmail.contoso.com`
- `autodiscover.contoso.com`
- `ams-exch01.contoso.com`
- `ams-exch02.contoso.com`

The good thing about certificate warnings is that the error is actually shown in the error message. The following certificate messages are possible:

- The SSL certificate is issued by a non-trusted certifying authority (CA)
- The SSL certificate is expired and thus no longer valid
- The name the client is using to contact the server is not included on the certificate (this error is shown in Figure 9-9)

Figure 9-9. SSL certificate warnings with a mismatch in server names

A good certificate is key to achieving the best results with Exchange 2013! This is not only true for internal communications but also for external communications. If your Exchange 2013 CASs are exposed to the Internet, you need to register both FQDNs (`webmail.contoso.com` and `autodiscover.contoso.com`) in public DNS; otherwise it won't work.

To test this from the Internet, you can use the Remote Connectivity Analyzer (RCA), which can be found on `www.testexchangeconnectivity.com`. Follow these steps:

1. When you open this tool, select Outlook Autodiscover under the Microsoft Office Outlook Connectivity Tests and click Next.

2. Enter your email address and credentials.

3. Select both of the following checkboxes:

   a. Ignore Trust for SSL.

   b. I understand that I must use the credentials of a working account from my Exchange domain to be able to test connectivity to it remotely. I also acknowledge that I am responsible for the management and security of this account.

4. Then enter the verification code.

5. Once done, click Perform Test and wait for the results to show up.

RCA will perform a variety of tests with respect to Autodiscover to see which of the services is actually working. The results are shown on the screen. You can expand all the various tests to check them in detail, as shown in Figure 9-10. As shown here, the RCA fails. But by expanding all the tests, you can see that RCA was able to resolve my Autodiscover FQDN; it was not able to open a connection on port 443, which is needed for SSL, of course. Most likely a firewall is still blocking this port, causing Autodiscover to fail.

Figure 9-10. *Failure of the Remote Connectivity Analyzer*

The main problem with RCA is that the average Exchange administrator is scared by the number of red Xs that seem to block anyone's ability to troubleshoot. Just expand all the various test steps in RCA, and read them carefully. This will point you in the right direction and help you troubleshoot your Exchange 2013 CAS connectivity problems.

But remember: SSL certificates, virtual directory settings, and public DNS are the main causes for connectivity problems!

Another great online tool for troubleshooting connectivity issues is the Outlook Connectivity Guided Walkthrough for Exchange On-Premises. This tool is created and maintained by Microsoft, and you can find it at `http://tinyurl.com/nm2jaw8`.

■ **Note** For testing purposes, you can enter the correct IP address and the FQDN in the local HOSTS file, but don't forget to remove these once done.

Branding Outlook Web App

This topic is not exactly a troubleshooting one, but the information here can be very helpful for troubleshooting purposes.

When using a load-balanced array of Exchange 2013 CASs, and you are testing your CASs from an external network, you might want to know which CAS you're connected with.

Personally, I find it helpful to brand Exchange 2013 OWA with a unique text string per server so I know in the blink of an eye what CAS I'm connected to, as shown in Figure 9-11.

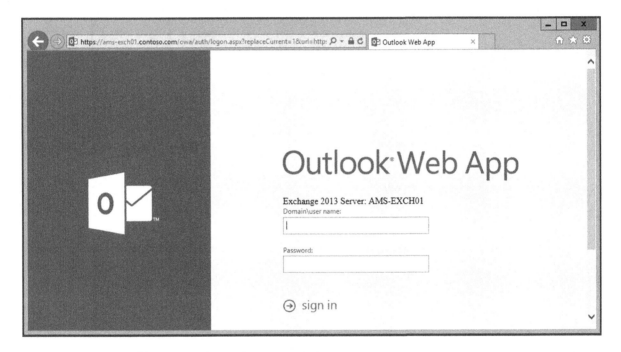

Figure 9-11. *A branded logon page of an Exchange 2013 CAS*

To achieve this, log on to the Exchange 2013 CAS, open Windows Explorer, and navigate to the `C:\Program Files\Microsoft\Exchange Server\V15\FrontEnd\HttpProxy\owa\auth` directory. Open the `logon.aspx` page with (for example) Notepad++.

In this file, scroll down to the `<div class="logonContainer">` section and add the servername text or any other identifyable text just before the `<div class= "signInInputLabel" id="userNameLabel" aria-hidden="true">` section, as shown in Figure 9-12.

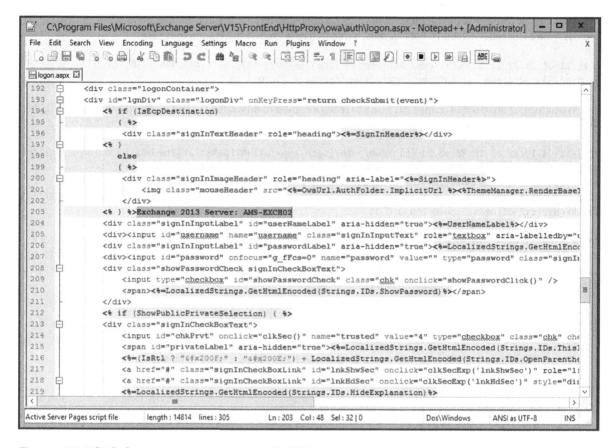

Figure 9-12. *Edit the logon.aspx page to customize the OWA logon page*

It's a perfect solution for troubleshooting purposes, but don't forget to remove this text string once you're finished. If you choose to keep it, remember that installing a future cumulative update of Exchange 2013 will overwrite your changes, so you need a proper backup.

Connectivity Log Files

All connections to the Exchange 2013 CAS are automatically logged in all kinds of log files. For example, all IIS-related connections, like OWA, Web Services, Autodiscover, PowerShell, or Outlook Anywhere, are logged in the default IIS log files.

You can find the default IIS log file in the directory C:\Inetpub\logs\LogFiles\W3SVC1. These log files are stored on a daily basis and can be very large in size. When you open a log file with Notepad++, for example, you'll see all kinds of connections with a date and time stamp, the source IP address the request is originating from, and the command that's used to retrieve the information.

Valid examples of these commands are:

- RPC_IN_DATA /rpc/rpcproxy.dll (for Outlook Anywhere)

- GET /owa/auth/logon.aspx (for an OWA logon request)

- POST /powershell (for a PowerShell command)

- GET /owa/healthcheck.htm (a health check performed by a load balancer or by Managed Availability)

Managed Availability is a frequent logger of information, and thus a log of information in the IIS log files is coming from Managed Availability. For example, a Client Access Probe will log something like:

```
2013-11-04 18:22:02 ::1 GET /ews/ &cafeReqId=fcc6475e-8934-4d76-a74c-a42b99639f56; 443 CONTOSO\
SM_dfd3256318d541269 ::1 AMProbe/Local/ClientAccess - 200 0 0 16
```

When logging on to the Exchange 2013 CAS to reach a regular mailbox, the request is logged as well. In the IIS log file you'll find something like:

```
2013-11-04 17:41:27 10.38.96.84 GET /owa/auth/logon.aspx url=https%3a%2f%2fwebmail.exchange15.nl%2fo
wa%2f%3fauthRedirect%3dtrue&reason=2&cafeReqId=d8fb8df2-2b28-47b7-954d-0857555f6587;
443 - 109.109.115.145 Mozilla/5.0+(Windows+NT+6.3;+WOW64;+Trident/7.0;+rv:11.0)+like+Gecko
https://webmail.exchange15.nl/owa/auth/logon.aspx?url=https%3a%2f%2fwebmail.exchange15.nl%2fowa%2f%3
fauthRedirect%3dtrue&reason=0 200 0 0 31

2013-11-04 17:41:32 10.38.96.84 POST /owa/auth.owa &cafeReqId=f9f2ba4f-001b-43cd-ad05-dcc08a3520c6;
443 contoso\administrator 109.109.115.145 Mozilla/5.0+(Windows+NT+6.3;+WOW64;+Trident/7.0;+rv:11.0)+
like+Gecko https://webmail.exchange15.nl/owa/auth/logon.aspx?url=https%3a%2f%2fwebmail.exchange15.nl
%2fowa%2f%3fauthRedirect%3dtrue&reason=2 302 0 64 46
```

In these examples, you'll see:

- The date and time stamp
- The source IP address (in this example, the source IP address is the load balancer IP address)
- The command that's executed
- The username
- The user's source IP address
- The public URL
- The success code that's returned by IIS

It's a lot of information that's logged into the IIS log files, but everything is logged here, and thus everything is traceable.

SMTP Tranport Routing Problems

Troubleshooting SMTP Transport routing issues can be difficult. When users hit routing problems, they always blame *your* Exchange 2013 servers. But it's always possible that the intended recipient's mail server has the problem. For example, the recipient's mailbox can be full and is hitting its quota, or the recipient is no longer working for this particular company and the email is bounced.

The average user doesn't care about this; the only thing he or she sees is an error message, and the only thing a user *does* know at this point is that the mail isn't working. Well, you can't blame the user, of course. But when users call your help desk, you have to ask them to send you the error message. That way, you can start the troubleshooting.

There are usually three scenarios:

- **Inbound SMTP** People on the Internet cannot send messages to recipients in your Exchange organization.

- **Outbound SMTP** Users in your Exchange organization cannot send messages to recipients on the Internet.

- **Internal SMTP** Users on your Exchange servers cannot send messages to other users or to a subset of users in your Exchange organization.

Inbound SMTP Messages

When people on the Internet are sending messages to recipients in your Exchange organization, the following steps occur:

- The sending SMTP server checks the public DNS servers for MX records that point to your Exchange servers. In our contoso.com environment, that would be the Exchange 2010 Edge Transport servers, but these can also be Exchange 2013 Client Access servers or third-party solutions like Microsoft Exchange Online Protection, Cisco Ironport, or other anti-spam vendors.

- The Edge Transport server accepts the request and checks if the sender is on a Realtime Blacklist (RBL). If not, it accepts the message and forwards it to the internal Exchange 2013 Mailbox server.

- The Exchange 2013 Mailbox server checks the recipient and forwards the message to the Mailbox server hosting the recipient's mailbox.

- The recipient's Mailbox server accepts the message and hands it over to the Mailbox Transport Delivery service, which delivers the message to the actual mailbox.

The chances that your own MX records are not configured correctly are small; otherwise, your Exchange servers wouldn't accept any mail at all.

The anti-spam solution can be an issue, though, when it comes to receiving messages via the Internet. If the sending organization is on a blacklist, your mail servers will check this and the connection from the sending mail server will be dropped; no messages from this mail server will be accepted. To check the most used blacklist engines, you can use the www.network-tools.com tool and select the Spam Blacklist Check.

Another possibility is that the sending organization doesn't have its SPF record or the reverse lookup configured correctly. These settings help Exchange servers in the ongoing battle with spam, but when not configured correctly, the Exchange 2013 servers can (accidentally) identify the sending organization as a spam-sending one.

When the message is accepted by the Edge Transport server, it is forwarded to the internal Exchange 2013 server. The Edge Transport server and the Exchange 2013 Mailbox server use a mechanism called *Edge Synchronization* to keep each other up to date. If this fails, messages are no longer sent between the two and the mail will stay in the queue on the Edge Transport server. But you won't notice this until these messages expire. The sender will receive an error message that the message cannot be delivered successfully. A typical timeout value is 48 hours. If you're lucky, the sender might give you or the intended recipient a call.

On the other hand, if inbound SMTP fails owing to Edge Synchronization issues, the outbound SMTP mail flow will fail as well and your internal users will see similar error messages.

When messages need to be delivered to the mailbox databases, they are stored in queues as well. Each mailbox database has its own queue, as shown in Figure 9-13.

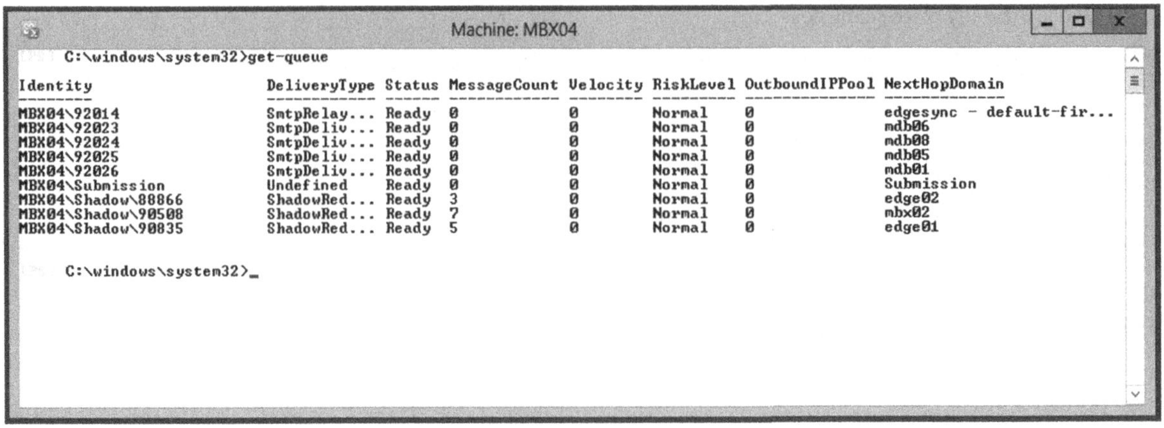

Figure 9-13. *Each mailbox database with it own queue for delivering messages*

When the Mailbox Transport Delivery service cannot deliver the message to the appropriate mailbox database, the messages stay in the corresponding queue and users will receive nothing in their mailboxes.

This can be very confusing if you have multiple Exchange 2013 Mailbox servers with multiple mailbox databases. For instance, if Mailbox server A cannot deliver messages owing to issues with the Mailbox Transport Delivery service, but Mailbox server B can, you'll see that message delivery sometimes fails and other times works.

Normally, Managed Availability should take care of problems like this, but when you're using a standalone Mailbox server—that is, not part of a DAG—you have to restart the Mailbox Transport Delivery service manually or remount the mailbox databases.

■ **Note** In the old NT4 days, you had to reboot the Windows Server for every small configuration change or for every minor problem that occurred. While this is no longer the case, it still looks like rebooting a server is a great refreshment, even for an Exchange 2013 server.

DSN or NDR Codes

When messages cannot be delivered to another mail server, whether it's an Exchange server or not, a Non-Deliver Report (NDR) is generated. An NDR is sometimes also referred to as a Delivery Status Notification (DSN), a Non-Delivery Notification (NDN), or simply a "bounce message."

When a mail server is generating an NDR, a code is used and this code can be key to troubleshooting the problem. Every problem has its own code, so looking at this code will help you find the solution. A list of NDR codes and possible causes is shown in Table 9-1.

Table 9-1. Common NDR Codes and Possible Causes

Code	Possible Cause
4.3.1	Out-of-memory or out-of-disk space condition on the Exchange server. Potentially also means out-of-file handles on IIS.
4.3.2	Message deleted from a queue by the administrator via the Queue Viewer interface in Exchange System Manager.
4.4.1	Host not responding. Check network connectivity. If problem persists, an NDR will be issued.
4.4.2	Connection dropped. Possible temporary network problems.
4.4.6	Maximum hop count for a message has been exceeded. Check the message address, DNS address, and SMTP virtual servers to make sure that nothing is causing the message to loop.
4.4.7	Message expired. Message wait time in queue exceeds limit, potentially due to remote server being unavailable.
5.0.0	Generic message for no route available to deliver a message or failure. If it is an outbound SMTP message, make sure that an address space is available and have proper routing groups listed.
5.1.0	Message categorizer failures. Check the destination address and resend the message. Forcing a rebuild of Recipient Update Service (RUS) may resolve the issue.
5.1.1	Recipient could not be resolved. Check the destination address and resend the message. Potentially email account no longer exists on the destination server.
5.1.3	Bad address.
5.1.4	Duplicate SMTP address. Use LDIFDE or script to locate duplicate and update as appropriate.
5.2.1	Local mail system rejected message, "oversize" message. Check the recipient's limits.
5.2.3	Message too large. Potentially the recipient mailbox is disabled due to exceeding mailbox limit.
5.3.3	The remote server has run out of disk space to queue messages, possible SMTP protocol error.
5.3.5	Message loopback detected.
5.4.0	Authoritative host not found. Check message and DNS to ensure proper entry. Potential error in smarthost entry or SMTP name lookup failure.
5.4.4	No route found to next hop. Make sure connectors are configured correctly and address spaces exist for the message type.
5.4.6	Categorizer problems with recipient. Recipient may have alternative recipient specified looping back to self.
5.4.8	Looping condition detected. Server trying to forward the message to itself. Check smarthost configuration, FQDN name, DNS host and MX records, and recipient policies.
5.5.0	Generic SMTP protocol error.
5.5.2	SMTP protocol error for receiving out-of-sequence SMTP protocol command verbs. Possibly due to low disk space/memory of remote server.
5.5.3	Too many recipients in the message. Reduce number of recipients in message and resend.
5.7.1	Access denied. Sender may not have permission to send message to the recipient. Possible unauthorized SMTP relay attempt from SMTP client.

For a complete view of all status codes used in SMTP, check RFC 1893 on the Internet Engineering Task Force (IETF) website on www.ietf.org/rfc/rfc1893.txt.

Reverse DNS Lookup and SPF

In order to fight spam, additional checks are created for handling inbound SMTP messages. Two of these checks are the *reverse DNS lookup check* and the Sender Policy Framework (SPF). Most people don't realize this, but these two options can be a cause of rejection or dropping of email messages.

Reverse DNS lookup is a relatively simple DNS check. When some email server (Server A) sends a message to another email server (Server B), Server B does a lookup for the IP address of Server A. It does this in reverse order. Normally an FQDN is used, and the corresponding IP address is requested from DNS, but when a reverse DNS lookup is performed, Server B will look up the FQDN based on the IP address of Server A.

So, besides having a normal DNS zone (also known as a *forward lookup zone*), it is strongly recommended you have a reverse lookup zone for your domain. It happens frequently that mail cannot be delivered because the receiving mail server is not accepting connections, owing to the lack of a DNS reverse lookup zone. Is that your problem? If messages from your Exchange server cannot be delivered because of this, it's your reverse lookup zone that's causing the problem.

A less strict check is performed by a technique called the Sender Policy Framework, or SPF. This is an open framework that you can read about at http://www.openspf.org/. The Microsoft implementation of SPF is called the Sender ID Framework, but it is very similar.

Sender ID filtering tries to determine if the sending SMTP server is actually allowed to send messages on behalf of the sender. Sender ID filtering uses an additional record in the public DNS to achieve this. In this DNS, record information is stored that indicates which servers are allowed to send mail on behalf of their users. Viewed from the other way around, if another SMTP server is sending mail on behalf of a user, and this information is *not* stored in DNS, it might well be a source of spam (spoofed messages). This record in DNS is an SPF record.

This is how it works: A user sends a message (1) to a recipient in your organization, and the user's SMTP server sets up a connection. When the EHLO and MAIL FROM (2) commands are sent, the receiving Exchange server tries to contact DNS to get the SPF record (3) and compare the data found in the SPF record with the name and IP address of the sending server to ascertain that there's a match (4). If there's a match ("pass"), an entry to the message header is added; but if there's no match ("fail"), there are multiple options:

- The message is rejected and nothing else happens.

- The message is stamped with an additional message header saying the sending ID failed and at the same time the Spam Confidence Level (SCL) is increased. Then the message is delivered to the mailbox (5)—if the SCL is below the threshold, of course.

This process is shown graphically in Figure 9-14.

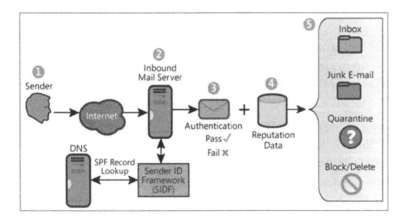

Figure 9-14. *Sender ID framework in Exchange Server 2013*

If you haven't configured the SPF records for your domain, it's just another step in potentially experiencing blocked messages. The policy can be set very strict, but then there's a risk of losing valid messages. Don't forget that not everybody is using SPF records.

If you want to test your SPF records, there's a test option available via the OpenSPF organization. If you suspect SPF is causing the problem, you can send a test message to `spf-test@openspf.net`. This message will be rejected by the mail server and a bounce message will be returned containing the results of an SPF test of your SMTP domain, as shown in Figure 9-15.

Figure 9-15. *The OpenSPF organization offers an SPF test option*

Creating an SPF record is not that difficult. Microsoft has a wizard available to do this, which can be found on `http://tinyurl.com/b3zpz`. Just follow the wizard, and the information that's needed inside the SPF record is automatically generated.

SMTP Headers

Every SMTP message consists of a message header and a message body. The message header contains all kinds of information regarding the message, such as:

- The receiving mail server, including its IP address and time stamp of the message

- The sending mail server, including its IP address and time stamp of the message

- Recipient information

- Sender information

- The message ID

- Server-specific message information; in the case of Exchange Server, these are called X-header information

For example, the message shown in Figure 9-15 has the following message header:

```
Received: from EXCH02.wesselius.local (10.38.96.22) by EXCH02.wesselius.local
(10.38.96.22) with Microsoft SMTP Server (TLS) id 15.0.775.35 via Mailbox
Transport; Wed, 6 Nov 2013 17:44:36 +0100
Received: from EXCH01.wesselius.local (10.38.96.21) by EXCH02.wesselius.local
(10.38.96.22) with Microsoft SMTP Server (TLS) id 15.0.775.35; Wed, 6 Nov
2013 17:44:35 +0100
Received: from SMTPHOST2.exchangelabs.nl (10.38.96.32) by
EXCH01.wesselius.local (10.38.96.21) with Microsoft SMTP Server (TLS) id
15.0.775.35 via Frontend Transport; Wed, 6 Nov 2013 17:44:51 +0100
MIME-Version: 1.0
From: Microsoft Outlook
<MicrosoftExchange329e71ec88ae4615bbc36ab6ce41109e@wesselius.local>
To: <jaap@wesselius.info>
Date: Wed, 6 Nov 2013 17:44:17 +0100
Content-Type: multipart/report; report-type=delivery-status;
boundary="ef1abc60-1e62-4e70-b838-06ea6c050b45"
X-MS-Exchange-Organization-SCL: -1
Content-Language: en-US
Message-ID: <ef4e38b2-845b-4733-835c-12344cfeabdd@SMTPHOST2.exchangelabs.nl>
In-Reply-To: <eb9bc7057a9549dd8726f7c585688f6c@EXCH02.wesselius.local>
References: <eb9bc7057a9549dd8726f7c585688f6c@EXCH02.wesselius.local>
Thread-Index: AQHO2w9NAghcyjLTWO2W/gE4sWjW+ZoYaL8u
Subject: Undeliverable:
X-MS-Exchange-Organization-AuthSource: SMTPHOST2.exchangelabs.nl
X-MS-Exchange-Organization-AuthAs: Internal
X-MS-Exchange-Organization-AuthMechanism: 05
X-MS-Exchange-Organization-MessageDirectionality: Originating
Return-Path: <>
X-MS-Exchange-Organization-Network-Message-Id: 14cedbb1-5c07-4a92-5a1b-08d0a9269c92
X-MS-Exchange-Organization-AVStamp-Enterprise: 1.0
```

You can clearly see that this message enters the Exchange environment on the server called smtphost2.exchangelabs.nl (which is an Exchange 2010 Edge Transport server), and is then forwarded to the Exchange 2013 server EXCH01.wesselius.local. This server forwards the message to server EXCH02.wesselius.local, the server where my actual mailbox is hosted.

Header information can help you identify the flow of the message. In the example above, it was just a normal message, transported encrypted via Transport Layer Security (TLS), so you won't find anything strange in there. When there are problems and a message is bounced several times, or it enters an SMTP loop, then the header information can become lengthy and it can be difficult to analyze.

The Google Apps Toolbox offers a tool to analyze header information and show it in a GUI. Just navigate with a browser to http://tinyurl.com/otdln6c and copy the entire header into the text box, then click the Analyse the Header Above button. It will show you the header information in a very friendly manner, as shown in Figure 9-16.

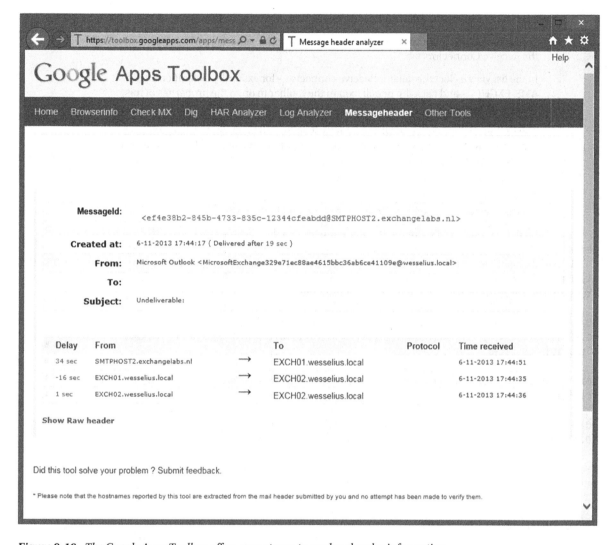

Figure 9-16. *The Google Apps Toolbox offers a great way to analyze header information*

Another great tool for analyzing message headers is the Message Header Analyzer from Microsoft, which you can download at http://tinyurl.com/otk553u.

SMTP Transport Log Files

One of your last options in troubleshooting Exchange 2013 message flow is the SMTP Transport log files. Every connector in Exchange 2013, whether it's a Send connector or a Receive connector, has the ability to log all processing that takes place on this particular connector. By default, protocol logging on the Send and Receive connectors is disabled in Exchange 2013 because of the amount of information that's logged onto the server.

To enable protocol logging for a default Receive connector, follow these steps:

1. Log on to the EAC as an administrator, and in the Feature pane, select Mail Flow and select the Receive Connectors tab.

2. In the list view, select the default Receive connector—for example, Default Frontend AMS-EXCH01—and click the pencil icon in the toolbar to open the properties of this Receive connector.

3. The Exchange Receive Connector window will open, and on the general page you'll see that the protocol logging level is set to None. Select the Verbose radio button and click Save to store the new setting.

4. To activate the new setting, the Transport service needs to be restarted. It is possible to use the Services MMC snap-in to achieve this, but it's also possible to use the `Restart-Service MSExchangeTransport` command in the EMS.

You'll find the protocol log files for the Receive connector in the `C:\Program Files\Microsoft\Exchange Server\V15\TransportRoles\Logs\FrontEnd\ProtocolLog\` SmtpReceive directory on the Exchange 2013 server.

When you open the log file, you'll find tons of information regarding messages entering the Exchange 2013 CAS, like date and time stamps, IP addresses, certificate information, actual SMTP commmands, and information that the Transport service answers to the sending server; for example:

```
2013-11-06T14:43:37.291Z,EXCH01\Default Frontend EXCH01,08D0A8364CC1775F,2,10.38.96.21:25,
10.38.96.31:45578,>,"220 EXCH01.wesselius.local Microsoft ESMTP MAIL Service ready at Wed,
6 Nov 2013 15:43:36 +0100",

2013-11-06T14:43:37.291Z,EXCH01\Default Frontend EXCH01,08D0A8364CC1775F,3,10.38.96.21:25,
10.38.96.31:45578,<,EHLO smtphost.exchangelabs.nl,

2013-11-06T14:43:37.291Z,EXCH01\Default Frontend EXCH01,08D0A8364CC1775F,4,10.38.96.21:25,
10.38.96.31:45578,>,250-EXCH01.wesselius.local Hello [10.38.96.31],
```

This kind of information is hard to read, but it can certainly help you identify problems in receiving SMTP messages. Of course, you need proper understanding of how SMTP works.

POP3 and IMAP4 Issues

POP3 and IMAP4 are relatively easy protocols to use. Once installed and configured, there's hardly any need to troubleshoot them. Only in freshly installed Exchange 2013s is some time needed to get it up and running, or to troubleshoot to determine why it's not working yet.

When Exchange 2013 is installed, both POP3 and IMAP 4 are installed, but they are not running and the startup mode of both services is set to manual. This is a common pitfall in every Exchange server deployment. To start them automatically during booting, you have to set these services to Automatic startup mode. The easiest way to achieve this is by using the services MMC snap-in.

You can also open a regular command prompt (don't forget the elevated privileges!) and use the following commands to change the startup mode:

```
sc config MSExchangePOP3 start= Automatic
sc config MSExchangeImap4 start= Automatic
```

Of course, it is also possible to use the EMS to achieve this:

```
Set-Service "MSExchangePop3" -StartupType Automatic
Set-Service "MSExchangeIMAP4" -StartupType Automatic
```

■ **Note** In Exchange 2013, the POP3 and IMAP4 services are running on the Client Access server and on the Mailbox server. The CAS acts as a proxy and proxies the request to the Mailbox server. So, the Mailbox server has its own service running. This service is called IMAP4BE for IMAP4 and POP3BE for POP3. (A different name is used to avoid conflicts when using a multi-role server.) These services have to be started as well, and their startup mode has to be set to Automatic also. The commands are identical to the commands as shown here.

A pitfall with both POP3 and IMAP4 is that the default settings are Secure Login (i.e., encrypted) while most clients by default use plain text login (i.e., unencrypted). Needless to say, this is not compatible. It is not good practice to use unencrypted POP3 and IMAP4 on the Internet (although widely used at almost every hoster!), since the Active Directory credentials used to log on are easy to capture. My recommendation is to use either SSL or TLS for IMAP4 and POP3 on the Internet. Not encrypted POP3 and IMAP4 can be used on the internal network, but there still is a risk, of course.

But if there are applications that force you to use unencrypted PlainTextLogin, you can use the Set-POPSettings command in EMS:

```
Set-POPSettings -Server AMS-EXCH01 -LoginType:1
```

The LoginType can have the following values:

- 1, or PlainTextLogin

- 2, or PlainTextAuthentication

- 3, or SecureLogin (which is the default)

■ **Note** Do not forget to restart the POP3 or IMAP4 service after making a change to the configuration of the service. Again, that's a common pitfall.

To test the POP3 or IMAP4 service, you can use the Telnet client on port 110 for POP3 and on port 143 for IMAP4, but this only works when using a PlainTextLogin.

To open a POP3 session using POP3, you can use the following command on the command prompt:

```
Telnet ams-exch01.contoso.com 110
```

When the service is running and accepting connection (beware of firewall issues!), you'll see the POP3 banner saying:

```
+OK The Microsoft Exchange POP3 service is ready.
```

At least you now know that the service is running and accepting connections. It is also possible to log on to a mailbox using POP3 via a Telnet client. Once logged on, you can use the following commands in the Telnet client to log on, for example to John's mailbox:

```
User john
Pass Pass1word
List
```

The `List` command shows the number of messages in the user's inbox. The console output is shown in Figure 9-17. When you are able to see this, you know that the POP3 protocol is running fine and that you can successfully access the user's mailbox.

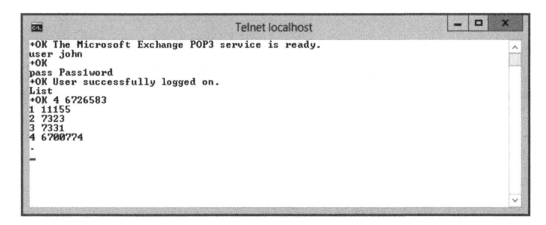

Figure 9-17. Logging in using POP3 with a Telnet client

You can use the `Quit` command in the POP3 session to log off from the mailbox in the Telnet client.

The same is possible for testing IMAP4 with a Telnet client, but instead of port 110 you have to use port 143:

```
Telnet ams-exch01.contoso.com 143
```

When the service is running, you'll see an IMAP4 banner saying:

```
* OK The Microsoft Exchange IMAP4 service is ready.
```

Logging on to a mailbox with IMAP4 in a Telnet client is a bit more difficult. Use the following commands in the Telnet client after setting up a successful connection to log on to John's mailbox, and you'll get a list of all available folders:

```
. login John Pass1word
. LIST "" "*"
```

Note that the command is [dot, space] *login <<username>> <<password>>*; you have to enter the dot and the space before the login command. If you omit either one, the login will fail! Figure 9-18 shows a successful logging onto John's mailbox using the IMAP4 protocol in a Telnet client

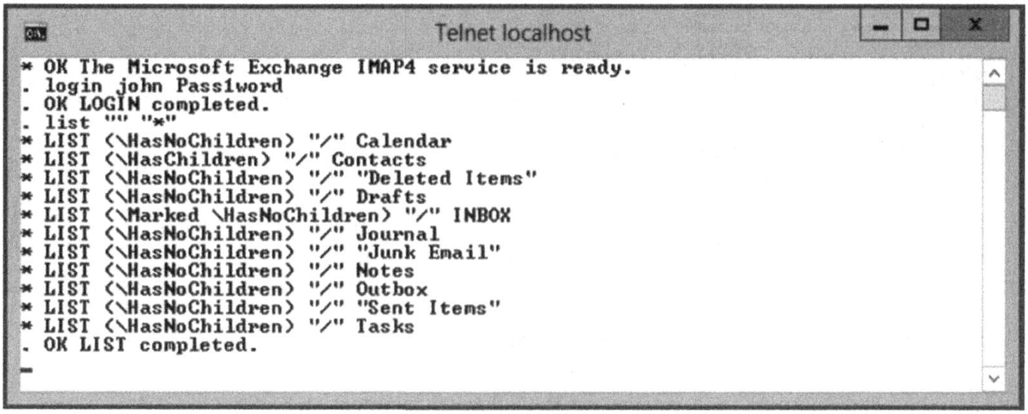

```
*  OK The Microsoft Exchange IMAP4 service is ready.
.  login john Password
.  OK LOGIN completed.
.  list "" "*"
*  LIST (\HasNoChildren) "/" Calendar
*  LIST (\HasChildren) "/" Contacts
*  LIST (\HasNoChildren) "/" "Deleted Items"
*  LIST (\HasNoChildren) "/" Drafts
*  LIST (\Marked \HasNoChildren) "/" INBOX
*  LIST (\HasNoChildren) "/" Journal
*  LIST (\HasNoChildren) "/" "Junk Email"
*  LIST (\HasNoChildren) "/" Notes
*  LIST (\HasNoChildren) "/" Outbox
*  LIST (\HasNoChildren) "/" "Sent Items"
*  LIST (\HasNoChildren) "/" Tasks
.  OK LIST completed.
```

Figure 9-18. *Login using IMAP4 to a mailbox using a Telnet client*

If you are still unable to log on, you can enable protocol logging. To enable this for POP3 and IMAP4, use the following commands in the EMS:

```
Set-PopSettings -ProtocolLogEnabled $true -LogFileLocation "C:\Pop3Logging"
Set-IMAPSettings -ProtocolLogEnabled $true -LogFileLocation "C:\IMAP4Logging"
```

Again, don't forget to restart the services on the Exchange 2013 server to activate the changes. Also important to note: if you have multiple Exchange 2013 CASs offering POP3 and IMAP4, you have to enable this on all those servers.

By using these log files, it is possible to check on a protocol level as to what's actually happening on the Exchange server.

Database Availability Group Problems

Managed Availability, as explained in Chapter 8, is constantly monitoring the DAG. When Managed Availability finds any problems via its use of probes and monitors, it takes appropriate action, such as restarting a particular application pool or service, or even performing a bugcheck on a server. Bug checking the server means deliberately bluescreening a server, causing it to reboot.

If you have to troubleshoot your DAG, despite Managed Availability, a good starting point is the `Test-ReplicationHealth` command in EMS. This command will test the health of the replication engine and show the results on the console, as displayed in Figure 9-19.

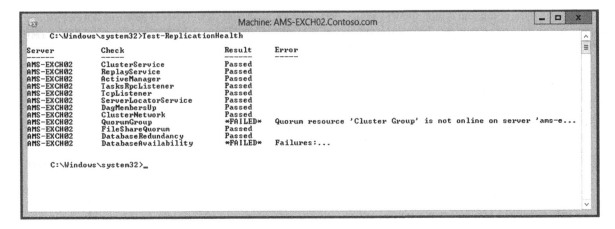

Figure 9-19. The Test-ReplicationHealth command shows the health of your DAG

To drill down into the failed QuorumGroup, you can use the following command in EMS:

```
Test-ReplicationHealth | where {$_.Check -like "QuorumGroup"} | fl
```

The result will provide details about the QuorumGroup check, as shown in Figure 9-20.

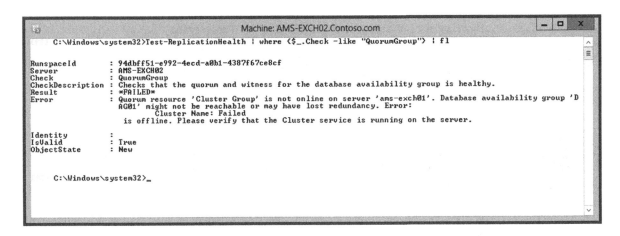

Figure 9-20. Drilling down into the Test-ReplicationHealth command

Although the DAG is typically managed using the EMS or the EAC, this is good moment to open the Failover Cluster Manager MMC snap-in and check the underlying cluster technology.

A typical problem concerns the IP address of the DAG. Both nodes need to be able to rewrite the IP address of the DAG, and therefore need permission to do so. If you create the IP address in Active Directory integrated DNS, you should also select the "Allow any authenticated user to update DNS records with the same owner name" option, as shown in Figure 9-21.

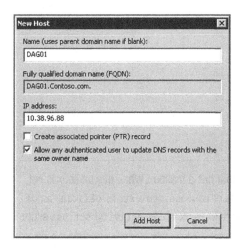

Figure 9-21. Don't forget the permissions option when creating the IP address of the DAG

It is perfectly safe to change this in a production environment during business hours, so you can delete the "old" IP address and create a new IP address in DNS.

When you open the Failover Cluster Manager, you'll see the cluster components in the Navigation pane on the left and the details of the cluster in the Details pane in the middle. There's an entry called Recent Cluster Events that shows the number of cluster problems in the last 24 hours.

With respect to the QuorumGroup error, as shown in Figure 9-19 and Figure 9-20, there are indeed entries in the Cluster Event log that you can find in the System Event log as well. One of the events is EventID 1214, from FailoverClustering, saying "You were not connected because a duplicate name exists on the network. If joining a domain, go to System in Control Panel to change the computer name and try again. If joining a workgroup, choose another workgroup name."

After some searching, it turned out that there actually were two DAGs on the same network, both called DAG01. There's no way to work around this, so the DAG needs to be rebuild, which means:

- Removing mailbox database copies

- Removing Mailbox servers from the DAG

- Removing the DAG, including removing the DAG Computer object from Active Directory and removing the IP address for DNS

When the DAG is fully removed, a new DAG can be created, as outlined in the "Creating the Database Availability Group" section in Chapter 5.

Test Commands in Exchange Management Shell

There are a lot of test commands available in Exchange Server 2013 that can be used in EMS:

- `Test-Mailflow`

- `Test-PowerShellConnectivity`

- `Test-MAPIConnectivity`

- `Test-POPConnectivity`

- `Test-OWAConnectivity`

- Test-WebServicesConnectivity

- Test-OutlookConnectivity

- Test-EdgeSynchronization

- Test-SMTPConnectivity

- Test-ServiceHealth

- Test-MRSHealth

■ **Note** Some of these test commands use an account in Active Directory that has a mailbox. When this mailbox is not available, you'll receive an error message like "Could not find or sign in with user contoso.com\extest_08f1c1a39ccd4." To create this test account, navigate to the $exscripts directory and run the New-TestCasConnectivityUser.ps1 script.

These tools are very helpful in troubleshooting your Exchange environment. However, some of them will be replaced in the future by the Get-ServerHealth command.

For OWA, this tool is already visible (in Exchange Server 2013 CU3); the Test-OWAConnectivity command is no longer functioning correctly, and it turns out that this command is deprecated.

To test the OWA health, you can use the following commands:

```
Get-ServerHealth -Identity NYC-EXCH01 -HealthSet OWA | Format-Table -AutoSize -Wrap
Get-ServerHealth -Identity NYC-EXCH01 -HealthSet OWA.Protocol | Format-Table -AutoSize -Wrap
```

The options Format-Table, -AutoSize, and -Wrap are used to get better readability, as can be seen in Figure 9-22.

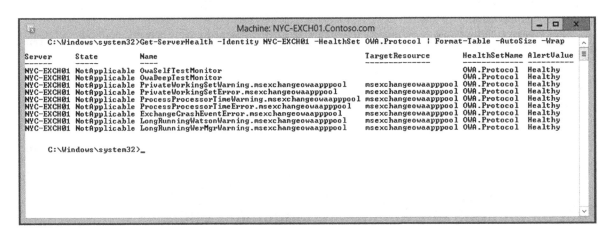

Figure 9-22. *Use the Get-ServerHealth command to retrieve the health status of OWA*

"What is a good starting point?" one might ask. That's a good question and it depends on the kind of help-desk calls that are raised, of course. If you are logged on to a particular Exchange 2013 server, the Test-ServiceHealth on that box is a good starting point since it returns information regarding the Exchange 2013 roles running on that server as well as the services that are *not* running on that server, as can be seen in Figure 9-23.

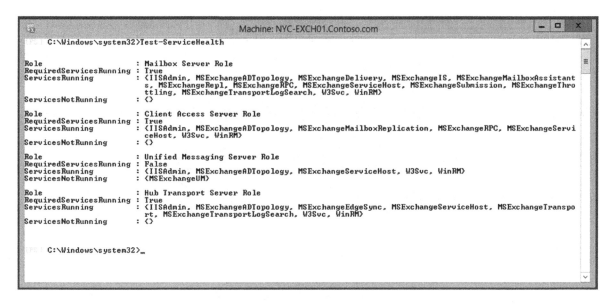

Figure 9-23. *The Test-ServiceHealth command returns information regarding the roles and services running on that server*

From this point, you can drill down if any issues are shown. If you are interested about the MSExchangeUM service not running as shown in Figure 9-23, UM was not configured at all on this particular server.

Performance Analysis of Logs (PAL)

When you run into performance issues, you have to start your troubleshooting with the Performance and Monitoring tool, as explained in Chapter 8. This tool is able to capture a lot of good information, but the problem is how to correctly analyze the information since it can be really overwhelming.

A great tool to analyze this information is the Performance Analysis of Logs, or PAL. PAL is a freeware tool that you can download on http://pal.codeplex.com.

PAL uses .NET Framework 3.5 and PowerShell 2.0. It analyzes the performance log files based on a number of thresholds as supplied by Microsoft (the tool is actually written by Microsoft employees). After analyzing the performance data, it is formatted in an HTML page that you can view using any browser. Besides giving a graphic representation of all the counters, it also provides a description of each counter, which can be seen in Figure 9-24.

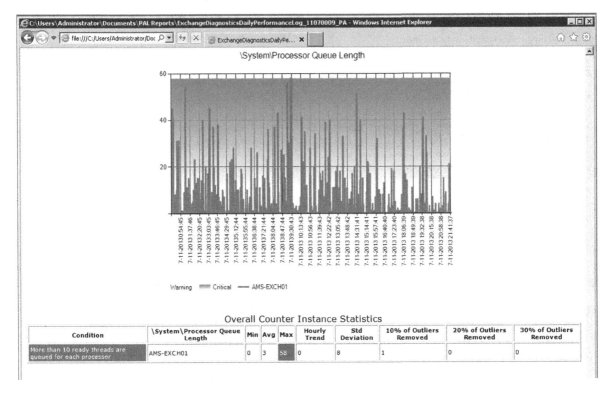

Figure 9-24. PAL is a great tool to analyze performance logs—in this case, it's Exchange Server 2010

There are a lot of templates for analyzing log files, like:

- Exchange 2007

- Exchange 2010

- Microsoft OCS 2007 R2

- Microsoft SharePoint 2010

- Windows Server 2012 Hyper-V

As you can see from this list, there's no template available yet for Exchange 2013. I recommend checking the http://pal.codeplex.com website to find Exchange 2013 updates.

Log Parser

As we've seen earlier in this chapter, analyzing log files like the protocol log files or IIS log files can be very difficult because of the amount of information stored in these log files. To make the task even worse, they consist of PlainText information, which is unreadable for normal administrators.

Log Parser 2.2 is a powerful, versatile tool that provides universal query access to text-based data such as log files, XML files, and CSV files, as well as key data sources on the Windows operating system, such as the Event Log, the Registry, the file system, and Active Directory. You tell Log Parser what information you need and how you want it processed. The results of your query can be custom-formatted in text-based output or can be persisted to more specialty targets like SQL, SYSLOG, or a chart.

Log Parser accepts the following input formats:

- XML - XML files (requires the Microsoft XML Parser)

- TSV - Reads tab- and space- separated values text files

- ADS - Reads information from Active Directory objects

- REG - Reads information from the Windows Registry

- NETMON - Makes it possible to parse NetMon .cap capture files

- ETW - Reads Event Tracing for Windows log files and live sessions

Log Parser uses a query language very similar to the standard SQL query language. For example, to get an overview of all users on a particular Exchange 2013 CAS that are accessing the CAS with the Autodiscover protocol to retrieve configuration information, you have to analyze the IIS log files where the cs-uri-stem contains the value "Autodiscover." This would be converted to a query such as:

```
"select cs-username, Count(*) as Posts FROM C:\inetpub\logs\LogFiles\W3SVC1\u_ex*.log WHERE
cs-uri-stem LIKE '%Autodiscover%' AND cs-username IS NOT NULL GROUP BY cs-username ORDER BY Posts desc"
```

The query can then be used by the Log Parser tool:

```
C:\Program Files (x86)\Log Parser 2.2>logparser "select cs-username, Count(*) as Posts FROM
C:\inetpub\logs\LogFiles\W3SVC1\u_ex*.log WHERE cs-uri-stem LIKE '%Autodiscover%' AND cs-username IS
NOT NULL GROUP BY cs-username ORDER BY Posts desc"
```

This will return something like:

```
cs-username                  Posts
---------------------------  -----
CONTOSO\SM_8809cea52643489cb 79991
CONTOSO\SM_bd6a0296b73a48438 29129
CONTOSO\SM_4377632d5a4746889 26740
CONTOSO\SM_61f3faf613ef49cb9 17926
CONTOSO\SM_47cfa4e81d4f43b6a 17141
CONTOSO\Administrator        45
Contoso\F5Mon1               14
CONTOSO\jaap                 14
contoso\jaapw                11
contoso\administrator        4
cs-username                  Posts
---------------------------  -----
CONTOSO\errol                4
CONTOSO\Cindy                4
CONTOSO\extest_f244d2d7ead04 1
contoso\f5mon1               1

Statistics:
-----------
Elements processed: 7861843
Elements output:    14
Execution time:     473.10 seconds (00:07:53.10)
```

That's very helpful, but unfortunately it's a command-line tool and the average Windows and Exchange administrator has a strong preference for GUI-based tools. Microsoft recognized this, and introduced the Log Parser Studio.

Log Parser Studio is a graphic tool that does the same thing. It comes with several predefined Exchange queries, but it is possible to create and use your own queries as well. For example, there's a query in the Log Parser Studio that retrieves the top 20 users in OWA on a particular Exchange 2013 CAS. This query looks like this:

```
SELECT TOP 20 cs-username AS UserID,
        cs(User-Agent) AS Application,
        cs-uri-stem AS Vdir,
        c-ip AS CLIENT,
        cs-method,
        Count(*)
FROM '[LOGFILEPATH]'
WHERE cs-uri-stem LIKE '%OWA%'
GROUP BY UserID, Application, Vdir, Client, cs-method
ORDER BY COUNT(*) DESC
```

If you run this query, you'll find the top 20 users in OWA. Unfortunately, there are no real users in this top 20, since most requests are coming from the load balancer performing its health check (by requesting the healthcheck.htm file in the /owa virtual directory) and Managed Availability performing its Customer Touch Point tests, as shown in Figure 9-25.

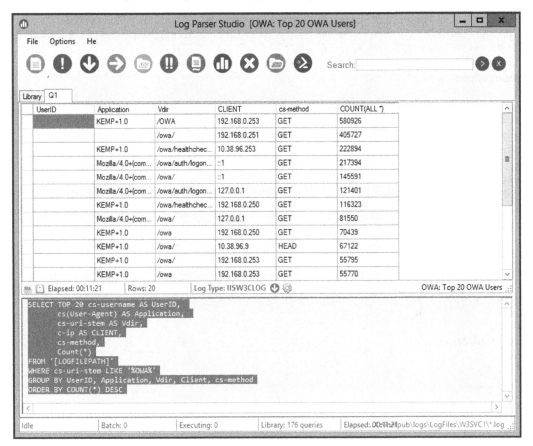

Figure 9-25. *Top 20 OWA users on an Exchange 2013 server*

As you can see in Figure 9-25, it took quite some time to query all the log files in the `C:\inetpub\logs\logfiles\W3SVC` directory. (If you are wondering about the different IP addresses shown in Figure 9-25, that's because there has been a VLAN change in my environment.)

Here's how to get more information regarding the Log Parser and the Log Parser Studio:

- There's a download link for Log Parser; visit the Microsoft TechNet site: `http://tinyurl.com/5w7d993`.

- Professor Windows has written a detailed blog (back in 2005!) about the Log Parser usage, which you can find on `http://tinyurl.com/mg7su5o`.

- For very detailed and in-depth information, there's a Log Parser Toolkit available, which can be purchased on the `Amazon.com` website: `http://tinyurl.com/mjx7roy`.

- When you want to download the Log Parser Studio, you can find it on the TechNet gallery on `http://tinyurl.com/q5xlzeg`.

The Exchange Community

Finally, the Exchange community can help you when working with and troubleshooting your Exchange 2013 environment.

Exchange Server has given birth to a strong user community that has traditionally been maintained by tech-savvy people. Quite a number of these people have received the Microsoft Most Valuable Professional (MVP) award. Examples of these Exchange communities and user groups are:

- Philadelphia Area Unified Communications User Group: `www.phillyexug.org/`

- Dutch UC User Group: `www.ucug.nl`

- MSExchange.org: `www.msexchange.org/`

- Microsoft Unified Communications User Group London: `http://mucugl.co.uk/`

The user groups typically organize local meetings at which various topics concerning Microsoft UC, including Exchange, are discussed. The organizers of these events are usually highly visible and most of the times receptive for receiving questions. You can use your favorite search engine to find a local user group in your area.

The social media are also a means for obtaining help when you face Exchange issues. You can drop a question on Twitter, for example, with the #MSExchange hashtag; most likely people will respond.

Facebook is an especially interesting social media. There's a vivid Exchange 2013 group on Facebook, hosted by fellow Exchange MVP Jason Sherry. You can find this group at `www.facebook.com/groups/MSEX2013`.

The Microsoft Exchange forum is an online support source where Microsoft staff monitor the chats closely and try to help with questions and problems. The forums are localized, so there's always one closeby, in your language. You can find the Microsoft Exchange forum on the Microsoft Technet Site:

`http://social.technet.microsoft.com/Forums/exchange/en-US/home?category=exchangeserver`

Summary

Troubleshooting your Exchange 2013 servers can be difficult, annoying, and time-consuming. But, you need to know your tools, and you shouldn't be afraid of command-line tools especially. Overall, you need to know your messaging environment.

Connectivity issues are always a cause of headaches. Most of these problems are caused by badly configured Autodiscover and virtual directory settings, but SSL certificate errors contribute to this as well.

Transport problems seem to be easier to troubleshoot, since the Transport service uses a lot of error codes when returning messages. But be careful: some errors are not caused by your Exchange environment and are instead an issue at the recipient's mail server. Or worse, the problem can be with your DNS configuration, in which case your Exchange server is fine, the recipient's mail server is fine, but the mail doesn't get delivered.

Microsoft offers a lot of tools to troubleshoot your environment, and you should use these tools on a regular basis, even if you don't have any thing go wrong. It's good to have some experience with the tools!

As said in earlier chapters, there are thin borders between monitoring your Exchange 2013 servers, and managing your Exchange 2013 servers, and troubleshooting your Exchange 2013 servers. If you have the first two in control, the third should be a lot easier!

Index

■ F

■ G, H

■ I, J, K

■ L

■ M

Get the eBook for only $10!

Now you can take the weightless companion with you anywhere, anytime. Your purchase of this book entitles you to 3 electronic versions for only $10.

s Apress title will prove so indispensible that you'll want to carry it with you erywhere, which is why we are offering the eBook in 3 formats for only $10 if ι have already purchased the print book.

nvenient and fully searchable, the PDF version enables you to easily find and ɔy code—or perform examples by quickly toggling between instructions and ɔlications. The MOBI format is ideal for your Kindle, while the ePUB can be ɪzed on a variety of mobile devices.

to www.apress.com/promo/tendollars to purchase your companion eBook.

Apress®
THE EXPERT'S VOICE™

ɔress eBooks are subject to copyright. All rights are reserved by the Publisher, whether the whole or part of the material is concerned, fically the rights of translation, reprinting, reuse of illustrations, recitation, broadcasting, reproduction on microfilms or in any other cal way, and transmission or information storage and retrieval, electronic adaptation, computer software, or by similar or dissimilar ɔdology now known or hereafter developed. Exempted from this legal reservation are brief excerpts in connection with reviews or arly analysis or material supplied specifically for the purpose of being entered and executed on a computer system, for exclusive use ɘ purchaser of the work. Duplication of this publication or parts thereof is permitted only under the provisions of the Copyright Law of ublisher's location, in its current version, and permission for use must always be obtained from Springer. Permissions for use may be ɪed through RightsLink at the Copyright Clearance Center. Violations are liable to prosecution under the respective Copyright Law.